Women, Adult Education, and Leadership in Canada
Inspiration, Passion, and Commitment

Information on how to obtain copies of this book is available at:

Website:	www.thompsonbooks.com
E-mail:	publisher@thompsonbooks.com
Telephone:	(416) 766–2763
Fax:	(416) 766–0398

Library and Archives Canada Cataloguing in Publication

Women, adult education, and leadership in Canada : inspiration, passion, and commitment / edited by Darlene E. Clover, Shauna Butterwick, and Laurel Collins.

Includes bibliographical references and index.

ISBN 978-1-55077-248-7 (paperback)

    1. Women in education--Canada. 2. Adult education--Canada. I. Clover, Darlene Elaine, 1958-, editor II. Butterwick, Shauna J. (Shauna Jane), 1950-, editor III. Collins, Laurel (Laurel Christina), editor

LC1762.W63 2015   370.82   C2015-907478-9

Editor: Jane McNulty
Design: Gary Blakeley, Blakeley Words+Pictures

This book is published in association with the Canadian Association for the Study of Adult Education L'Association Canadienne pour l'Etude de l'Education des Adultes.

Every reasonable effort has been made to acquire permission for copyrighted materials used in this book and to acknowledge such permissions accurately. Any errors called to the publisher's attention will be corrected in future printings.

The photo on page 46 is used in compliance with Crown copyright on protected works managed by the Department of National Defence/Canadian Armed Forces (DND/CAF) regulations. The photo on page 84 is used by permission of Division de la gestion de documents et des archives, Université de Montréal. Fonds de l'Association des femmes diplômées des universités de Montréal (P0107) 1FP06857.

We acknowledge the support of the Government of Canada through the Canada Book Fund for our publishing activities.

Printed in Canada.

1 2 3 4 5   20 19 18 17 16

Women, Adult Education, and Leadership in Canada Inspiration, Passion, and Commitment

Edited by:
Darlene E. Clover, Shauna Butterwick,
and Laurel Collins

THOMPSON

Contents

List of Contributors

Marlene Atleo is Associate Professor and Coordinator of Adult and Post-Secondary Education at the University of Manitoba. She is of the House of Klaaq-ish-peethl/Himix-klaaq of Ahousaht, Vancouver Island, BC. She does Aboriginal adult education to promote dialogue and right relations between Aboriginal and non-Aboriginal Canadian lifeworlds.

Lorraine Bell is a PhD student in Leadership Studies at the University of Victoria. Her research interest focuses on museums as sites of non-formal and place-based adult education for socio-ecological change. She is currently co-editing an edited volume titled *Adult Education and Museums: Animating Social and Cultural Change*.

Kate Braid has written, edited, and co-edited 11 books of prize-winning poetry and non-fiction, including *Journeywoman: Swinging a Hammer in a Man's World*, a memoir of her 15 years as a construction labourer, apprentice, carpenter, and contractor. In 2012 she was declared a "Remarkable Woman of the Arts" in Vancouver.

Susan M. Brigham is a Professor in the Faculty of Education at Mount Saint Vincent University, Halifax, Nova Scotia. Her research interests include lifelong learning/adult education, Africentricity in education, teacher education, migration, and diversity issues. Susan's most recent co-edited books include *Building on Critical Traditions: Adult Education and Learning in Canada* and *Africentricity in Action*. She is Chair of the Alexa McDonough Institute for Women, Gender and Social Justice.

Shauna Butterwick is a Professor in the Department of Educational Studies at the University of British Columbia. A feminist perspective on women's learning as it occurs in many different contexts has been central to her research, much of which has been conducted in partnership with community groups.

Erin Careless is a Doctoral Candidate at Mount Saint Vincent University, Halifax, Nova Scotia. She is a contract faculty member in the Adult Education department of St. Francis Xavier University, and teaches part-time at MSVU. Erin's research interests include critical feminism, (step)mothering, technology in education, and social media.

Darlene E. Clover is a Professor in the Faculty of Education at the University of Victoria. Her areas of interest include women and leadership; feminist and arts-based adult education; and critical education in arts and cultural institutions. She is co-editor of a volume titled *Adult Education and Museums: Animating Social and Cultural Change* (in press).

Laurel Collins is an interdisciplinary PhD Candidate in Sociology and Leadership Studies at the University of Victoria. Her research interests include theories of violence and nonviolence; embodiment; social movement learning; and radical adult education. She teaches courses in Social Justice Studies and Political Sociology.

Linda Cullum explores the lives, experiences, and labour of working-class women and men in 20th-century Newfoundland and Labrador, and examines the intersection of gender and class within and across relations of power. One of her current research projects is The Girls' Friendly Society in Newfoundland, 1883-1950.

Jan Duerden is a Lecturer in the Department of English and Modern Languages at Thompson Rivers University, Kamloops, British Columbia. Her interests include phenomenological research methods and women's experiences of post-secondary education, particularly adult female learners' experience of returning to post-secondary education.

Maren Elfert is a PhD Candidate in the Department of Educational Studies at the University of British Columbia. Before coming to UBC she worked for the UNESCO Institute for Lifelong Learning in Hamburg, Germany.

Leona M. English is a Professor of Adult Education at St. Francis Xavier University. She is co-author of *Feminism in Community: Adult Education for Transformation*, to be published by Sense (2015). She received the Houle Award for her critical pedagogy work and is presently co-editor of *Adult Education Quarterly*.

Cheryl Gosselin is a Professor in the Department of Sociology at Bishop's University in Sherbrooke, Québec. She teaches a variety of courses including feminist social theory, gender studies, Québec society in a comparative perspective, and sociology of the body. Her research focuses on minority communities of Québec and their mobilization efforts to maintain the vitality of their populations.

Patricia A. Gouthro is a Professor in the Graduate Studies in Lifelong Learning program at the Faculty of Education at Mount Saint Vincent University in Halifax, Nova Scotia. Her research interests include fiction writing, citizenship, and critical feminist issues in adult education. She is Principal Investigator on a SSHRC grant that explores creative literacies.

Susan M. Holloway is an Associate Professor in the Faculty of Education at the University of Windsor. Her research interests include multiliteracies, adult education, and critical theory. She is Co-investigator on a SSHRC grant exploring creative literacies and has developed a web-based Multiliteracies Project.

Catherine J. Irving works at the Coady International Institute of St. Francis Xavier University, Antigonish, Nova Scotia. She runs the Institute's Marie Michael Library, and teaches research methods and information activism. Her research interests include libraries and resource centres in adult education, and community feminist learning and activism.

Jennifer Kelly is a Professor in the Department of Educational Policy Studies at the University of Alberta. Her areas of research are sociology of education, race, racialization, youth culture, and politics of education. She is the author of two books: *Under the Gaze* and *Borrowed Identities*. She is co-author of *Work and Learning: An Introduction*.

Mary Victor Kostandy is a PhD student in the Department of Educational Studies at the University of British Columbia. Before moving to UBC, she worked as an instructor in the Professional Educator Diploma program at the American University in Cairo, Egypt.

Laurie McGauley is a sessional instructor in the Women's Studies and Inter-Arts programs at Laurentian University. Her areas of interest are community-based art, activism, social justice, and participatory democracy. She is the founder of Myths and Mirrors Community Arts, one of Canada's first community arts organizations.

Catherine McGregor is an Associate Professor in the Faculty of Education at the University of Victoria. Her research interests include women in leadership, diversity, and socially just educational leadership. Her recent research highlights the importance of Indigenous leadership in educational programming and formal education.

Shahrzad Mojab is a Professor of Adult Education and Women's Studies at OISE/University of Toronto. She is internationally known for her work on war, displacement, violence, and women's learning. She is the editor of *Marxism and Feminism; Women, War, Violence, and Learning* and the co-editor of *Educating from Marx: Race, Gender and Learning*.

Winnie Ng, labour rights activist and scholar, is currently the Unifor Sam Gindin Chair in Social Justice and Democracy at Ryerson University in Toronto. She is a former union organizer with immigrant workers in garment factories and hotels, and a labour educator and regional director with the Canadian Labour Congress.

Sylvia Parris hails from Mulgrave, Guysborough County, Nova Scotia. She is committed to lifelong learning in both the formal and informal realms. Sylvia holds two graduate degrees: Master of Education (St. Mary's University) and Master of Arts in Education in Lifelong Learning: Africentric Leadership. Sylvia is currently the Chief Executive Officer of the Delmore "Buddy" Daye Learning Institute.

Thashika Pillay is a Doctoral Candidate at the University of Alberta. Her scholarship focuses on educational policy, migration studies, intersectionality, and critical, anti-colonial, and African feminisms. Her work intersects with issues of social justice, citizenship, and Indigenous knowledge systems and re-centres marginalized onto-epistemological perspectives.

Carole Roy is Associate Professor in the Department of Adult Education at St. Francis Xavier University. Her research interests include women's collective resistance and older women activists. She is currently researching documentary film festivals as sites of learning and community building, and co-editing a volume on community-based learning and the arts.

Kathy Sanford is a Professor in the Faculty of Education at the University of Victoria. Her research interests span gender issues, learning in professional programs, libraries and museums, assessment, and literacy. She works collaboratively with teachers and pre-service teachers in schools and community organizations for educational change.

Suzanne Smythe is an Assistant Professor of Adult Literacy/Adult Education in the Faculty of Education at Simon Fraser University. Her research interests include the entanglements of research, practice, and policies in adult digital literacies; digital equity; and adult basic education. She is completing a multi-site ethnography of adult digital learning in public spaces.

Michèle Stanton-Jean, O.Q., is Guest Scholar in the Centre de recherche en droit public, Faculty of Law at Montréal University. She was the Québec government representative within the Permanent Delegation of Canada to UNESCO from 2011-2014 and President of the Canadian Commission for UNESCO from 2006-2010. One of Québec's 10 "Women of the Year" in 1979, she was named "Career Woman of the Year" in 1981 and won the 2010 YWCA Women of Distinction Award.

Katie Stella is a Master of Education student at the University of New Brunswick and is in the final stages of thesis completion. Deriving from a genuine curiosity for understanding people, their experiences, and the knowledge they form, Katie's research covers women's learning, and practices of activism in the non-profit sector.

Nancy Taber is an Associate Professor in the Faculty of Education at Brock University. She teaches critical adult education, and learning gender in a militarized world. Her work often draws on her experiences serving in the Canadian military as a Sea King helicopter air navigator. Nancy is co-editor of *Building on Critical Traditions: Adult Education and Learning in Canada* and guest editor of an issue on the state of feminism in the *Canadian Journal for the Study of Adult Education*.

Ashley Taylor is Visiting Assistant Professor, Educational Studies at Colgate University in the United States. She specializes in the philosophy of education and disability studies, and is interested in pedagogies of social justice, disability in civic education, and intersections of race, gender, and ability. Ashley's recent work appears in *Hypatia* and *Philosophy of Education*.

Kim Villagante is an interdisciplinary artist, community arts educator, and graduate of UBC's Visual Arts and Art History program. She was awarded the Vancouver Mayor's Arts Award in Community-Engaged Arts in 2013, and has been working as an arts-based facilitator engaging youth around topics of anti-oppression. Passionate about the potential of art in telling stories that are often unheard, her music and art centres the lives of queer people of colour.

Helen Woodrow is an adult educator and historian whose research interests have encompassed literacy practices in coastal Newfoundland, practitioner research, and community publishing. Her current research is focused on the community work of the founding members of the Women's Institute in the Labrador Straits.

Alannah Young Leon, PhD, is Anishnabe Midekway and Nehiy/naw Cree from Treaty One and Treaty Five territories, currently living in unceded Coast Salish territories. Her leadership studies focus on creating partnerships with Indigenous Elders to articulate local Indigenous peoples' protocols, tribal womanist legal traditions, and developing Indigenous land-based pedagogies. Alannah is a Sessional Instructor in the Faculty of Education at the University of British Columbia.

Sajedeh Zahraei completed her PhD in the Faculty of Social Work at the University of Toronto. She has been working in the mental health field for the past 20 years. Her research interests include social determinants of immigrant and refugee mental health, and women, war, violence, and trauma.

In March 2015, Donna Chovanec, a co-editor of this volume, died. Donna was a stalwart feminist, a dedicated activist, and a brilliant scholar. She was an inspiration to all the women activists, students, and adult educators with whom she came in contact. She was an inspiration to us. She made the world better because she was in it.

We are deeply saddened by her death, but cherish the time we had to work with and know her. This book is dedicated to Donna, and all she has done for women and adult education in Canada and the world.

Foreword

"Feminism is dead." This is the headline of a new study reported in the *Daily Mail* as I write this. Last year, Lillian Davis pondered the question "Is feminism dead, dying, or outdated?" in *ModViv*, a daily online newsmagazine (August 1). Clearly, feminism is proving hard to kill—over 14.5 million sites online today purport to address the "Is feminism dead?" question.

For me, this question ceased to have much meaning at all when I came to know Shauna Butterwick and Darlene Clover, two of the editors of *Women, Adult Education, and Leadership in Canada*. For both women, I think it's fair to say, feminism is not a thing separate from themselves that can be taken off or declared "dead." Rather, it is a way of breathing, of being in the world. In Chapter 1, Shauna refers to the "feminist language of critique and the feminist language of possibility." The work of both women entwines these languages, with a special emphasis on animating—and celebrating—the inspiring possibilities that they see around them in women's lives and in women's learning.

When I first met her in the early 1990s, Shauna was hard at work in the community, where she usually can be found, collaborating with a group of women who were living in poverty and seeking ways to be taken seriously in their efforts to access good job training (they kept getting sent either to "life skills" classes or to menial jobs). Later in her career I watched from a rather safer academic office as Shauna went night after night to a dodgy part of the inner city, encouraging a group of women to express their difficult stories through community theatre. Never shy of a fight with authority over unfairness, Shauna once surprised her colleagues by marching with students against her own university to protest a proposed policy that would have doubled their fees. Like Shauna, Darlene is a devoted cultural activist who works with and through the arts. When I first met her she was focusing on environmental adult education. I still smile at recalling how wonderfully she startled a roomful of British academics with her passion about transforming Earth-human relations. She has also transformed much academic work, showing how the arts—visual, textile, spoken, and sound—can be a powerful mobilizer. Back in 2002, I recall her working with a group to make quilts protesting a gas-burning power plant. At one conference that she convened, she arranged clotheslines to be strung throughout the foyer, displaying quilted and other artistic representations of community research projects. I found her in tears in the middle of this riot of colour and threads, overcome by the stories they conveyed.

As you may appreciate, the paths taken by Shauna and Darlene are among the most difficult, lengthy, often frustrating, and sometimes least-celebrated ways of doing research and academic work in general. Both women have made a life-lasting impression on me and many others for their ingenuity in finding creative ways to rally community activism, and for their courage in speaking out on issues that those less energetic may consider too unfashionable, or perhaps too difficult to tackle—to live feminism, in other words. True to their collaborative roots, Shauna and Darlene worked on this book in collaboration with Laurel Collins, an early career researcher, and with Donna Chovanec. Donna is a keenly felt absent presence here, a most generous and spirited adult educator who is deeply missed by those of us privileged to have known her. The book itself presents an inspiring array of women—both the chapter authors and in the women they describe—who, like the editors, have lived to help others learn together how to make life better for everyone.

For any adult educator, these stories are fascinating to read. The chapters here reveal not only the critical role of women and their unique approaches to mobilizing adult education and social change, but also the substantial contribution of Canadian perspectives and approaches to developing adult education as a global movement. Some may still see Canada as a very young country with a harsh climate, a dispersed population, and what Margaret Atwood called the "malevolent north." Its powerful neighbour to the south can easily obscure international understandings of Canada"s achievements and special challenges, and the useful lessons for other countries here. What does it take to build a democratic society in a young country roughly the size of the United States but with a population less than 12% of America's, in which peoples from over 200 countries and cultures can co-exist peacefully with one another and their natural environments, and enjoy equal life chances? Despite the onslaughts of neo-liberalism and the pressures of supra-national organizations, the basic welfare state notion still survives in Canada. Its education system is one of the best in the world (scoring just below the frequently celebrated Finnish system in international assessments such as PISA, for those who put faith in these). Canada's struggle to acknowledge and work towards reparation of the oppression inflicted on its Aboriginal peoples is unique globally, and its French-English relations have been a valuable study for other countries confronting sovereignty movements. And in a time of disturbing moves elsewhere to close borders, Canada continues to employ a comparatively open approach to welcoming immigrants and grappling with ways to tolerate many voices, including those that may not be so tolerant in return.

This is the stuff of these chapters, for adult education infuses the development of strong communities that value freedom, peace, sustainability, and well-being for all. The central themes in Canada's rich history of adult education are of collective action and experiments in radical social change. Initiatives created here, such as the 1920s Antigonish movement and the 1940s Farm Radio Forum, have been imported around the world. This year is the 100th anniversary of the Women's Institute, another iconic movement in Canada's adult education history, which has been commemorated in various events here in the United Kingdom in the past few weeks. Women consistently have been at the heart of these key initiatives, catalyzing citizens' political participation, extending urban universities' reach into farflung areas, fighting for equality, defending public spaces, and, generally, developing civil society.

For me personally, this book is like coming home, reading the words of so many women I have known who have been key leaders in advancing adult education across Canada in recent decades. The chapter authors not only represent top scholars of adult education, who happen to do their work in Canada. These authors are also the people who have kept the associations going, coordinated the conferences, initiated community events—put up the clotheslines and carried the pickets—to make things really happen in the field of adult education and in social change, with global reverberations.

I am honoured to be asked to write the Foreword for this volume. I heartily commend it to readers as an important—as well as illuminating and entertaining—book, to savour and to share.

Tara Fenwick
Stirling, UK, October 2015

Introduction

This edited volume is unique, the first of its kind. Women across Canada have always been part of adult education and learning in formal, non-formal, and informal spheres, and played leadership roles in communities, social movements, and myriad institutions, agencies, and organizations. To date, however, there has never been a book dedicated to their lives and work. This volume brings together writings by new and established faculty members and researchers, community educators, activists, students, and change-makers.

Darlene E. Clover, Shauna Butterwick, and Laurel Collins

Women power is a formidable force.
—*Gro Harlem Bundtland, 1992*

Effective today, the National Association of Women and the Law (NAWL) is being forced to close its office, lay off its staff, and cease major consultations and advocacy on women's legal issues as an outcome of the Harper government's devastating changes to the mandate of Status of Women Canada. This closure is a grave blow to the continuing struggle for women's equality.
—*NAWL Press Release, 2007*

Until very recently...the world was run by men and writing about and by men who, consequently, wrote us, and our role and place in their world.
— *Isabel Allende, 2003*

Pedagogy and learning have become vital spaces of encounter and new kinds of contact zones where histories, including gender histories which have otherwise been subject to enforced forgetting, have perhaps a small chance now of being written.
—*Angela McRobbie, 2009*

These four quotations about power provide a pertinent frame for a book that explores the past and present of feminist and women's adult education and leadership in Canada. In 1992, Former President of Norway Gro Harlem Brundtland emphasized the significance of women's power in the struggle for gender and ecological change. Moving forward to 2007, the press release by the National Association of Women and the Law (NAWL) is a disturbing reminder of another type of power, that exerted by a deeply conservative government over the lives of countless women across Canada. Author Isabelle Allende renders visible men's power to tell and control women's stories, while Angela McRobbie reminds us of the power of education and learning, and the opportunity we have to write ourselves as women into history.

The Gendered Terrain

While much progress has been achieved over the decades with respect to women's rights, we still have a long way to go. Recent events on campuses across this country illustrate entrenched sexist beliefs and practices. For example, the men's hockey program at the University of Ottawa was suspended following allegations of sexual assault (Pedwell, 2014), and four male student leaders resigned over a sexually explicit Facebook chat about the female head of the student federation. Misogynistic social media posts by male students at Dalhousie's Dentistry School came to light, and at Saint Mary's University in Halifax and at UBC in Vancouver, student orientation week involved students leading chants that encouraged underage sex and rape. Canada's former Governor-General and current Chancellor of the University of Ottawa, Michaëlle Jean, commented on what she saw as the "rape culture" infecting university campuses across the country.

While some decried this abuse, others argued that these activities were harmless. McRobbie (2009) explores what underpins this latter reaction and is deeply concerned about "the guise of modern and enlightened 'gender aware' forms of governmentality" (p.2). In 2006 Taber and Gouthro brought to our attention the belief held by many young women and men that "women have already attained equality so feminism is no longer needed" (p. 56). In 2011, a study by Plan Canada demonstrated that while "Canadian teenagers may talk the talk on gender equality...they also harbour some marked stereotypical views of appropriate roles and behaviours for men and women" (Baluia, 2011, p. A3).

University campuses are not alone in the practice of misogyny; it is rife in other powerful institutions such as Canadian fire brigades, police forces, and the military. There is a culture of denial among the leaders of these institutions, including the CBC. Jian Ghomeshi, a popular CBC radio host, was eventually terminated, long after senior administrators became aware of his violent sexual proclivities. As of the time of publication of this book, he is facing four counts of sexual assault.

As we focus our gaze on contemporary gender problems and challenges, we must remember that colonization, a highly abusive, patriarchal force, has been active in Canada for hundreds of years now. It has taken its toll on all Aboriginal peoples, but especially women. For example, the recent *Truth and Reconciliation Report* (*T&R*) (2015) notes, among many other things, how the replacing of "existing forms of Aboriginal government with relatively powerless band councils" disempowered Aboriginal women in particular, "who had held significant influence and powerful [leadership] roles in many First Nations" (pp. 1-2). The legacy of this colonial patriarchy, as Doyle-Bedwell (2012) argues, is that if you ask an Aboriginal woman today "if she sees herself as a leader, she will likely respond in the negative" (p.192), although these women do much of the work required to move their communities forward. The *T&R* report also draws attention to how the Canadian educational system worked to ensure that men acquired "the habits and modes of thought of white men" (p.3), which has transformed relations between Aboriginal men and women.

Over the past two decades in particular, it has come to light that hundreds of Indigenous women have been murdered or gone missing in British Columbia alone. Kalbfleish (2010) notes that for years, "the police did not pursue these unsettling disappearances, leaving the loss of each woman and its attendant ambiguous circumstances to be marked only by the women's friends and family" (p. 280). Unlike his predecessor, Prime Minister Justin Trudeau has promised a full government iquiry into this national shame. The government's failure to respond has been duly noted by the United Nations Committee on the Elimination of All Forms of Discrimination Against Women (CEDAW, 2015), who subsequently conducted an inquiry and, like other feminist organizations, called for the Canadian government to conduct a public inquiry and implement an action plan.

Putting Power Back into Empowerment

Women, adult education, and leadership in Canada are centred between these problematic political and exclusionary forces and the landscape of despair and hopelessness left in their wake, and the potential and determination of women and feminist educators, learners, leaders, activists, and change-makers. These individuals are responding to a challenge by Shrilatha Batliwala (2014) for forms of feminist leadership and pedagogy that put power back in empowerment.

This edited volume details a range of feminist and women's learning practices and spaces, as well as pedagogical, activist, and leadership work motivated in the pursuit of emancipation, justice, and change. The authors highlight a wide diversity of critical, provocative, creative, historical, and contemporary ideas with, about, by, and for women. In so doing, they tell different stories from past eras, reveal a multitude of contexts, and employ distinctive conceptual sites and lenses. They expose the multifaceted challenges that women have faced, and continue to face, as they negotiate the cul-de-sacs, broken pavements, and deep ditches inherent in the game of power, profit, and patriarchy. Importantly, this book also draws attention to women's acts of commitment, passion, resourcefulness, creativity, wisdom, sheer cheek, and what Manicom and Walters (2012) call "possibilities" along the road to gendered, pedagogical, and social change. Through their stories, the authors help us to appreciate the women who teach, learn, lead, and act—at times overtly, at other times subversively, but always purposefully and courageously—upon the Canadian stage.

The Canvas of Hope and Possibility

> Here is the road, maybe a thousand miles long, and the woman walking down it isn't at mile one. I don't know how far she has to go, but I know she is not going backward, despite it all—and she is not walking alone.
> —Rebecca Solnit, 2014

As we paint these bleak, gendered realities onto the Canadian canvas, we are also reminded of the words of Ursula Franklin, a professor at the University of Toronto who once rebuffed a particularly critical conference participant by asking: "Having taken the dim view, now what?" Her question reminds us to be cognizant of the less than shadowy side, the side that celebrates progressive gains made, and still being made, by women across this country. For example, Canada at the moment has two progressive women premiers. Kathleen Wynne in Ontario is a lesbian and an adult education graduate (Ontario Institute for Studies in Education, OISE). Rachel Notley ousted the long-governing Conservative party in Alberta, painting a New Democratic Party face onto the legislature of one of Canada's most regressive provinces

Women in Canada have won the legal right to choose what they do with their own bodies, even in the face of neo-conservative religious fundamentalist moralizing and fuelling of anti-choice sentiments.

Canada was one of the first countries to legalize same-sex marriage and thereby unmask the bias, ignorance, and injustice of hetero-normativity. That being said, missing from this volume is a chapter specifically dedicated to the adult education and/or leadership work of lesbian and transgender women in Canada, although some authors in this volume align with these identities. While a shortcoming to be sure, it provides a fertile area for future volumes on feminist adult education and leadership in this country.

Framing the Debate: What Is the Solution?

This volume has three introductory chapters and four parts, each with a number of chapters. Interspersed between the chapters are "vignettes," profiles of Canadian feminist organizations and educators, activists, and leaders. Many of the women profiled are no longer alive, but they all were or are pioneers in their own way, courageous and determined women whose struggles we wanted to honour. We realize there exist countless others, and we leave the work of honouring others to the women who succeed us in moving the feminist and women's adult education and leadership agenda forward.

Following this introductory chapter is Chapter 1, "Feminist Adult Education: Looking Back, Moving Forward," written by Shauna Butterwick and guided by the spirit of Donna Chovanec and the solidarity of Darlene Clover and Laurel Collins. It provides a challenge to the traditionally male-focused history of adult education in Canada. Providing a feminist framework for this book, Butterwick emphasizes the importance of both the feminist language of critique and the feminist language of possibility. She describes the essential role of women's and feminist contributions, and the importance of understanding adult learners' contexts in this post-feminist era in which sexist policies and practices and gender inequality persist. The chapter concludes with responses to the question, "What is the solution?"

Following this chapter is a vignette about Donna Chovanec, who was one of the original editors for this volume. Donna's pedagogy, research, and advice were deeply informed by her feminist spirit.

Chapter 2, "Making Waves: Feminist and Indigenous Women's Leadership," by Darlene E. Clover and Catherine McGregor, provides another important framework for this book. The authors take up Blackmore's (1999) acknowledgement that women "have long been troubled by the notion of 'leader' and the [masculinist] images it conveys" (p. 2). They explore dominant discourses of leadership and archetypes of leadership, troubling salvation, traits-based orientations, and assumed masculinities, including "feminine" conceptions that maintain stereotypes. The chapter concludes with key aspects of Indigenous women's and feminist leadership that re-politicize and re-position leadership as a powerful means for gender, social, and ecological change.

Chapter 2 is followed by a vignette about Ellen Woodsworth, a long-time participant in feminist activism, social justice, and community organizing. Ellen served two terms as Vancouver City Councillor and was the first out lesbian City Councillor in Canada. She co-chaired the Women's Task Force, which wrote the Gender Equality Strategy for the City of Vancouver—the first city in Canada to have such a policy.

Part I Leadership and Activism

Part I, *Leadership and Activism*, begins with Marlene Atleo's Chapter 3, "All My Relations: Networks of First Nations/Métis/Inuit Women Sharing the Learnings." This chapter interrupts dominant colonial and sexist portrayals of Indigenous women, pointing to their past, present, and future contributions to revitalizing and maintaining communities and cultural understandings. We learn how the Idle No More Movement was initiated by women adult educators alongside other young women, all of who courageously challenged the federal government's colonial practices using social media to great effect.

Following Chapter 3 is a vignette about Laura Hughes, a World War I peace activist who led the Women's International League for Peace and Freedom and who later engaged in labour reform in response to factory women's working conditions.

Solnit (2014) reminds us that although violence does not necessarily have "a race, a class, a religion or a nationality...it does have a gender" (p.21). This is where Nancy Taber begins Chapter 4. In *"Women Military Leaders in the Canadian Forces: Learning to Negotiate Gender,"* she brings to bear a feminist anti-militarist perspective, problematizing the ways in which gender and militarism intersect in society, with an overall privileging of men, masculinity, militarism, and militaries. She calls on us to recognize that militaries are not isolated entities, and illustrates how adult learning theory can inform current understandings of women and militarism through new narratives of leadership.

The vignette following this chapter explores the contributions of Paz Buttedahl, an academic scholar who was actively engaged in international relations and who began the Masters program at Royal Roads University in Human Security and Peace-building.

For Grey and Sawer (2008), a distinct power of social movements is their ability to "introduce new ways of looking at the world and challenge the rationale and operation of existing systems" (p. 4). In Chapter 5, "Exploring the Learning and Wisdom of Elder Social Activists in Atlantic Canada: Learning Liberation," Shauna Butterwick and Maren Elfert illustrate how Elder women's social activism and learning challenge false binaries between private and public realms and the prominence of power-oriented, confrontational notions of masculinist leadership. The authors remind us that to truly transform relations of domination, our actions and pedagogies must be built through solidarity, offer counter-narratives, and be grounded in action and hope for a better world. The courage, tenacity, and leadership of Flora MacDonald, the first woman to run for the leadership of a national party in Canada, are described in the vignette that follows this chapter.

In Chapter 6, "Black Women's Africentric and Feminist Leadership: Voices from Nova Scotia," Susan M. Brigham and Sylvia Parris highlight understandings of Africentric leadership through the eyes of ten feminist and womanist adult educators who graduated from an Adult Education/Lifelong Learning program. Black feminist leadership is linked to daily concerns, such as education and health; acknowledges women's common history; seeks freedom from injustice; and emphasizes the importance of education and new knowledge creation to empower oppressed people by building on a relational ontology of I/We.

In Chapter 7, Cheryl Gosselin takes us back to 1950s and 1960s Québec, a time of great change, nationalism, and discontinuity, but also a time of active mobilization to advance women's rights. She explores how L'Association des femmes diplômées des universités de Montréal (AFDUM) fought for gender equality in the work force by lobbying, promoting the principle of equal pay for equal work, and inspiring women to enter post-secondary education, move outside the home, and take up leadership roles in politics and other public arenas. Gosselin illustrates how this early feminist work paved the road for women leaders n Québec today.

In the next vignette, we learn about Marie Thérèse (Forget) Casgrain, who began her political career as President of the League for Women's Rights. She later became the first woman in Canada to lead a political party in Québec.

The Federated Women's Institute of Canada (WI) is perhaps the best known, non-formal site of adult education in Canada. In Chapter 8, "Disrupted Discourses in the Women's Institute Organizations of Canada: Celebrated Stories," Katie Stella takes us into the world of this rural organization committed to initiating national programs for women, using a feminist post-structuralist lens to explore the complexity of women's learning within this site. Stella highlights celebrated stories of unity and inclusion, but also argues the need to shift our thinking away from women's learning as viewed by WI as merely harmonious and value-free, to a recognition of the importance of solitude, silence, resistance, and power as successful ways to operate within these organizations.

The final vignette profile subject in Part I, Florence O'Neill, was also involved with the provision of non-formal adult learning opportunities, particularly to poor marginalized fishing communities in Newfoundland. In her Doctorate from Columbia University, she developed an island-wide cohesive program for adult education, a vision that informed her work as Director of Adult Education for the province of Newfoundland.

Part II Pedagogies for Change

Alannah Young Leon's Chapter 9, "Weaving Indigenous Women's Leadership: Pedagogies, Protocols, and Practice," begins Part II, *Pedagogies for Change*. This chapter continues the theme of Indigenous women's leadership and strategic engagement with colonialism. The chapter shares conversations with Indigenous women at a Tribal Indigenous land-based health education program called the Medicine Camp in rural Manitoba. Through this program, Tribal Midewiwin matriarchs' transmission of knowledge contrasts with the assimilationist Canadian state, providing understandings of Indigenous pedagogies based on protocols and practices related to Indigenous laws and legal traditions.

In the first vignette in Part II, the contributions of Verna J. Kirkness are showcased. A Cree woman from Manitoba, Kirkness is a key leader and the author of reports about Aboriginal control of Aboriginal education in Canada. She has also provided a clear vision for the education and hiring of Indigenous teachers and the development of Indigenous language programs.

If, as Fryer (2010) argues, "our first promise of freedom consists of the...extension of citizenship" (p.23), then what must be said when full citizenship is denied? This is a question that Sajedeh

Zahraei and Shahrzad Mojab take up in Chapter 10, "War, Diaspora, and Learning: Arab Iraqi Refugee Women." This chapter tells a story of war, displacement, and dispossession through the eyes of Arab Iraqi refugee women in Canada. Using the context of Iraq's recent history and Western colonialist interventions, the authors challenge notions of "liberating" and "saving" Iraqi women and demonstrate the contradictory effect of racialized and gendered displacement, loss of status, and the ongoing violence of social exclusion. The combined forces of neo-liberalism and securitization serve to keep refugee women at the borders of Canadian society, denying them access to substantive citizenship rights and employment.

In Chapter 11, "Nonviolent Adult Education: Violence and Nonviolence in the Context of Women's Adult Education in Canada," Laurel Collins illustrates how theories of nonviolence can provide a lens through which to examine educational institutions, structures, and practices. She explores concepts of violence and nonviolence and the intersections between violence against women, systemic and institutional violence, nonviolent communication education (NVC), peace education, and the creation of nonviolent educational spaces. Collins provides suggestions for how NVC education, in combination with feminist adult education, can provide tools that support the needs of women learners.

For Simon, Dippo, and Schenke (1991), Canadian unions are "a way in which workers have responded and can respond to the desire for a better life" (p. 128). Winnie Ng's Chapter 12, "Building Solidarity for All: Voices of Women of Colour, Anti-Racism Leaders, and Labour Educators," explores how labour education must employ more substantive ways in which to sustain and further the contributions and issues experienced by racialized women and other equity-seeking members of labour unions. From her long experience in the labour movement, Ng provides a critical reflection on existing practices and strategies of anti-racism education within the movement, and draws on the voices of women of colour activists and educators to give us a re-imagining of labour education in Canada aimed at solidarity and labour renewal.

In the next vignette, we are introduced to the Canadian Congress for Learning Opportunities for Women (CCLOW). For several decades, this key feminist adult education organization provided leadership and policy advocacy and conducted multiple research projects on a broad array of topics relevant to women's learning.

Jennifer Kelly and Thashika Pillay recognize in Chapter 13, "African-Canadian Women, Leadership, and Adult Education: Reclaiming a Past," the absences and silences in Canada's leadership and adult education histories. Using a critical feminist analysis of the newspaper column, "Our Negro Citizens" (ONC) written by Reverend George W. Slater, Jr., and published in the *Edmonton Bulletin* and *Edmonton Journal* between 1921 and 1924, the authors explore socio-historical representations of African-Canadian women engaged in public adult education. In particular, they illustrate how newspapers act as power brokers and sites of public adult education, creating through word and image new social and discursive realities and constructs of Black women and Black communities in Edmonton, Alberta.

The tireless commitment to honouring the history and experiences of peoples of African and Caribbean heritage and to mentoring and enabling intergenerational transfer of knowledge is the focus of the next vignette about Edmonton-based Jeannette Austin-Odina.

In Chapter 14, "Dialogue as Interdependence: Disability, Gender, and Learning across Difference," Ashley Taylor offers another dialogue across difference, in this case differences of ability, wherein she argues that the social positioning and experiences of participants relative to gendered norms of ability and able-bodiedness are of central concern. Taylor orients dialogic exchange as a means of developing cross-positional interdependence, arguing that this view acknowledges women's social connections and their dependence on one another for the construction of narratives, as well as their embeddedness in abled and gendered webs of political, economic, and cultural meanings and social power.

Part III Pedagogy and the Imagination

Part III, *Pedagogy and the Imagination*, begins with Chapter 15, "Imagining the Possible: Feminist Arts-Based Adult Education and Leadership." In this chapter, Darlene E. Clover and Laurie McGauley examine the Occupy Wall Street movement's belief that "the imagination is the most subversive thing the public can have" (Mohanty, 2012, p. vii). They illustrate how women and feminist artists, adult educators, and researchers in communities and universities across Canada are developing and using innovative, creative, and dynamic practices to strengthen the fraying social, cultural, and environmental fabrics of neo-conservative Canada. They argue that the strength of women's arts-based practices lies in their capacity to simultaneously disturb yet affirm, represent yet conceal, respect individuality yet encourage collectivity, and unsettle yet celebrate and amuse.

The vignette that follows Chapter 15 features Barbara Clague, who worked for many years with the Pacific Association for Continuing Education (PACE) and who later served as Administrative Assistant to the Minister of Advanced Education, and then to the Minister of Aboriginal Affairs in British Columbia.

Dorothy Smith (1987) once argued that "as we learn more about our women's history we discover that a powerful intellectual and artistic current moves like an underground stream" (p. 22). This idea resonates throughout Chapter 16, "The Political Fashion Shows of Filipina Activists: Creating Defiant Imagination through Creative Processes." Authors Shauna Butterwick and Kim Villagante explore visual and performative art created by Filipina activists at the Philippine Women's Centre of BC (PWCBC), a feminist group located in Vancouver. Using Marxist-feminist and transnational feminist theory, they illustrate how PWCBC 's arts-based practices work to reveal interlocking dimensions of gender inequity, political engagement, social and economic justice, and labour rights. The PWCBC fashion shows not only name injustices, but they also offer a language of possibility and hope.

Chapter 17, "Women Working for Libraries: Learning and Social Change," was authored by Catherine J. Irving. Durrani (2014) calls for public libraries that can make "a significant contribution to a society based on principles of equality, human rights and social justice" (p.8) and this is what Irving illustrates—how libraries and women librarians in Antigonish, Nova Scotia were central to a wide range of educational efforts aimed towards the betterment of the working classes. She explores the vital roles these women played in promoting and serving the goals of the Antigonish Movement, by supporting and encouraging women's learning, public activism, and engagement.

In the vignette that follows Chapter 17, we learn more about the women of the Antigonish Movement, which occupies a central place in the history of Canadian adult education. It portrays how a group of tireless women collected and sometimes wrote materials for study clubs, documented their activities, and created and distributed newsletters to keep the different subgroups connected.

As Canadian author Margaret Lawrence (1983) once suggested, as we grow older, we should become not less radical but more so. The chapter and vignette that follow show us just what this looks like. In Carole Roy's Chapter 18, "More than Laughter: Raging Grannies and Creative Leadership," we learn how this unique group of senior feminist activists, who refuse to simply sit quietly in their rocking chairs, have transformed protest into an art form. Through leadership practices such as satirical songs, whimsical costumes, cheekiness, and a deep knowledge about the social and environmental issues they address, the Grannies transform our understandings of senior women's power and place on the Canadian landscape. The next vignette provides brief profiles of how some members of the Raging Grannies challenge stereotypes of grandmothers and bring a playful and imaginative approach to public protests.

Hannah Arendt's belief that "storytelling reveals meanings" is captured in Chapter 19, "Feminism and Femininities: Learning about Gender and Women's Leadership through Fiction" by Patricia A. Gouthro and Susan M. Holloway. The authors draw upon research on women fiction writers and their own experiences as educators to explore what fiction can tell us about issues related to gender. They share how women writers explain their creative learning processes and in so doing, broaden how we understand adult learning and re-value the art of storytelling as a pedagogical tool. The chapter illustrates how the concept of gender is, and can be, taught through fiction, and its impact on the development of female identity.

Although public museums are ubiquitous pedagogical institutions that have been pressured to move beyond elitism and to join the struggle for social change (Barrett, 2011), Janes (2009) laments their lack of ability to engage with Canada's most pressing social and environmental problems. But Lorraine Bell, Darlene E. Clover, and Kathy Sanford challenge this idea in Chapter 20, "Women and Adult Education in Public Museums and Art Galleries: Women in the Cultural Sphere," which illustrates how women museum-based adult educators are becoming key players in the struggle for social and ecological justice. While recognizing that problematic traditions linger, they provide examples of how women are designing and using exhibitions and arts-based practices to make important contributions to our understandings of the place and role of museums in Canada, as well as the wider world of cultural adult education practice and political activism.

Part IV Structures and Agency

The first chapter in Part IV, *Structures and Agency*, deals with women's needs and aspirations as learners. Jan Duerden's Chapter 21, "Adult Female Learner: Is That a Real Thing?" argues that as post-secondary institutions in Canada grapple with shifting enrolments within the traditional student demographic, they are being required to focus on non-traditional student groups. This requirement must include new discussions about student engagement and support. Through the lived experiences of seven adult female learners, Duerden explores the challenges and possibilities involved in returning to university.

Appearing after Chapter 21 is a vignette about Anne Ironside, whose life exemplifies a creative dance between conceiving a vision and creating structures to enable that vision. Ironside directed the First Women's Resources Centre and persuaded the government of British Columbia to fund similar centres for all B.C. colleges. She was also the first woman to become president of the CAAE.

In Chapter 22, "'Don't Relegate Women to the Nursery and Kitchen': Women and the Memorial University Extension Service," Helen Woodrow and Linda Cullum use archival documents, secondary sources, and interviews with women to illustrate how the Memorial University Extension Service operated as a vehicle of transformation for women in Newfoundland in the second half of the twentieth century—both as workers in the organization and as citizens in the province's communities. The authors explore structured educational programs, literacy work, and direct training of rural women in terms of its goal of the "betterment" of home, family, and women.

"It is very much like a trapeze artist trick. Everything depends on the connection of the two trapeze artists...so that one or both is not dropped" (Gilbert and Sameh, 2002, p. 185). In Chapter 23, "Critical and Creative Transformative Learning: 'Longing for the Sea' in Feminist Non-Profit Organizations," Leona M. English explores the trapeze act of feminist non-governmental organizations (NGOs) in Canada today. She illustrates how they are oriented, by and large, to social transformation and to structural changes, frequently combining advocacy and service within the complexity of multi-faceted social and gender issues. She suggests that the effect of NGOs on women's lives can be transformative, and that this fact needs better recognition in the transformative learning literature that is too often silent in the area of feminist community-based NGOs.

Developing an educated citizenry was the objective of Citizen's Forum (CF), a joint project of the Canadian Association for Adult Education (CAAE) and the CBC. This program ran for 20 years and owed much of its success and longevity to Isabel Wilson, who served as the National Secretary, helping to produce more than 300 pamphlets for the CF study clubs. Wilson is profiled in a vignette following Chapter 23.

In Chapter 24, "'Neither Kind nor Patient': Canadian Women Literacy Educators Working in the Spaces of Neo-Liberalism," Suzanne Smythe discusses the complexity of practices and skills required by women in order to support adult literacy learning in a landscape of inequalities. She draws upon literacy education reports, research projects, policy visions, and curricular documents to elaborate a feminist analysis of adult literacy as "women's work." She argues that a feminist analysis of literacy education elucidates why these issues matter to the quality of literacy instruction, to hidden pedagogies and practices in the field, and to the salience of political resistance.

Ruth Isabel McKenzie is the subject of the next vignette. Like Isabel Wilson, Ruth McKenzie was a key player in the CAAE, serving as the National Editor and Research Director of the weekly CBC National Farm Radio Forum.

Hawthorne and Klein (1999) defined the use of new information and community technologies for women's empowerment as cyberfeminism. In Chapter 25, "Mommy Blogs: A Feminist Community of Practice," Erin J. Careless invites us into a world where mothers are using social media as sources of voice and empowerment. She argues that blogging for mothers, as a form of online journaling, makes public their experiences, rendering visible their reproductive work and learning/educating practices in previously unprecedented ways.

In Chapter 26, "Swinging a Hammer in a Man's World: Learning, Adapting, and Celebrating," Kate Braid tells the story of her experience as the first woman to graduate from the British Columbia Institute of Technology (BCIT) with a red seal ticket, to teach at BCIT full time, and to be voted to the executive of the Vancouver Carpenters' Union. Woven throughout Kate's personal narrative is a larger discussion of women's persistent underrepresentation in the trades and in the educational programs that enable more women to choose jobs in the trades and to survive and thrive in this area of work. The important role of advocacy groups, such as Women in Trades—a group that Kate helped to found in Vancouver in 1979— is also examined.

We give the final word in this volume to Michèle Stanton-Jean, the keynote speaker at the June 2015 conference of the Canadian Association for the Study of Adult Education in Montréal. Using a narrative style similar to Braid's, Stanton-Jean tells a captivating story in Chapter 27, "My Long Journey in Adult Education: From the 'Me' to the 'We.'" She shares the challenges and successes associated with her involvement in adult education since 1966 and her leadership in the Québec policy arena. She describes her growing awareness of women's inequality and of adult education as a significant means to expand opportunities for women. She concludes with what she sees as future challenges for women's adult education.

Staying in the province of Québec, we present our final vignette on Relais-femmes. Based in Montréal, this organization exercises a mandate to liaise between women's groups and academic researchers and to provide training in action research.

References

- Antrobus, P. (2000). Transformational leadership: Advancing the agenda for gender justice. *Gender and Development,* 85(3), 50-56.
- Arendt, H. Retrieved August 05, 2015, from http:///www.quotationspage.com/quote/riy1.html.
- Barrett, J. (2011). *Museums and the Public Sphere.* Oxford: Wiley-Backwell.
- Batliwala, S. (2013). *Engaging with Empowerment: An Intellectual and Experiential Journey.* New Delhi: Women Unlimited.
- Blackmore, J. (1999). *Gendered Lives: Becoming Educators, Feminist and Leadership. Troubling Women: Feminism, Leadership and Educational Change* (pp.62-84). Buckingham: Open University Press.
- Blatchford, C. (2015). Troubling report on "sexualized culture" in Canada's military may overstate problem. Retrieved June 01, 2015, from http://news.nationalpost.com/full-comment/christie-blatchford-troubling-report-on-sexualized-culture-in-canadas-military-may-overstate-problem.
- Butler, J. (1990). *Gender trouble: Feminism and the Subversion of Identity.* New York & London: Routledge.
- CEDAW, (2015, March 6). Report of the inquiry concerning Canada of the Committee of the Elimination of Discrimination against Women under article 8 of the Optional Protocol to the Convention on the Elimination of All Forms of Discrimination against Women. New York: United Nations Convention on the Elimination of all Forms of Violence Against Women.
- Doyle-Bedwell, P. (2012). And so I turn to Rita: Mi'kmaq women, community action, leadership and resilience. In C. Kenny & T. Ngaroimata Fraser (Eds.), *Living Indigenous leadership: Native Narratives on Building Strong Communities* (pp.192-203). Vancouver: UBC Press.

- Durrani, S. (2014). *Progressive Librarianship: Perspectives from Kenya and Britain, 1979-2010*. London: Vita Books.
- Fryer, R.H. (2010). *Promises of Freedom: Citizenship, Belonging and Lifelong Learning*. Leicester: NIACE.
- Grey, S. & Sawer, M. (2008). *Women's Movements: Flourishing or in Abeyance?* London & New York: Routledge.
- Janes, R. (2009). *Museums in a Troubled World*. Milton Park, Abingdon, USA: Routledge.
- Hawthorne S & Klein, R. (1999. *Cyberfeminism: Connectivity, Critique and Creativity*. North Melbourne: Spinifex Press Pty Ltd.
- Kalbfleish, E. (2010). Bordering on feminism: Space, solidarity and transnationalism in Rebecca Belmore's Vigil. In C. Suzack, S. Huhndorf, J. Perreault & J. Barman (Eds.), *Indigenous Women and Feminism: Politics, Activism, Culture* (pp.278-297). Vancouver: UBC Press.
- Kesler Gilbert, M. & Sameh, C. (2002). Building feminist educational alliance in an urban community. In N. Naples & K. Bojar (Eds), *Teaching Feminist Activism: Strategies for the Field* (pp.185-206). New York & London: Routledge.
- Laurence, M. (1983). My finest hour. Retrieved May 20, 2015, from http://canlit.ca/pdfs/articles/canlit100-Final(Laurence).pdf.
- Manicom, L. & Walters, S. (Eds.) (2012). *Feminist Popular Education in Transnational Debates*. New York: Palgrave MacMillan.
- McRobbie, A. (2009). *The Aftermath of Feminism: Gender, Culture and Social Change*. London: Sage Publications Ltd.
- Mohanty, C. (2012). Series editor forward. In L. Manicom & S. Walters (Eds.), *Feminist Popular Education in Transnational Debates*. New York: Palgrave MacMillan.
- NAWL (2007). Harper government working to silence women. Retrieved October 10, 2014, from http://nawl.ca/en/library/entry/harper-government-working-to-silence-women.
- Pedwell, T. (2014). Former Governor-General Michaelle Jean calls out "rape culture"infecting country's campuses and society. The Canadian Press. Retrieved May 31, 2015, from http://news.nationalpost.com/news/canada/former-governor-general-michaelle-jean-calls-out-rape-culture-infecting-countrys-campuses-and-society.
- Simon, R., Dippo, D. & Schenke, A. (1991). *Learning Work: A Critical Pedagogy of Work Education*. Toronto: OISE Press.
- Smith, D. (1987). *The Everyday World as Problematic: A Feminist Sociology*. Toronto: University of Toronto Press.
- Solnit, R. (2014). *Men Explain Things to Me*. London: Granta Publications.
- Taber, N. & Goutro, P. (2005). Women and adult education in Canadian society. In T. Fenwick, T. Nesbit & B. Spencer (Eds.), *Contexts of Adult Education: Canadian Perspectives* (pp.58-67). Toronto: Thompson Educational Publishing.
- Trigg, M. (Ed). (2010). *Leading the Way: Young Women's Activism for Social Change*. New York & London: Rutgers University Press.
- Walby, S. (2011). *The Future of Feminism*. Cambridge: Polity Press.
- Yuen, J. (2015). Hydro One firing TFC fan after vulgar comment to reporter. Retrieved August, 04, 2015, from http://www.torontosun.com/2015/05/12/hydro-one-firing-tfc-fan-after-vulgar-comment.

People demonstrate in Montréal in 2015 to highlight International Women's Day, which is celebrated on March 8 every year around the world.
THE CANADIAN PRESS/Graham Hughes.

1

Feminist Adult Education
Looking Back, Moving Forward

> Feminism ... is a movement to end sexism, sexist exploitation and oppression.
>   — bell hooks, 2015

Adult education and feminism, as social movements, are both oriented to praxis, defined as "reflection and action directed at the structures to be transformed" (Freire, 1970, p. 126). They are also oriented to an appreciation for how adult learning—specifically, critical inquiry into the structures and mechanisms of domination—is a core activity of movements for social justice.[1] Despite a mutual history and shared sensibility, feminist thought and action are seldom considered to be part of what counts as the "foundation" of adult education, that is, its history, philosophy, and scholarship.

Shauna Butterwick

There have been debates within the Canadian Society for the Study of Adult Education (CASAE) about the fragmentation of adult education knowledge due to differing interests and perspectives. In 2003, these debates led to a major review of CASAE conference proceedings, the *Canadian Journal for the Study of Adult Education*, and adult education Master and PhD thesis abstracts to analyze the extent to which feminism and an orientation to women's equality had influenced studies within the field (Butterwick, Fenwick, and Mojab 2003). The idea that feminist approaches are marginal is challenged by hooks (2015), who argues that feminism is a movement for everybody, as "feminist change has touched all our lives in a positive way" (p. xiv).

In some sense there has been a single story told about the foundation and history of adult education in Canada, a story in which well-known male leaders and initiatives in our field figure prominently while women's and feminist contributions remain for the most part invisible or marginalized. Addressing this oversight is a central motivation of this book. As Chimamanda Ngozi Adiche, a Nigerian novelist, notes in her TED talk titled "The Danger of the Single Story," the problem with single stories is not that they are untrue, but rather, that they are incomplete. A single-story approach is evident in dominant notions of what counts as the major contributions to our field of practice and study.

This chapter offers a feminist framework for this book, a way to think through women's contributions to adult education and to understand the needs and capacities of women as adult learners. It outlines some key feminist theories and how they contribute to what many consider to be a central truth about adult education, that is: we cannot understand adult learners' capacities, motivations, and struggles unless we understand their contexts. More specifically, this chapter attempts to bring feminist theory to bear on how individuals are "inextricable from the society in which they live" and how "they develop in ways intrinsic to themselves *but moulded by the discriminatory forces of society within which they function*" (Baumgartner 2001, para 20, emphasis added).

The Location of the Speaker Is Epistemologically Significant

hooks' definition of feminism appears simple. However, given that feminism is dynamic, undergoes constant change, and includes diverse perspectives and debates, providing a feminist framework for adult education is not a simple or straightforward matter. A feminist exploration of adult education is a decidedly personal project. As Bracken and Nash (2010) note, "gendered scholarship is deeply personal because we cannot escape ourselves in our own projects; it is what we study and analyze, but it [is] also *who we are*" (emphasis in original, p. 351). Given my social location and genealogy, this chapter will feature unique inclusions and exclusions. The concept of "home" is for many the most significant site of learning and my feminist sensibilities reflect my experiences as the daughter of white Canadian middle-class parents who married post-World War II. My parents' immigrant history also informed my upbringing.[2] My feminist education was further shaped by my observations of feminist movements that began in the 1960s and 1970s and by my participation in feminist activism in the 1980s, 1990s, and onward. I also learned about feminism through formal education; graduate school was a significant time for me, as was my first position teaching in a women's studies program after completing graduate studies. My engagement with feminist ideas and practices has been and continues to be a lifelong learning process, and I am often reminded of the partiality and limitations of what I know. Black feminists and Indigenous movements have been particularly important to my education and to my journey of decolonization, helping me understand my history and location as a member of Canadian settler society.[3]

To achieve the objective of offering an entry into feminist perspectives related to adult education, this chapter is organized around two larger inquiries: "What is the problem?" and "What is the solution?" In "What is the problem?," a number of issues are examined, including: naming women's oppression; the challenges of applying a more complex, intersectional, and nuanced type of analysis when seeking answers; researchers' subjectivity along with processes or methodologies of creating knowledge; and claims that we live in a post-feminist era. In "What is the solution?," some key themes embraced by feminist pedagogy are explored. In discussing these questions, I have included references to the contributions of feminist scholars whose ideas and explorations have influenced my thinking; I hope they are also relevant to readers of this book.

What Is the Problem?

Feminist theory and feminist movements are radical and revolutionary. One of the most significant contributions made by feminist thought is a deeper understanding of gender: "a set of overlapping and often contradictory set of cultural descriptions and prescriptions referring to sexual difference which arise from and regulate particular economic, social, political, technological and other non-discursive contexts" (Van Zoonen, 1994, p. 4). How gender as a social construct operates depends on history, culture, politics, location, and so on.

This notion of gender and how it positions women as "Other" was central to Simone de Beauvoir's immensely influential feminist treatise *The Second Sex* (1949) and her notion that woman is made, not born. To say that women are "Other" is to say that they are defined only in relation to men. Men, on the other hand, are not similarly identified; that is, they are not "Other" in relation to women.

As subjects, women are alienated, most particularly from their bodies and reproductive capacity. Women's alienation from themselves as human beings with full rights and responsibilities was also a concern of Betty Friedan, who explored women's unhappiness, referred to as "the problem that has no name." *The Feminine Mystique* is considered the start of the "second wave" of the American Women's Liberation movement.[4] While Friedan's work has been challenged for its omission of race and class analysis, its focus on the white middle class, and its usefulness only to American women given the fact that few other countries experienced this "wave," this text did nonetheless contribute to an understanding of just how powerful the structures of gender socialization were and how they dictated what women should expect of themselves and how they should feel fulfilled.

The lack of legal, structural, and institutional initiatives to address women's inequality was clearly identified as "the problem" in the Canadian Royal Commission on the Status of Women (1977), which was initiated in 1967 by Prime Minister Lester Pearson, but only in the wake of major advocacy work undertaken by multiple women's organizations. The Commission's report was tabled in Parliament in 1970 with 167 recommendations. In 1971, the Office of the Status of Women was established. We are now approaching the 50th anniversary of the Commission, and while some gains have been made in relation to women's equality, there remain major gaps in several important areas, including the lack of a national child care policy; growing levels of poverty, most particularly for women; and continuing violence against women (most particularly Aboriginal women), as we noted in the introduction to this book. These concerns are detailed in the West Coast Leaf's Report Card (2014) on Canada's submission to CEDAW (Convention for the Elimination of all forms of Discrimination Against Women). This UN Convention, which enshrines significant protections for women and girls under international human rights law, was ratified by Canada in 1981.

Which Women?

Black, Hispanic, and Indigenous feminists ask the question "Which women?" in response to the white middle-class worldview underpinning earlier feminist contributions, such as those of Friedan. These scholars and activists have identified how other dimensions of women's social location, such as race and class, are just as significant as gender in shaping their lives. Patricia Hill Collins' *Black Feminist Thought* (1991) examined the problem of the assumed whiteness of feminist writing in the 1960s, 1970s, and 1980s. Collins also challenged Afrocentrism for its masculinist assumptions. Crenshaw (1989) wrote about intersectionality and how multiple mechanisms of sexism, racism, classism, ableism, homophobia, and so on, operate simultaneously (not independently) to create systems of oppression. For Ferree and Tripp (2006), intersectionality means:

> that privilege and oppression, and movements to defend and combat these relations are not in fact singular. No one has a gender but not a race, a nationality but not a gender, an education but not an age. The location of people and groups within relations of production, reproduction, and representation [...] is inherently multiple (p. 10).

In *Sister Outsider* (1984), Audre Lorde takes up the challenge of recognizing and understanding the implications of the various differences among women.

> Certainly there are very real differences between us of race, age, and sex. But it is not those differences between us that are separating us. It is rather our refusal to recognize those differences, and to examine the distortions which result from our misnaming them and their effects upon human behaviour and expectation (p. 115).

The writings of Judith Butler (1990, 1993) pushed thinking farther along this continuum, challenging the binary notions that underpinned feminist understandings of the differences between sex and gender. The concept of woman, from Butler's perspective, cannot be understood as a concrete category; rather, gender identity is "an unstable fiction," one that is performed through "repetition and ritual" (1993, p. xv).

What and How Can She Know?

Adult learning education is fundamentally about knowledge—uncovering it, acquiring it, and challenging its dominant forms. The relationship between feminism and knowledge has been a core concern of feminist scholars for decades. A question posed by Canadian feminist philosopher Lorraine Code (1991), considered outrageous at the time, was, "What can she know?" Code, among others (see Gilligan 1982; Miller 1976; and Smith 1974), argued that the sex of the knower was epistemologically significant, a direct challenge to claims of neutrality that were fundamental to many other disciplines and the scientific method. Code and others argued that masculinity and its associated power and authority mattered a great deal when it came to knowledge claims. Canadian feminist sociologist Dorothy Smith approached this question by exploring women's everyday worlds. In *The Everyday World as Problematic* (1987), Smith argued that the everyday world of women was the starting point of creating feminist knowledge. Women's standpoint or knowledge, however, as with all standpoints, is always partial and cannot be taken for granted. Some standpoints dominate and are not identified as partial; this exclusionary perspective was central to Smith's methodology for exploring the social and institutional relations organizing the everyday. The traditional sociological approach, Smith observed, reflects a masculine worldview in which spheres such as paid work, politics, and formal organizations are on the radar, but feminized spheres such as child care, sexual reproduction, domestic labour, and affective relations are not.

> Feminist standpoint epistemologists have challenged the differential power that groups have to define knowledge, and they argued that marginalized groups hold a particular claim to knowing. At the core of standpoint epistemology is their assertion that they represent the world from a particular socially situated perspective, which represents epistemic privilege or authority (Doucet and Mauthner, 2013, p. 37).

Alison Jaggar's (1989) deliberations about feminist epistemology, and the relationship between emotions and knowledge, provide another important contribution. She outlines how emotions have been associated with women and positioned as outside of and in opposition to reason and rationality, considered to be the foundation of scientific knowing. In contrast to these arguments, Jaggar asserts that emotions, particularly those of "underclass" groups, are key to the development of critical social theory. For example, feelings of anger, dismay, and sadness in response to a situation can signal the existence of oppressive and unfair discriminatory structures and practices that can lead to critical inquiry into these injustices.

What counts as knowledge has also been a concern for Ellsworth (2005), who challenged notions of knowledge as a "thing," something that can be achieved. She argued for a more active and ongoing definition of knowledge as making sense of what she called "knowledge in the making" (p. 5). This involves "the embodied sensation of making sense, the *lived experiences* of our learning selves that make the thing we call knowledge" (p. 1, emphasis in original).

Is Feminism Still Relevant?

Despite multiple decades of significant change to sexist policies and practices, rapidly expanding feminist scholarship, and multiple studies conducted on girls and women's educational needs and experiences, gender inequality persists, indicating deeply rooted patriarchal and misogynist perspectives related to girls and women.

> Gender inequality ... remains among the greatest challenges of our times. Fed by deeply embedded discrimination against women and girls, it is wrong and costly, whether it interrupts economic progress, undercuts peace or restricts the quality of leadership. Ending it should be foremost among global and national goals. (*UN Women Annual Report, 2012-2013*, p. 4)

While advancements in women's status in Canada have occurred, most significantly through the efforts of feminist activists who pushed women's issues onto the public policy agenda, women still do not have equal pay for work of equal value and discrimination in the workplace and domestic violence abound (Marsden, 2012). Despite these realities, it is not unusual to encounter arguments that feminism, as a social and liberatory movement, is no longer relevant, because some people perceive women to be now equal to men and discrimination to be non-existent. Walby's (2011) claim that "feminism is not dead ... [it] is still vibrant ... [and] taking new forms" (p. 1) was instrumental in the publication of a 2015 special issue on feminism and adult education for the *Canadian Journal for the Study of Adult Education*. As editor of that issue, Nancy Taber took up Walby's assertion and asked readers and colleagues, "Is feminism 'still vibrant' for Canadian adult educators?" (p. iv). The response was a resounding "yes."

The claim to feminism's irrelevancy is somewhat paradoxical. It illustrates, in some respect, the successful outcomes of feminist movements that were instrumental in changing certain laws and cultural practices, including women's right to vote, our right to education, our right to be free of violence both outside of and within intimate relationships, and the right to control our bodies, to name a few. This claim to irrelevancy also illustrates, however, how the history of feminist struggles is not well known and how that absence of knowledge, or in some respects amnesia, is an outcome of oppressive practices that seek to both devalue and rewrite history. As feminist historian Anne Firor Scott (1984) observed, "Selective and partial vision will doubtless always be part of the historical enterprise, but perhaps by taking thought we can at least reduce its incidence" (p. 8).

Women's rights were hard fought-for and are now under threat by neo-liberal agendas and conservative politics that reinforce a kind of rabid individualism whereby an individual's success and failure are viewed as entirely a matter of individual choices and agency with little attention paid to structural dimensions that shape locations of privilege and penalty. In her examination of the effects of neo-liberalism, Mohanty (2013) speaks to its impact on movements for social justice. She draws attention to how neo-liberal agendas have undermined the public domain, which has become "denuded of power and histories of oppression" (p. 971). In this process, individualism dominates approaches to democratic decision making. As a result of neo-liberal sensibilities, the idea that "the personal is political," a foundational argument of feminism, becomes delinked. Politics is now only about addressing personal concerns and any sense of collective responsibility is diminished.

> Questions of oppression and exploitation as collective, systematic processes and institutions of rule that are gendered and raced have difficulty being heard when neoliberal narratives disallow the salience of collective experience or redefine this experience as a commodity to be consumed. If all experience is merely individual, and the social is always collapsed into the personal, feminist critique and radical theory appear irrelevant—unless they confront these discursive shifts (Mohanty, 2013, p. 971).

What Is the Solution? Women's Empowerment and Feminist Pedagogy

Feminism was and is centrally concerned with analyzing the mechanisms of women's oppression, but it has also been oriented to understanding and providing learning contexts and processes that empower women. Feminist pedagogy, as Briskin (1994) has argued, is a standpoint, rather than a technique or specific method. "Feminist pedagogy starts from the acknowledgement of women's oppression and speaks to the gendered character of the classroom, of interactions between students and teachers, of the curriculum itself" (p. 443). Ellsworth (1989, 1992) also speaks about the importance of understanding feminist pedagogy as a relational art that can explore difference and create conditions for open exploration of identity.

Centuries ago, the lack of formal education available for girls and women was a key issue for feminists such as Mary Wollstonecraft (1789). Most of the discussion within feminist pedagogy today continues to focus on formal education. But, as English and Irving (2015) remind us, "[to] focus on classroom experience is valid, but it does not encompass feminist learning in the community, where much political learning occurs" (p. 2). The 20th century bore witness to a diverse collection of feminist movements, which were important sites of learning from which emerged many aspects of feminist pedagogy, in particular the notion of consciousness-raising (CR). In CR groups, women came together to share their experiences and to critically analyze how the "personal is political" (Hanisch, 1970), that is, to understand how their everyday experiences of discrimination were related to systemic sexist practices grounded in the structures and practices of patriarchy. Feminist efforts led to legislative and public policy changes in some parts of the world that opened doors to education (mainly for white and middle-class girls and women) that had previously been closed. In many locations around the world, however, doors remain closed to women's education because of sexist, racist, and classist practices that are reinforced by capitalist globalization.

Tisdell (2000) outlines the historical context of feminist adult education and the different foci of psychological, structural, and post-structural approaches. A psychological orientation emphasizes the development of women's voices and the importance of supportive contexts that enable women to speak about their experiences and to see themselves as knowers and knowledge creators. Feminist research in the late 1970s and 1980s fuelled this psychological orientation, in particular, the work of Belenky, Clinchy, Goldberger, and Tarule (1986), who examined how "women's self-concepts and ways of knowing are intertwined" (p. 3).

Critiques of psychological orientations pointed to their individualistic orientation and lack of attention to structural issues, and to how these theories were race-blind. As noted above, the differences that exist among women, and in particular how race and gender shaped social relations within and outside classrooms, became a key focus of feminist pedagogical discussions (e.g., Ellsworth, 1989). Again, as noted, the contributions of feminists of colour (e.g., Collins, 1991), Indigenous educators (e.g., Graveline, 1994), Third World feminists (e.g., Mohanty, 2003), and queer feminists (e.g., Butler, 1990) have been a key factor in creating a deeper understanding of difference and of how dominant and Eurocentric ways of thinking, ways that maintain dominant-subordinate relations, can persist within classrooms despite "good" intentions. As scholars of colour called for feminist pedagogy to focus on race and its intersection with gender and class, in a similar way, queer theorists have called attention to sexuality, challenging the heterosexual bias of feminist scholarship, including feminist pedagogy.

Post-structural approaches have raised concerns about the oppressive outcomes of dichotomous thinking, pointing to how certain binaries (male/female, black/white, rational/emotional, subjective/objective) contribute to injustices by positioning one side of the pairing as the norm by which the

Illustration: Courtesy of Jill Laxamana.

"Mail Order Brides." A political fashion show sketch by Vancouver-based custom clothing designer Jill Laxamana.

10

"other" side is judged as inferior or subordinate (Tisdell, 2000). Using these frameworks, feminist pedagogues invite students to analyze dominant discourses and notions of identity. Carpenter (2012) acknowledged the contributions of post-structural approaches, but sought to bring more emphasis to the particular social and material conditions of women's lives. "These conditions and our relation to them have to be interrogated as a source of knowledge and the conditions have to be historicized and understood as relations" (pp. 30-31).

Voice and Empowerment in Feminist Pedagogy

Voice and empowerment remain important ideas for feminist pedagogy; a key question emerging from these ideas is, "Under what conditions can and do women speak their truths?" In Hayes and Flannery's (2000) explorations of women as learners, they paid particular attention to the significance of creating conditions for and listening to women's stories and narratives about learning. Razack (1998), however, challenges "uncritical reliance on stories" (p. 47) and draws attention to the failure to understand that the risks taken to tell stories are not equally shared.

> When we depend on story telling either to reach across differences or to resist patriarchal and racist constructs, we must overcome at least one difficulty: the difference in position between the teller and the listener, between telling the tale and hearing it. (p. 36)

Paying attention to the concept of risk is also important in understanding how, for some learners, the risks of learning are significant (Horseman, 1999). Rockhill (1987) studied women's ambiguous motivations and sensibilities with respect to learning and found that women's desire for further education can result in violence when it is perceived to be a threat within patriarchal societies. The risk associated with learning was a key theme in *Educating Rita*, a film that explored a working-class woman's desire for further education and the dismissive and sometimes violent reaction to these hopes on the part of her family. Risks are also part of the lived experience of adult educators who are racialized and who see their authority and motivations challenged. (Brown, Cervero, and Johnson-Bailey, 2000) The backlash experienced by women learners was a concern in Stalker's (2001) study of women's struggles to access learning. She concludes that misogyny, that is, a hatred and denigration of women, "creates a useful, sharper theorization from which to explicate obstacles to women's participation in tertiary education" (p. 288).

The social relations between learners and teachers are key issues in feminist adult education. For hooks (1994), feminist teachers should practice "engaged pedagogy" in which reciprocity and mutuality are important goals. Part of an engaged pedagogy also involves honouring the role of emotions in knowledge and learning. Feminist approaches to adult education are also oriented to the embodied aspects of learning. As Haraway (1988) observed, "I am arguing for a view from a body, always a complex, contradictory, structuring and structured body versus the view from above from nowhere from simplicity" (p. 584). Lawrence (2012) also called for "reclaim[ing] the body as a source of knowledge" (p. 10), as did Yakhlef (2010), who drew attention to how the body is "an active producer of culture, at the same time being a product thereof" (p. 411).

Feminist Popular Education

A term commonly used by many feminist adult educators who have worked in Latin America is "feminist popular education." This term aims to bring attention to learning that occurs in nonformal and informal settings. Feminist popular education has been defined as "intentional and facilitated processes of collective learning and knowledge production that enable and provoke self- and social transformation toward the realization of contextually determined feminist goals" (Manicom and Walters, 2012, p. 3). Feminist popular education creates what Manicom and Walters call "pedagogies of possibility" (p. 3), imaginings of "what might become thinkable and actionable when prevailing relations of power are made visible, when understandings shake loose from normative perspectives and generate new knowledge and possibilities of engagement" (p. 4).

Arts-Based Feminist Adult Education

The role of arts-based activities in the development of feminist consciousness through popular education is receiving more attention (e.g., Butterwick and Lawrence, 2009; Clover and Sandford, 2013; Clover and Stalker, 2007; Clover, Stalker, and McGauley, 2004). Arts and creative expression can enrich "knowledge in the making" (Ellsworth, 2005, p. 5) and support "more reflexive and transformational learning" (McGregor, 2012, p. 310). Creative expression can enable a "defiant imagination" and an "alternative analysis and reflection" (Clover and Stalker, 2007, p. 15). For further discssions of this topic, see the chapters in Section III of this volume.

Conclusions

Feminist approaches to adult education offer both a language of critique, exploring the origins of women's subjugation and exclusion, and a language of possibility, that is, ways of creating learning environments that enable and support women. As noted at the beginning of this chapter, context matters; bringing a feminist framework to our adult education policies and practices means that we understand how structures and practices of discrimination based on sexist, racist, classist, ablest, homophobic, and transphobic thinking impact adult learners' lives, desires, and opportunities for further learning. Feminist pedagogy is a unique approach, a standpoint that must be reflexive and dynamic in order to reflect the plurality of learning environments, including women's homes and communities, workplaces, cooperatives, literacy classes, and social movements, to name a few.

Feminist contributions to adult education have been and continue to be significant. The dynamics of feminist thought will continue to inform the work as deeper understandings are developed about the ideologies, structures, and policies that fuel various forms of oppression. The colonial project continues to inform many institutions and sites of adult learning. One of the next challenges, for me as a feminist adult educator, is the process of decolonizing, of undertaking an examination of how deeply our sensibilities of social justice have been framed by colonialism.

Endnotes

[1] This chapter is dedicated (as is this book) to Donna Chovanec. Donna was to be co-author of this chapter; she died on March 4, 2015 many years after her original diagnosis of cancer. For Donna, feminism proved to be a powerful framework for understanding the obstacles many women face in living as full human beings and for directing attention to structures and practices that needed to change.

[2] My mother immigrated to Canada in her teens; my father was a fourth-generation immigrant.

[3] As Paulette Regan (2010, p. 11) asks, "How can we, as non-Indigenous people, unsettle ourselves to name and then transform the settler–the colonizer who lurks within." The process of decolonizing my own thinking and practices is a lifelong journey that involves recognizing how I am someone whose good fortune in relation to economic, social, and cultural security is linked to the colonization of First Peoples. I work in an academic institution where a colonial perspective is deeply ingrained in our thoughts and actions.

[4] While the concept of first wave, second wave, and third wave feminism has been a common approach used to describe feminist movements (Frederick, n.d), there is debate about the usefulness of these divisions, particularly because they suggest a kind of discontinuity that some academics have challenged.

References

- Adiche, C. (n.d.) The danger of the single story. Retrieved from http://www.ted.com/talks/.

- Baumgartner, L. (2001). Four adult education theories and their implications for practice. *Focus on Basics*, 5 (B), 29-34.

- Belenky, M.F., Clinchy, B.M., Goldberger, N.R., and Tarule, J.M. (1986). *Women's Ways of Knowing—The Development of Self, Voice, and Mind.* New York: Basic Books.

- Bracken, S. and Nash, H. (2010). Struggles for utopia(s): gender and sexuality in adult and continuing education. In C. Kasworm, A. Rose and J. Ross-Gordon (Eds.) *Handbook of Adult and Continuing Education* (pp. 351-358). Thousand Oaks, CA: Sage.

- Briskin, L. (1994). Feminist pedagogy: Teaching and learning liberation. In L. Erwin and D. MacLennan (Eds.) *Sociology of Education in Canada: Critical Perspectives on Theory, Research and Practice* (pp. 443-470). Toronto: Copp Clark Longman, Ltd.

- Brown, A.H., Cervero, R.M., and Johnson-Bailey (2000). Making the invisible visible: Race, gender and teaching in adult education. *Adult Education Quarterly*, 60(4), 273-288.

- Butler, J. (1990). *Gender Trouble: Feminism and the Subversion of Identity.* New York: Routledge.

- Butler, J. (1993). *Bodies That Matter: On the Discursive Limits of Sex.* London: Routledge.

- Butterwick, S., Fenwick, T., and Mojab, S. (2003). Canadian adult education research in the 1990s: Tracing liberatory trends. *Canadian Journal for the Study of Adult Education*, 17 (2), 1-19.

- Butterwick, S., and Lawrence, R. L. (2009). Creating alternative realities: Arts-based approaches to transformative learning. In Mezirow, J. and Taylor, E. W. (Eds.), *Transformative Learning in Practice. Insights from Community, Workplace, and Higher Education* (pp. 35-45). San Francisco, CA: Jossey-Bass.

- Carpenter, S. (2012). Centering Marxist feminist theory in adult learning. *Adult Education Quarterly*, 62 (1), 19-35.

- Clover, D. and Sandford, K. (Eds.). (2013). *Lifelong Learning, the Arts and Community Cultural Engagement in the Contemporary University.* Manchester: Manchester University Press.

- Clover, D. and Stalker, J. (Eds.). (2007). *The Arts and Social Justice: Re-Drafting Adult Education and Community Cultural Leadership.* Leicester: NIACE.

- Clover, D. E., Stalker, J., and McGauley, L. (2004). Feminist popular education and community leadership: The case for new directions. In *Adult Education for Democracy, Social Justice and A Culture of Peace: Proceedings of the Joint International Conference of the Adult Education Research Conference (AERC) and the Canadian Association for the Study of Adult Education (CASAE)* (pp. 89-94), University of Victoria.

- Collins, P. H. (1991) *Black Feminist Thought: Knowledge, Consciousness, and the Politics of Empowerment.* New York: Routledge.

- Crenshaw, K. (1989). Demarginalizing the intersection of race and sex: A black feminist critique of antidiscrimination doctrine, feminist theory and antiracist politics. *Chicago Legal Forum*, 139–167.

- Code, L. (1991). *What Can She Know? Feminist Theory and the Construction of Knowledge.* Ithaca, NY: Cornell University Press.

- de Beauvoir, S. (1949). *The Second Sex.* Paris: Editions Gallimard.

- Doucet, A. and Mauthner, N. (2006). Feminist methodologies and epistemologies. In C. D. Bryant and D. L. Peck (Eds.) *Handbook of 21st Century Sociology*, Volume 2. Thousand Oaks, CA: Sage.

- Ellsworth, E. (1989). Why doesn't this feel empowering? Working through the repressive myths of critical pedagogy. *Harvard Educational Review*, 59(3), 297-323.

- Ellsworth, E. (1992). Teaching to support unassimilated difference. *Radical Teacher*, 42, 4-9.

- Ellsworth, E. (2005). *Places of Learning: Media, Architecture, and Pedagogy.* New York: Routledge.

- English, L. and Irving, C. (2015). Feminism and adult education: The nexus of policy, practice, and payment. *Canadian Journal for the Study of Adult Education*, 27 (2), 1-15.

- Ferree, M.M. and Tripp, A.M. (2006). *Global Feminisms: Transnational Women's Activism, Organizing and Human Rights.* New York: New York University Press.

- Frederick, J. (n.d.). Breaking the waves: Continuities and discontinuities between second and third wave feminism. Retrieved from: http://www.feministezine.com/feminist/historical/Second-and-Third-Wave-Feminism.html.

- Freire, P. (1970). *Pedagogy of the Oppressed*. New York: Bloomsbury.
- Friedan, B. (1963). *The Feminine Mystique*. New York: Norton and Company.
- Gilligan, C. (1982). *In a Different Voice: Psychological Theory and Women's Development*. Cambridge, MA: Harvard University Press.
- Graveline, F.J. (1994). Lived experiences of an aboriginal feminist transforming the curriculum. *Canadian Women's Studies*, 14(2), 52-55.
- Hanisch, C. (1970). The personal is political. In *Notes from the Second Year: Women's Liberation. Major Writings of the Radical Feminists*. New York: Radical Feminism.
- Hayes, E. and Flannery, D. (Eds) (2000). *Women as Learners—The Significance of Gender in Adult Learning*. San Francisco: Jossey-Bass.
- Haraway, D. (1988). Situated knowledges: The science question in feminism and the privilege of partial perspective. *Feminist Studies*, 14(3), 575-599.
- hooks, b. (1994). *Teaching to Transgress—Education as the Practice of Freedom*. New York: Routledge.
- hooks, b. (2015). *Feminism Is for Everybody: Passionate Politics*. New York: Routledge.
- Horseman, J. (1999). *Too Scared to Learn—Women, Violence, and Education*. Toronto: McGilligan.
- Jaggar, A. (1989) Love and knowledge: Emotion in feminist epistemology. *Inquiry: An Interdisciplinary Journal of Philosophy*, 32 (2), 151-176.
- Lawrence, R. (2012). Bodies of knowledge: Embodied learning in adult education. *New Directions for Adult and Continuing Education*, 134. San Francisco: Jossey-Bass.
- Lefebvre, H. 1969). *The Sociology of Marx*. New York: Vintage Books.
- Lorde. A. (1984). *Sister Outsider. Essays and Speeches*. Freedom, CA: Crossing Press.
- Manicom, L. & Walters, S. (Eds.) (2012). *Feminist Popular Education in Transnational Debates: Building Pedagogies of Possibility*. New York: Palgrave Macmillan.
- Marsden, L. (2012). *Canadian Women and the Struggle for Equality*. Don Mills, Ontario: Oxford University Press.
- McGregor, C. (2012). Arts-informed pedagogy: Tools for social transformation. *International Journal for Lifelong Education*, 31 (3), 309-324.
- Miller, J. (1976). *Toward a New Psychology of Women*. Boston, MA: Beacon Books.
- Miles, A. (Ed.). (2013). *Women in a Globalizing World: Transforming Equality, Development, Diversity and Peace*. Toronto: Inanna Press.
- Mohanty, C. (2003). *Feminism Without Borders: Decolonizing Theory, Practicing Solidarity*. Durham: Duke University Press.
- Razack, S. (1998). *Looking White People in the Eye: Gender, Race and Culture in Courtrooms and Classrooms*. Toronto: University of Toronto Press.
- Regan, P. (2010). *Unsettling the Settler Within: Indian Residential Schools, Truth Telling and Reconciliation in Canada*. Vancouver, BC: UBC Press.
- Rockhill, K. (1987). Literacy as threat/desire: Longing to be SOMEBODY. In J. Gaskell and A. McLaren (Eds.) *Women and Education* (pp. 315-332). Calgary, AB: Detselig Enterprises.
- Royal Commission on the Status of Women in Canada (1977). *Report of the Royal Commission on the Status of Women in Canada*. Ottawa, Canada.
- Scott, A.F. (1984). On seeing and not seeing: A case of historical invisibility. *The Journal of American History*, 71 (1), 7-21.
- Smith, D. (1974). Women's perspective as a radical critique of sociology. *Sociological Inquiry*, 4, 1–13.
- Smith, Dorothy. 1987. *The Everyday World as Problematic: A Feminist Sociology*. Milton Keynes, England: Open University Press.
- Stalker, J. (2001). Misogyny, women and obstacles to tertiary education: A vile situation. *Adult Education Quarterly*, 51(4), 288-305.
- Taber, N. (2015). A critical engagement with the current place of feminism in canadian adult education. *Canadian Journal for the Study of Adult Education*, 17 (2), iv-vii.
- Tisdell, E. (2000). Feminist pedagogies. In E. Hayes and D. Flannery (Eds.), *Women as Learners* (pp. 155-183). San Francisco: Jossey-Bass.
- UN Women (2013). *Annual Report, 2012-2013*. Retrieved 05/10/15 from http://www.unwomen.org/~/media/Headquarters/Attachments/Sections/Library/Publications/2013/6/UNwomen-AnnualReport2012-2013-en%20pdf.pdf.
- Van Zoonen, L. (1994). *Feminist Media Studies*. London: Sage.
- Walby, S. (2011). *The Future of Feminism*. Cambridge: Polity Press.
- West Coast Leaf (2014). *CEDAW 2015 Report Card*. Retrieved 08/04/2015 from http://www.westcoastleaf.org/wp-content/uploads/2014/10/2014-CEDAW-Report-Card.pdf.
- Wollstonecraft, M. (1789). *A Vindication of the Rights of Women: With Strictures on Political and Moral Subjects*. Boston: Thomas and Andres.
- Yakhlef, A. (2010). The corporeality of practice-based learning. *Organizational Studies*, 31(4), 409-430.

This vignette was prepared by Mary Kostandy.

Donna Chovanec, one of the original co-editors of this volume, died in March 2015. This book is dedicated to her memory. Donna was a stalwart feminist, a dedicated activist, and a brilliant scholar. She inspired all the women activists, students, and adult educators with whom she came in contact, including us. She made the world better because she was in it. May her legacy endure in our minds and hearts forever.

Donna was born on July 8, 1956 in Edmonton, Alberta. She had two younger siblings and lived next to her grandparents, with whom she was very close. Donna had four children: three daughters, Alejandra, Carolina, and Amelia, and one son, Esteban. In 1978 she obtained a Bachelor of Social Work degree from the University of Calgary. After obtaining her degree, Donna was employed for 12 years as a social worker in a pediatric rehabilitation unit at Glenrose Hospital in Edmonton, where she worked with families of pre-schoolers with development disabilities.

Donna obtained a Master of Education degree in Adult and Higher Education in 1994. Her Master's thesis was titled *The Experience of Consciousness-Raising in Abused Women*. In writing her thesis, she collaborated with women at an abused women's drop-in centre who were also anti-violence activists in Edmonton. As a graduate student, Donna joined a planning committee for the 1995 Adult Education Research Conference, served as an assistant to the editors of the adult education textbook *Learning for Life*, and became the Intercultural Education Undergraduate Program Student Advisor. She also worked as a part-time senior research officer for the Alberta Alcohol and Drug Abuse Commission (AADAC) for over 12 years, and participated in evaluation projects for Community and Family Services in Edmonton.

Donna earned her PhD in 2004. Her research, which she later published as a book, *Between Hope and Despair: Social and Political Learning in the Women's Movement in Chile*, documented the learning and educational processes within the women's movement in the city of Arica in northern Chile. Donna's research revealed that the development of a critical and gendered consciousness among women is one of the main ways by which women learn their way out of victimization and violence to become advocates or oppositional agents.

As a faculty member in Educational Policy Studies at the University of Alberta, Donna continued to conduct research into learning for social change, social movements, qualitative research, feminist and critical pedagogy, and women's issues. She also served as the Board Chair of the Learning Centre Literacy Association and the Secretary of the Edmonton-Strathcona Provincial New Democratic Party Association. She co-founded the Centre for Community Organizing and Popular Education (CCOPE).

Donna struggled courageously with cancer and, following her initial diagnosis, carried on with all her activities and a ten-year plan fueled by her strong will and her positive and optimistic attitude. As her health declined towards the end of her life, the students to whom Donna was passionately committed would come to her house to discuss their work. Her family and friends also gathered around her and took care of her as she has always taken care of them. On March 4, 2015, Donna lost her battle against cancer. Days after she passed away, her students and friends created a Facebook page about her titled "Celebrating the Life of Donna Chovanec."

References

- Chovanec, D. (n.d.a). Donna M. Chovanec. Retrieved April 22, 2015, from http://www.edpolicystudies.ualberta.ca/en/People/Faculty/Chovanec.aspx

- Chovanec, D. (n.d.b). Home Page. Retrieved April 22, 2015, from http://www.ualberta.ca/~chovanec/chovanec.html

- Chovanec, D. (2010, December 3). Faculty and Instructors: Dr. Donna Chovanec. Retrieved April 22, 2015, from http://cde.athabascau.ca/faculty/donnac.php

- H. K. (2015, March 11). Eulogy for Donna Maureen Chovanec. Speech presented at the Mass of Christian Burial. Edmonton, Alberta.

Carole James was elected MLA for Victoria-Beacon Hill in 2005 and served as Leader of the Official Opposition for seven years.
Photo courtesy of Carole James, MLA.

2

Making Waves
Feminist and Indigenous
Women's Leadership

Leadership, like adult education, is pervasive, has many definitions and manifestations, and is therefore often misunderstood. Leadership has been articulated by men for the most part and, thus, is steeped in an ethos of masculinity and "Machiavellian" individualized notions of power—to direct, to dominate, to be the hero of one's own story of the world. These dominant imaginings of leadership tend to be narrowed to administrative tasks and management processes, or habitually diminish leaders to biological traits that essentialize both men and women, and reduce leadership to a parody. However, to us, the authors focusing on leadership in this volume, as well as feminists working in social and private arenas across this country, leadership is an essential component of the change we/they want to make and, as such, requires interrogation, understanding, and re-articulations.

Darlene E. Clover and Catherine McGregor

We begin this chapter by situating ourselves in "leadership," and then outline briefly some common amorphous definitions of leadership and leaders. From there, we explore various dimensions of some of the dominant "heroic" and "post-heroic" discourses and archetypes related to leadership, troubling and exposing salvation- and traits-based orientations, individualizations, and assumed masculinities, as well as problematics associated with so-called "feminine" descriptors and conceptions.

The purpose of mapping this historical terrain is to make evident the discursive traces that manifest the contemporary need for feminist/Indigenous forms of leadership. We argue that we need to find a new place from which to operate—a pivot point if you will—that recognizes the fluid and emergent nature of women's leadership practices, and that this messy, complex space is made even more problematic by discourses that continually work against the goals of justice, central to women who lead in today's world. It is the role of the feminist/Indigenous leader to interrupt and disrupt such ways of thinking and doing. Essentially, we offer feminist leadership as an emergent art, one that centers social change in its performance.

In the final section, we focus on emerging Indigenous women's and feminist leadership discourses. We avoid definitions in favour of explorations of the nature of the "change" toward which these discourses aim, some of their essential components, their links to adult education, and their combined potential to re-politicize and re-energize efforts to advance gender, social, and ecological justice and transformation in Canada today.

Situating Ourselves

We are both professors in Leadership Studies in the Faculty of Education, University of Victoria (UVic). I (Darlene) was the International Coordinator of a global environmental adult education program for five years with the International Council for Adult Education (ICAE). I worked collectively with educators worldwide to develop an educational theory and practice around an issue that had been overlooked in adult education, but which has come to have major gender and life-support system consequences (e.g., Klein, 2014). When I came to the University of Victoria in 2002, I was placed in Leadership Studies. To help update this area, I developed a course on women, learning, and leadership. The first question I ask the women students enrolled in this course is to identify a "leader." Responses roll out quickly: Mahatma Ghandi, Martin Luther King, and Nelson Mandela. The significance of these male leaders notwithstanding, their gender stands in sharp contrast to the topic of the course. When I draw attention to this, students look sheepish, offering up Margaret Thatcher to appease the gods of omission. This sets in motion interrogations of the gendered nature of leadership, as well as the constraints imposed by my question. I see feminist adult education and leadership as complementary strategies. Each is open to and enhances possibility within a steadfast commitment to empowerment, transformation, justice, and sustainability. This goal shapes the means.

I, Catherine, am a "recovering" politician—a term I use with a degree of irony and pride—having served as Member of the Legislature and Cabinet Minister in the British Columbia government from 1996-2001. As a politician, I experienced first hand the gendered, patriarchal practices of political leadership, and continue to see these experiences and characterizations echoed in the media around women in politics today. I've been active in the New Democratic Party (NDP) for more than 20 years, and have served in both local and provincial capacities. In 2004, I worked with feminist colleagues in the party to bring in a preferential selection system for women and "minority" candidates for the NDP in BC. This action seemed particularly significant as it followed the research related to women's adult education and learning in politics that we had recently completed, which traced the impact of a new electoral reservation system in India (Clover, McGregor, Farrell, and Pant, 2011). My experiences in both formal and informal roles of leadership within the NDP, and then as a researcher working in the field of gender and leadership, have suggested other pathways for envisioning how feminist and post-modern approaches to leadership might alter existing socio-political organizational cultures and practices. In my current work with women and men in leadership roles, I consistently look for ways to disrupt discourses that fail to identify the complex terrain of women's experience in becoming leaders.

Defining Leadership

There exist "almost as many definitions of leadership as there are persons who have attempted to define the concept" (Stogdill, 1974, p. 259). Summerfield (2014) suggests that there is an easy definition, but Blackmore (2013) reminds us "leadership is something we all recognize, but find difficult to define" (p. 139). This comment is personified in the assortment of definitions of leadership Batliwala (2013) outlines in *Engaging with Empowerment*. For example, General H. Norman Schwarzkopf defines leadership as "a combination of strategy and character. If you must be without one, be without the strategy." John Maxwell argues that "leadership is influence—nothing more, nothing less." Warren Bennis describes leadership as "a function of knowing yourself, having a vision that is well communicated, building trust among colleagues, and taking effective action to realize your own leadership potential" (p. 178). For Ciulla, "leadership…is a complex moral relationship between people, based on trust, obligation, commitment, emotion and a shared vision of the good" (cited in Batliwala, 2013, p. 178).

Attempts to define a "leader" are equally amorphous: "Managers have subordinates—leaders have followers" (Murray Johannnsen); "If you inspire others to dream more, learn more, do more and become more, you are a leader" (John Quincy Adams); "The superior leader gets things done with very little motion. He [sic] imparts instruction not through many words but through a few deeds. He [sic] keeps informed about everything but interferes hardly at all" (Lao Tse, cited in Batliwala, 2013, p. 177).

Pervasive in many definitions of leadership are terms such as greatness, visionary, decision makers, inspirational, assertive, powerful, in control, and rational, contributing to what Bennis (1959) once characterized as "the slipperiness and complexity of leadership" (p. 260). Despite their elusive nature, most definitions do include some normative threads that we can trace. The majority of definitions come from men working within management and organizational theory frameworks and, therefore, the masculine pronoun "he" is either used, or at least sufficiently inferred, to indicate that "real" leaders are male. The leader is usually a charismatic individual, a singular heroic figure and, therefore, by extension, "leadership is an act of heroism" (Batliwala, 2014, p. 176). Leaders have a heightened "moral" character, with the capacities and power to direct the behaviour and actions of others. Ford (2005) sums up this concept of leadership as embedded in American discourses that semantically privilege "an ideology of celebrating individualistic…strong, masculine characters who lead" (p. 241), a concept proliferated and normalized globally through, in particular, Hollywood films' combined power of narrative and image.

Feminine Leadership

Turock (2008) "reminded us that women who did not conform to masculine models were [frequently] eliminated from studies that invariably concluded leadership was predominantly a male endowment" (p. 120). But the social turbulence of the 1960s and 1970s saw the focus shift to concentrate on the differences between men and women as leaders. The majority of these studies began from a male standard, although a number of women did attempt their own definitions, taking up what Lau Chin, Lott, and Sanchez-Hucles (2007) called a "feminine stance." Feminine leadership is typically positioned around so-called female attributes or traits characterized as caring, compassion, emotion, service, and nurturing, to name but a few. Loden defines feminine leadership as a style that "emphasizes cooperation over competition; intuition as well as rational thinking in problem solving, team structures where power and influence are shared within the group…interpersonal competence; and participatory decision making" (cited in Batliwala, 2013, p. 226). Other definitions include notions of self-worth, "feminine talent," integrity, and consultation. These traits and attributes are not a problem in and of themselves, but they frequently fall within socially acceptable categories assigned to women and, thereby, essentialize and homogenize women's nature and maintain problematic gender binaries (Muhr and Sullivan, 2013). This gendered normativity can result in recriminations and condemnations such as women leaders being "worse than men." Feminine definitions also avoid reference to feminism, and therefore, "to gender power and women's lack of access to formal positions of authority" (Batliwala, 2013, p. 180). Moreover, these attempts by women to redefine and re-orient leadership around traits underestimate how men have dominated leadership in the public spheres of influence "for so long, 'doing masculinity' and 'doing work' have been conflated, such that everyone (men and women) experiences subtle pressure to 'do masculinity'... in order to be perceived as competent" (Fletcher, 2004, p. 653).

Heroic and Post-Heroic Archetypes and Discourses of Leadership

The scope of literature about leadership makes selecting leaders to profile in a short chapter a challenge. Our selections below, therefore, are guided by Huber and West's (2002) four distinctive phases of leadership theory. The first two phases focus on the individual (often described as the "great man"), and on how individual behaviours or personalities demonstrate leadership, typically described as "traits-based" theories. Phase three involves situational leadership theories (where leadership practice is dependent upon context or might be shared or distributed). Finally, stage four emphasizes more transformational leadership theories. While the first two phases of leadership theories have historically shaped the leadership canon, particularly in terms of their patriarchal frames, theories in the latter two categories have become predominant in contemporary leadership scholarship—although, as will become apparent, these too feature both explicit and implicit assumptions in which male experience and knowledge are privileged.

Charismatic and Transactional Leadership

The notion of charismatic leadership comes from the work of Max Weber, and is the one we are most familiar with; it is notable in the definitions above and is the normative answer to the "name a leader" game. Northhouse (1997) summarized charismatic leaders as "individuals who are special and who make others want to follow the vision they put forward" (p. 135). Charismatic leaders are most frequently defined as deeply moral, ethical, and motivated to do the "right" thing. These leaders have an overwhelming presence and a gift for communication. Charismatic leaders have made positive changes in the world, but they have equally wreaked havoc. We must be cautious of the disempowerment, and resulting weaknesses, inherent in placing or seeing power as localized in one individual.

A second discourse of leadership that falls under the heroic moniker is transactional. This type of leadership is a process described as the practice of an exchange of benefits: compliance with a leader's direction is rewarded with financial or personal gain. Transactional leadership is a strong fit for what can be described as "management science" and "rational choice theory" that were the dominant ways of thinking about leadership after the Second World War (Witzel, 2012). Given this history, transactional leadership might be considered outdated, yet it remains current and useful in the context of contingency leadership, a very similar concept that presents leadership as dependent upon and constrained within exigency. Contingency leadership theory builds on the transactional stance by acknowledging the to-ing and fro-ing between contexts and among diverse groups of people as essential to the "doing" of leadership, although it does not sufficiently describe the role of leaders as potential change agents, or what is known as the transformational stance.

Transformational Leadership

Transformational leadership theory marks the beginning of what is known as the "post-heroic" period of leadership. As Collinson (2005) argued:

> It is now increasingly common to view effective leadership as "post-heroic," "shared," "quiet," … "follower-oriented" and/or "project team-based" where leaders act as "servants" rather than as commanders and controllers.… Leadership is increasingly seen as being distributed up, down and across hierarchies (p. 1422).

Burns (1979) is usually credited with the birth of transformational theory. Born of an era when human values began to supersede organizational structure, Burns argued that moral agency was central to effecting how leaders could shape organizations to better respond to human needs, goals, and desires: "Leaders induc[e] followers to act for certain … wants and needs, the aspirations and expectations—of both leaders and followers" (p. 19). Furthermore, leaders and followers in transformational leadership contexts engage in mutually beneficial activities, expected to transform both leader and follower.

Transformational leadership theory has become the dominant paradigm in management and organizational theory, as well as academic scholarship, in large part because it describes the complexity of human engagement within organizational structures, procedures, and operations. As such, it has signalled important changes in leadership studies and offers new spaces in which to think about how to engage in, with, and through leadership. In many ways this theory parallels ideas in adult learning, such as levelling teacher/leader-learner/follower power dynamics through more learner/follower-centred approaches. Yet its heroic roots remain very much a product of gendered, racialized, and patriarchal histories, naturalized as histories of progress, social change, and "greater" inclusion. Antobus (2000) also sees an important omission within the discussions of transformative social change in transformational leadership; that is, the notion of justice, and particularly, gender justice.

Distributed and Democratic Theories of Leadership

Two other important post-heroic leadership theories are known as "distributed" and "democratic." Distributed leadership, according to Spillane (2005) is "first and foremost about leadership practice rather than leaders or their roles, functions, routines, and structures.… Leadership practice is viewed as a product of the interactions of … leaders, followers, and their situation" (p. 206). The emphasis on practice is a key point that illustrates how this theory relies on leadership as a social construction (in contrast to leadership as a personal attribute or personality trait). Scholars like Gronn (2002) have taken this idea even further, emphasizing conjoint agency, characterized as enactments of activity that construct leadership as a shared, fluid and emergent, collectively constructed product of social interactions. Bolden (2011) claims there are three essential features or beliefs behind distributed leadership: a concept of leadership as an emergent property of interactions; an openness to how leadership is conceived and practised; and expertise shared among multiple participants. He (2011) suggests this makes distributed leadership theory relevant to particular fields of study, including education and nursing (both highly "feminized" professions), in which shared activity is valued and understood to be normative.

Democratic leadership can be considered a subset of distributed leadership, with an emphasis on how leadership should be shared according to the principles that guide its practice. Themes such as participation, self-determination, inclusion, and shared deliberation are key to democratic leadership. Credited as the first scholar to study democratic leadership, Lewin (1950) theorized it as a process of engagement that emphasizes the quality of the environment created in an organization in which such leadership is practised. In this sense, formal leaders create the conditions in which such ongoing and purposeful deliberation occurs within the organization in order for change to take place. Furthermore, the democratic leader engages others in processes that not only build capacity for reasoning, but also a caring for all who participate in the collective work (Gastil, 1994). This concept of democratic leadership as predominantly an attribute of the leader stands in sharp contrast, however, to Woods' (2004) belief that democratic leadership involves democracy-creating facilitation and "democracy-doing," which is dispersed and can be initiated from within the broader organizational structure by anyone, a type of organic or emergent governance. Among other things, this concept places an emphasis on the "who" of democratic decision making as key to meeting organizational goals. This emphasis is particularly important when considering the role that leaders can play in creating more equality in terms of decision making. What becomes troublesome, however, is a consistent failure to problematize the notion of "democracy," which in the Canadian context has excluded Indigenous peoples as well as other voices—a consequence of our country's having been shaped by and through colonialism, patriarchy, and "first-past-the-post" politics.

Muhr and Sullivan (2013) highlight the underlying "hetero-normative" nature of all the heroic and post-heroic leadership discourses. These underlying gendered understandings and traits-based concepts emphasize, perpetuate, and privilege particular expressions of gender. Muhr and Sullivan argue that we need to "queer" leadership as a means to "do gender" unassigned to an identity category, based on using feminine as well as masculine competencies.

Blackmore (2013) asserts that what is usually absent in the above discourses "is any recognition of the theoretical or political position from which these approaches to leadership are derived" (p. 140). Put another way, conspicuous in its absence in the definitions, archetypes, and discourses above is the nature of the change that leadership aims to bring about, as if what needs to be changed is irrelevant in the quest for best practices (e.g., Batliwala, 2013). However, what needs to be changed is the pivot around which feminist and Indigenous women's/feminist leadership revolve.

Waves of Justice and Change: Feminist and Indigenous Women's Leadership

Women's leadership is pervasive; it is performed in different ways, at different levels, and in different arenas such as the community, the state, Band councils, civil society, the streets, schools, adult and higher education, cultural institutions, as well as within the family (e.g., Antrobus, 2000; Batliwala, 2013; Grundy, 1999; Tsosie, 2014). As Santamaría (2013) notes, "One needs only to consult traditional oral history or even historical written record for evidence of leadership under the rule of capable

Indigenous women in the world" (p. 3). As fluid and indirect products of social struggle, feminist leadership and Indigenous women's/feminist1 leadership[1] have no hard or fast definitions, although they draw from, or align with, some of the more progressive or egalitarian elements of the discourses outlined above. However, feminist and Indigenous women's/feminist leadership discourses have a number of distinctive, inter-woven components and re-conceptualizations that enable us to think about leadership in more socially purposeful and political ways. Central to the goal of these discourses are issues of oppression, power/empowerment, justice, inequity, and gender. As such, they support feminist adult education in its struggle to create a new, more just social order, by being nested in critical feminist and post-colonial theory, by troubling leader identity, by being above all action-oriented, and by being disobedient and making waves where they are situated.

Similar to adult education, leadership in feminist emancipatory discourse is viewed as a means, not an end. This framing is significant because it moves us away from a singular focus on the normative question of what leadership "is," and its endless entanglement of definition versus re-definition, towards a more important and central question: What is "the nature of change leadership seeks to bring?" (Batliwala, 2013, p. 179). This nature of change question re-politicizes and re-contextualizes leadership within what Furman (2012) calls the "extra-personal." The extra-personal is the sphere of the material reality of the lives of women and of others such as the Indigenous peoples of Canada who have faced systemic marginalization. This is a messy, complicated, and difficult sphere dominated by capitalist, neo-conservative, patriarchal, and neo-colonial understandings and practices that, by design and carelessness in near equal measure, have perpetuated a series of injustices and inhumanities. Within this context, feminist leadership becomes an active, living demonstration of a politics of resistance, an action-oriented practice of anti-oppressive reflexivity that dares to name, to confront, and also to exercise strength and vision (Batliwala, 2013; Furman, 2012). Leadership, therefore, becomes not a series of techniques or processes but a social action, a purposeful process of engaging a group around problematic forces to render these forces visible and to bring about, as much as possible, their demise. Leadership is an active process of rending visible "the political agenda it pursues" (Batliwala, 2013, p. 207). Feminist movements are of course regenerative traditions of leadership enacted on local and global stages and, most often, highly visible and public examples of purposeful leadership by women acting both individually and collectively.

Batliwala (2013) argues that feminist leadership "must begin at home, from within the organization, movement, or any other location from which women are attempting to change the larger reality... to create alternate models of power within their own structure" (p. 190). Furman (2012) calls this the intrapersonal level of leadership. On the one hand, it calls into question notions of "the leader," illustrating how the power(ful) positioning of an individual can produce domesticated and obedient followers who learn to think and act in ways that consciously and unconsciously maintain patriarchy and other oppressive social arrangements. We can equate this notion of "a leader" with Freire and Macedo's (1995) idea of "professional authority" in adult education, the right of power and control in the learning environment by virtue of positionality. But Batliwala (2013) also believes it is a myth to assume that "a leader," just like "an educator," will always simply reproduce patriarchal, hierarchical structures and practices of oppression, although she acknowledges that this is a "sticky" area because being in a position of leadership does involve one's own use and practice of power. Indeed, as Blackmore (2013) reminds us, any emancipatory or radical intent can be readily subverted by discursive processes and discourses that simply reproduce normative hierarchies of institutional and social practice. Batliwala suggests that we think about a feminist leadership role as something that is and must be earned, an authority bestowed upon a particular woman by others in recognition of her abilities and knowledge and understanding "of systemic social justice issues" (Furman, 2012, p. 203). This knowledge is seen as representative of the issues at hand, and the knowledge and aims of the group, so that the leader may speak and act on their behalf when required. We can equate this idea in many ways with what Freire and Macedo called "knowledge authority," a consciousness of the world one aims to change, and a demonstrated commitment to using this knowledge towards the creation of socially just regimes. Earned authority necessitates what Furman (2012) defines as and what feminist adult educators would call "praxis," a process of self-knowledge, of critical self-reflection on one's own power, position, and authority. Dialogue with others is key to praxis, but so too is a continuous reflection of how different approaches and decisions may privilege some perspectives, or generate bias towards others. Self-reflexivity enables feminist leaders, such as adult educators, to work carefully, consistently, respectfully, and fairly with others. Particularly important, however, is the ability of the feminist leader to help other women develop their own capacities to deal with what Batliwala calls "the messy, frightening, dangerous but exhilarating business of feminist social transformation" (p. 224). This ability means not seeing everyone as the same, but rather valuing the different ideas and skills that each individual brings to the table and working with this collection of abilities and attributes to raise the level of potential for systemic change (Silverman, 1995). This brings us to the notion of empowerment as it is embedded in feminist leadership.

The Meaning of "Empowerment" in Feminist Leadership

Let us begin with a statement of what is decidedly not empowering. What is not empowering is to assume that, for example, women leaders must speak on behalf of all women, or that Indigenous women leaders must speak on behalf of their communities. These assumptions rely on monolithic categorizations, subjectives, and identities defined through race, class, ability, sexuality, and so forth (Blackmore, 1999). But whether enacted in public, institutional, or private spheres, a central component of feminist leadership is power because "leadership is first and foremost about power—it is about holding power (position), exercising power," and in the case of feminist leadership, about "changing the distribution and relations of power" (Batliwala, 2013, p. 189).

Although often framed as something that is purely negative, power in feminist leadership needs to be re-positioned in terms of its nature and purpose. Power is "stepping forward to challenge sexism and discrimination" (Antrobus, 2000, p. 55). It is a willingness, often in the face of controversy or at great personal risk, to speak out in "defence of women's and human rights" (p. 55). Enacting power pedagogically in leadership enables women to unmask, as noted above, systems and practices that control, oppress, and marginalize other people, even within their own institutions, and to name what influences the agenda and the barriers and biases this entails (Batliwala, 2013, p. 192). But power is also based on agenda setting, on imagining different ways of working as well as a different world. Feminist leadership is, therefore, about leveraging within people a sense of agency, a way of thinking in a problem-solving and decision-making context in order to arrive at just, responsible, and appropriate choices and actions. Agency entails "the strategic skills, experience, insight, et cetera that can be marshalled and mobilised towards the transformation agenda that has been collectively adopted. Power is the recognition of what we, the change makers, bring to the table" (p. 195). This approach makes the practice of leadership, like feminist adult education, a "continual and complex theoretical and practical process of learning" to contest, to accept, to use, and to position power as the means to make change (Pessoa de Carvalho and Rabay, 1999, p. 1). It makes the feminist practice of leadership an art, a creative process that includes risk-taking, forethought, reflection, testing, shaping, and acting to change the world.

Going further, Batliwala (2013) reminds us that feminist leadership has a "greater concern with creative collective leadership models, rather than individual heroines" (p. 183). Nevertheless, we need to broaden how we think about the approaches and methodologies employed by women as these approaches and methodologies can become oppressive and self-defeating. Collective decision making is a strength that builds teams and respect, but it can prove to be oppressive, disabling, and ineffective if it discounts the ability of an individual to take on an issue and run with it when required (Blackmore, 1999). There are moments of possibility, moments that require action by those best positioned to take it. In other words, we need to see particular methodologies such as cooperation, sharing, and re-distribution not as inherent biological traits or as the only methods of leadership, but as means aligned with and corresponding to the goals of gender justice and social change to be used when appropriate. The different methods and approaches are a constellation of responses, processes, and principles that aim to broaden, deepen, contextualize, politicize, and democratize leadership practice, with the aim of ameliorating the "social and economic circumstances [of women] in Canada" (Silverman, 1995, p. 276).

For Yee (2011), Indigenous women have always been leaders. She notes:

> My mother, grandmother and aunts were all vocal Onkwehonwe women who rarely shied away from an opportunity to speak out against the discrimination of women, and taught me the importance of owning your sex in its entirety. I owe the strong, vocal voice I carry today to these courageous females who still refuse to be silenced (p. 22).

Indigenous leadership as articulated by women and feminists across Canada builds on the "nature of change" but adds a new and important dimension for this new century: What does it mean to live on Indigenous land? Epistemologically, this question imparts to leadership the opportunity to open up conversations about the problematic and limited understandings that Canadians have of Indigenous peoples, particularly women, both historically and in contemporary society. Politically, it brings into play the policies and practices that have led to this ignorance and that prevent self-determination. It creates opportunities to question the hegemony of forces and power relations that have impoverished nations within a nation, that have shaped Indigenous communities historically, and that have caused inequities in Indigenous gender roles in household, community, and society (Tsosie, 2014). Ontologically and ecologically, this question gets to the heart of the "heroic" myths of struggle against a hostile environment in an empty land. It challenges us to re-think the implications of human-Earth and fellow human being-Spirit disconnections with respect to human dignity and other lives on this planet. Wilson (2008) situates this work in a discourse of relationality that exemplifies reciprocal, community, and mutual benefit "rooted in relational accountabilities" (p. 11), and includes visions that reconnect people to the land, the ancestors, and spiritual values and beliefs. In this sense, although this discourse of relationality dovetails with Furman's (2012) dimension of action/reflexivity as ecological, it strengthens Furman's idea by positioning leadership as relationally centred, spiritually informed, and culturally and linguistically nested within "traditional" ways of knowing that aim for gender, social, and ecological justice and transformation (Santamaría, 2013; Ahnee-Benham and Napier, 2002). Going further, central to Indigenous women's and feminist leadership is a commitment to working as allies and change agents across movements, communities, and institutions to create a broader base of equity among otherwise marginalized, ostracized, or oppressed peoples, and to create systems that give voice to diverse identities and subjectivities (Tsosie, 2014).

Final Thoughts and Conclusions

Feminist and Indigenous women's/feminist leadership are emerging, fluid processes practised in personal and public spheres. Situated in terms of contending and complex gendered and social forces and emerging from struggle, they have no singular, overarching site or definition. However, feminist and Indigenous women's concepts of leadership take as their starting point the pervasiveness of women's leadership. These concepts are theoretically informed, place gender and social justice and change at their core, and thereby make waves intended to disrupt the shoreline of the status quo. When we begin with the question of the "nature" of change that leadership seeks to bring about, we understand methodologies and techniques not as "naturalized" gender attributes, but as means that advance agendas to dismantle oppression of all kinds and imagine very different relations in its place.

Endnotes

1   Indigenous scholars use both feminist and women's leadership and therefore, we follow suit.

References

- Acker, J. (2006). Inequality regimes: Gender, class and race in organizations. *Gender and Society*, 20(4), 441-464.
- Ahnee-Benham, M. and Napier, L. (2002). An alternative perspective of educational leadership for change: Reflections on Native/Indigenous ways of knowing. In K. Leithwood, Ph. Hallinger, G. Furman, K. Riley, J. MacBeath, and P. Gronn (Eds.). *Second International Handbook of Educational Leadership and Administration*, pp. 133-165. Dordrecht, The Netherlands: Kluwer Academic.
- Antrobus, P. (2000). Transformational leadership: Advancing the agenda for gender justice. *Gender and Development*, 85(3), 50-56.
- Batliwala, S. (2013). *Engaging with Empowerment: An Intellectual and Experimental Journey.* New Delhi: Women Unlimited.
- Bass, B. (1998). *Transformational Leadership: Industry, Military, and Educational Impact.* Mahwah, NJ: Erlbaum Associates.
- Bass, B. M., and Avolio, B. J. (1994). *Improving Organizational Effectiveness through Transformational Leadership.* Thousand Oaks, CA: Sage.
- Bennis, W. (1989). On becoming a leader. Reading, MA: Addison-Wesley Publishing.
- Blackmore, J. (2013) A feminist critical perspective on educational leadership. *International Journal of Leadership in Education: Theory and Practice*, 16(2), 139-154.
- Blackmore, J. (1999). *Dealing with Difference. Troubling Women: Feminism, Leadership and Educational Change* (pp. 187-202). Buckingham: Open University Press.
- Bolden, R. (2011). Distributed leadership in organizations: A review of theory and research. *International Journal of Management Reviews*, 13, 251-269.
- Burns, J. M. (1978). *Leadership.* New York: Harper & Row.

- Collinson, D. (2005). Dialectics of leadership. *Human Relations*, 58(11), 1419-1442.
- Clover, D.E., McGregor, C., Farrell, M., and Pant, M. (2011). Women learning politics and the politics of learning: A feminist study of Canada and India. *Studies in the Education of Adults*, 43(1), 18-33.
- Fletcher, J. K. (2004). The paradox of postheroic leadership. *The Leadership Quarterly*, 15, 647–661.
- Ford, J. (2005). Examining leadership through critical feminist readings. *Journal of Health Organization and Management*, 19(3), 236-251.
- Furman, G. (2012). Social justice leadership as praxis: Developing capacities through preparation programs. *Educational Administration Quarterly*, 48(2), 191-229.
- Gastill, J. (1994). A definition and illustration of democratic leadership. *Human Relations*, 47(8), 953-975.
- Gheradrdil, S. (1994). The gender we think, the gender we do in our everyday organizational lives. *Human Relations*. 47(6), 591-610.
- Gronn, P. (2002). Distributed leadership as a unit of analysis. *The Leadership Quarterly*, 13(4), 423-45.
- Grundy, Shirley (1999). Educational leadership as emancipatory praxis. In J. Blackmore and J. Kenway (Eds.). *Gender Matters in Educational Administration and Policy*, pp. 165-177. London: Falmer Press.
- Huber, S. and West, M. (2002). Developing school leaders: A critical review of current practices, approaches and issues and some directions for the future. In K. Leithwood and P. Hallinger (Eds.). *Second International Handbook of Educational Leadership and Administration Part 2* (pp. 1071-1099). Dordrecht, The Netherlands: Kluwer.
- Lau Chin, J., Lott, B. and Sanchez-Hucles, J. (Eds.) (2007). *Women and Leadership: Transforming Visions and Diverse Voices*. Oxford: Blackwell Publishing.
- Muhr, S. and Sullivan, K. R. (2013). None so queer as folk: Gendered expectations and transgressive bodies in leadership. *Leadership*, 9(3), 416-435.
- Northouse, P. (1997). *Leadership Theory and Practice*. Thousand Oaks, CA: Sage.
- Pessoa de Carvalho, M.E. and Rabay, G. (1999). Women and politics in Paraiba, Brazil: Participation, learning and empowerment. *40th Annual Proceedings of the Adult Education Research Conference*. Northern Illinois University, Dekalb, Illinois.
- Santamaria, L. M. J. (2013). Indigenous women's leadership: "We are the one's we have been waiting for." Accessed from: https://www.academia.edu/4206188/Indigenous_womens_leadership_We_are_the_on es_we_have_been_waiting_for.
- Spillane, J. (2005). Distributed leadership. *The Educational Forum*, 69(2), 143-150.
- Silverman, E. (1994). Women in women's organizations: Power or pouvoir? In H. Radtke and H. Stam (Eds.), *Power/gender: Social Relations in Theory and Practice* (pp. 270-286). London: Sage Publications.
- Summerfield, M. (2014). Leadership: A simple definition. *American Journal of Health Systems*, 71, 251-253.
- Tsosie, R. (2014). Native women and feminist leadership: An ethics of culture and relationship. In C. Suzack, M. Hundorf, J. Perreault, and J. Barman, J. (Eds.), *Indigenous Women and Feminism: Politics, Activism and Culture*. Vancouver: UBC Press.
- Turock, B. (2008). Women and leadership. *Journal of Library Administration*, 32(3-4), 115-137.
- Witzel, M. (2012). *A History of Management Thought*. Routledge. New York and Great Britain.
- Wilson, S. (2008). *Research Is Ceremony: Indigenous Research Methods*. Fernwood Publishing: Winnipeg, Canada.
- Woods, P. A. (2004). Democratic leadership: Drawing distinctions with distributed leadership. *International Journal of Leadership in Education*, 7(1), 3-26.
- Yee, J. (2011). I'm an Indigenous Feminist—and I'm Angry. *Our Times*, 30(1), 22-23.

This vignette was prepared by Shauna Butterwick.

Ellen Woodsworth was born in Toronto in 1948 and embarked on a long and continuous journey of feminist activism, social justice, and community organizing. She was greatly influenced by her parents, particularly her mother Jean Ross Woodsworth, who was the National YWCA representative on the founding board of the National Action Committee for the Status of Women and executive director of a number of YWCAs. Jean also worked for Roby Kidd and was editor of a CAAE publication. She was awarded the Order of Canada and the Order of Ontario.

Ellen completed her BA in sociology, during which time she was elected head of the speaker's bureau. She used her office as the first women's centre on campus. In 1971, she took part in the Abortion Caravan for women's right to choose, chaining herself in the House of Commons. In 1972, she moved to Toronto and co-founded The Other Women Newspaper, one of the first Canadian women's liberation newspapers oriented to women's global struggles and lesbian feminist issues. She co-created and ran CORA the Women's Liberation Bookmobile, which travelled all over Ontario. She also joined the Toronto Wages for Housework Campaign, which became a founding member of the International Wages for Housework Campaign.

She returned to Vancouver and, among other roles, worked as the Coordinator of the BC Action Canada network fighting free trade agreements. For 10 years she was a seniors' organizer at the Downtown East Side Seniors Centre, helped organize the Women's Memorial March, which brought attention to women's issues in the Downtown East Side, and chaired the Bridge Housing Society for Women, which built housing and space for the Downtown East Side Women's Centre. In 1999, she was hired as the Coordinator of the Seniors' Summit, a broad-based coalition that organized two provincial conferences to raise awareness of seniors' issues; she fought and saved the seniors' bus pass and started WE*ACT (Women's Elders Action Project).

Ellen served as Vancouver City Councillor from 2002 to 2005 and from 2008 to 2011 and was the first out lesbian City Councillor in Canada. She co-chaired the Women's Task Force, which wrote the Gender Equality Strategy for the City of Vancouver—the first city in Canada to have such a policy. In 2004, she co-founded and served as Secretary of the World Peace Forum. She established the LGTTBQ and women's advisory committees and succeeded in getting the City of Vancouver to join the Canadian Coalition of Municipalities Against Racism and Discrimination. The first Stonewall celebration and forum in Vancouver City Council chambers was led by Ellen and another Councillor; since then, City Hall has continued to host Gay Pride celebrations in Vancouver. In 2011, she launched Women Transforming Cities (WTC), which is now an international society (www.womentransfromingcities.org). In 2012, Ellen chaired the sold-out WTC conference. WTC organized monthly cafés that led to the identification of eleven key ways to make cities work for women and girls based on an intersectional analysis; these key strategies were outlined in the Hot Pink Paper Municipal Election Campaign that Ellen coordinated.

At the federal level, Ellen represented WTC in the creation of "Advancing Equity and Inclusion: A Guide for Municipalities" and the Up for Debate national coalition, which highlighted women's issues in the lead-up to the October 2015 Canadian federal election.

References

- www.ellenwoodsworth.com

Photo courtesy of Ellen Woodsworth.

Leadership and Activism

3

All My Relations
Networks of First Nations/Métis/Inuit
Women Sharing the Learnings

Indigenous women of Canada have been significant leaders, moving towards social justice and self-determination for First Peoples. This chapter illustrates that throughout colonization, Indigenous women have continued to do the work of cultural revitalization and have actively resisted the racist and sexist foundations of Canada's colonial relationship to Indigenous peoples. Indigenous women have been and continue to be central to survivance, a term used in the Indigenous community to express survival in the face of genocidal forces. First Nations/Métis/Inuit women have been the mainstays of Indigenous survivance in Canada since time immemorial.

Marlene R. Atleo

In this chapter, I share some observations about the key roles that Indigenous women of Canada play in social movements for justice and self-determination. Their leadership is an extension of the significant and continuing role that Indigenous women play, and have played, in cultural revitalization. This perspective has emerged from my participation in and observations of an adult lifetime living in a colonized community that is undergoing mobilization and revitalization. I am ?eh ?eh naa tuu kwiss, a member of the Ahousaht First Nation and the House of Klaakishpilth, a home economics educator, a salmon industry worker, and a professor. Indigenous women are raising consciousness at every level of the lifeway, and education—formal, informal, and adult—is a primary force for transformational change in Aboriginal and non-Aboriginal public and private settings. I seek to interrupt social perceptions of Indigenous women that ignore their activism and their key role in cultural revitalization and social movements for justice.

It is within the home and within cultural spaces that I begin the pursuit of real understanding, and so this chapter starts by referencing examples of community/lineage practices invested in Indigenous young women. These young women inherit expectations of full, productive lives as a respected/ful relation: daughter, sister, grandchild, aunt, cousin, niece, friend, and, later, worker, wife, and mother, as well as grandmother and lineage elder. I then consider the notion of critical consciousness, particularly the notion of "two-eyed seeing" (Archibald, 1997; Atleo, 2001) that is crucial to Indigenous survival, before exploring the vital role played by Indigenous women in the Idle No More movement. I go on to discuss Indigenous women's roles and leadership activities in light of the colonial history of Canada, its impact on Indigenous women, and the influence of the work of Indigenous women artists. In the final part of the chapter, I draw attention to the role of education and to the contributions of several key Indigenous women who have inspired a new generation of leaders.

Valuing the Lives of Women: Aitstootla (ꞔ iičtʼuuła)

Against the background of the Indian Act, First Nations, Métis, and Inuit women have ever laboured to create bridges on which to live and walk between the cultural shores. Much of this work has involved and continues to involve consciousness raising, adult learning, childrearing, and institutional development on the highways and in the byways coast to coast to coast in what some call Turtle Island. Often the women who become the educators and leaders in local communities are those who have developed a strong connection to their own roots in terms of language, culture, and family at some level that has been re-kindled (Atleo and Fitznor, 2010). Even those women who went to residential schools have reclaimed and revitalized their understanding of their cultures through language that affirms their lives and gives them insight.

Women in familial relationships reproduce themselves culturally. While Indigenous women may be hidden from public view, their works are not (Voyageur, Newhouse, and Beavon, 2011). For example, in the last 40 years, Nuu-chah-nulth women from the 14 First Nations of these West Coast people have relied on practice, cultural roles, and lifeways to revitalize ways to socialize their children, rebuild governance structures, reclaim relations, rename themselves, and reoccupy their territories (Moore, 2013). Retelling the stories and re-embodying the songs and dances with which to ground social innovation was the gift of revitalization of the 60s and 70s. Coming of age ceremonies for young women—known as Aitstootla (ꞔ iičtʼuuła)—was revived publicly along the West Coast to provide socio-cultural orientation and to declare the value of these girls (Atleo, 2001). In fact, all across Canada there has been a revival of these types of ancient practices—referred to as community witnessing—that aim to support Indigenous girls in understanding their worth, thus forming a foundation of heritage and expectations over the lifespan (Anderson, 2011; *Two Row Times*, 2014). Aboriginal women educators who embraced remnants of their heritage language and culture through these coming of age ceremonies felt they were able to succeed in the mainstream because of just such a foundation (Atleo and Fitznor, 2010). For example, in the book *Jingle Dancer* (Smith, 2000), a young urban girl anticipates her coming of age in the powwow tradition by gathering components of a jingle dress. Her relatives give her items with which to construct the dress and they share their wisdom, skill, stories, and love with her. She is thus empowered to dance at the next powwow when she comes of age. Similarly, for Inuit women, the art of womanhood is crystallized by three tools: the *ulu*, or woman's knife; the *kudlik*, or stone lamp that lights and heats the igloo; and the *amau-ti,* or mothers' parka, which carries the babies. These are visible technologies mastered by Inuit women to cope with the cold in which their cultural rights and traditions can be exercised (Watt-Cloutier, 2015).

It is the continuity of Indigenous knowledge, values, experience, and relations that residential school policy under the Indian Act sought to interrupt (Miller, 1996). The arms of generations of Indigenous mothers across the continent were kept empty because the vital Indigenous socialization that they could offer was denied to them. Instead, generations of children were stolen and sent to residential schools; contemporarily, the child welfare system continues to remove Indigenous children from their homes and communities, thus perpetuating the national anthropological myth that Indigenous peoples were and are disappearing.

Cultivating Critical Consciousness and Ways of Seeing

The cultural revitalization work of Indigenous women is a form of critical adult education that interrogates the socio-cultural myths that reduce the horizon of social consciousness and enables social justice and equities to promote societal change and transformation. Critical adult education is about creating consciousness and self-consciousness out of mystifications and stories; it is fundamentally about seeing. To be able to "see" what is happening before our very eyes through the lens of colonial oppression, cultural desire, and yearning for revitalization and relief from the intergenerational tensions of chaos and despair requires a specially grounded focus. Jo-ann Archibald (1997, 2004) and I (Atleo, 2001; 2009, 2013) have written about "two-eyed seeing," which, I maintain, is a phenomenological orientation or perceptual shift between two grounds. It is also a metaphor that captures a profound difference in how Indigenous peoples see when we look. Different ways of viewing the world was also the central concern of W.E.B. Du Bois (1903), who identified "double consciousness" as a Black lived experience in the United States. This concept was extended by hooks (2004), who described how a Black person had to be able to read the in-tensions of those in power to remain safe. Women of colour, such as hooks, have called for the creation of multiple lenses or ways of seeing as a response to marginalization through cognitive and cultural imperialism.

Interrogating traditional and contemporary mythologies develops a critical consciousness that promotes multiple ways of seeing and knowing. Marie Battiste, a Mi'kmaq educator, revolutionized Canadian Aboriginal education in the 1990s with the notion of "cognitive imperialism" (Battiste, 1986), a critical conceptualization of education based in "cultural imperialism" (Carnoy, 1974). She argues that cognitive imperialism disclaims other forms of knowledge, thus promoting a public discourse informed by racism and colonialism. Welton (2005, p. 102) suggests yet another way to think about this. He uses the term "cunning pedagogies" to describe "the Jesuit attack pedagogy [which was] aimed primarily at undermining the lifeworld foundations of Indian ways of life."

Dr. Marlene Atleo's chitulth (fish knife)—almost 50 years of use in cutting salmon.

Photo courtesy of Dr. Marlene Atleo.

Survivance

Developing critical consciousness and ways of seeing is key to survivance, a term used in the Indigenous community to express survival in the face of genocidal forces (Dorion, 2010; Visenor, 2000; Powell, 2002; Truth and Reconciliation Commission, 2015). For children transitioning into young adulthood and its social realities, survivance involves engaging with a liminal or third space, an ever-shifting social space where the oppressive legacies of colonialism imposed by the Indian Act and the cultural revival and aspirations of self-determination meet. Engaging with the tensions of this social space requires the kind of critical consciousness suggested by Freire (1970; 2000). Survivance (Visenor, 2000; Powell, 2002) is a unique cultural response by Indigenous peoples wherein critical consciousness counters genocidal contexts by activating traditions, affirming presences, and embracing rights and responsibilities. In survivance, all manner of narratives are used for meaning making. Customs are reclaimed and race gives way to relations; cultural reason prevails over English discursive logic. Survivance is about evoking resistance, humour, and courageous action by individual people and communities in a one-ness born of a common frame of mind and community spirit. The discourse of survivance shows how oppression operates and how it must be countered to create a discursive space in which to dialogue so as to develop common ground out of common interest (Powell, 2002).

Indigenous Women's Social Capital

To appreciate Indigenous women's leadership in cultural revitalization and movements for self-determination, I now turn to a brief history of colonization within Canada and an overview of how Indigenous women were positioned, beginning with the fur trade. During this time, many "tender ties" were developed in which Aboriginal women became the "country wives" of fur traders, thereby establishing the evolution of a Métis Nation. By 1870, however, European women began to arrive and the country wives were abandoned. Their currency or social capital disappeared along with the fur trade (Van Kirk, 1996). Before 1951, through the Indian Act, Indigenous women were treated like inventory on a ledger; they were transferred to other bands or given over to the non-Aboriginals they married. Before changes were made to the Indian Act in 1951, their movement was greatly restricted; it was also impossible for them to gather together with others without the presence of the Indian Agent or to leave the reserve without the issuance of a "red card" that provided legal authority. The amendments of 1951 were largely in keeping with the post-World War II human rights movement. While human rights were gained by Indigenous women who were married to non-Indigenous men, non-indigenous women who married registered Indians under the Act became status Indians by law. Fiske (1995) maintains that changes to the Indian Act provided a means to reorder Indian bands along patriarchal lines and to keep reproductive Indigenous females off the rolls. While the offspring of Indian men would have to be accounted for on the ledger, the children of Indian women who left their reserves became the property of their non-Indian husbands, and thus no longer a responsibility of the government (Lawrence, 2000).

For the past 30 years, there has been a slow releasing of Indigenous will as the shackles of the Indian Act have been shaken off and social justice demands have been asserted. First Nations, Métis, and

Inuit women have begun to move publicly and relentlessly to once again fill their arms and homes and hearts with life. Two significant examples of their public engagement are the Idle No More (INM) movement and "Rock the Vote," an initiative to encourage voting in federal elections (I say more about these topics below).

All My Relations in Cyberspace

As mentioned earlier, survivance is a key element of movements for cultural revitalization and self-determination. Survivance requires engagement rather than an "idleness" born of the inertia of oppression. The perception of "idleness" refers to a state of frustrated agency that Indigenous peoples faced in light of the oppressive structures that bound Indigenous peoples in a state of non-action. Historically, it had been illegal to gather, dance, or wear regalia (Miller, 1996). This notion of idleness was central to the Idle No More (INM) movement, which is led by Indigenous women.

Nowhere has that pan-Indigenous cultural expression of resistance been better used for educational purposes across Canada than by the INM movement that began in the fall of 2012. The trigger for the movement was Bill C-45, which violated treaty and land rights and which was introduced without rigorous Indigenous consultation. The INM movement signified that ironic play of tropes in which Indigenous and non-Indigenous peoples seem to be caught. On the one hand, the Indian Act policy and practices imposed by the government provide the legislative framework; on the other hand, Indigenous peoples maintain a totally different perspective, resulting in miscommunication or communicative inaction, a stalemate in which the pragmatics of living the ideals of expectations for nationhood, sovereignty, and self-governance never meet (Coates, 2014).

At the time that Bill C-45 was announced in 2012, the Assembly of First Nations (AFN) was focused on educational reform and the government's inadequate response to their proposals, as evidenced by its Senate Report and the First Nations Education Act. The AFN subsequently held a special assembly during the first week of October. At that assembly, differing perspectives with respect to how to move forward arose between treaty and non-treaty members. The discussion was tabled until December 4-6, 2012, at which time the Chiefs in Council developed a list of demands to set before the government. On December 12, the 450-page Omnibus Bill was passed and the dam broke.

Prior to the outrage over Bill C-45, Indigenous women had been engaged on many fronts, but what was significant about their leadership of INM in the fall of 2012 was their savvy use of social media. Their actions were part of a wave in a series of international technologically-powered social movements, including Occupy (seeking economic democracy and liberatory social change) and the Arab Spring (an anti-dictatorship, pro-democracy movement in Egypt) (La Botz, 2012). Many of these women were second-generation activists; they knew the histories, they had witnessed the defeats and triumphs of their elders, and they embodied the same passions, but they were better oriented as a result of post-secondary education and political experience. They set out to educate, raise consciousness, and bring the people along with them in a peaceful manner, rather than to score points and position themselves in the political arena.

In his book *#IDLENOMORE and the Remaking of Canada*, Coates (2015) elaborates on the contributions and backgrounds of key Indigenous women in INM and the ways in which they employed social media to great effect. Through Coates, we learn about freshly minted Cree lawyer Tanya Kappo, who is a political leader, writer, National Aboriginal Award winner, lawyer, negotiator, and the daughter of Harold Cardinal. Tanya and her mother Margaret Kappo, a social worker and community leader, wrote on #inm about their readiness for activism now. Doctor of Laws and author Sheila McAdams (McAdams, 2015) had been living on the land; she was concerned about her father's fishing sites and was working to integrate her roots, education, and law to envision a truly grounded future in which Cree laws can support Cree formal institutions and aspirations. A certified life skills coach and counselor embedded and active in the urban Aboriginal community in Saskatoon, Jessica Gordon promoted self-reliance and life choices in the Aboriginal community. Anti-racism educator Sheelah Mclean is a self-reflective non-Indigenous ally whose work with Indigenous environmentalist Priscilla Settee and anti-racist educator Verna St. Denis at the University of Saskatchewan helped her begin to understand her students more fully and thus participate in the INM movement (USASK, 2014). Nina Wilson, Kahkewistahaw First Nation citizen and Registered Dietician, worked actively with the David Suzuki Foundation in the early phases of organizing INM. Nina tweeted about becoming disenchanted with the hijacking of the processes of the movement by those who had been involved with Occupy and Defenders of the Land. Jessica, Sheelah, and Nina were the adult educators who, along with lawyers such as Tanya Kappo and Pam Palmater, brought this issue forward to their networks (Caven, 2013; Favel, 2012).

Dancing with the Red Dress/Vamp

In addition to social networking, round dances and flash mobs were happening across Canada to draw attention to INM. In *The Winter We Danced*, the Kino-nda-niimi Collective (2014) describes how these activities were key demonstrations of the INM movement, illustrating the self-control within the Aboriginal community and how this movement served as a continuation of Indigenous agitation for social justice and rights in Canada that goes back centuries.

A powerful use of creative expression during that period was the *Red Dress* installation by Winnipeg Métis artist Jaime Black, who sought to "evoke a presence through the marking of absence" (Black, 2014, n.p.) by drawing attention to the racialized nature of the violence inflicted on missing and murdered Aboriginal women. The limp red dresses hung prominently in outdoor settings. For Black, as for many Aboriginal women, this event took place at the nexus of the economic, personal, political, and social. Black taught in Opaskwayak, exhibited at the Shaman Gallery, and is a mentee with Mentoring Artists for Women's Art (MAWA)[1].

Another artist whose work contributed to INM is Métis activist Christi Belcourt. She follows in her father Toni Belcourt's footsteps, creating a stained-glass window entitled *GINIIGAANIIMENAANING* (which means "looking ahead"). This window was installed in the Centre Block of the Canadian Parliament in 2012. The work commemorates the Residential School Survivors and the 2008 Apology by Prime Minister Stephen Harper. Belcourt expresses her environmental philosophy with paints. She conceived the project known as "Walking with Our Sisters" (Belcourt, 2015), a memorial to missing and murdered Aboriginal women and those who did not come home from residential schools. The almost 2,000 pairs of moccasin vamps (tops) in this travelling installation are memorials of love. The installation organizes a ritual space where participants may witness and participate in the deep history of the erasure of Aboriginal women. Here, the "vamp" is an Aboriginal symbol of investment and exultation, of recognition and respect by the participants. It offsets the negative connotation of the "vamp" as a fallen women, evoking the limerance—that is, the simultaneous compulsion and attraction response—to the innocent/vamp stereotype of the Indigenous woman (Householder, 2007). This project proclaims the Indigenous perspective rather than the Euroheritage perspective of Aboriginal women.

Jackie Travers is another artist whose work contributed to INM. She is a Manitoba Aboriginal multimedia artist (Uniquely Manitoba, 2014) who is using her local profile to raise Indigenous political awareness and to organize Aboriginal voters. Travers' prints, signage, and T-shirts are an active component in raising awareness of the issues related to both the Winnipeg mayoralty campaign and to the campaign titled "Winnipeg Indigenous Rock the Vote in the 42nd Federal Election October 19, 2015" on Facebook. Given their immense talents and their diverse art forms, these three visual artists significantly enhance the promotion of awareness of First Nations/Métis/Inuit women's issues.

Photo courtesy of M. Atleo.

A cedar and beach sedge basket by Elsie Little Atleo Robinson showing the Nuu-chah-nulth story of the thunderbird and whale.

Dancing All A-round

The women of INM will be the first to say that the liberation of Indigenous peoples through education about the movement is a continuation of the work done by the many leaders who have gone before, such as the Indigenous women who were on "the cusp of contact" with settlers. Barman (2010) recalls that during the Gold Rush in British Columbia in the mid-1800s, Aboriginal women demonstrated an agency that was remarkable to the men who were caught unawares. The "Kittys," or dancehall girls, demanded to be treated with social respect and deference between dances. As dancehall girls during the Gold Rush, they could earn considerable money; they therefore learned the requisite language, manners, and dress and demanded social equality even if it was not always reciprocated. These entrepreneurial women began to carve out spaces in which succeeding generations could be heard.

In the spirit of such gender autonomy, the strong women of Saddle Lake, Alberta (Carlsen, Steinhauer, and Goyette, 2013) began their quest to have their status returned, modelling strong positions for subsequent demands by Lavelle (Ojibwa), Bedard, (Six Nations), Lovelace (Maliseet), and McIvor (Lower Nicola). The history of their activism was surely well known by #INM contributors Kappo, Houle, and Makokis. Morley, Alberta lawyer Rachel Snow also contributed to INM; she is the daughter of international ecumenical activist Reverend John Snow, who for decades hosted the international gatherings in Morley that brought Indigenous of spirit peoples from around the world together to share, to grow, and to overcome assimilationist tendencies (Snow, 2005).

Re-Kindling through Education

The greatest gains by Indigenous women over the last 40 years have been in education. For example, Fisher River's own Verna Kirkness (2013) made her mark by participating in the writing of Indian Control of Indian Education at the national level and the "Wabung" (Our Tomorrows) education manifesto for Manitoba. In the 1970s, she worked in Manitoba and then moved to the University of British Columbia to lead the Native Teacher Education Program (NITEP). Kirkness went on to create a Masters program, initiate the First Nations House of Learning, and in general champion the education of Aboriginal peoples in British Columbia and across Canada. Her lifelong engagement with education as a teacher, bureaucrat, professor, writer, speaker, innovator, fundraiser, and visionary makes her an excellent role model.

The Opaskwayak Cree Nation in Manitoba produced an abundance of elders and educators with post-graduate degrees who facilitated the development of the University College of the North (UCN) that is unique in Canada. UCN is a college with a provincial charter, an Elders Council consisting of Aboriginal and non-Aboriginal elders, and a Teacher Education program called Kenanow[2] which means "all of us," bringing the communities of the north and the land together in a curriculum of relationships. The dialogue among the women of the Elders Council and the Learning Council is central to its success.

Many First Nations communities have developed child and family welfare systems based on delegated authority whereby the community administers provincial child and welfare policies and laws with less money from Aboriginal and Northern Affairs Canada (AANAC). Cindy Blackstock has been a tireless fighter for the rights of the Aboriginal child. In 2006, Métis lawyer Mary-Ellen Turpel-

Lafond was appointed as the first Children and Youth Representative in British Columbia; she has been reappointed for another five-year term. For many years Debbie Foxcroft of the Nuu-chah-nulth Tribal Council was head of the USMA (which means "precious one") child services (Moore, 2013) and she is now the president of the Tribal Council. Everywhere, First Nations/Métis/Inuit women are creating new social institutions and transforming old ones.

For example, Mary Simon (1997) vaulted into the spotlight at the Earth Summit in Rio, expounding on the ecology of the Arctic. She retired in 2012 after four decades leading the Inuit people and six years as head of the Inuit Tapiriit Kanatami (the National Inuit organization of Canada). Mary began her life on the land but moved to a larger community with a school. After her highly celebrated lifetime of public service, she returned to the community to ensure that children are spending time on the land and with the language. Simon is clear that Inuit people need to be engaged with their governance because she maintains that others cannot be depended upon. Similarly, Inuit leader Minnie Grey (2010) watched her widowed mother move from the land to town to make a new life for her family. While Minnie learned how to live on the land as a child, she later participated in building public institutions to serve her people. She recounts the many initiatives in which she and other Inuit women participated because all the roles filled by professionals and bureaucrats in mainstream governance were part of the role that Inuit women have played traditionally. The Honourable Ethel Blondin-Andrew is the first Aboriginal woman elected to the House of Commons. A Tulita-born Dene women, she is the chairperson of the Sahtu Secretariat Inc. (SSI), an organization created by the Sahtu region's seven land corporations "to ensure the Sahtu land claim (signed in 1994) is properly implemented." (Quenneville, 2013, n.p.). Blondin-Andrew has moved from the land to the boardroom but continues to hunt moose with her husband on the land. "The right to be cold," to live on the land where the cold dictates cultural strategies, is what Sheila Watt-Cloutier (2015) wants. She travels tirelessly to promote environmental equities for her people and she knows what it is like to move away from the land and then come back to see it changed, diminished by outside forces. These women leaders are examples of how one needs to be of the land in order to understand the deep needs of those peoples that have cultural and spiritual relationships with the land.

Creating Dance Halls for Future Generations

First Nations/Métis/Inuit women have been the mainstays of Indigenous survivance in Canada since time immemorial. During the fur trade, they were the ones who socialized non-Aboriginal men to live in the bush and they became mothers of the Métis nation. During the Gold Rush, they were the ones who could dance with the best of them and who began to understand the ways of non-Indigenous society. Today, Aboriginal women are lawyers, accountants, professors, stockbrokers, industrial managers, CEOs of corporations, social workers, nurses, doctors, PM6s (top bureaucrats), MLAs, MPs, Chancellors and Vice Presidents of universities, midwives, X-ray technicians, health workers, community leaders, and all manner of important contributors to the communities in which they live. Aboriginal women are transforming institutions and creating new ones. It is those women who remember their traditions who will have insight into their futures. With education, political and economic participation will come. The histories and wisdom of mainstream Western society cannot provide the insights for the synergies needed to live as Indigenous peoples in historical territories and homelands. There is a growing need to expose the lies of colonialism about Indigenous women and to trust their leadership to model survivance so that their families might survive, thrive, and participate as full members in Canadian society.

Endnotes

[1] https://mawa.ca/about

[2] https://www.ucn.ca/sites/academics/facultyeducation/programs/bacheloreducation/Pages/Kenanow-Bachelor-of-Education-Program.aspx

References

- Anderson, K. (2011). *Life Stages and Native Women: Memory, Teaching and Story Medicine*. Winnipeg, MB: University of Manitoba Press.

- Archibald, J. (1997). *Coyote Learns to Make a Storybasket: The Place of First Nations Stories in Education*. Unpublished doctoral dissertation. Burnaby, BC, Simon Fraser University.

- Archibald, J. (2004). *Indigenous Storywork*. Vancouver, BC: UBC Press.

- Atleo, M.R. (2001). *Learning Models in the Umeek Narratives: Identifying an Educational Framework through Storywork with First Nations Elders*. Unpublished doctoral dissertation. Vancouver, BC: University of British Columbia.

- Atleo, M.R. (2013). The zone of Canadian Aboriginal adult education: A social movement approach. In T. Nesbit, S. M. Brigham, N. Taber, & T. Gibb (Eds.). *Adult Education and Learning In Canada* (pp. 1-26). Toronto, ON: Thompson Publishers.

- Atleo, M.R. (2009). Understanding Aboriginal learning ideology through storywork with elders. *Alberta Journal of Educational Research*,Vol.55, No.4, pp. 452-467.

- Atleo, M.R. & Fitznor, L. (2010). Aboriginal educators discuss recognizing, reclaiming and revitalizing their multi competences in heritage/English language usage. *Canadian Journal of Native Education*, 32(1), 13-34.

- Barman, J. (2010). Indigenous women and feminism on the cusp of contact. In C. Sazack, S. M. Huhndorf, J. Perreault, & J. Barman (Eds.). *Indigenous Women and Feminism: Politics, Activism, Culture* (pp. 92-108). Vancouver, BC: UBC Press.

- Battiste, M. (1986). Micmac literacy and cognitive assimilation. In J. Barman, Y. Hébert, & D. McCaskill (Eds.). *Indian Education in Canada*, Volume 1: The Legacy (pp. 23-45). Vancouver, BC: UBC Press.

- Belcourt, C. (2015). Home. http://www.christibelcourt.com

- Black, J. (2014). The red dress project. An aesthetic response to the more than 1000 missing and murdered Aboriginal women in Canada. http://www.redressproject.org/?page_id=27.

- Carnoy, M. (1974). *Education as Cultural Imperialism*. New York, NY: David McKay Co., Inc.

- Carlsen, N, Steinhauer, K., & Goyette, L. (2013). *Disinherited Generations: Our Struggle to Reclaim Treaty Rights for First Nations Women and their Descendants*. Edmonton, AB: University of Alberta Press.

- Caven, F. (2013). Being idle no more! The women behind the movement. *Cultural Survival CSQ*. Issue: 37-1. Retrieved from: http://www.culturalsurvival.org/publications/cultural-survival-quarterly/being-idle-no-more-women-behind-movement.

- Coates, K. (2015). *#IDLENOMORE and the Remaking of Canada*. Regina, SK: University of Regina Press.

- Dorion, L. M. (2010). *Opinawasowin: The Lifelong Process of Growing Cree and Metis Children*. Unpublished Integrated Studies Project for the degree of Master of Arts–Integrated Studies. Athabasca, AB: Athabasca University. Retrieved from: http://www.communityschools.ca/documents/FinalPaperMAIS701-5.pdf.

- Du Bois, W. E. B. (1903). *The Souls of Black Folk*. New York, NY: Dover Publications.

- Favel, F. (2012, Dcc. 9). Silence is assimilation, not what our people want. *The Battleford-News Optimist*. Retrieved from: http://www.newsoptimist.ca/opinion/editorial/silence-is-assimilation-not-what-our-people-want-1.1572247.

- Fiske, J. (1995). Political status of native Indian women: Contradictory implications of Canadian state policy. *American Indian Culture and Research Journal*, 19(2) 1-30. http://www.law-lib.utoronto.ca/diana/whrr/cfsearch_advanced. cfm?sister=utl&page=0.

- Freire, P. (1970, 2000). *Pedagogy of the Oppressed*. London: Bloomsbury Academic.

- Gordon, J. (2015). Profile: LinkedIn: http://firstnationstories.com/?tag=jessica-gordon.

- Grey, M. (2010). From the tundra to the boardroom to everywhere in between: Politics and the changing roles of Inuit women in the arctic. In C. Sazack, S. M. Huhndorf, J. Perreault, & J. Barman, (Eds.). *Indigenous Women and Feminism: Politics, Activism, Culture* (pp. 21-28). Vancouver, BC: UBC Press.

- hooks, B. (2004). *Rock My Soul: Black People and Self-Esteem*. Washington, DC: Washington Square Press.

- Householder, M. (2007). Eden's Translations: Women and temptation in Early America. *Huntington Library Quarterly*, Vol. 70, No. 1, 11-36. Retrieved from: http://www.jstor.org/stable/10.1525/hlq.2007.70.1.11 .

- Kino-nda-nimi Collective, The (2014). *The Winter We Danced: Voices from The Past, the Future, and the Idle No More Movement*. Winnipeg, MN: Arbeiter Ring Publishing.
- Kirkness, V. (2013). *Creating Space: My Life and Work in Indigenous Education*. Winnipeg, MB: University of Manitoba Press.
- La Botz, D. (Winter, 2012). From Occupy Wall Street to Occupy the World: The emergence of a mass movement. *New Politics*, Vol. XIII (No. 4). Retrieved from: http://newpol.org/content/new-politics-vol-xiii-no-4-whole-number-52.
- Lawrence, B. (2000). Regulating native identity by gender. In M.A. Wallis & S. Kwok (Eds.). *Daily Struggles: The Deepening Racialization and Feminization of Poverty in Canada* (pp. 59-72). Toronto: ON: Canadian Scholars' Press Inc.
- McAdams, S. (2015). *Nationhood Interrupted: Revitalizing Nêhiyaw Legal Systems*. Calgary, AB: Purich Publishing.
- Miller, J. R. (1996). *Shingwauk's Vision: A History of Native Residential Schools*. Toronto, ON: University of Toronto Press.
- Moore, J. (2013). *The Hidden Voices of Nuu'chah'nulth Women*. Unpublished doctoral dissertation. Christ Church, New Zealand: Canterbury Christ Church University.
- Powell, M. (2002). Rhetorics of survivance: How American Indians use writing. *College Composition and Communication*, 53(3), 396-434.
- Quenneville, G. (2013) Ethel Blondin-Andrew proves you can go home again. *Up Here Business*. Retrieved from: http://upherebusiness.ca/post/34707058458.
- Settee, H. (2014). *Tipachimowin: Students and Professors Share Stories About their Winnipeg Education Centre Experience*. Unpublished Master of Education thesis. Winnipeg, MB: University of Manitoba.
- Simon, M. (1996). *Inuit: One Future, One Arctic*. Peterborough, ON: The Cider Press.
- Simon, M. (1997). *Inuit: One future–One Arctic*. Courtenay, BC: The Cider Press.
- Smith, C. L. (2000). *Jingle Dancer*. New York. NY: HarperCollins.
- Snow, J. (2005). *These Mountains Are Our Sacred Places: The Story of the Stoney People*. Calgary, AB: Fifth House Ltd..
- Truth and Reconciliation Commission (TRC) (2015). *Honouring the truth, reconciling for the future: Summary of the final report of the Truth and Reconciliation Commission of Canada*. Winnipeg, MB. Retrieved from: http://www.trc.ca/websites/trcinstitution/File/2015/Honouring_the_Truth_Reconciling_for_the_Future_July_23_2015.pdf
- *Two Row Times* (March 24, 2014). Our future standing proud: Oherokon rites of passage. Retrieved from: http://www.tworowtimes.com/arts-and-culture/our-future-standing-proud-oherokon-rites-of-passage/
- Van Kirk, S. (1996). *Many Tender Ties: Women in Fur-Trade Society, 1670-1870*. Norman, OK: University of Oklahoma Press.
- Visenor, G. R. (2000). *Fugitive Poses: Native American Indian Scenes of Absence and Presence*. Lincoln, NB: University of Nebraska Press.
- Voyageur, C. J., Newhouse, D., & Beavon, D. (2011). *Hidden in Plain Sight: Contributions of Aboriginal Peoples to Canadian Identity and Culture*. Volume 2. Toronto, ON: University of Toronto Press.
- Welton, M. (2005). Cunning pedagogics: The encounter between the Jesuit missionaries and Amerindians in 17th-century New France. *Adult Education Quarterly*, 55 (2), 101-115.
- Watt-Cloutier, S. (2015). *The Right To Be Cold: One Woman's Story of Protecting Her Culture, The Arctic and the Whole Planet*. Toronto, ON: Allen Lane, Penguin Random House, Canada.
- Uniquely Manitoba (2014). 10 years anniversary award winner: Jackie Travers. *Rising Star*. Retrieved from: http://www.uniquelymanitoba.ca/resources/pages/files%5Crisingstar/RS%20Jackietraverse.pdf
- USASK (2014). *Sheelah Mclean: A Call to Action*. Department of Native Studies. Saskatoon, Saskatchewan. Retrieved from: http://artsandscience.usask.ca/nativestudies/news/news.php?newsid=3522.

WILPF
MANIFESTO
2015

WOMEN'S INTERNATIONAL LEAGUE FOR
PEACE & FREEDOM

This vignette was prepared by Laurel Collins.

Laura Hughes lived in Toronto in her twenties, during the First World War, and was an outspoken and dedicated pacifist. She combined education and activism in her work with the Women's International League for Peace and Freedom (WILPF), and was the league's link to the international peace movement. She organized reading circles, monthly study sessions, and visiting speakers, and she provided information about where to get anti-war reading material that could not be purchased in Canada. She taught other feminists about war profiteering and about the potentially permanent loss of civil liberties during war. The majority of Canadian women who sustained their peace activism throughout World War I, as well as in the years afterwards, were informed by and deeply committed to a combination of pacifism, feminism, and socialism, and most often they were maternalists. For example, Francis Beynon, Violet McNaughton, and Gertrude Richardson all saw women as having special talents and obligations as mothers to create a moral, peaceful world. Less common were women such as Laura Hughes, who also held pacifist, feminist, and socialist ideals, but who did not express women's peace efforts in terms of their role as mothers or their essential feminine nature. Her pacifism was quite radical, and she focused her criticism on capitalist structures and on church and government officials for their involvement in profiting from war by selling armaments to both sides.

Laura Hughes also spoke to many women's groups about women's suffrage, factory conditions, and the exploitation of children. She went undercover to investigate working as a factory girl in a war plant, and her first-hand experience of the degrading working conditions and lack of adequate labour laws inspired much of her later work. She subsequently published a paper exposing the abusive working conditions for women in the mills, and campaigned for labour law reform. She spoke frequently at Toronto labour conventions and became the Vice-President of the Toronto Labour Party.

During the war, Laura also operated a feminist, pacifist clearing house, and corresponded with women across Canada. In order to avoid censorship and arrest, she and the WILPF framed their mission in terms of peace education focused on post-war concerns about ensuring that there was never a subsequent war. But, despite their claims, she and the WILPF were in reality engaged in a movement to stop the war. In her correspondence, she wrote about women's power to bring about substantial social change. She and her WILPF colleagues laid the groundwork for the mobilizations in the 1920s and built networks of women engaged in social activism. Laura Hughes died in 1966.

References

- Lunde, L. H. (1931-1967). Laura Hughes Lunde papers, Special Collections and University Archives, University of Illinois at Chicago.

- Roberts, B. A. (1985). "Why do women do nothing to end the war?": Canadian feminist-pacifists and the Great War. Ottawa: Canadian Research Institute for the Advancement of Women.

- Socknat, T. (1989). For peace and freedom: Canadian feminists and the interwar peace campaign. In J. Williamson & D. Gorham (Eds.), *Up and Doing: Canadian Women and Peace* (1st edition, pp. 48-65). Toronto: Women's Press.

Vignette: Laura Hughes, 1886-1966

Captain Nancy Taber in front of a Sea King helicopter at CFB Shearwater, Nova Scotia, 1997.

4

Women Military Leaders in the Canadian Forces
Learning to Negotiate Gender

As a child, I grew up in a proud military family. My father was in the Canadian Navy, so we were transferred every few years, back-and-forth across the country, with him deploying frequently. When I was 17 years old, I enthusiastically joined the Canadian Air Force. I was looking forward to an exciting career that would challenge me, with opportunities for travel and new experiences. I began with a basic training officer course and then started my undergraduate degree at Royal Military College. Upon graduation and commissioning as an officer, I trained as an air navigator and Tactical Coordinator (TACCO) of a Sea King helicopter, after which I was deployed on a destroyer at sea.

Nancy Taber

Despite the challenges of being a woman in a masculine institution, I enjoyed my time in the military. However, near the end of my short service engagement (SSE) contract (four years of university plus nine years' service), I began to question my place in the military. At sea, my cabin-mate and I had long conversations about what it was like to be women military members, even while we hated being categorized as "women" and definitely distanced ourselves from anything perceived as "feminist." We just wanted to be military members. Yet we always felt so visible; while we were accepted as aircrew and recognized for our competence, we were typically in the extreme minority and, in one case, the only two women on ship.

When I completed my SSE contract, I resigned, deciding to pursue my Master of Education in adult education degree and experience life as a civilian. Progressing through my Master's and PhD studies, I increasingly problematized gender and militarism in my life, in the military, and in society as a whole, and this problematization has now become central to my research program. Furthermore, my positioning in the academic discipline of adult education helped me theorize how gender is learned and how military culture functions pedagogically as it intersects with societal discourses and ruling relations.

There is much work on gender in the military, but there is little published that explores gender and the military through a learning lens, particularly as it relates to Canada. I do so in this chapter due to my particular life path, one that has taken me to an unexpected place as an academic feminist. I also recognize the irony of using my own service as a way to forefront my critique of the military and militarism. Sasson-Levy, Levy, and Lomsky-Feder (2011) explore this privileged positioning in their research about the experiences of female Israeli ex-soldiers who engage in anti-war protest. They suggest that "as military veterans, they [their participants] gain a new alternative political and moral power for women, but at the same time when women use their military service to criticize the military, they reaffirm the republican ethos that grants a legitimate political voice only to those who contribute to the security of the collective" (pp. 741, 742).

Gender and the Military through a Learning Lens

It is important to note that I am neither arguing that militaries should be outright abolished, nor that woman cannot serve successfully. I know several women from my time in the Canadian Forces (CF)[1] who are still in the military; although they often recognize that they faced challenges due to their gender, they have worked for their promotions through the ranks and are, as senior officers, in leadership roles. I also know military men who believe firmly in women's rights and equality, and are allies to them. Feinman (2000) would term their approaches as feminist egalitarian militarism, aligning with liberal feminism, which "use[s] equal rights discourse and policies to insist that women play a full and unimpeded role in the military" (p. 1). However, my approach comes from a feminist antimilitarist perspective (Enloe, 2000, 2007; Feinman, 2000) that problematizes the ways in which gender and militarism intersect in society, with an overall privileging of men, masculinity, militarism, and militaries. It must be recognized that militaries are not isolated entities; "military matters and, beyond them, the organization of military society are continually mixing in human cultural evolution" (Caforio, 2006, p. 3). This chapter, therefore, explores the ways in which gender, leadership, and learning intersect in the lives of women in the Canadian military, and what I see as the implications of this intersection for Canada as a whole.

Communities of Practice Learning Theories

My theoretical stance blends feminist antimilitarism with legitimate peripheral participation (LPP) in communities of practice (CoP) learning theories. LPP focuses on situated learning as it relates to "the relations between newcomers and old-timers…. It concerns the process by which newcomers become part of a community of practice [and] move toward full participation in the sociocultural practices of a community" (Lave and Wenger, 1991, p. 29). Wenger, McDermott, and Snyder (2002) describe CoPs as "groups of people who share a concern, a set of problems, or a passion about a topic, and who deepen their knowledge and expertise in this area by interacting on an ongoing basis" (p. 4). Members of CoPs participate in organizational culture, engage in joint enterprise, and negotiate meaning, and are involved in learning that is "an experience of identity … a process of becoming" (Wenger, 1998, p. 215).

Lave and Wenger's (1991) ideas have been taken up, further developed, and critiqued by various scholars (e.g., Barton and Tusting, 2005; Fuller, Hodkinson, Hodkinson, and Unwin, 2005; Taber, Plumb, and Jolemore, 2008). They have also been applied in postmodern ways to explore "communities of masculine and feminine practice" (Paechter, 2003, p. 72). In previous research involving military mothers (Taber, 2011), I examined how masculine and feminine military communities of practice functioned in complex ways to marginalize women and maintain a masculine militaristic status quo. My purpose here is not to explore how female military members can move more successfully towards full membership, but to examine how learning theory can inform current understandings of women, militaries, and militarism. I do so by detailing the history of women in the Canadian military, examining the contemporary discourse of equality in the Canadian Forces, and problematizing female officers' narratives of leadership.

A Brief History of Women in the Canadian Military

Although military organizations vary from country to country, they feature unique characteristics that differentiate them from other organizations, as they require increased allegiance, obedience, and availability on the part of members (Soeters, Winslow, and Weibull, 2006). Militaries are greedy institutions that blur professional and personal life, with members dedicated to live and die for their country (Coser, 1974; Segal, 1986; Taber, 2011). Furthermore, military organizations are gendered in that they tend to exclude and devalue women. This has a concomitant negative impact on women's participation in these organizations (Feinman, 2000; Franke, 1997; Kronsell, 2005).

Women's involvement in the Canadian military has changed over the decades, starting with their complete exclusion and moving to complete inclusion, at least officially. Canadian women worked as nursing sisters beginning in the late 1800s, but were not eligible for military membership until women-only units were established during World War II. As these units were disbanded, women served in mixed units in support roles (but were still released if they married or became pregnant). Eventually, women were allowed to serve in combat roles but not on submarines (Dundas, 2000; Symons, 1990). In 2000, this final restriction on women's service was eliminated (Government of Canada, 2013). Each of these changes resulted from legislation that required the Canadian Forces to integrate women more fully (Symons, 1990; Davis, 2007a). The trajectory of newcomer to old-timer, from peripheral to full participation, was established in policy. But the reality of women's lives, both civilian and military, demonstrates that discourses of equality are complex and often misleading.

Contemporary Discourses of Women as "Equal"

In contemporary Canadian society, discourses of equality circulate in ways that promote the idea that all Canadians are equal. However, this notion of equality is based on neo-liberal capitalist notions that position citizens as individual consumers and entrepreneurs (Brodie, 2008). In a similar manner, the Canadian military is perceived as progressive: "The CF takes pride in being a leader in the field of equality and women's rights and is actively recruiting women for dynamic, rewarding positions" (Government of Canada, 2012, para. 1). As military members, women have access to secure employment, good pay, comprehensive benefits, and guaranteed pensions. They are full citizens (Feinman, 2000) and "their achievements contribute to the full and equal inclusion of women in our society and national institutions" (Government of Canada, 2012, para. 16). Ostensibly, "there is truly no limit to career opportunities for them [women] in the Canadian Forces" (para. 2). However, women make up only 15 percent of the Regular Force and Primary Reserve and 10 percent of those deployed internationally (Government of Canada, 2013). Furthermore, they tend to be clustered in traditional occupations, underrepresented in leadership roles (Davis, 2007a), marginalized (Gouliquer, 2011), sexually harassed (Gouliquer, 2011), and sexually assaulted (Mercier and Castonguay, 2014).

Interestingly, the CF does state that there is a need for research into "systemic barriers" (Government of Canada, 2012, para. 15) in order to "level the playing field for women" (para. 16). However, systemic barriers cannot be overcome by leveling any field; to do so, one must radically change the field itself. Lieutenant-Colonel Karen Davis's (2009) research can be used to further illuminate this discourse of equality: "The persistent denial of women as women in the military, whether perceived as a *gender neutral* or *gender blind* perspective, raises important considerations regarding not only the contribution of women to the Canadian Forces (CF), but also how sex and gender is constructed and understood by the CF" (italics in original, p. 431).

The discourses of "dichotomous gender difference" and "gender neutrality" in the above quotation exist alongside each other, obscuring the ways in which the CF as an organization is gendered in itself (Harrison, 2002; Taber, 2009; Davis and McKee, 2004; Poulin, 2001; Winslow & Dunn, 2002). A Defence Women's Advisory Organization (DWAO) was created, in accordance with Canada's Employment Equity Act passed in 2002, to address issues related to women's service and bring them to the attention of the military leadership (House of Commons, 2013). In the transcript of her report to the Standing Committee on the Status of Women (House of Commons, 2013, n.p.), the DWAO military co-chair continually refers to "systemic issues" which, when she is questioned, she defines as "a trend or pattern" typically related to harassment. This categorization overlooks the gendered nature of military culture. She also states that "women are wired a bit differently,"[2] furthering the idea that dichotomous and homogenous gender attributes or differences exist and these, therefore, help to explain what is taking place. Her approach contrasts with that of Lieutenant-Colonel Karen Davis (the author of the research cited above), who critiques the "warrior culture" of the CF in her appearance before the committee, particularly with respect to the combat arms, describing this culture as founded on "assumptions that women and men are different; men are strong, women are weak; women are protected, men protect women; women are emotionally unstable, men are more stable for fighting in war."

Davis (2009) in fact advocates for improving the recruitment and retention of women, pointing to the importance of having more women in leadership roles and having leaders "better understand the value of greater gender diversity" (House of Commons, 2013). Her ideas can be applied to how women learn to become military members: they imply that women's standing will improve if they have trajectories to full participation as leaders and are able to engage in changing the gendered nature of the institution from within. However, if women (and men) learn to become military members in a warrior culture that values militarized masculinity, must their legitimate peripheral participation also value this culture? Indeed, "women who have taken on leadership roles in hegemonic masculine institutions, such as becoming military leaders…often have downplayed their femininity [preferring instead to be] seen as a soldier, just like all the men" (Kronsell, 2005, p. 292).

Narratives of Successful Leadership: An Unwanted "Spotlight"

In her edited volume about female Canadian military officers, Davis (2007c) highlights their successes while also exploring how, "without exception, they have had to reconcile and negotiate experiences that are unique from their male peers, based on the fact that they are women" (p. viii). Chapter authors in Davis's volume discuss how their leadership experiences intersect with their embodied-ness as women. A common thread throughout the narratives is the unwanted presence of a "spotlight" that followed them throughout their careers simply because they were women. They wanted to be judged impartially, without prejudice or preference. Interestingly, though, they most often accept the fact that they are naturally different because of their gender, subscribing somewhat to the idea of a gender dichotomy, but they do not want to be treated differently. They are undeniably successful, demonstrating that women can become old-timers as full military members. However, their trajectories depended on learning to negotiate gender in specific ways. As Davis (2009) argues, "their leadership experience in the military is as much about negotiating the perceptions of those around them in reference to their 'gender' as it is about leadership style per se" (p. 436). Although some authors discuss gender in more critical ways than others, the volume as a whole—which I would classify as feminist egalitarian militarism—helps illuminate their gendered experiences.

Reiffenstein (2007), an artillery officer in the combat arms, critiques the common organizational perception that the CF is gender neutral. While she agrees that certain occupations may have achieved some form of gender integration, she worked in a "gender asymmetric environment," where she was a "token woman" who was "frequently singled out for the wrong reasons" (p. 4). She critiques the idea that, as told by the Chief of Defence Staff during his speech to the Women in Defence and Security luncheon, "gender is no longer an issue" (p. 2), explaining "many subtle and underlying cultural influences have not been seriously addressed from a gender perspective" (p. 7). In particular, Reiffenstein relates the story of a young university student "who wants to be an infantry officer but does not want the stigma of being the first female officer in the regiment" (p. 7). As Davis (2007a) asks in relation to operational roles as a whole, "How does a woman find her place and her pride in a tradition to which women have no history?" (p. 83). This question demonstrates how policies that allow for full membership of women do not necessarily reflect the realities of women's experiences and decision-making processes. Reiffenstein emphasizes that "gender integration was a leadership issue. It was not about male or female, it was about accepting soldiers for who and what they are" (Reiffenstein, 2007, p. 2). Full members must make changes, but these same full members have benefited from the system as it is, based on its warrior culture.

Forgues (2007) examines her career as a "lone woman pilot," stating that "being 'one of' anything generates a great deal of interest in your activities and abilities" (p. 29). Mulkins (2007) discusses how she is under a "ubiquitous microscope" (p. 40) as the first woman to command a Canadian ship. She explains, "While this scrutiny and associated judgement by others never caused any particular anxiety, it was an everpresent factor, which, even when it was benign or even well intentioned, likely cast the complexion of my command in a slightly different light than that of my male peers" (Mulkins, 2007, p. 35). Similarly, Forgues asks: "Was I there because there was some sort of nebulous quota for women pilots that needed to be filled or did I genuinely merit the wings I wore? That was an added pressure that virtually none of the men I ever flew with had to experience" (Forgues, 2007, p. 29).

Mulkins discusses the leadership differences between position power and personal power, arguing that attaining power through rank alone will only get a leader so far. Personal power "depends on the favourable reception by others of one's personality traits" (p. 39). She states that it is "more important to maintain strong 'personal power'" (p. 40). In other words, full membership cannot be achieved by organizational promotions alone.

At times the argument that women should be included as leaders extends from the need for equality to one of difference (i.e., that "feminine" leadership qualities, which are equated with women, are needed). For instance, Speiser-Blanchet (2007), a tactical helicopter pilot who worked with the combat arms as a "rare woman" (p. 49) in an "annoying spotlight" (p. 56), argued that "women are particularly well suited to this interactive, team-oriented environment [of an aircraft], where communication and teamwork are vital to the success of the mission" (p. 45). Interestingly, this assertion equates women's successes in certain environments with the fact that they are a result of natural gender differences.

Similarly, Febbraro's (2007) research is prefaced upon specific categories of masculinity (task-oriented leadership), femininity (person-oriented leadership), and androgyny (a blend of the two). Using terms such as masculinity and femininity tie leadership to gender, whereas if Febbraro had simply used the two foci of task and person, gender would have been separated out to some extent. The women in her study felt a blend of masculine and feminine approaches were best. Furthermore, "Women must accommodate to the military and the military must accommodate to women" (Febbraro, p. 119). However, it seems that the military is not doing much accommodating. Speiser-Blanchet (2007) explains her "greatest challenge as a female leader [was] adjusting to a male culture" (p. 53), as she was engaged in "learning to deal with perception issues and coping with some form of the ubiquitous spotlight that followed the women wherever we went" (p. 53).

The experiences of these female military leaders demonstrate that women may be officially allowed full membership, but attaining it is much more difficult than for men. If women are expected to conform as they move from newcomer to old-timer, learning to negotiate their gender in very specific ways and trying to hide from while not resenting the spotlight, it is difficult to enact change. Women can become leaders, but only if they accommodate themselves to the military. Arguably, as these narratives of leadership are provided by successful military women, it is possible for women to attain full membership and old-timer status. However, the distinct ways in which they were required to learn to negotiate their gender points to the differences in the service trajectories of men and women.[3]

Several authors in Davis's (2007) volume call for military members to learn more about the intersection of leadership and gender in the military as well as in society. Reifenstein (2007) argues that diversity training programs should be rethought. Davis (2007a) explains that there is a need for a "broader understanding of the social and historical processes that influence the persistent labeling of women's sexuality and social behaviour in male dominated cultures...such understanding is an important aspect of professional development and success for women in masculine cultures such as the CF" (p. 73). Davis first achieved this understanding when she attended university, just as I did when learning about feminist theory in a Master of Education course (Taber, 2005).

Although I was involved in continuous formal and informal educational courses during my military career, including diversity training, it was not until I encountered the discipline of adult education that my learning took on a societal, critical lens. Perhaps this learning was so powerful because it allowed me to learn about theory through my own experiences. Thus, as with the Israeli military members in Sasson-Levy, Levy, and Lomsky-Feder's (2011) research, I could explore how "the gender regime of the military" shaped my "military service" and "political voice" (p. 759). In retrospect, I would classify my perspective when I joined the military as stemming from an initial belief in feminist egalitarian militarism. As I neared the end of my service and then entered academia, my political voice gradually shifted to encompass feminist antimilitarism. Entering a scholarly community of practice, on a trajectory of learning from student to professor, opened up new ways of thinking, enabling me to negotiate the meanings of gender and militarism with a critical stance. So, while educational opportunities within the military can help deepen members' understanding of gender, it is doubtful that members will ever do so in any radical sense, and they are certainly not about to critique militarism and its masculinized presumptions.

Conclusion

The military is a very specific organization requiring unwavering and continuous dedication. It is a calling, a vocation as opposed to just a job, which demands that CF members embody certain forms of duty, honour, and service before self (Taber, 2009). As such, the CF can be considered a community of practice in itself, with members engaged in the joint enterprise of defending the country through the "ordered, lawful application of military force" (National Defence, 2003, p. 4). Meaning is officially not negotiated but mandated in a manual that "codifies...what it means to be a Canadian military professional" (National Defence, 2003, p. 2), wherein identity is "collective" and "revolves around three concepts...voluntary military service, unlimited liability, and service before self" (p. 20).

However, CoPs do not equate simply with organizations and neither meaning nor identity can be mandated in a straightforward manner. Certainly, the way in which Speiser-Blanchet (2007) discusses her experiences with her aircrew indicates that they may have been a CoP. People can participate in a multitude of CoPs, learning to negotiate meaning, particularly with respect to gender, in differing ways. As members of various CoPs, women (and men) can engage in meaning making by interacting with newcomers, old-timers, and those at various positions on the learning trajectory. There is some space for engaging in formal and informal critiques of masculinity and its concomitant implications for women (as well as men who may not be judged as "masculine" enough). However, what may be more difficult is critiquing militarism itself. How can militarism be separated out from militaries? As Canadian leaders attempt to construct Canada as a "warrior nation" (McKay and Swift, 2012), planning expensive celebrations of the War of 1812, WWI, and WWII (Chase, 2014; McKay and Swift, 2012), and privileging military service over other forms of contributions to the nation (Taber, in press), militarism becomes even more difficult (but important) to critique.

Sasson-Levy, Levy, and Lomsky-Feder (2011) explore how "women's struggle for equal participation in the military is often criticized as reinforcing militarism, encouraging the militarization of women's lives and, in a roundabout way, even legitimating the use of force" (p. 759). Certainly, some feminist antimilitarists are pacifists who believe in the abolition of militaries; however, others support the judicious use of militaries while arguing that militarized masculinity must be eliminated (see Feinman, 2000). It is clear that any examination of gender, women, and the military is complex. This chapter demonstrates the ways in which, although officially equal, women leaders continue to be marginalized within the Canadian Forces. Furthermore, exploring how they negotiate militarized masculinity on a daily basis can help illuminate larger discourses of gender, equality, and militarism. By applying learning theories to their experiences, adult educators can increase their understandings of the ways in which gender and militarism intersect with leadership in Canada, which in turn may influence adult education teaching and scholarship.

Endnotes

[1] In 2013, the name of the Canadian Forces (CF) was changed to the Canadian Armed Forces (CAF). I use the term CF in this chapter as it applies to most of the time frame I discuss and the references which I use.

[2] This phrasing is disturbingly similar to that of General Tom Lawson, then Chief of the Defence Staff, in response to the "External Review into Sexual Misconduct and Sexual Harassment in the Canadian Armed Forces." He stated that "we're [men] biologically wired in a certain way and there will be those who believe it is a reasonable thing to press themselves and their desires on others" (*The Globe and Mail*, 2015, para. 4). This chapter was written before this review was published. There were a number of recommendations in the review. They include "cultural change" and "strong leadership." Furthermore, "improving the integration of women, including in positions of senior leadership, is necessary to cultural reform.... [T]here is an undeniable link between the existence of a hostile organizational culture that is disrespectful and demeaning to women, and the poor integration of women into the organization. Increasing the representation of women in the CAF, including in the highest positions of senior leadership, is therefore key to changing the culture of the organization" (Deschamps, 2015, p. vii).

[3] I recognize that the use of terms such as "women" and "men" represent a problematic gender binary. In an article about experiences of military mothers (Taber, 2011), I further discuss the complex performances of masculinity and femininity by women and men. For the purposes of this chapter, I use the binary terms to reflect the language used by the authors in Davis' (2007) volume.

References

- Brodie, J. (2008). We are all equal now: Contemporary gender politics in Canada. *Feminist Theory*, 9(2), 145-164.
- Caforio, G. (2006). Introduction. In Caforio, G. (Ed.), *Handbook of the Sociology of the Military,* (pp. 3-6). New York: Springer.
- Chase, S. (2014, February 19). Defence department fears public wrath over spending on war commemorations. *The Globe and Mail*, p. A4.
- Coser, L. A. (1974). *Greedy Institutions: Patterns of Undivided Commitment*. New York: The Free Press.
- Davis, K. (1997). Understanding women's exit from the Canadian Forces: Implications for integration? In L. Weinstein and C. White (Eds.), *Wives and Warriors: Women in the Military in the United States and Canada* (pp. 179-198). Westport: Bergin and Garvey.
- Davis, K. (2007a). From ocean ops to combat ops: A short history of women and leadership in the Canadian Forces. In K. Davis (Ed.), *Women and Leadership in the Canadian Forces: Perspectives and Experiences* (pp. 69-91). Winnipeg: Canadian Defence Academy Press.
- Davis, K. (2007b). Introduction. In K. Davis (Ed.), *Women and Leadership in the Canadian Forces: Perspectives and Experiences (*pp. vii-xiv). Winnipeg: Canadian Defence Academy Press.
- Davis, K. (Ed.). (2007c). *Women and Leadership in the Canadian Forces: Perspectives and Experiences*. Winnipeg: Canadian Defence Academy Press.
- Davis, K. (2009). Sex, gender and cultural intelligence in the Canadian Forces. *Commonwealth and Comparative Politics*, 47(4), 430-455.
- Davis, K. and McKee, B. (2004). Women in the military: Facing the warrior framework. In F.C. Pinch, A.T. MacIntyre, P. Browne, and A.C. Okros (Eds.), *Challenge and Change in the Military: Gender and Diversity Issues* (pp. 52-75). Winnipeg: Canadian Defence Academy Press.
- Deschamps, M. (2015). *External Review into Sexual Misconduct and Sexual Harassment in the Canadian Armed Forces*. Marie Deschamps, External Review Authority.
- Dundas, B. (2000). *A History of Women in the Canadian Military*. Montréal: Art Global.
- Enloe, C. (2000). *Maneuvers: The International Politics of Militarizing Women's Lives*. Berkeley: University of California Press.
- Enloe, C. (2007). *Globalization & Militarism: Feminists Make the Link*. Lanham: Rowman & Littlefield Publishers, Inc.
- Febbraro, A. R. (2007). Gender and leadership in the Canadian Forces combat arms: Perspectives of women leaders. In K. Davis (Ed.), *Women and Leadership in the Canadian Forces: Perspectives and Experiences* (pp. 93-138). Winnipeg: Canadian Defence Academy Press.
- Feinman, I. R. (2000). *Citizenship Rites: Feminist Soldiers and Feminist Antimilitarists*. New York: New York University Press.
- Forgues, S. (2007). Building trust and credibility at home and abroad. In K. Davis (Ed.), *Women and Leadership in the Canadian Forces: Perspectives and Experiences* (pp. 15-33). Winnipeg: Canadian Defence Academy Press.
- Franke, L. B. (1997). *Ground Zero: The Gender Wars in the Military*. New York: Simon & Schuster.
- Fuller, A., Hodkinson, H., Hodkinson, P., and Unwin, L. (2005). Learning as peripheral participation in communities of practice: A reassessment of key concepts in workplace learning. *British Educational Research Journal*, 31(1), 49-68.
- Government of Canada. (2013). Backgrounder: Women in the Canadian Armed Forces. Retrieved from http://www.forces.gc.ca/en/news/article.page?doc=women-in-the- canadian-forces-cf/hgq87xxi.

- Gouliquer, L. (2011). *Soldiering in the Canadian Forces: How and Why Gender Counts!* Unpublished PhD Dissertation. Montréal: McGill University.

- Harrison, D. (2002). *The First Casualty: Violence against Women in Canadian Military Communities.* Toronto: James Lorimer & Company Ltd., Publishers.

- House of Commons. (2013). Standing Committee on the Status of Women, Number 058, 1st Session, 41st Parliament.

- Kronsell, A. (2005). Gendered practices in institutions of hegemonic masculinity: Reflections from feminist standpoint theory. *International Feminist Journal of Politics*, 7(2), 280-298.

- Lave, J., and Wenger, E. (1991). *Situated Learning: Legitimate Peripheral Participation.* Cambridge, England: Cambridge University Press.

- Mercier, N. and Castonguay, A. (2014, May 5). Our military's disgrace: A special investigation. *Macleans Magazine* (pp. 18-26).

- Morton, D. (1999). *A Military History of Canada: From Champlain to Kosovo* (4th ed.). Toronto: McLelland & Stewart Inc.

- Mulkins, M. (2007). Command at sea: July 2003-June 2005. In K. Davis (Ed.), *Women and Leadership in the Canadian Forces: Perspectives and Experiences* (pp. 35-44). Winnipeg: Canadian Defence Academy Press.

- National Defence. (2003). Duty with honour: The profession of arms in Canada. A-PA-005-000/AP-001. Ottawa: Chief of Defence Staff.

- Paechter, C. (2003). Learning masculinities and femininities: Power/knowledge and legitimate peripheral participation. *Women's Studies International Forum*, 26(6), 541-552.

- Poulin, C. (2001). "The military is the wife and I am the mistress": Partners of lesbians in the Canadian military. *Atlantis: A Women's Studies Journal*, 26(1), 65-73.

- Reiffenstein, A. (2007) Gender integration: An asymmetric environment. In K. Davis (Ed.), *Women and Leadership in the Canadian Forces: Perspectives and Experiences* (pp. 1-10). Winnipeg: Canadian Defence Academy Press.

- Sasson-Levy, O., Levy, Y., and Lomsky-Feder, E. (2011). Women breaking the silence: Military service, gender, and the antiwar protest. *Gender & Society*, 25(6), 740-763.

- Segal, M. W. (1986). The military and the family as greedy institutions. *Armed Forces and Society*, 13(1), 9-38.

- Soeters, J., Winslow, D., and Weibull, A. (2006). Military culture. In G. Caforio, (Ed.), *Handbook of the Sociology of the Military* (pp. 237-254). New York: Springer.

- Speiser-Blanchet, J. (2007). "There's no hell like tac hel!" In K. Davis (Ed.), *Women and Leadership in the Canadian Forces: Perspectives and Experiences* (pp. 45-58). Winnipeg: Canadian Defence Academy Press.

- Symons, E. (1990). Under fire: Canadian women in combat. *Canadian Journal of Women and the Law*, 4(2), 477-511.

- Taber, N. (2005). Learning how to be a woman in the Canadian Forces/unlearning it through feminism: An autoethnography of my learning journey. *Studies in Continuing Education*, 27(3), 289-301.

- Taber, N. (2009). The profession of arms: Ideological codes and dominant narratives of gender in the Canadian military. *Atlantis: A Women's Studies Journal*, 34(1), 27-36.

- Taber, N. (2011). "You better not get pregnant while you're here": Tensions between masculinities and femininities in military communities of practice. *International Journal of Lifelong Education*, 30(3), 331-348.

- Taber, N. (2013). A composite life history of a mother in the military: Storying gendered experiences. *Women's Studies International Forum*, 37, 16-25.

- Taber, N. (in press). Official (masculinized and militarized) representations of Canada: Learning to be a "good" citizen. In N. Taber (Ed.), *Gendered Militarism in Canada: Learning Conformity and Resistance.* Edmonton: University of Alberta Press.

- Taber, N., Plumb, D., and Jolemore, S. (2008). "Grey" areas and "organized chaos" in emergency response. *Journal of Workplace Learning*, 20(4), 272-285.

- The Globe and Mail. (2015, Jun. 17). Top soldier under fire after "biologically wired" comment on sexual misconduct. *The Globe and Mail.* Retrieved from http://www.theglobeandmail.com/news/politics/top-soldier-under-fire-after-biologically-wired-comment-on-sexual-misconduct/article24996098/

- Wenger, E. (1998). *Communities of Practice: Learning, Meaning and Identity.* New York: Cambridge University.

- Wenger, E., McDermott, R., and Snyder, W. (2002). *Cultivating Communities of Practice: A Guide to Managing Knowledge.* Boston: Harvard Business School Press.

- Winslow, D. and Dunn, J. (2002). Women in the Canadian Forces: Between legal and social integration. *Current Sociology*, 50(5), 641-667.

This vignette was prepared by Mary Kostandy and Shauna Butterwick.

Paz Buttedahl was born in Chile in 1942. Her father died when she was ten and she was sent to Catholic boarding school in Argentina, where several family members lived. Boarding school, according to her daughter Maria, was something Paz greatly enjoyed. At boarding school, she developed plans of becoming a nun. As a novice, she was given an opportunity to teach children and her experiences teaching and inherent problems with authority diverted her from the original plan. After finishing her schooling, Paz returned to Chile and worked in television, where she became involved in a number of professional activities, including doing film reviews for the Catholic church. At 25 she married for the first time and had two children. The marriage was short-lived. While separated from her first husband, she travelled to Florida to complete her doctorate in adult education and there she met her second husband, Knute Buttedahl.

Paz's career was multifaceted but her vision of global peace and justice sustained all of her engagements. Paz (which means "peace" in Spanish) worked with United Nations Education, the Scientific and Cultural Organization, the U.S. Agency for International Development, and the Organization of American States. She also worked with the Center for National Security Studies and it was during this engagement that she began to link sustainable development to human security, which she saw as living without fear. Her partner, Knute, shared her life mission. He played an important role in the creation of the International Council for Adult Education (ICAE), for which Paz served as the Latin American program officer. Knute was also a co-creator of the Canadian Association for the Study of Adult Education (CASAE). Together, Paz and Knute managed Buttedahl Associates, an educational consulting business, and they also both worked with the Canadian International Development Agency (CIDA) and the International Development Research Centre (IDRC) in Ottawa. In the 1980s and 1990s, they were employed as professors of adult education at the University of British Columbia (UBC).

In 1984, while Paz was on faculty at UBC, she invited Paulo Freire to the campus to teach a course on his philosophy. Paz had connected with Freire earlier while doing international work. Paz left UBC to work in Ottawa with the IDRC but later returned and assumed the role of Director of International Relations at UBC's Faculty of Education. To Paz, working for peace involved more than stopping war; it also involved the development of an equitable and sustainable society on all levels and it was this vision that informed her creation of a Master of Arts in Human Security and Peace-building at Royal Roads University in Victoria, British Columbia. She continued to work tirelessly, even while dealing with a cancer diagnosis and treatments, until she took her last breath on October 8, 2006.

Paz was a lively, dynamic, and passionate person and a warm and approachable educator. She made a difference in the lives of all who made her acquaintance. She worked incessantly for peace and justice in developing countries. She had a particular talent for bringing people from very different backgrounds together. Along with her partner Knute, Paz left a memorable legacy in Adult Education and International Development in Canada and around the globe.

References

- Hall, B. L. (2000). Knute Buttedahl: Celebrating life. Newsletter of the Canadian Association for the Study of Adult Education. Retrieved from http://casae-aceea.ca/~casae/sites/casae/files/bwCASNLA00w.pdf

- Island Lives: Buttedahl made a global difference. (2007, October 26). CanWest MediaWorks Publications Inc. Retrieved from http://www.canada.com/story_print.html?id=1d78be7f-bd5e-485f-9726-310d5afb80b2&sponsor

- Paz Buttedahl: Obituary. (2007, October 13). *Vancouver Sun*. Retrieved March 26, 2015, from http://www.legacy.com/obituaries/vancouversun/obituary.aspx?n=paz-buttedahl&pid=96058546

Sister Joan O'Keefe, Congregational Leader of the Sisters of Charity (Halifax) and Chancellor of Mount Saint Vincent University.
Photo courtesy of Dean Casavechia.

5

Exploring the Learning and Wisdom of Elder Social Activists in Atlantic Canada
Learning Liberation

Social movement learning (SML), "sustained civic involvements in the instigation of collective social change" (Frank, 2002, p. 111), is a significant arena of adult education. Since the 1990s, academics have paid increasing attention to SML. Welton (1993) examined the learning challenges inherent in social movements and Foley (1999) took note of learning associated with voluntary activities and social and political struggles. In 2006, Hall and Turray published *State of the Field Report of Adult Learning Research—Social Movement Learning,* recommending more systematic analyses of SML. In 2013, Hall, Clover, Crowther, and Scrandett (2013) sought to make visible "the extraordinary scope, diversity, range of actors, breadth of means and methods and indefatigable energy of those who are immersed in the educational work [...] that is the world of social movement education and learning." (p. x).

Shauna Butterwick and Maren Elfert

In presenting this chapter, we share the same motivations as the above authors but call for more attention to *women's* SML. Some time ago, feminist adult educator Jane Thompson (1983) found that women's learning needs, leadership, and pedagogical practices tended to be ignored by the male-dominated field of adult education. From our perspective, a similar process has contributed to a lack of attention to women's SML, a process akin to what Dorothy Smith called "a peculiar eclipsing" (1978, p. 281). For example, compared with the breadth of engagement with Freire's (1970) ideas about conscientization and education for empowerment, much less recognition is given to the pedagogical dimensions (such as consciousness raising) of women's liberation movements, one of the most significant movements for social change to emerge in the last century (Butterwick, 1987). As Scott (1984, p. 7) observed, "Selective and partial vision will doubtless always be part of the historical enterprise." She then asked, "What must happen to bring some hitherto unseen part of past reality into visibility?"

We seek to offer a correction to that invisibility. We begin by noting some key concepts within feminist scholarship that inform our understandings of women's SML. We then provide an overview of some of the studies of women's SML in our field before turning our attention to the stories of a group of elder women social activists from Atlantic Canada. These elders' profiles offer many insights into the lifelong and life-wide learning that informed their social activism.

Our own social activist history has shaped our understanding of this topic. Shauna's passion for adult education and learning was informed by her feminist activism focusing on such issues as violence against women and women's access to employment-related programs. Maren's interest in the political nature of women's learning was triggered by her involvement in family literacy programs in Germany and Europe. As academic middle-class women of European ancestry, we recognize that we occupy privileged race and class positions and that this privilege is related to various colonizing practices and policies.

Women's Social Movement Learning: The Politics of Recognition

As we have stated, attention to consciousness-raising, a key pedagogy of feminist social activism, has been mostly absent from studies of SML in our field. Central to this pedagogy, which has many similarities to Freire's ideas about conscientization, is a process by which women come to understand how their own personal struggles and lived experiences are not isolated nor unique but are, rather, powerfully shaped by larger structures and forces of oppression. From this process emerged the well-known phrase "the personal is political" (e.g., Brownmiller, 1999; Hanisch, 2006). Feminist scholars have studied this aspect of SML in detail, drawing attention to how consciousness raising is an example of radical democratic impetus given its non-hierarchical and inclusive approach (Cornell, 1996). Feminist scholars have also explored coalition building and the need to recognize the differences and power inequalities among women (Mohanty, 1998; Reagon, 1998; Keating, 2005), as well as the importance of developing what Sandoval (2000) called "differential consciousness," which is an orientation towards adaptation to different contexts.

As noted in the introduction, the peculiar eclipsing of women from dominant sociological frameworks and theories was the focus of Dorothy Smith's scholarship. Like Smith, we have considered the mechanisms of this marginalization and believe it is linked to the narrow and masculinist lens which has dominated discussions of what constitutes SML. Women's ways of working, as Mayo and Thompson (1995) observed, have been "based on the importance attributed to personal knowledge by the women's liberation movement" (p. 127). According to Fraser (1997), Habermas's theorizations of what counts as the public sphere and who participates in that sphere have contributed to the misrecognition of popular education and participatory grassroots activism of marginalized groups. We believe these spaces, which Fraser called "the subaltern," are key to the development of oppositional discourses, positions that challenge dominant conceptions of inequalities.

How social activism is conceputalized was also a concern of Stall and Stoecker (1998). They noted how the masculine "Alinsky model" of social activism, with its outcome- and power-oriented approaches, strong leadership, confrontation, and professionalism in the "public sphere," has dominated understandings of social activism such that less recognition is given to women-centred models of community work, which are oriented to relationship building and collaboration. Rather than seeing these approaches as dichotomous, however, Stall and Stoecker argued that, in reality, the boundaries between them are blurred. Kilgore (1999) challenged the individualistic assumptions informing studies of SML, and pointed to the significance of "collective identity, group consciousness, solidarity and organization" (p. 191). What counts as social activism was also a concern of Gouin (2009), who observed that "women engage in social transformation in ways that are rarely recognized in traditional conceptions of protest or revolution" (p. 159).

In our discussion of women's SML, we have employed the following broad definition of social activism: "acting to bring about social, political, economic, or environmental change for a more just, sustainable and peaceful world" (Whitmore, Wilson, and Calhoun 2011, p. 8).

Feminist Studies of SML: A Wealth of Knowledge

Feminist scholarship exploring SML in the field of adult education is growing and we have endeavoured to locate this research in adult education books, journals, and conference proceedings. We cannot do justice to all the contributions, given the limitations of space. Instead, we offer a brief overview of studies of women's SML which illustrate the different foci of these inquiries. For example, the role of the arts and creative expression in women's political and social movement engagement has been a focus of several studies, and this area of inquiry is expanding rapidly (e.g., Clover, Stalker, and McGauley, 2004; Roy, 2004; West and Stalker, 2007; Butterwick and Lawrence, 2009; Clover, 2013). Feminist adult education researchers have examined the creation of critical consciousness through feminist consciousness-raising groups (Butterwick, 1987), the development of identity and moral agency (Parrish and Taylor, 2007; Sandlin and Walther, 2009), and women's learning within and opposition to war and violence (Mojab, 2010). Earlier investigations focused on the role of feminist organizations in social movements (Ferree and Martin, 1995), while more recent studies have examined women's advocacy groups and their social structure (English, 2005) and the role of grassroots organizations in the development of political consciousness (Gouthro, 2012). The powerful role that the Internet has played in creating virtual networks and feminist organizations' use of communication technologies are new areas of inquiry (Irving and English, 2010).

Women's contributions to national liberation movements (Chovanec, 2009), environmental movements (Clover, 1995; Walter, 2007), and the apartheid movement in South Africa (Walters, 1996) illustrate the key role that women's activism has played in these new social movements. Feminists have also drawn attention to the caring dimension of activism (Hart, 1992), to learning and activism that occur in the private sphere (Gouthro, 2009a, 2009b), and to the less desirable outomes of SML, including burnout (Zielińska, Lowzan, and Prusinowska, 2011). The internal workings of social movements have also been explored, including the challenges arising within feminist coalition politics (Butterwick and Selman, 2006) and the importance of bringing an anti-colonial and anti-racism framework in which to consider movements for social action (Gouin, 2009). The embodied and emotional aspects of activism have also been examined (Ollis, 2008).

Women's social movement learning, we suggest, can be considered a response and a resistance to Charles Taylor's (1991) notion of the "malaise of modernity," which Reichenbach (2002) describes as an eroding belief in political action. Hannah Arendt (1998, p. 54) also addressed the loss of the public realm as an aspect of what she calls "world alienation." When people withdraw from the public realm, Arendt argued, it means that they believe that "the world will not last"; it means, in other words, that they have given up on the world.

Women's social movement learning and social activism can be understood as a form of resistance to this malaise and a search for authenticity, which Vannini (2007) described as "being true to one's self" (p. 65). Reichenbach (1998) linked authenticity with the capacity for agency, change, and emancipation, which involve both an inward and an outward journey. The feminist pedagogy captured in the phrase "the personal is political" speaks to the search for such authenticity as well as social justice. Feminist social activists are resisting the individualism and political disengagement that aligns with Taylor's malaise of modernity.

A key dimension of this malaise is the loss of hope. Freire (1998, p. 8) described hope as "an existential, concrete imperative [and] an ontological need [that] demands an anchoring in practice." In response to critics who challenged his emphasis on hope, Freire agreed that, while hope was necessary, it was not enough. "Alone, it does not win. But without it, my struggle will be weak and wobbly. We need critical hope the way a fish needs unpolluted water" (Freire, 2004, p. 2).

Learning about SML from Elder Activists

The social activism of a group of elder activists from the Atlantic region of Canada provides a rich source of insight about women's SML, illustrating how this learning begins early in life and involves incidental and on-the-job learning as well as learning through formal education. The stories of their social activism also speak to how working collectively and embracing hope and vision are key to sustaining the challenging work of social activism. These women were the focus of a project initiated by Dr. Liz Burge.[1] Between 2007 and 2011, she interviewed 27 elder women activists and created web-profiles of these women,[2] hoping to contribute to intergenerational learning between younger and older activists.

Social Movement Learning Begins at Home

These elders began their activist learning early and their mothers were significant role models. Sister Angelina Martz's activism was informed by the Christian values instilled in her by her mother who, during the Depression, responded generously to unemployed workers who often came to the family farm looking for food and shelter: "They were always treated with the greatest respect and given more than many would give." She entered a religious order and found a place there to continue this commitment, bringing her energies and vision to social housing and environmental concerns. Similarly, Phyllis Artiss spoke about her mother and her family as a significant influence on her personal development. As a faculty member at Memorial University for over 40 years, her activism was oriented to supporting Aboriginal students. Yvonne Atwell's[3] mother played a central role in her belief that everyone should be treated equally, a philosophy that fueled her decision to fight the racial discrimination experienced by African Nova Scotians.

Speaking Truth to Power

For many of these elder activists, "speaking truth to power" (Bristol et al., 1955) was central to their engagements. Speaking out, for many, was a turning point. Sister Angelina Martz described the first time she felt compelled to speak out: "I have something important to say and I must say it." She also prayed for strength as this was her first act of public speaking. For others, speaking truth to power is about publically identifying oneself as a feminist. This was the case for Nancy Riche, a leading Canadian activist for workers' rights. "From that first day when I stood up and said, 'I'm a feminist'... I thought it was important to put it out there all the time." For Marian Perkins, who worked with recovering alcoholics and their families as well as women prisoners, her first public speaking act involved making an anonymous call to a radio program. Being the voice for others as well as oneself is often a key motivation for social activists. In describing her work related to housing, food banks, and other issues related to poverty, Sister Kathrine Bellamy believed she was just an informant and "a voice for [people living in poverty]." Speaking out, saying "This is wrong, this has to change," even when a case seems hopeless, was equally important for Sister Angelina Martz.

It was risky for these women to speak out and take action at a time when women were repeatedly told that their proper place was in the home, certainly not in the public sphere. For Maria Bernard, whose social activism concerned women's rights, particularly in francophone minority communities, speaking up at public meetings and conferences was viewed by others as a major transgression. Many of these activists were often the only women present in public discussions of the issues with which they were concerned, and they were often the lone voices challenging dominant perspectives. They faced backlashes as well (see Faludi, 2006; Zingaro, 2009). For example, when Yvonne Atwell decided to run for public office, she recalled how people "made racist comments, sexist comments, like 'Who do you think you are?' and 'You don't know the issues.'"

Social Activism: An Inner and Outer Journey

The notion of being true to oneself or being authentic is a key element of becoming a social activist (Frank, 2002). This is evident in these elders' references to "doing the right thing," the importance of attending to "the inner voice," finding the "moral anchor," "finding the truth," and "being respected as a person." Many activists, such as Kathy Sheldon, whose community activism in Newfoundland involved building up women's leadership skills, spoke about their desire to encourage other women to discover their true selves and "pursue some of the things that they want to do, and not to be tied down to the traditional roles that other people thought they should be filling." Similarly, Yvonne Atwell wanted to help women "to critically examine the dynamics of their lives"; she reflected on the importance of "providing the opportunity for them to hear their own voice, and to be able to say 'I can do this.'" Sister Angelina Martz described her social activism as an experience that gave her "a sense of my own being that I didn't have."

Creating meaning out of personally experienced injustice is also a central aspect of women's social movement learning (Hanisch, 1999; Brownmiller, 1999). For Stella Lord, a sociologist and university professor involved in poverty-related activism, being true to oneself involved "coming to terms with my own experience of inequality, my sense of identity, and my search for autonomy and meaning." A search for authenticity involves building coherence between one's private and public lives. This was important for Ann Brennan, whose social activism was triggered by patriarchal attitudes towards women in the rural area where she lived: "We have to make social change personally before we can make it publicly, become strong in our own personal centre." Looking back at her 40 years of community activism in the African Nova Scotian community and provincial politics, Yvonne Atwell described how "being a social activist is a way of living every day." Similarly, Betty Peterson noted, "I cannot imagine living in this world without working for social change."

Developing Social Activism Knowledge and Skills

As noted, for many of these social activists, their SML began early in life when they observed their families' and particularly their mothers' responses to social injustice. Learning was core to their activism, as was acquiring interpersonal, practical, and analytic knowledge and skills. "My way of being a feminist and activist has been to learn skills," reflects Mary Lou Stirling, a university teacher

Sister Angelina Martz receives the John Peters Humphrey Human Rights Award for decades of commitment to justice.

(and later professor) and activist for women's rights. The everyday practical skills of activism are not to be dismissed. Sister Joan O'Keefe described the importance of learning how to "hand deliver key letters to city councilors." Social actions such as demonstrations and protests are significant moments and spaces for SML, community building, and networking. Betty Peterson's learning for social action was richly informed by her participation in the civil rights movement in the United States, and later, after she moved to Halifax, by her work with the Innu First Nation. She had vivid recollections of a demonstration with chants, speakers, music, and thousands of people in New York and how these elements contributed to a strong sense of belonging to a larger movement. Similarly, Phyllis Artiss recalled the "totally amazing" experience of singing, dancing, marching, debating, sharing stories, eating together, and listening to inspiring speeches at the Women's Conference in Gander in 2000. Other elders similarly recalled the power of their encounters through group experiences at conferences and debates with many other women, often from different contexts and countries.

Women's social movement learning is also embodied and emotional (Jaggar, 1989). Anger, in particular, is an important emotion that spurs many social activists to take action. This was true for Sister Joan O'Keefe, long-time coordinator of the Guardian Angel and Single Parent Centre in Halifax. While her anger was key to taking action, O'Keefe also argued that it was important to "act with deliberation, [and] not just react." As noted earlier, speaking up is often associated with strong emotions, including anxiety, but there is also joy and a sense of agency and growing self-confidence. Engaging in social action is more organic than planned. As Joan Hicks noted: "I don't think most of us plan on becoming social activists. I think we get involved because something moves us to act."

Higher education also plays an important role in SML, particularly the knowledge and skills needed for critical analysis. For Madeleine Gaudet, an activist for seniors' affordable housing and later for improved working conditions for nurses, a labour relations training course proved to be pivotal: "It was just as if I had been shot from a cannon!" For Stella Lord, studying media relations helped her to become more effective and to "gain a deeper understanding of the forces that were shaping our world and Canada." Yvonne Atwell also described learning about human rights and developing skills for critical analysis through higher education. Viola Robinson, who advocated for the rights of Mi'kmaq people and Aboriginal and treaty rights in Nova Scotia and Canada, spoke of the importance of "establish[ing] the issue precisely: is it discrimination? Racism? Inequality? Violence?" As a final example, Stella Lord described the role of higher education as key to developing her knowledge of the "underlying structures and legacies of capitalism, patriarchy, and colonialism." She observed that "as you become a little more exposed to the outside world and a little more knowledgeable, you begin to put a finger on what's wrong with this picture."

Social movement learning is also about understanding the processes of change, appreciating how it is often slower than desired and usually involves educating the public. This was true for Edith Perry who, for most of her life, was involved in politics, labour issues, and women's rights in Prince Edward Island. She noted that "it's more complicated and more difficult to change policy and how things are done because you have to educate yourself and everyone else around you." Moving from charity to social justice is a crucial dimension of social movements for liberation. As Sister Joan O'Keefe observed: "Charity is … 'feel good' … it gives me a warm feeling. But justice is the hard work." Edith Perry recognized how charity was an obstacle to change: "The system in Canada . . . is based on the charity model, not the social justice model." In her work in academia, Mary Lou Stirling noted the "big paradox" between helping and fairness and how it took her decades to more fully comprehend and resolve this tension. For Stirling, social movement learning was also about learning from failures (Meyers, 2011): "You may fail, but you'll learn from failure to go on and do things better."

We Can't Do It Alone: Sustaining Social Activism

Building personal and social relationships as well as networks are key to sustaining engagement in social activism. Solidarity, collaboration, and affiliating with people who share similar values and concerns can provide a sense of comfort and meaning. "Social activism … brings you together—connecting, learning, growing" (Yvonne Atwell). Phyllis Artiss also pointed to the importance of networking and how she "developed a strong sense of community around our shared values and activities." Similarly, Kathy Sheldon forged strong attachments to friends and people who had encouraged and supported her: "The first thing I learned is how strong the ties and friendships are between women and how much support and encouragement we give one another." Social justice work cannot be done alone (Kilgore, 2009). As Edith Perry reflected: "The number one point is you have to be part of a group." Ann Bell, who started her activism as a member of the nurses' union and later led the provincial Advisory Council on the Status of Women, was convinced "that collaboration with like-minded colleagues is necessary to create change." Additionally, many of these activists discussed the principles of compassion, caring for others, and trust.

While aspects of collaboration, relatedness, and care are important to social movement learning, so too are dealing with the realities of confrontation and conflict (Hirsch and Fox Keller, 1990; English, 2005). Kathy Sheldon experienced a major conflict in her life as an activist. Some of her colleagues in the Women's Institute refused to work with feminists because, for them, feminist activism meant "going beyond the private domestic sphere into the public policy sphere." Kathy recalled receiving nasty letters, and how the conflict caused some women to leave the Women's Institute. Sustaining engagement in social action is challenging on other fronts as well; there are many disappointments.

As Kathy Sheldon noted, "No matter what you decide and do, it hardly ever reaches the people who need it the most." And so it is important to value the "small victories." Similarly, Sister Dorothy Moore encouraged others to "never give up on themselves" and spoke of the joy and hope she felt when she witnessed an Indigenous child who could speak her Native language: "Here is our future generation keeping us alive!" For Marian Perkins, her activism was sustained through "the exhilaration and inner satisfaction of knowing you are doing the right thing."

Going Forward: Lessons Learned

We encourage readers to examine these elder women's profiles for themselves; they are full of insight about women's social movement learning. Reading them can serve as a kind of intergenerational exchange. These stories highlight how social movement learning is essentially lifelong and life-wide. Social movement learning begins in our families and communities, where as children we learn from our elders, particularly our mothers, about acting with moral courage. Social movement learning is about sharing stories about what inspires us to fight against social justice. This learning is both an inward and an outward journey. Moments of transgressive action, of crossing the private-public boundary and speaking truth to power, are significant internal and external turning points in the lives of social activists. At the heart of feminist activism and of many social movements is the process of converting private troubles into public issues (Mills, 1959). These moments, for many social activists, can be transformational (Touraine, 1985). Sustaining our engagements in movements for social justice is challenging and remaining hopeful is essential. Hope, as Freire (1998) reminded us, is "an existential concrete imperative" (p. 8).

While we may not bear witness to changes in policy, it is important to recognize that social change is already occurring through social action. Speaking up or speaking truth to power is both a rehearsal for change and a moment of transformation. Engaging in social movements requires that we develop a variety of skills and knowledges, including analytic, interpersonal, and practical skills through on-the-job learning as well as higher education. The struggle for social justice is also a spiritual and emotional process and, finally, it is a collective journey.

Women's social movement learning, as exemplified in these elder women's activist stories, remind us of Margaret Mead's oft-quoted message: "Never doubt that a small group of thoughtful, committed citizens can change the world. Indeed, it is the only thing that ever has."[4] In order to truly transform relations of domination, our actions must be ones of solidarity, not charity, and they must be grounded in hope. Being hopeful is a direct confrontation to claims that exploitation based on race, gender, and class, which underpins capitalist globalization, is inevitable and natural. We are hopeful that "hearing the moral impulse in others' stories enables us to become part of their struggle to re-enchant a disenchanted world" (Frank, 2002, p. 116).

Endnotes

1 Now retired, Burge was formerly a professor at the University of New Brunswick.

2 The full profiles can be found as a free e-book at https://womenactivists.lib.unb.ca.

3 Yvonne Atwell is one of the women portrayed in Gouthro (2009a).

4 Please see the website of the Institute for Intercultural Studies, http://www.interculturalstudies.org/faq.html#quote, in lieu of a reference for this quote.

References

- Arendt, H. (1998). *The Human Condition* (2nd ed.). Chicago and London: University of Chicago Press.

- Bristol et al. (1955). *Speaking Truth to Power: A Quaker Search for an Alternative to Violence*. Prepared for the American Friends Service Committee.

- Brownmiller, S. (1999). *In Our Time: Memoir Of A Revolution*. New York: Dial Press.

- Butterwick, S. (1987). *Learning Liberation: A Comparative Analysis of Feminist Consciousness Raising and Freire's Conscientization Method* (Unpublished master's thesis). University of British Columbia, Vancouver.

- Butterwick, S. and Lawrence, R. L. (2009). Creating alternative realities. Arts-based approaches to transformative learning. In J. Mezirow and E. W. Taylor (Eds.). *Transformative Learning In Practice. Insights From Community, Workplace, And Higher Education* (pp. 35-45). San Francisco: Jossey-Bass.

- Butterwick, S. and Selman, J. (2006). Embodied metaphors: Telling feminist coalition stories through popular theatre [Special issue]. *New Zealand Journal of Adult Learning*, 34(2), 42-58.

- Chovanec, D. M. (2009). *Between Hope And Despair: Women Learning Politics*. Halifax: Fernwood.

- Clover, D. E. (1995). Gender, transformative learning and environmental action. *Gender and Education*, 7(3), 243-258.

- Clover, D. E. (2013). Aesthetics, society and social movement learning. In B. Hall, D. Clover, J. Crowther, and E. Scandrett (Eds.), *Learning and Education for a Better World: The Role of Social Movements* (pp. 87-100). Rotterdam: Sense Publishers.

- Clover, D.E., Stalker, J., and McGauley, L. (2004). Feminist popular education and community leadership: The case for new directions. In *Adult Education for Democracy, Social Justice and a Culture of Peace* (pp. 89-94). *Proceedings of the International Gathering of the Canadian Association for the Study of Adult Education and the Adult Education Research Conference*, University of Victoria.

- Cornell, D. (1996). Rethinking consciousness raising. *Southern Journal of Philosophy*, 35, 109-126.

- English, L. (2005). Narrative research and feminist knowing: A poststructural reading of women's learning in community organizations. *McGill Journal of Education*, 40(1), 143-155.

- Faludi, S. (2006). *Backlash: The Undeclared War Against American Women*. New York: Three Rivers Press.

- Ferree, M. M. and Martin, P. Y. (1995). Doing the work of the movement: Feminist organizations. In M. J. Ferree and P. Y. Martin (Eds.). *Feminist Organizations: Harvest Of The New Women's Movement* (pp. 3-23). Philadelphia: Temple University Press.

- Foley, F. (1999). *Learning In Social Action: A Contribution To Understanding Informal Education*. London, UK: Zed Books.

- Frank, A. W. (2002). Why study people's stories? The dialogical ethics of narrative analysis. *International Journal of Qualitative Methods*, 1(1), 109–117.

- Fraser, N. (1997). *Justice Interruptus: Critical Reflections on the Postsocialist Condition*. New York: Routledge.

- Freire, P. (1970). *Pedagogy of the Oppressed*. New York: Continuum.

- Freire, P. (1998). *Pedagogy of Freedom: Ethics, Democracy, and Civic Courage*. Lanham, MD: Lowman & Littlefield.

- Freire, P. (2004). *Pedagogy of Hope: Reliving Pedagogy of the Oppressed*. New York: Continuum.

- Gouin, R. (2009). An antiracist feminist analysis for the study of learning in social struggle. *Adult Education Quarterly*, 59(2), 158–175.

- Gouthro, P. A. (2009a). Life histories of Canadian women as active citizens: Implications for policies and practices in adult education. *Canadian Journal for the Study of Adult Education*, 21(2), 19-36.

- Gouthro, P. A. (2009b). Neoliberalism, lifelong learning, and the homeplace: Problematizing the boundaries of "public" and "private" to explore women's learning experiences. *Studies in Continuing Education*, 31(2), 157–172.

- Gouthro, P. A. (2012). Learning from the grassroots: Exploring democratic adult learning opportunities connected to grassroots organizations [Special issue]. *New Directions for Adult and Continuing Education*, 135, 51-59.

- Grosz, E. (1994). *Volatile Bodies: Toward a Corporeal Feminism*. St Leonard's, UK: Allen & Unwin.

- Hall, B. and Turray, T. (2006). A review of the state of the field: Social movement learning. Retrieved from http://www.ccl-cca.ca/pdfs/AdLKC/stateofthefieldreports/SocialMovementLearning.pdf.

- Hall, B., Clover, D., Crowther, J. and Scandrett, E. (Eds.) (2013). *Learning and Education for a Better World: The Role of Social Movements*. Rotterdam: Sense Publishers.

- Hanisch, C. (1970). The personal is political. In *Notes from the Second Year: Women's Liberation. Major Writings of the Radical Feminists*. New York: Radical Feminism.

- Hanisch, C. (2006). The personal is political. Retrieved from http://www.carolhanisch.org/CHwritings/PIP.htm.

- Hart, M. U. (1992). *Working And Education for Life. Feminist and International Perspectives on Adult and Continuing Education*. NewYork: Routledge.

- Hirsch, M. and Fox Keller, E. (1990). *Conflicts in Feminism*. New York: Routledge.

- Irving, C. and English, L. (2010). Community in cyberspace: Gender, social movement learning, and the Internet. *Adult Education Quarterly*, 30, 1–17.

- Ismail, S. (2009). Popular pedagogy and the changing political landscape: A case study of a women's housing movement in South Africa. *Studies in Continuing Education*, 31(3), 281-295.

- Ismail, S. (2015). *The Victoria Mxenge Housing Project: Women Building Communities through Social Activism and Informal Learning*. Cape Town, South Africa: UCT Press.

- Jaggar, A. (1989). Love and knowledge: Emotion in feminist epistemology. *Inquiry—An Interdisciplinary Journal of Philosophy*, 32(2), 151–176.

- Keating, C. (2005). Building coalitional consciousness. *NWSA Journal*, 17(2), 86-103.

- Kilgore, D.W. (1991). Understanding learning in social movements: A theory of collective learning. *International Journal of Lifelong Education*, 18(3), 191-202.

- Mayo, M. and Thompson, J. (1995). *Adult Learning, Critical Intelligence and Social Change*. Leicester, UK: NIACE.

- Meyers, B. (2011). *Walking with the Poor: Principles and Practices of Transformational Development*. Maryknoll, NY: Orbis Books.

- Mills, C. W. (1959). *The Sociological Imagination*. Oxford and New York: Oxford University Press.

- Mohanty, C. T. (1998). Feminist encounters: Locating the politics of experience. In A. Phillips (Ed.). *Feminism and Politics* (pp. 460-471). New York: Oxford University Press.

- Mojab, S. (Ed.) (2010). *Women, War, Violence and Learning*. London: Routledge.

- Ollis, T. (2008). The "accidental activist": Learning, embodiment and action. *Australian Journal of Adult Learning*, 48(2), 316-334.

- Parrish, M. M.,and Taylor, E. (2007). Seeking authenticity: Women and learning in the Catholic worker movement. *Adult Education Quarterly*, 57(3), 221-247.

- Reagon, B. J. (1998). Coalition politics: Turning the century. In A. Phillips (Ed.). *Feminism and Politics* (pp. 242–253). New York: Oxford University Press.

- Reichenbach, R. (1998). The postmodern self and the problem of developing a democratic mind. *Theory and Research in Social Education*, 26(2), 226-237.

- Reichenbach, R. (2002). A-teleological Bildung and its significance for the democratic form of living. *Journal of Philosophy of Education*, 36(3), 409-419.

- Roy, C. (2004). *The Raging Grannies: Wild Hats, Cheeky Songs, and Witty Actions for a Better World*. Montréal PQ: Black Rose Books.

- Sandlin, J. A. and Walther, C. S. (2009). Complicated simplicity: Moral identity formation and social movement learning in the voluntary simplicity movement. *Adult Education Quarterly*, 59(4), 298-317.

- Sandoval, C. (2000). *Methodology of the Oppressed*. Minneapolis: University of Minnesota Press.

- Scott, A.F. (1984). On seeing and not seeing: A case of historical invisibility. *The Journal of American History*, 71 (1), 7-21.

- Smith, D. (1978). A peculiar eclipsing: Women's exclusion from man's culture. *Women's Studies International Quarterly*, 1, 281–295.

- Smith, D. (1987). *The Everyday World as Problematic—A Feminist Sociology*. Toronto: University of Toronto Press.

- Stall, S. and Stoecker, R. (1998). Community organizing or organizing community? Gender and the crafts of empowerment. *Gender and Society,* 12(6), 729-756.

- Taylor, C. (1991). *The Malaise of Modernity*. Toronto: House of Anansi Press.

- Thompson, J. (1983). *Learning Liberation: Women's Response to Men's Education*. London: Croom Helm.

- Touraine, A. (1985). An introduction to the study of social movements. *Social Research*, 52 (4), 749-787.

- Vannini, P. (2007). The changing meanings of authenticity: An interpretive biography of professors' work experiences. *Studies in Symbolic Interaction*, 29, 63-90.

- Walter, P. (2007). Adult learning in new social movements: Environmental protest and the struggle for the Clayoquot sound rain forest. *Adult Education Quarterly*, 57(3), 248-263.

- Walters, S. (1996). Training gender sensitive adult educators in South Africa. In S. Walters and L. Manicom (Eds.) *Gender in Popular Education: Methods of Empowerment* (pp. 23-39). London, Zed Books.

- Welton, M. (1993). Social revolutionary learning: The new social movements as learning sites. *Adult Education Quarterly*, 43 (3), 152-164.

- West, N., and Stalker, S. (2007). Journey to a (bi)cultural identity: Fabri art/craft and social justice in Aotearoa, NewNealand. In D. Clover and J. Stalker (Eds.), *The Arts and Social Justice: Re-Crafting Adult Education and Community Cultural Leadership* (pp. 125–143). Leicester, UK: NIACE.

- Whitmore, E., Wilson, M., and Calhoun, A. (2011). *Activism That Works*. Halifax and Winnipeg: Fernwood.

- Zielińska, M., Kowzan, P., and Prusinowska, M. (2011). Social movement learning from radical imagination to disempowerment? *Studies in the Education of Adults*, 43(2), 251-267.

- Zingaro, L. (2009). *Speaking Out: Storytelling for Social Change*. Walnut Creek, CA: Left Coast Press.

This vignette was prepared by Darlene Clover.

Flora MacDonald was born and raised in Cape Breton, Nova Scotia. Growing up during the Depression in one of Canada's poorest areas, she became keenly aware of the hardships people faced. Her father was a trans-Atlantic telegraph operator and this provided her with a portal into the larger world of Canadian politics and international affairs. She shared her name with and was inspired by the 18th-century heroine who aided Bonnie Prince Charlie's flight from the English. In their communiqué of her death, Equal Voice (2015) noted that "Flora entered the political arena at a time when women were a rarity. But she had talent and determination and this has assured her a place in Canada's history books as a woman of firsts" (n.p.).

Flora served in a variety of political roles for more than 15 years, but became the first and only woman to win the federal riding of Kingston and the Islands, securing this riding in 1972, thus becoming the only woman elected of 107 Progressive Conservative Members of Parliament. Flora held this seat for some 15 years, "during a dynamic time in Canada's political history" (Equal Voice, 2015, para 6). But this was not her only first. "Three years later, she became a candidate for the national party's leadership, the first and only woman in a crowded leadership race." (ibid., para 7)

Innovation defined Flora's campaigns as well as her political life. "She adopted a grassroots approach to fundraising decades before it became popular with Canada's political parties, launching something called 'The Dollar for Flora' campaign. Nearly 20,000 Canadians, many of them not wealthy, contributed. She also dared to differ with her male counterparts on key issues, including capital punishment and abortion." (ibid, para 8)

Also during her political career, Flora brokered an arrangement to facilitate the immigration to Canada of 60,000 Vietnamese refugees displaced by the war in Vietnam. She also oversaw a set of complex security arrangements, including the provision of falsified Canadian passports, in aid of U.S. diplomats who were in hiding during the Iranian hostage crisis. Having more than proved her mettle, she went on to serve as federal Minister of Communications.

As a former Canadian foreign minister, Flora was frequently in demand to speak on behalf of charities such as Oxfam, CARE, and Doctors Without Borders. She was appointed by the UN Secretary-General as a member of the Eminent Persons Group, and she worked closely with former NDP leader Ed Broadbent.

Following her political life, Flora became engaged in international humanitarian work. She served as Chair of the Board of the International Development Research Centre from 1992 to 1997. She eventually formed her own non-governmental organization titled Future Generations Canada (the overall goal of Future Generations is to promote community-led development in partnership with government). The Canadian focus, under Flora's leadership, was on supporting girls and women to become educated and promoting their civic participation as equal decision makers. Her engagement with Future Generations Canada also involved setting up village schools in Afghanistan where girls could be educated. She shaped the future of hundreds of Afghan girls and communities as indelibly as her contribution here in Canada has affected the lives of untold thousands of Canadians.

References

- Adapted from a July 28, 2015 Communiqué by Equal Voice entitled: Equal Voice mourns the loss of the Hon. Flora MacDonald, trailblazing giant for electing more women in Canada, 2015. Retrieved from http://equalvoice.ca/speaks_article.cfm?id=984

- Martin, Patrick (2015). Obituary: Conservative Trailblazer Flora MacDonald dies at 89. *The Globe and Mail* (July 26). Retrieved from http://www.theglobeandmail.com/news/politics/conservative-trailblazer-flora-macdonald-dies-aged-89/article25714535/

- Future Generations: Empowering Communities to Shape Their Futures (Website). Retrieved from http://www.future.org/Civil-Society

Our individual stories offer a rich palette, and when combined they reflect a colourful collaborative sharing of multi-centric knowledge.
Photo © Paul D. Smith/Shutterstock.

6

Black Women's Africentric and Feminist Leadership Voices from Nova Scotia

[S]he who thinks [s]he is leading and has no one following is only taking a walk. —Malawian proverb

What images flashed in your mind when you read the book title, *Women, Adult Education, and Leadership in Canada*? Who comes to mind and where are these women in your kinship line? In this chapter, we look at Black women and feminist leaders and leadership through the lenses of Womanism and Black feminism. Acknowledging the importance of Black Canadian feminism which "begins with ourselves, our stories, both old and new" (Wane, 2007, p. 298), we share in this chapter some historical and present-day stories from and about Black women.

Susan M. Brigham and Sylvia Parris

One of the stories we share in this chapter is of Viola Desmond, an African Nova Scotian woman who stood against racial inequality in 1946 and whose legacy lives on.[1] Our present-day stories are drawn from the transcripts of a study involving ten women who self-identified as African Nova Scotian. These feminist educators worked in formal, nonformal, and informal contexts, including a public school, a college, a public library, and the community at large. The women were interviewed two years after they graduated from a Master of Education degree program in Adult Education/Lifelong Learning, which focused on Africentric leadership (hereafter referred to as the Africentric cohort). The program was the first of three Africentric cohorts. Each cohort consisted of 20 students of African descent, all of whom received scholarships. The cohorts were taught largely by professors of African descent. We present a "polyvocal" (multi-voice) collective story of the ten women through four themes: safe with my community in the Africentric cohort; cocooned by Africentricity; leadership and community capacity entwined; and relationships as learning points. Our chapter is informed by Womanism/Black feminism and Africentric discourses. We conclude our chapter with a discussion of implications for adult educators.

The context of this chapter is Nova Scotia, home to the oldest established Black communities in Canada, founded by descendants of Black Loyalists, former slaves, Black Refugees (referred to as the Chesapeake Blacks) from the United States, and Maroons from Jamaica, all of whom arrived in the 1700s and 1800s. These Black communities were cut off from many services. The Black churches (such as the African Baptist Church) and their affiliated committees, auxiliaries, and institutes, in which women played central roles, helped to fulfil the social, economic, and spiritual needs of Black communities, while also fighting for change. As Hamilton (1993) argued, "Black women both individually and collectively developed a tradition and a spirit of self-reliance and self-help which have greatly contributed to the survival of African people in Nova Scotia" (p. 191).

Black Feminism, Africentricity, and Adult Education

In some Black communities, feminism is not seen as inclusive of all women. Some of us, therefore, speak of Womanism, rather than Black feminism. The term "Womanist," as defined by Alice Walker, invokes the Black vernacular and describes the characteristics and attitudes of a Womanist:

> From *womanish*. (Opp. of "girlish," i.e. frivolous, irresponsible, not serious.) A black feminist or feminist of colour. From the black folk expression of mothers to female children, "you acting womanish," i.e., like a woman. Usually referring to outrageous, audacious, courageous or *willful* behavior (sic). Wanting to know more and in greater depth than is considered "good" for one. Interested in grown up doings. Acting grown up. Being grown up. Interchangeable with another black folk expression: "You trying to be grown." Responsible. In charge. *Serious*. (1983, p. xi; emphasis in original).

However, others in Black communities use the term Black feminism, particularly in academic circles. Canadian Black feminism explores

> how oppression impacts and complicates the lived realities of Black women located within the various social categories. ... it focuses importantly on commonalities and shared histories to show how Black women's lives have been shaped by regional, social and political differences, yet can draw from their collective ancestry to re-imagine new possibilities for Black women's empowerment. (Wane, 2007, pp. 302-303)

Hill Collins (1990) adds that "Black feminist thought demonstrates Black women's emerging power as agents of knowledge [and] Afrocentric feminist thought speaks to the importance that knowledge plays in empowering oppressed people" (p.221). Black feminism acknowledges that those who live in a particular situation are best situated to speak, educate, and transform that situation. She further explains that in certain contexts Black women are labeled "Other" and are perceived as outsiders. However, Hill Collins provides the example of how, in the past, Black women became "insiders" to white society as a result of their presence in white homes as housekeepers and nannies. Yet "these same Black women knew they could never belong to their white 'families.' In spite of their involvement, they remain 'outsiders'" (1986, p. 35). She refers to this as the "outsider within" phenomena. In contemporary times in certain institutional structures, Black women must negotiate their "outsider within" status and their identities, identities that can be oppositional. The first person voice of Black women enlivens that analysis. Hill Collins writes, "Outsiders within occupy a special place—they become different people, and their difference sensitizes them to patterns that may be more difficult for established sociological insiders to see" (p. 53). As Black women share their stories, they become the consummate leader-adult educator. This is summed up in the Ethiopian proverb: "[S]he who learns, teaches."

Asante (1998) argued that the philosophy of living as Africentric beings, grounded in relationships and knowledge of history and self, "standing in our own cultural spaces" (p.8), operationalized Africentric leadership. Ontologically this places an emphasis on the I/We relationship, as opposed to the I/You of Western perspectives, which emphasizes the individual (Chilisa, 2012). Epistemologically, a Black woman's standpoint that contains elements of Africentricity and Black feminism, emphasizes the simultaneous intersection of multiple realities.

Women's contributions to community building and leadership have largely been ignored, silenced, downplayed, or devalued in the historical accounts. This absence of voice has contributed to the reproduction of the idea that women are not "true" leaders or leaders of significance. Moreover, as long as leadership is conceptualized within a dichotomous framework of superior and subordinate, recognized only within the traditional arenas such as the so-called public sphere, and restricted to a context that ignores race, class, and gender, Black women's leadership will continue to be delegitimized. Given limited access to traditional sources of power and decision making, Black women have taken up leadership roles in non-traditional ways and contexts (Gilkes, 1985). However, Black women, too, have a history of leadership in the struggle against oppression, racism, and sexism and in their fight for education, employment opportunities, safe and healthy living and work conditions, housing, and fair treatment in the workplace and in the justice system. These activist efforts have occurred in many community sites, such as churches, ladies' auxiliaries, women's clubs and institutes, workplaces, and homes. It is Black women's common history, their collective radical spirit, and their deliberate quest for freedom that has transformed communities. Looking back to the brutality of slavery in North America, Angela Davis (1971) reminds us of the Black enslaved woman's "indispensable efforts to ensure the survival of her people" (p. 87). In addition to working alongside men in the fields, women also performed domestic labour for the slave community, such as "ministering to the needs of the men and children around her (who were not necessarily members of her immediate family)"; in doing this work, "she was performing the only labour of the slave community which could not be directly and immediately claimed by the oppressor" (p. 87). Thus, from the centre of the Black community, she was "assigned the mission of promoting the consciousness and practice of resistance" (p. 87). Her very survival activities were a form of resistance. Such is the legacy of Black women's leadership.

A legacy from Nova Scotia 70 years ago, only recently revived, that reflects a Womanist/Black feminist perspective is Viola Desmond's story. This story, while read about recently by many, has been spread via storytelling throughout African Nova Scotian communities for 70 years. The core themes of resilience, self-reliance, success, and resistance reinforced the Black communities' sense of self and empowered and fortified Black women as they embraced Womanist/Black feminist leadership.

The Story of Viola Desmond

Viola Desmond, who embodied the kind of critical lens required in leadership, paid a price that has only recently been reconciled. The story as told in a book written by Viola Desmond's sister, Wanda Robson (2010), sheds light not only on Viola, a woman gifted with leadership qualities, but also on the women around her—leaders in their own right—who supported Viola. On November 8, 1946, Viola Desmond was forcibly removed from her seat at a movie theatre in New Glasgow by a police officer and the theatre manager because she was Black and sitting in the Whites-only downstairs section rather than in the balcony. She was jailed, tried without counsel, and fined not for sitting in a Whites-only section, but rather for not paying one penny in tax. Pearleen Oliver,[2] an activist for racial justice, persuaded Viola to hire a lawyer with the help of the Nova Scotia Association for the Advancement of Coloured People (NSAACP) to fight her conviction. Carrie Best,[3] a Black woman activist, journalist, and author in Nova Scotia who founded the newspaper *The Clarion*, ran the story on the front page of her paper on December 31, 1946. Viola's case went to the Supreme Court of Canada, but because her lawyer applied for a judicial review rather than an appeal of the original conviction, Viola's case (of tax evasion of one penny, and no mention of the racial issues) was dismissed. It was 64 years later, in 2010 that Viola Desmond (who had passed away in 1965), her family, and all African Nova Scotians were issued an apology by the Premier of Nova Scotia, Darrel Dexter, for the "racial discrimination she was subjected to by the justice system in November of 1946" (p. 170). At the same time, the Lieutenant Governor of Nova Scotia, Mayann E. Francis, proclaimed the Royal Prerogative of Mercy Free Pardon of Viola Irene Davis Desmond, which acknowledged that Viola had never committed a crime, that she had been fighting against racial segregation, and that she had not received justice. Viola's case inspired others to fight for justice. Indeed, who is to say that she did not inspire Rosa Parks,[4] who nine years later, in 1955, refused to give up her seat in the coloured section of a bus to a white passenger in Montgomery, Alabama, and was arrested for civil disobedience in violating segregation laws? Rosa Parks became a symbol for the American Civil Rights movement, while Viola Desmond became a symbol for racial justice in Canada.

Wanda Robson's book is sprinkled with stories of Viola's unassuming determination, ambition, and strength. Viola did not see herself as a skilled public speaker and she therefore refused to be a NSAACP spokesperson and go on a speaking tour about the Roseland Theatre incident and the subsequent trials. Nonetheless, she stood up for justice. Robson gives examples of Viola's tenacity, sharing the story of when she (Wanda) was left penniless by a husband who had money but refused to support his wife and their three young children. Viola had guessed that Wanda was in trouble and made her way to Massachusetts where Wanda was living. Upon entering Wanda's house she declared:

> "You can't live this way. No lights and no heat. I'm going to town hall." I [Wanda] said, "It's Saturday. They won't be open." She went to the town hall. Inside, she found a meeting going on. She opened the door and said, "I want to speak to the head of social services." The Mayor told her, "You can't come in. We're having a meeting." And Viola said, "Oh, yes, I can. Yes, I can. I can come in here because I have something to say. It's about my sister." And she named me. ... And Viola turned to the Mayor and said, "My sister's living down there. No heat, no lights. It doesn't matter whose fault it is. She has children." And the Mayor said, "Well—we can't discuss that right now—it's the weekend, and we'll have to deal with that the first of the week." And Viola said to him, "Well, children die on the weekend, too." The meeting was adjourned. When she got back to where I lived, there was a truck already there. Lights were on. And they were fixing the stove. (p. 89)

Wanda Robson (2010) says this of her sister:

> Who is to say that by sticking to her goals, maintaining a successful beauty shop, and training other women in black beauty culture while setting very strict standards—who is to say that she was not making significant positive racial and feminist achievements—things only she could accomplish? I say she was. (p. 113)

Similarly, some of our ten research participants were reticent to claim to be leaders in the traditional sense; yet before, during, and after attaining their Master of Education degree they were taking on leadership roles in their communities, in paid and volunteer positions. They have not always been acknowledged for their diverse leadership abilities in these positions, for as Numosa[5] reminds us: "It's very challenging for women because they take on so many roles that no one clearly accepts are distinct, requiring specific types of skills and each one of those skills and roles needs to be valued in and of itself." The multiple skills and knowledge women develop, acquire, and apply in leadership positions must be recognized if women are to be acknowledged as leaders. A traditional assumption is that leadership positions are assigned to men. Therefore, when Black women do take up leadership roles, it is assumed that this happens because there is not a man to do it. However, as the Chinese proverb encourages us to consider, "Man is the head that leads the family, woman the neck that turns the head."

The message delivered by Mayann E. Francis, former Lieutenant Governor of Nova Scotia (2006-2012), the first African Nova Scotian to serve as Lieutenant Governor, conveys the importance of family and community and of acting in a Black Feminist/Womanist way (as leaders). In her speech at York University in 2014, as she received an honorary Doctor of Laws degree, she shared this of her personal and professional journey, stating: "I was a Black woman armed with education, foundations of values, respect, and faith taught to me by my family and the community of Whitney Pier" (YFile, 2015, para. 10 and 11). She called on educational institutions to rally with community to provide a holistic education, while proclaiming to the graduates: "You have to decide on your own whether you will be a passive or active participant in the life of your community, regardless of where that community is. It is too easy to step back, watch and complain" (para. 10 and 11).

Our research participants frequently echoed this sense of responsibility to community, of taking action to improve circumstances, and of looking to the future. For example:

> I got a message from community, from my parents, from my young life that it was important for you to be involved in community. Yes, and the Catholic faith around it, but very clearly from my parents, like, it is important you respect elders in the Black community, it is important that you give back to your community. [My parents would say]: "You're not doing anything this morning and you see 'so and so' has three kids. Go down there and help them with the laundry." (Jane)

> It is our responsibility to make our community a better place and not just geographically but our racial community a better place. ... Anytime I help my kids [the students at school], you're helping the community. You want to build capacity in your community anyways. [It's] about responsibility to those coming after us. And I always believe that we should set a good example, teach them, impart any knowledge or wisdom, support and validate and guide and nurture. We have a responsibility and an obligation to do so. And that's where my idea of Africentricity comes from. (Harriet)

> I have always been an individual who could make an influence for families. I could make an influence in how decision makers perceived programming to remind decision makers of what they had left out. To be a role model, as an artist, a scientist, as a person who values all forms of literacy and sees literacy where people [see] deficits. My form of leadership is not an elected position or an appointed position. My form of leadership is "See your world and act." (Numosa)

Other participants expressed the importance of developing a critical lens. For example, Selma noted how she "didn't want to look at things like the norm. I would look at things and ask how I can change them or present them in a unique way." The actions of these Black women are those of activists who utilize individual influence, the engagement of the collective community, their historical and contemporary grounding in faith, and a sense of criticality to transform Black communities. Drawing on a philosophy of living as Africentric beings, the women underscore the importance of the I/We relationship, placing a high value on human unity, communality, collectivity, and social justice. These women also reposition the appreciation of knowledge and the contributions of the Black community. Through their stories, we have heard that you are never too young to learn or too meek to lead. The composite story we present below continues the thread of activist leadership, emphasizing the "connection to the past, and acknowledgement of Black women's heterogeneity, and of our collective ancestry, [which] is central to Black Canadian feminisms" (Wane, 2007, p. 297).

The Composite Story of Black Feminist Leaders

We use this composite story to represent the collective voice, which is a key tenet of Africentricity. The composite story captures and conveys the first person collective voice of the ten African Nova Scotian women who shared their stories with us. Both authors (Brigham and Parris) conducted a thematic analysis of the interview transcripts. Once we compiled the verbatim quotes of the research participants that reflected those key themes, we put them together without attributing the quotes to a specific person. No one voice is privileged over another. While each of the sentences in the collective story may come from a different person's transcript, they are strung together one after another in a polyrhythmic voice. In this collective story, the women reflect predominantly on their experiences in the Africentric cohort. These reflections emphasize adult education that embraces Africentricity; centres Black women, including their past and present, individual and collective experiences; and enlarges an understanding of leadership. The composite story defines leadership within adult education as seeking change and embracing an approach to learning and leadership steeped in the survival and resilience well known to African Nova Scotians. It underscores Africentric leadership as "based on responsibility, admiration and love" (Warfield-Coppack, 1995, p. 38). Following the composite story, we conclude our chapter with a summary and recommendations regarding Africentric perceptions of leadership and adult education.

The Story ... Safe with My Community in the Africentric Cohort

Because we all felt safe and respected and our opinions were heard, I learned so much. Making those connections with other members of the class was just so empowering. To understand not only the struggles but also the contributions [of Black people] and to know that we are still here, we are still standing, and we are thriving. It didn't feel like teacher and student [where] you're sitting and writing [and the teacher is standing]; it was more like a circular model. Like we all had something to contribute. I was able to participate where I felt I needed to and where I felt that I could provide a different perspective than my classmates. Part of having voice is not just the opportunity to speak and express ... it is having the safe space of expression. I would take the initiative to make some of the courses more important to me. I think of lively discussions, which were great because everyone had an opinion and we were not afraid to share it. And no one really dominated the sessions, which was really rare, especially in a group of twenty. We [learner and educator] were together in this. And it is more like working together as opposed to, "I'm coming in to help you." All in all, the program meant a great deal. It was a chance to work with some like-minded students. It was something that a normal university program doesn't give you.

The Story ... Cocooned by Africentricity

The fact that we were studying Africentricity [meant] you had to incorporate your whole self, not just a segment of yourself; you had to share all the different components that made you, you. I think the Africentricity model is the main model and then you can take it and put any kind of lens over it with those principles at the core ... you would get a really inclusive and holistic program. The highlight for me in all the classes was the class discussion. It was just so phenomenal, so vibrant, and sometimes so controversial. That comfort of knowing it was African Canadian educators and professionals [as peers and educators]. I felt that cohesiveness would remain and it was the case. I saw [the Africentric cohort] as a unique opportunity to engage with other committed African Nova Scotians to make a difference in the lives of youth and families.... This is the modality that delineates how I see my purpose in life. It's not just a question of skin colour; it's more that I choose Africentric philosophy. [The Africentric cohort] was more reflective. It was far more engaging because it was reflective. It tweaked my interest and encouraged me to learn more.

The Story ... Leadership and Community Capacity Entwined

Even though I have always been outspoken about my beliefs in the workplace, I felt I had more of a responsibility in my workplace to stand up when I saw something, especially when it related to African Nova Scotians ... and I felt I had a responsibility to address it one way or another and I actually did during the [Africentric cohort] program a few times in my workplace. Where my interest is in research ... I could perhaps do something around research and curriculum and with my background in community development I could mesh them all together and develop programs. But to focus not on self, but on the collective, the community ... that's what Africentricity means to me. I believe that the African Nova Scotian community requires researchers who [are] leaders and not leaders who happen to do a bit of research on the side. I think the primary focus of the [Africentric cohort] program is on people who are the active problem solvers and part of that active problem-solving process is through research. I never was a critical thinker. I never was taught and I never felt that my voice mattered... Coming out of this program I have become a critical thinker. It has meant me being more confident in who I am as an African Nova Scotian woman, parent, and educator and feeling that one person can make a difference. I gained a lot of tools to make a difference as far as the community is concerned, being an advocate on behalf of persons in communities and a person who will go forward and make change especially when it comes to education. And now that I have the tools, I cannot sit idle. My conscience will not allow me to do that.

The Story ... Relationships as Learning Points

One of the best parts of the [Africentric cohort] program was being in a classroom with 20 other people who had the same or similar experiences and background. I feel a strong sense of affiliation and belonging with those guys [classmates]. We saw different aspects of each person and when you do that over and over again, you get to know them and respect them and you feel like that's my brother, that's my sister and not just a classmate. We shared a lot of struggles that we were going through in the workplace and in the community, and we asked for solutions, help, and advice from each other. ... The work [load in the course was heavy] and I was thinking I can't do it, but [my classmates] really rallied and gave support and we pressed on. I related to [the teacher] a lot because she reminded me of my mother. I respected her more because she reminded me of my mother and I was in awe of her. [The Africentric cohort] has helped me in so many ways ... [like] when I'm dealing with people who I know have power, you look for your opportunity to make a point of influence and it will serve you well because the relationship will be what is fostered as opposed to your disagreement with how or why they did things. The [Africentric cohort] program was a once-in-a-lifetime experience. Africentric principles should guide you at all times and it's that we all have a responsibility to each other. Now that I know what I know, I have a responsibility to act.

Conclusion: Africentric Perceptions of Leadership and Adult Education

An Africentric perception of leadership from Black women's positions brings Black women's perspectives from the margin to the centre, raises awareness about women's leadership and resistance outside the traditional arena, and offers valuable insights into the field of adult education. Contextualizing Black women's leadership by looking at historical examples and current experiences through collective stories of Black women—in this case, graduates from the Master of Education in Lifelong Learning/Adult Education with a focus on Africentric leadership program—helps us to better understand Black women's social and political realities and their valuable contributions to Canadian society. The composite story presented above also suggests andragogical principles in formal adult education graduate programs in each of the story headings: Safe with My Community in the Africentric Cohort; Cocooned by Africentricity; Leadership and Community Capacity Entwined; and Relationships as Learning Points. While the Africentric cohort is no longer in place (at least for now), the model was used for six years at Mount Saint Vincent University and resulted in demonstrated success for the learners (see Brigham, 2007; Parris and Brigham, 2010; Brigham and Parris, 2011). The Africentric cohort points to suggestions for other adult education programs, both formal and nonformal. For instance, we suggest that as adult educators and leaders we need to be mindful of creating safe learning environments in which people see themselves reflected, supported, and validated. This includes re/dis/covering, analyzing, and celebrating stories of Black women leaders, past and present.[6] Until adult education programs become more inclusive of diverse ways of knowing, histories, theories, philosophies, and methods, a cohort learning model such as the Africentric cohort for specific groups can offer such a learning environment. Indeed, a cohort learning model can offer opportunities for learners of all backgrounds to build a sense of community, develop leadership skills and relationships that go beyond the curriculum, and support collective success. The composite story suggests that we ensure leadership, both positional and influential, embraces the Womanist/Black feminist reflection action process, and that we weave relationship building and nurturing into all components of both leadership and adult education. We conclude this chapter as we began, with similar reflection questions: Ten years from now, what images of women do you think will be in a future reader's mind when reading the book title, *Women, Adult Education, Learning, and Leadership in Canada*? Who are these women and what is their kinship line?

Endnotes

[1] In 2010, Viola was issued a posthumous Free Pardon by the Lieutenant Governor and an apology by the Premier of Nova Scotia. At that time the Premier declared Viola "an inspiration, a role model, a true Nova Scotian, and ... a Canadian hero," adding "Mrs. Desmond should be remembered as a leader for her time" (Robson, 2010, p. 171). In 2012, Viola was depicted on a commemorative stamp issued by Canada Post. In February 2015 Nova Scotia celebrated the first Heritage Day named Viola Desmond Day. Her photo is displayed in the Nova Scotia Legislature.

[2] Dr. Pearleen Oliver was an activist who for decades fought against racial discrimination. For example, she was involved in the successful protest to end the ban on Black women in nursing schools in Canada. She was a founding member and an executive member of the NSAACP. In 1976 she became the first woman moderator of the African United Baptist Association. Among her awards, she received the inaugural YMCA Community Leader Award, an Honorary Degree from Saint Mary's University (1990), and an Honorary Doctor of Humane Letters from Mount Saint Vincent University, Halifax, NS (1993) (Colaiacovo, 2008, p. 5).

[3] Carrie Best was a recipient of the Order of Canada and the first posthumous recipient of the Order of Nova Scotia (Colaiacovo, 2008). She was depicted on a commemorative stamp issued by Canada Post in 2011.

[4] Among her many awards and accolades Rosa Parks received an Honorary Doctor of Humane Letters from Mount Saint Vincent University, Halifax, NS in 1998.

[5] All names are pseudonyms to protect the confidentiality of the research participants.

[6] Some of the principles are being applied in an Africentric cohort program in Acadia University's Master of Education in Counselling Program (2015-18) in which all 20 students are African Nova Scotian and all are receiving scholarships (DBDLI, 2015). Another outgrowth of the Africentric cohort were the Africentric literacies workshops held at Mount Saint Vincent University in 2012, which explored literacies through spoken word and poetry, storytelling, song, music (including drumming), Black literature, and quilting. This two-day event (co-chaired by Susan Brigham and Kesa Munroe Anderson) was part of the Literacies as Ways of Knowing series, and engaged educators and community members in co-learning (MSVU, 2012).

References

- Asante, M. (1998). *The Afrocentric Idea*. Philadelphia, PA: Temple University Press.

- Brigham, S. and Parris, S. (2011). Diversity in adult education: Lessons learned from a master of education program in studies of lifelong learning with a focus on Africentric leadership. *The Joint International Conference of the Adult Education Research Conference (AERC) 52nd National Conference and the Canadian Association for the Study of Adult Education (CASAE) 30th National Conference*. Ontario Institute for Studies in Education at the University of Toronto, ON, June 9-13, 2011 (pages 62-69).

- Brigham, S. (2007). Our hopes and dreams enrich its every corner: Adult Education with an Africentric focus. In Laura Servage and T. Fenwick (Eds). *Learning in Community. Joint International Conference of the Adult Education Research Conference (AERC) 48th National Conference and the Canadian Association for the Study of Adult Education (CASAE) 26th National Conference,* Halifax, Nova Scotia, June 6-9, 2007 (pages 79-84).

- Chilisa, B. (2012). *Indigenous Research Methodologies*. London: Sage.

- Colaiacovo, T. (Ed.) (2008). *The Times of African Nova Scotians: A Celebration of Our History, Culture and Traditions.* Halifax: Effective Publishing.

- Davis, A. (1972). *Reflections on the Black Woman's Role in the Community of Slaves*. The Massachusetts Review, 13(1/2), 81-100.

- Delmore Buddy Daye Learning Institute (DBDLI). (2015). *Spring Newsletter: Community Update*. Retrieved August 13, 2015 from: http://dbdli.ca/newsletter-spring-2015.

- Gilkes, C. T. (1985). Together in Harness: Women's Traditions in the Sanctified Church. In M. Malson, E. Mudimbe-Boyi, J. O'Barr, and M. Wyer (Eds.) *Black Women in America: Social Science Perspectives* (pp. 223-244). Chicago, IL: The University of Chicago Press.

- Hamilton, S. (1993). The women at the well: Black Baptist women organize. In L. Carty (Ed.) *And Still We Rise.* (pp. 189-203). Toronto: Women's Press.

- Hill Collins, P. (1986). Learning from the Outsider Within. *Social Problems*, 33(6), 14-32.

- Hill Collins, P. (1990). *Black Feminist Thought: Knowledge, Consciousness, and the Politics of Empowerment*. Boston, MA: Unwin Hyman.

- Mount Saint Vincent University (MSVU). (2012). *What's Happening*. Retrieved August 13, 2015 from: http://www.msvu.ca/en/home/aboutus/WhatsHappening/literacyseries/schedule/default.aspx.

- Parris, S. and Brigham, S. (2010). Exploring cultural worldviews through African Canadians' lifelong learning experiences: Lessons for post-secondary institutions. *The International Journal of Diversity in Organizations, Communities, and Nations*, 10(4), 207-216.

- Reece, R. (2007). Canadian Black Feminist Thought and Scholar-Activist Praxis. In N. Masaquoi and N. Wane (Eds.) *Theorizing Empowerment; Canadian Perspectives on Black Feminist Thought.* (pp. 266-295). Toronto: Inanna Publications and Education Inc.

- Robson, W. (2010). *Sister to Courage: Stories from the World of Viola Desmond, Canada's Rosa Parks.* Wreck Cove, NS: Breton Books.

- Walker, A. (1983) *In Search of Our Mothers' Gardens: Womanist Prose.* San Diego, CA: Harcourt Brace Jovanovich.

- Wane, N. (2007). Canadian Black Feminist Thought: Re-imagining New Possibilities for Empowerment. In N. Masaquoi & N. Wane (Eds.) *Theorizing Empowerment; Canadian Perspectives on Black Feminist Thought.* (pp. 296 – 314). Toronto: Inanna Publications and Education Inc.

- YFile (2015). Stay true to your principles, former lieutenant-governor of Nova Scotia tells grads. Retrieved June 10, 2015 from: http://yfile.news.yorku.ca/2014/06/23/stay-true-to-your-principles-and-embrace-change-former-lieutenant-governor-of-nova-scotia-tells-grads/

Madame Florence Fernet-Martel (1979), first president (1949-1951) of l'Association des femmes diplômées des universités de Montréal.
© Division de la gestion de documents et des archives, Université de Montréal.

7

L'Association des femmes diplômées des universités de Montréal Higher Education for Gender Equality, Leadership, and Change in 1950s and 1960s Québec

L'Association des femmes diplômées des universités de Montréal (AFDUM), was founded in 1949 by a small group of French-speaking female graduates in the Montréal area. The initial members wanted to start an association that could advocate for women's equal rights and treatment in the areas of education and the labour force. L'Association activities consisted of holding monthly meetings, arranging for guest speakers, initiating working committees to generate empirical facts about women's status in education and the economy, and producing memoirs for various royal inquiries, including the Commission on Québec Education (1962), the Royal Commission on Bilingualism and Biculturalism (1963), and the Royal Commission on the Status of Women in Canada (1968).

Cheryl Gosselin

As feminist activists, the AFDUM's members were committed to ensuring equal gender rights for women by pressuring municipal, provincial, and federal governments for legislative changes in education and the labour market. Discontented with focusing solely on narrowly constructed "women's concerns," the AFDUM pursued broader political and nationalist issues, such as disarmament, preservation of the French language, and the development of the Québec nation state. Many of the AFDUM's members were from Québec's most notable political families, such as Thérèse Casgrain and Claire Kirkland-Casgrain, both staunch feminists. All were professional women, such as Lise Fortier, a medical doctor, Suzanne Barrière, a lawyer, Monique Béchard, a psychologist, and Suzanne Coallier, a chartered accountant. The goals of the AFDUM were:

> To stimulate university women's interest in public life; to give them the opportunity to meet other university graduates; to allow the general public to recognize university women as representatives of the academic, professional world; and to let it be known that French Canadian women were not just wives and mothers, but had talents outside the home.[1] (My translation)

The history of this group of university-educated Francophone women is interesting for a number of reasons. Their 1950s gender equality ideas reveal the inappropriateness of using the traditional timeframe of the so-called first and second wave women's movement in Canada to study the trajectories of Québec feminism (Gosselin, 2006), the first wave occurring in the late 19th and early 20th centuries and the second beginnng in 1967 until the 1980s. The AFDUM used its demands for women's equal opportunity in higher education and the labour force as points of entry into society-wide calls for socio-political reforms. Additionally, the association's activism of the 1950s and 1960s became an important part of the women's movement in 1967. In this way, the AFDUM was able to combine a quest for women's individual rights through liberal feminist discourses with the nationalist pursuit for a new collective identity for all Québecers. In so doing, the association was able to carve out a space for what it called "la femme dans les affaires publiques" (women in public affairs).

Context: Gender as a Site of Contested Space

Through a content analysis of the AFDUM's archival documents,[2] I take you, the reader, on a journey back to the 1950s and 1960s of Québec to show how one group of university women used higher education as a negotiating tool to enhance women's position in the political realm and in all areas of public and professional life, and at the same time made a space for women's leadership among the nationalist social changes that developed in the 1950s, which became the Quiet Revolution of Québec of the 1960s.[3] The subsequent narrative will reveal my argument by exploring the AFDUM's discourses and activism related to women's rights to education, employment, and equality in marriage and civil rights reform, as well as its views on the links between liberal feminism and Québec nationalism. But first, it is important to establish the social context for Québec women living in the 1950s. We should ask our sources the following questions: What were French Québec women doing during the pre-1950s era? How did gender roles and social expectations change in the 1950s? What circumstances led to the formation of the AFDUM? How did the nationalist fervour of the 1960s Quiet Revolution provide a backdrop to the association's demands for individual equality rights through higher education and insert women's leadership skills into the new interventionist state?

Between 1945 and 1960, changing socio-economic and ideological conditions altered Québec women's lives in radical ways. The changes began with married women's participation in World War II and continued with the expansion of these women's labour market opportunities, increasing educational choices, declining church influences on daily life, a diffusion of ideas regarding the modernity of society and culture, and the presence of various women's organizations such as the AFDUM. Other transformations in the post-war period included the increasing burdens of women's "double day"—productive and reproductive work—and the use of contraception as a reality for the majority of women in Québec and Canada (Gauvreau and Gossage, 1997).

These socio-economic and ideological transformations signalled new and different gender relations between women, men, and the state. While women's lives in post-war society represented a discontinuity with the past and reflected the desires for a new social order, significant economic, legal, and attitudinal obstacles persisted in such a way as to limit women's full and equal participation in society. The labour market discriminated against women by refusing to grant status and salaries equal to those of men. At the same time, traditional elites and conservative clerics clung to the dominant conception of femininity as passive and subordinate to masculinity. They chastised working mothers for neglecting their duties to home and the French Canadian nation. Indeed, married women were regarded as legal and social non-entities.

Québec's Civil Code, established in 1866, ensured women's inferior legal status through guarantees of the husband's broad powers over his wife's person and property (Clio Collective, 1987). The Civil Code's marriage laws institutionalized masculine power in the uncontested control a husband could exert over his wife and children, which extended to his right to administer and dispose of the couple's *communauté des biens* (common property). Women in certain civil and legal categories, however, were exempt from this repressive matrimonial regime. Single women, of course, held the same civil status as men. Mostly wealthy, upper class women chose to enter a marriage with a premarital, notarized contract stipulating the separation of her property from her husband's, but she still needed his approval before she could do anything with her assets. Eventually, legal reforms in the 1960s, due to feminist pressures resulted in changes to the gender relations among wives and husbands so that women married under a "common property" regime could administer assets they earned from salaried work and did not need a husband's authorization before proceeding with any contractual affairs. These reforms were indicative of shifting gender relations at the time caused by women's increasing participation in all areas of public life.

Between 1941 and 1971 the percentage of women in the labour force steadily increased. The level of Québec women's participation went from 21,95% in 1941 to 33,65% in 1971 (Barry, 1977). At the same time, married women also increased their participation in paid employment. In 1941, only 8% of working women were married. In 1951 the rate rose to 17% and by 1971, 48% of female workers were married. Despite the introduction in 1944 of a federal family allowance program which was designed, in part, to encourage women with children to leave the labour force after the Second World War, throughout the 1950s, more and more married women were drawn into the work force as the economy expanded, especially in the tertiary sector. At the same time, university trained women were appointed to careers in Québec's expanding public labour force; namely in the health and educational fields. Many of these women likely engaged in a "two-phase work history" (Strong-Boag, 1994), whereby young wives remained in their jobs until their first child was born. At that time they generally quit, or labour codes forced them to, and returned to paid work only when children were old enough to look after themselves.

The backdrop to women's increasing labour force participation was a number of reforms to education for women and girls, which took place throughout the 1950s. The Roman Catholic Church, highly patriarchal in nature, held a near monopoly over the school system for French Québecers. Women's only avenue to higher education was domestic science, or home economics as it is sometimes called, instruction. This exclusion was based on the Church's belief that motherhood was the one honourable career for a woman and thus she did not require a post-secondary education of any kind. If a Francophone woman wanted to go to university she had to enrol in one of the English institutions at the time, McGill or Bishop's University, or leave the province to complete her education elsewhere.

Beginning in the 1950s, however, women's associations and progressive thinking social scientists began to side-step the church and demand from the government, a secular school system and more democratic choices for women in education. The result was the establishment of a public secondary school system in the mid-1950s, which legitimated the same education for girls and boys. Restructured programs now permitted female students to receive a high school education, which gave them the ability to do further studies at college and university or enrol in commercial courses for direct access to the job market.

Thus a number of competing interests produced a crisis in gender relations between women and men at the time which would eventually lead to the formation of a new social order. The church, state, school structures and market forces attempted to regulate women's gendered lives with ideologies, social systems and legal codes that sought to institutionalize a permanent gender hierarchy based on male control and female submission. But because gender is never uniform or stable, but intersects with class, civil status, race, and ethnicity and so forth, the control of women's destinies could never be homogeneously obtained. Thus, the gendered status quo of the 1950s was challenged by dissenting voices of reform coming from various women's groups, some of them feminist, professionals, career and working class women, and other advocates for a more modern and democratic society based on gender equality. Gender became a site of contested ground for women to speak out, in their collective voice, against the discriminatory practices and attitudes they experienced as they attempted to carve out a space for women in the public domain including the work force and education.

The AFDUM: The Importance of Women's Education for Gender Equality

In Québec the post-World War II period was marked by heated and controversial calls for major reforms to the entire Francophone educational system, including adult and higher education. Expanding secularization and industrialization of society as well as new employment opportunities required educational attainments that the current curriculum could not fulfill. Throughout the 1950s neo-nationalist groups argued that more schooling was needed to prepare boys and girls for entry into the labour force, while social reformers believed schools should be sites for teaching individuals about how best to prepare for the diverse demands of a modern Québecois society. Women's organizations contended that women needed more educational openings if they were to achieve gender equality in a democratic Québec. One of these groups to adopt the principle of granting women formal equality in education was, of course, L'Association des femmes diplômées des universités des Montréal. Much of the AFDUM's discourse on expanding French women's educational rights was framed in comparison to English-speaking Québec women's wider choice for higher-educational opportunities.

The AFDUM worked to recruit Francophone young women to university who would then be eligible for a variety of full-time careers. Members of the association accomplished this task in several ways. They provided information about access to higher education hoping to recruit as many girls as possible to enrol in university. Recruitment activities included holding career fairs, public lectures and information sessions and offering scholarship programs. The concern of the association was that not enough young women were taking advantage of a university degree and what it had to offer. Many girls preferred commercial or technical courses which was no surprise given the fact that they required little time and financing. These courses also reflected public attitudes which positioned women's quest for higher education as detrimental to future family roles. But L'Association members, whose own lives were indicative of changing gender status combined with the needs of a modern Québec, were outspoken in their views that "secretarial courses" only led to short-term employment and little financial security. The AFDUM petitioned the provincial government directly to request state support for women's higher education through expanded opportunities and funding. These calls reflect the changing nature of the state's role in public services during the 1950s. While education was still very much dominated by the Catholic Church, the Québec government was assuming more of the functions of building and financing the province's schools. During this time an intense debate took place between advocates for a more integral education for girls, similar to the one boys received, and partisans of instruction based on women's feminine and familial roles (i.e. Thivierge, 1982). On one side of the discussion were church officials and their supporters who argued that schooling for girls should remain separate from boys. They believed young women should be instructed in the art of housekeeping through domestic science schools and family institutes. This kind of secondary school education was compatible with women's nature, argued church leaders, and was required so they could assume their future roles as wives and mothers. On the other side of this war of ideas was the AFDUM, led by member Monique Béchard, a sociologist, who believed that if women were to achieve their full human potential they needed an education beyond high school which would open doors to all aspects of intellectual and professional life. The purpose was not to deny women the gender roles of wife and mother but to give them the opportunity to have a professional career as well. The AFDUM's appeals for women's higher educational needs were grounded in a liberal, equality feminism. The group believed a state supported educational system would provide equal treatment and opportunities for both sexes. Once this equal playing field was established, then women would be able to reach their full rights and capacities as humans. The association wanted women to put their higher education to good use through exercising their rights on the job. The liberal feminism of the AFDUM also became the platform to demand formal equality for women in the work force.

Advancing Women's Rights through "Equal Pay for Equal Work"

Throughout the 1950s, women's lives were changing rapidly, particularly with the expansion of their labour force participation, so the activities of the AFDUM reflected these vagaries. One of the most important liberal feminist goals of the association at this time was to fight for the right to work in professions of a woman's choosing and receive equal remuneration with men. The association carried out its objectives in several ways. Firstly, the AFDUM maintained contacts among university trained, professional women throughout the province. This task was accomplished by building a coalition of women's professional and cultural associations which served as a resource for information on opportunities in traditionally defined male areas of employment. A network of professional women was also created to chart the career paths and map the progress of female "firsts." In addition, the AFDUM studied the availability of careers for female graduates and held numerous conferences on the topic. The coalitions, networks and information all became part of the association's attempts to bring attention to the secondary status of women in the formal economy and eventually change it.

The AFDUM was not just concerned with individual success, but with the issues faced by all women in the labour market. It should come as no surprise that L'Association pressed for more institutionalized measures as part of its reforms for gender equality in the workplace. It lobbied the state to ensure women's access to government positions and agencies. For example, association members sent a letter to then Prime Minister Louis Saint-Laurent demanding that he nominate a Québec woman to the Senate (e.g. AFDUM Fonds, 1951). In 1955, at the request of women's groups across the country including the AFDUM, the federal government established la division de la main-d'oeuvre feminine du ministère du travail du Canada to study the issues faced by female workers, especially older women, and create more equitable salary and working conditions in the areas where they were employed. Members of the association believed that female representation in government ministries, school boards and municipal committees was crucial to women achieving gender equality in the formal economy.

But asking male leaders to promote women's interests was not a method the AFDUM knew it could solely rely on to achieve all its goals. Members wanted to ensure the legal right of female university graduates to an occupation of their choosing. To accomplish this, they pressed for economic rights through provincial and federal legislation. Two types of statutes were sought. In concert with other women's groups, the AFDUM, speaking out at an adult education forum, demanded equal pay for equal work laws which could be regulated by a federally appointed female section in the Ministry of Labour:

> [As] the advocates of equal pay [we] do not ask that women be paid the same as men if they are away from work or do not do equivalent work. What we ask is that women be given equal pay when they do equal work (CAAE, 1950, n.p.).

L'Association also argued that anti-discrimination laws were needed to counter traditional attitudes about women's inability to perform identical jobs to men. At the same time, AFDUM was well aware that an increasing number of mothers simply could not "attend to the early training and education of her young children" due to the need to work, and needed help in the form of public day care facilities as "not all individuals are cast in the same mould ... many women find their homes run more efficiently if they go out to work" (CAAE, 1950, n.p.).

The actions of the AFDUM were based on the perceptions that women's subordinate status was systemic throughout the work force and that the inequalities they experienced were substantive. As liberal feminists, the members believed that only state interventions could guarantee women's equality through the principle of individual rights. To achieve this principle, they advocated the need for legislation, which would guarantee these rights, coupled with strategies of inclusion to promote opportunities in the formal economy and representation in state structures. But since women were also treated unfairly because of their gender, the AFDUM recognized the need for different actions in the area of motherhood and thus demanded that equality rights necessitate gender specific provisions in the form of day care. Universal rights combined with attention to women's gender expectations defined the liberal, equality rights feminism of the AFDUM. While little action by federal or provincial governments to these demands would be taken until the sixties, we could interpret the association's 1950s ideas and actions surrounding women's status in education and the workplace as a prelude to its leadership activities in the building of the 1960s Québec nation-state and participation in the organized feminist movement of the time.

The AFDUM and Women's Leadership

The sixties brought enormous events of significance for Québec society including women's rights. The year 1960 is viewed as an important marker in the history of Québec because it signifies the beginning of massive socio-economic and political reforms commonly referred to as the "Quiet Revolution" (i.e. Dickinson & Young, 1993; Behiels, 1985). Finally, after a decade and a half of industrialization and urbanization as well as challenges to traditional nationalist beliefs, the Québec people were ready for their own secular and modern nation-state with an accompanying, new nationalist ideology of legitimation. Led by the provincial Liberal Party, reforms in all sectors of society and at every level were put swiftly into place.

The rapid implementation of these changes attests to the fact that 1960 may not represent such a revolutionary year in the history of contemporary Québec after all. True, the sixties were a period of social and political upheavals for all Western democracies. But far from being a spontaneous event in Québec, it is now generally recognized that the previous decade was the period when the vestiges of the old customary ways of life and values were finally replaced by different expectations and social imperatives of modernity. Thus, the Quiet Revolution can be viewed as an index, and not a cause, of radical social and cultural changes that were taking place in the preceding decades. Not one part of Québec society or its citizens was left untouched by the sweeping reforms of the provincial Liberals, including women. The 1960s were also important for women's rights; although similar to the Quiet Revolution they did not strike like a lightning bolt in the lives of women. For some, life appeared to remain the same while others, influenced by expanding telecommunications, believed the world was accelerating at too fast a pace. One thing was certain among AFDUM members: their politics would have to change. The 1950s had been a time of growing awareness about the number of injustices and inequalities experienced by women, but there had been no institutional mechanisms to ensure that women's rights would permanently be put in place. Now with the 1960s growth of a Québec interventionist state, women's groups had the tools to turn their consciousness-raising into action. Would the newly formed nation-state give women individual liberties and enlarge their opportunities in the public sphere or would it be an obstacle to achieving gender equality? The AFDUM and other advocacy groups would quickly find out.

The AFDUM used the wave of reform in the province to actualize its feminist analysis of the inequalities experienced by women throughout society. The outcome of the Quiet Revolution was the creation of state organized social and economic institutions along with the growth of a centralized government bureaucracy. The association envisioned the Québec state as an ally in the expansion of women's individual rights. Members of the AFDUM themselves acted as leaders in directing government officials to promote women's interests. The association believed state institutions and bureaucracy could be used as instruments in opening up the public sphere for women. The resulting social and economic equality for women would benefit not just the individual, but would foster national progress as well. This last point reveals how the AFDUM combined its liberal feminist and nationalist dreams. The group's quest for women's individual rights was situated within the promises of Québec's pursuit for the new nation-state's collective autonomy.

Amid the atmosphere of reform, we find members of the AFDUM carrying out leadership roles in various professions and government posts. These members included Thérèse Baron, sous-ministre adjoint à l'Éducation (assistant to the Education Minister), Jeanne Beauvais, Consultante en main-d'œuvre au gouvernement fédéral (consultant in the Canadian Department of Labour), Marthe Bellefleur, professeure, École des hautes études commerciales (professor at the school of business, Montréal University), Dr. Claire Turgeon Knaack, pathologist as well as the previously mentioned Thérèse Casgrain and Claire Kirkland Casgrain. As leaders among professional, public sector and government women, each one used her position to encourage more women to enter the public realm by acting as role models. They worked to amass empirical evidence about gender inequalities suffered by women as the basis for demanding legislative reforms in education and the formal economy. Their university education provided members with the ability to participate in various formal inquiries on language, education and women's rights.

We can ask ourselves if the generation of women reformers belonging to the AFDUM and other advocacy groups were successful in their struggles for women's equality rights. In the absence of an organized feminist movement, these groups did succeed in creating an alternative view of gender relations between women and men. Eager to redress the historical wrongs experienced by women, reformists constructed various political agendas to achieve meaningful social justice. The motivations of the AFDUM were based on an analysis of the structural and ideological forces that constrained women's lives. Central to their commitments to a just society was obtaining equality rights for women. Throughout the 1950s, these activists formulated and reformulated their ideas about how best to achieve gender equality and when the reforms of the Quiet Revolution were unleashed in the 1960s, members were ready to incorporate their demands into the newly formed Québec interventionist state. Unfortunately, the nation building project of the Quiet Revolution initially sought to maintain, rather than reform, the traditional gender order and women's position in it. But, since the modernization forces of the Quiet Revolution changed the landscape of Québec and its people, so too were gender relations affected. There was no turning back. From the perspective of the AFDUM, Québec's modern and democratic nation state must include the political recognition of women's equality. So when a new phase of the pan-Canadian women's movement began with the announcement of the Royal Commission on the Status of Women in 1967, the members of the association were primed and ready (i.e. Dumont, 1992). It should come as no surprise that the AFDUM would call on the federal state for legislation and policy since the group already had a well-established record of requesting reforms for women's rights within the context of a provincial, interventionist state. L'Association members used their leadership roles once again, this time in collaboration with feminist organizations across the country, to demand full citizen status for all women.

In conclusion, the university-educated women of the AFDUM are our foremothers in the continual battle for gender justice. This group of university women used their higher education as a liberal feminist platform to enhance women's position in the political realm and all areas of public/ professional life. At the same time, the members became leaders in the struggles to make a space for women among the social and economic changes that developed in the 1950s and later became the Quiet Revolution of Québec in the 1960s.

We honour these women and their education and leadership legacies and visions in particular, their recognition that we must take women as a starting point for our feminist political struggles, and political struggles must be feminist. However, as a category we now know that the category of "women" must be set within a series of diverse and hierarchical relations. It must be interpreted through the more complex web of class, race, sexual orientation and abelism, and situated within broader local, national and global social issues and contexts such as family, economy, politics, culture, and religion. But the possibilities brought about by the past acts of feminist leadership and educational re-visioning for empowerment and change, live on in Québec.

Endnotes

[1] Archives of the Université of Montréal, Association des femmes diplômées des universités de Montréal Fonds, P107, Box 278, "Assemblée préliminaire, procès-verbal," le 27 mai, 1949.

[2] The nature of these documents consist of information on organizational structures such as constitutions and by-laws, membership criteria, financial records, and the minute books of meetings; in addition to speeches, writings, publications, and formal studies about ideas and views on a variety of subject matter pertaining to women's and Québec nationalist issues in the form of correspondence, newspaper clippings, reports and resolutions, government reports, monthly bulletins, and briefs to various royal commissions.

[3] This work is based in part on my 2002 PhD thesis entitled *Vers L'avenir, Québec Women's Politics between 1945 and 1967: Feminist, Maternalist and Nationalist Links*. History Department, Montréal University.

References

- l'Université de Montréal Archives. Fonds de l'Association des femmes diplômées des universités de Montréal (Accessed in 2000).

- Barry, F. (1977). *Le Travail de La Femme au Québec*. Montréal: Les Presses de l'Université du Québec.

- Behiels, M. (1985). *Prelude to Québec's Quiet Revolution: Liberalism versus Neo-Nationalism, 1945-1960*. Montréal and Kingston: McGill-Queen's University Press.

- CAAE (1950). *Citizens' Forum: Equal Pay for Equal Work: Are Women Getting a Fair Deal?* Toronto: Canadian Association for Adult Education.

- Clio Collective (The) (1987). Dumont, Micheline, Michèle Jean, Marie Lavigne, and Jennifer Stoddart, *Québec Women: A History* (Trans. by R. Gannon and R. Gill). Toronto: The Women's Press.

- Dickenson, J. and Young, B. (1993). *A Short History of Québec*, 2nd Edition. Toronto: Copp Clark Pitman Ltd.

- Dumont, M. (1992). The origins of the women's movement in Québec. In C. Backhouse and D. Flaherty (Eds.), *Challenging Times: The Women's Movement in Canada and the United States* (pp. 72-89). Montréal and Kingston: McGill-Queen's University Press.

- Gauvreau, D. and Gossage, P. (1997). Empêcher la famille: Fécondité et contraception au Québec, 1920-1960. *Canadian Historical Review*, 78(3), 478-510.

- Gosselin, C. (2002). Vers L'avenir, Québec women's politics between 1945 and 1967: Feminist, maternalist and nationalist links. Unpublished PhD Thesis, History Department, Université de Montréal, 2002.

- Gosselin, C. (2006), Remaking Waves: The Québec Women's Movement in the 1950s and 1960s. *Canadian Woman Studies*, 25(3,4), 34-40.

- Strong-Boag, V. (1994). Canada's wage-earning wives and the construction of the middle class, 1945-1960. *Journal of Canadian Studies*, 29(3), 5-25.

- Thivierge, N. (1982). *Écoles Ménageres et Institut Familiaux: Un Modèle Féminin Traditionnel*. Québec: Institut Québécois de recherché sur la culture.

This vignette was prepared by Mary Kostandy.

Thérèse Casgrain was born on July 10, 1896 in Montréal. Her mother was Lady Blanche MacDonald, an active patron of many charities. Her father, Sir Rodolphe Forget, was a lawyer, financier, and conservative politician. In 1916, she married Pierre Casgrain, a lawyer, liberal politician, Speaker of the House of Commons, and Secretary of State under Prime Minister Mackenzie King. She had four children.

In 1921, Thérèse was one of the founding members of the provincial Franchise Committee for Women's Suffrage in Québec. From 1928 until 1942, she became a president of the League for Women's Rights (Ligue des droits de la femme) which succeeded in winning the right to vote for women at the provincial level. She was also a member of the National Health Council and the National Welfare Council. In the 1930s, Casgrain hosted Fémina, a Canada-Radio program. She was one of the presidents of the Women's Surveillance Committee for Wartime Prices and Trade Board during World War II. In the 1942 federal by-election, Thérèse became the Independent Liberal candidate in the Charlevoix-Saguenay riding, the seat that was held earlier by her father and then by her husband. She ran many times for public office federally and provincially. In 1946, Thérèse joined the Co-operative Commonwealth Federation (CCF) Party, which later became the New Democratic party (NDP). In 1948, she was chosen as the national vice-chair of the CCF and in 1951, she became the first woman in Canada to head a political party in Québec. From 1951 to 1957, Thérèse served as the leader of the Québec Wing and became president of the NDP in Québec.

In 1961, Thérèse founded the Québec branch of the Voice of Women to protest against nuclear arms and promote world peace. In 1960, she founded the League for Human Rights and in 1966 she established the Fédération des femmes du Québec. She served as president of the Québec Medical Aid to Vietnam Committee and the French section of the Canadian Adult Education Association. Thérèse served as vice-chairperson of the Consultative Committee on the Administration of Justice in Québec and in 1969, became president of the Canadian Consumers Association for Québec and was part of a successful lobby to create a Minister for Consumer Affairs.

In 1970, Thérèse was appointed by Prime Minster Pierre Trudeau to the Senate as an independent for nine months until she reached the mandatory retirement age of 75, after which she fought against compulsory retirement in jobs. She was awarded a "Woman of the Century" medal by the National Council of Jewish Women of Canada (1967) as well as a medal by the Société de Criminologie du Canada. She was appointed Officer of the Order of Canada, and in 1974, was made Companion of the Order. In 1979, Thérèse received the Governor General's Award in Commemoration of the Persons Case in recognition for her effort for women's suffrage in Québec. Thérèse received honorary Doctor of Laws (LL.D.) degrees from the Université de Montréal in 1968; McGill, Trent, and Queens in 1974; Waterloo, Bishop's, Notre Dame (BC), Mount Saint Vincent, York, and Ottawa in 1979; Concordia in 1980; and Windsor in 1981.

Thérèse continued to fight actively for the rights of Canadians until her death in Montréal in 1981 at the age of 85. The Thérèse F.-Casgrain Fellowship for Research on Women and Social Change in Canada was created in 1982 in her name by the Thérèse F.-Casgrain Foundation to perpetuate her memory and to continue her legacy.

References

- Karsh, Y. (n.d.). Marie Thérèse (Forget) Casgrain. Retrieved April 26, 2015, from https://www.collectionscanada.gc.ca/women/030001-1339-e.html

- Stoddart, J. (2008, March 24). Thérèse Casgrain (M. Lambert & A. Mcintosh, Eds.). Retrieved April 26, 2015, from http://www.thecanadianencyclopedia.ca/en/article/therese-casgrain/

Photo courtesy of Library Archives of Canada.

Members of the Women's Institute enjoy a hillside picnic in 1910. The first Women's Institute in Lambton County was formed in 1905.
© Lambton County Archives (2015).

8

Disrupted Discourses in the Women's Institute Organizations of Canada Celebrated Stories

Too often women's organizations are looked on as "tea party" groups—where women get together for an afternoon or evening of pleasantries and small talk. Well, yes, the Women's Institute can do that as well, but far more often we get together and extend a helping hand to make great things happen: and not only in our own communities. —British Columbia Women's Institute, 2014

It was fitting that I visited the birthplace of the first-ever Women's Institute organization in Stoney Creek, Ontario on the very weekend I was presenting a talk at the Canadian Association for the Study of Adult Education's (CASAE) annual conference on this same topic. I could not pass up the opportunity to visit the home of Janet and Erland Lee, a site that hosted one of the most critical meetings that one hundred women had attended a century prior to my arrival.

Katie Stella

At that meeting in Stoney Creek on February 19, 1897, Adelaide Hoodless addressed a group of women farmers on the importance and future of "domestic science," or what was also known as "home economics." Hoodless was, in fact, committed to educating rural women about raising the standard of knowledge and homemaking after her infant son had died from contaminated milk. She believed that if she had known about safe food practices, her son's death could have been prevented. One week following her address, the first Women's Institute in Canada was born.

Sitting atop Ridge Road, surrounded by the rich agricultural landscapes of the Lee home, I realized that for me, this site captures the essence of this rural women's organization and its struggle for change through, with, and by women's knowledge. This chapter is influenced by my own personal connections to the Women's Institute that included generations of my family members who were committed members (and many continue to be so), and by my position as a feminist academic reclaiming a lost history of the Women's Institute that has yet to be told. As a feminist poststructuralist, I strongly believe that we must celebrate the hidden stories that have been so often passed over, for they have indeed reshaped our contemporary reality. In unearthing the de-popularized stories of the Women's Institute in Canada, this chapter explores the celebrated stories of resistance, unity, individualization, and inclusion that are not typically told by historians. Throughout the chapter, I interchangeably use "WI" and "Institute" to refer to the Women's Institute as a provincial body, and federally as the Federated Women's Institute of Canada (FWIC).

Changing Histories

The Women's Institute (WI) is one of the longest standing women's organizations in the world and its origins are proudly rooted in rural Canada dating from 1897. Similar to the WIs of England—powerful and contradictory forces in their own right—and Farmer's Institutes (FI), spaces that offered farm men an opportunity to share agricultural best practices, the WI organized farm women and wives, seeing value in opportunities to socialize and share experiences among like-minded women. While group socials were common in their initial gatherings, the WI agenda eventually grew over the years to cover complex topics that included safe food practices, public administration, matters that impacted the family and farming, government lobbying, and women's rights activism.

As a means for rural women to enact change collectively, which was seen as a critical way to promote women's equality, the WI developed into an organizing body and a platform for raising the standard for women. With the power of women's voices rising up against opposition, the Institute spread throughout Ontario, and by 1909, British Columbia and Alberta had formed their own branches. Manitoba formed its first WI in 1910, and Saskatchewan, Québec, New Brunswick, and Prince Edward Island followed in 1911. Nova Scotia then followed in 1913, Yukon in 1956, and the North West Territories in the 1960s (Ambrose, 2000). Given such successful growth, establishing a federal body in 1919 called the Federated Women's Institute of Canada (FWIC) became necessary to offer the provincial Institutes a unified voice at the national level. In 1933, FWIC joined the global women's organization Associated Country Women of the World (Darroch-Lozowski, 1996; Thompson, 1987). What began in Canada in 1897 has now spread to over 70 countries worldwide (MacKeracher, 2009).

Critical of the Institute's instant success and of Hoodless's intentions in forming a WI, Kechnie (2003) purports that the Institute was created to serve the interests of men in the Farmer's Institute in order to revive their failing organization. Furthermore, Hoodless is criticized for serving the interests of the leaders of the Ontario Department of Agriculture (ODA) and their country reform, which would see younger generations remaining in the countryside to raise their families. During this time in Ontario, rural communities faced depopulation as a result of young women leaving the homestead for promising lives in urban regions. Rural living did not offer the modern conveniences that urban areas could, and many young women departed their rural life for employment opportunities in larger cities. Depopulation was part of the ODA's country reform, and as a result, the Ontario Agriculture College (OAC) was entertaining the establishment of a women's extension department which would offer domestic science courses to promote homemaking as a desirable option for young women.

Although many history texts document the Institute as a grassroots organization that experienced spontaneous growth, Kechnie (2003) interprets their history much differently. Prior to her address to women farmers on the evening of February 19, 1897, Kechnie argues that Hoodless had formulated a longstanding goal of establishing a domestic science school for women. Her address in Stoney Creek, Kechnie asserts, was no more than a tactic to recruit rural women to the idea that formal training for women's domestic work was necessary in validating their contributions to the world of (predominantly men's) work; if men had the opportunity for formal training facilitated through the FI, Hoodless would argue that women should have the opportunity for a separate women's organization—the WI. To critics, the movement that sought to raise the standard of homemaking via WIs would create provincial awareness around enhancing domestic studies, which would lead to increasing enrollment in the Ontario Agriculture College's women's extension department of domestic sciences.

At the time that the first couple of Women's Institutes were formed in Ontario in 1897, the Farmer's Institute was experiencing a state of flux, with enrollment declining due in part to a lack of interest among men who felt the evening meetings had become rather boring. In 1900, three years after the WI was born, George C. Creelman, Superintendent of the Farmers Institute, was tasked with revitalizing the FI and increasing its enrollment. To fulfill these tasks, Creelman required help from farmers' wives in encouraging their husbands to participate in an improved FI that would organize more lively functions and socials. Farmers' wives would supply food and drink and offer an entertaining social evening that everyone could enjoy. As enrollment numbers in the FI eventually increased, and keeping in mind the ODA's agenda for encouraging young families to remain in the countryside, Creelman pressed for farmers' wives to expand the number of WIs in the province. At the time, there were only two branches in Ontario, despite three years having passed since the establishment of the Stoney Creek WI. With help from the leaders of the ODA and the OAC, Creelman promoted the expansion of the WIs throughout Ontario and Canada.

Kechnie argues that Hoodless was an ideal spokesperson pursued by the leaders of the Farmer's Institute, the Ontario Agriculture College, and the Ontario Department of Agriculture to serve their patriarchal interests. Hoodless had little to do with the expansion of the WI and, therefore, Kechnie critiques the glamorizing of the WI's instant success and associates their origins and development alongside a political agenda that stripped them of their grassroots feminist history and placed their founding years under the auspices of patriarchal country reform.

If the WI had begun the way Kechnie (2003) interprets its beginnings, we should celebrate their resistance to hegemonic governmental agendas and superimposed neo-liberal influences that impacted feminist organizations and feminist practices of the day. For without deviating from a political agenda, we may be speaking about the WI in the past tense; however, we are here celebrating the emergence, pursuit, and accomplishments of the WI and shedding new light on this feminist rural organization. Whether you adopt Kechnie's (2003) interpretation of the WI's political beginnings, or the version proposed by Grey Otty (1961), Ambrose (2000), Darroch-Lozowski (1996), and Thompson (1987) about a grassroots rural women's group that would become one of the oldest women's non-profit organizations globally, what is certain is the WI's role in prolific social change and activism.

Organizing and Gathering: Choosing A Pattern and Assembling the Fabric

It is common to see WI members at local fairs selling tickets for hand-made quilts, or offering their expertise in handicrafts and hands-on craft workshops. Less visibly, the WI is also active in passing along resolutions to governments that request new standards in various categories for local and national regions. A non-inclusive list of such resolutions includes naming provincial flowers and implementing home economics courses in Canada; supporting the need for a university in the Niagara Peninsula, which would later become Brock University; and lobbying for the Marital Property Act. Their cause is widespread, but their roots remain intact: "For Home and Country."

How can an organization established in 1897 hold the same values in modern times? While progress has been made for women's rights since the 19th century, feminist adult educators are still writing about gender inequalities, the wage gap between women and men, the underrepresentation of women in Parliament, and the perpetual effects of marginalizing women's issues (e.g., Walby, 2011; Gouthro, 2007; English, 2005). Studying the WI in Canada, I noticed an alarming trend in what the mothers of the Institute were advocating for in the early days, compared to issues of today. Canada's contemporary economic and social landscape is experiencing a mirror image of the issues that affected rural Canada in the 1900s: the outmigration of young generations for work in urbanized markets, an alarming illiteracy rate among Canadians, women struggling to gain status as equal citizens, technology and policy advances that have stripped rural regions of their control over farming practices, and the education of families on the topics of food production and consumption. These trends were on the agenda in the early years of the WI, and several of these topics are relevant in Canada and throughout the world today. The issues that impact women must be addressed at all levels, from the individual to the national, and, fittingly, the motto "For Home and Country" remains relevant and evident throughout the global WI organization. One could argue that this relevance is equivalent to the contemporary feminist mantra, "the personal is the political," and I will return to this comparison later in this chapter.

The WI's Purpose, Mission, and Structure Today

The Institute continues to be a non-sectarian, non-partisan, and non-racial organization (Canadian Legal Information Institute, 2010) with a strong presence of religion throughout organizational documents and presidential messages highlighting the organization's attachment to traditional and historical practices. Despite their traditionalist core, the Institute takes a progressive stance in that each provincial body individually defines their own purpose, mission, and vision statement instead of adopting a national unified message. This characteristic sheds light on the organization's individuality and autonomy in making decisions relevant to each province's rural agenda. Although the WI's purpose statements vary by province, each statement conveys themes related to enhancing the quality of life for women, families, and communities through education, and advocating for change at the economic, social, and agricultural levels.

Structurally, the Institute is comprised of members, branches, districts, and a provincial and federated body. Members belong to a given branch, branches belong to a given district, and these branches and districts together comprise the provincial WI organization. Overseeing the federal body is the FWIC. The Institutes consist of a president, vice president, secretary, treasurer, directors, and administrative staff, and at the branch, provincial, and federated levels, a member is chosen to represent conveners whose interests are tied to different industries and sectors. These sectors include Agriculture, Canadian Industries, Citizenship and Legislation, Education, Home Economics and Health, and International Affairs.

Each year, an annual provincial convention is held to promote the successes of the past year, hear addresses from government officials and keynote speakers, facilitate learning opportunities through workshops, and pass resolutions. Democracy is deeply woven into the practices of the Institute and very apparent during each annual convention. The resolutions presented from the various provincial districts are discussed and voted upon at the convention, and the final resolutions are passed to respective government departments to develop policy. The resolution process is by no means a seamless and harmonious event despite what much of the literature says about women's learning and/or decision making and leadership (Belenky, Clinchy, Goldberger, and Tarule, 1986; Carfagna, 1995; Jordan, Kaplan, Baker Miller, Stiver, and Surrey, 1991; Lyons, 1987). These conventions feature contention, debate, and humour, and a majority vote before a decision is made. Resolutions do not always pass and can require decades of pressing the issue at the provincial and federal levels.

The Complexity within the Women's Institute: Cutting, Sewing, and Piecing

Operating in accordance with a set of constitutions and by-laws, the WI is governed by the Women's Institute handbook. This committedly democratic organization has the public administration skills to operate successfully at a level to which policy officials and government bodies can relate. Previous research claims that women's organizations operate in a non-hierarchal structure with non-bureaucratic ways (see Fondas, 1997) and that women tend to exercise an inclusive and process-oriented leadership style (Meinhard and Foster, 2003; Rosener, 1990). The WI does not shy away from the fact that their operations are democratically and bureaucratically situated within a rigid set of procedures and regulations (Perriton, 2009). This insight supports previous research on women's social action organizations in Atlantic Canada, where women have learned to negotiate the binary of feminism and bureaucracy (English, 2004). Feminist social action organizations must juggle aspects of this binary, with its tensions and interdisciplinary challenges. These challenges can include organizational leaders' management of daily pressures that impact board members and volunteers who feel obligated to work overtime due to diminishing government funds (English, 2004). They also include organizational leaders being confronted by criticisms from feminist literature and ideology on how to be a good feminist, and facing the challenge of maintaining social action status by partitioning themselves off from government reliance. Purist views of feminism maintain that feminist organizations must remain collectivist and empowering in order to counter bureaucratic paradigms (Ashcraft, 2000); however, the reality is that feminist groups can adopt structure, hierarchy, and governmental models of organization while also maintaining their feminist values (English, 2004). The WI has elevated their organization since 1897 from the rural to the international stage, and this speaks volumes to their operational mandate and organizational integrity in adopting their own strategies for expansion.

The pressures on women's groups are endless, but they have not reshaped their relationship with their provincial and federal governments. Government officials often speak at Institute conventions and events. Staying connected with decision makers offers the Institute a strategic government alliance and promotes the WI as a relevant advisor on rural women's issues. Following World War II, non-profit groups formed part of a wider social welfare system responsible for delivering a variety of social services to their communities (Meinhard and Foster, 2003). These services were once the responsibility of community groups such as the WI that had previously received considerable public funding for these expanded responsibilities. These responsibilities no longer fall within the government's social services reform, but to maintain oversight into rural matters and to remain legitimate in the eyes of public officials, the Institute must remain close to the state.

The Institute's complex growth is a result of the boundaries of structure and process intersecting with participatory and collective practice. It is hoped that this insight into the WI's operational integrity can relieve tensions that feminist groups experience when faced with choosing between a binary of decisions on how to expand their organization. Equally so, this insight can lead to new discourses and new regimes of truth (Foucault, 1980) that better represent women's work in the public sphere, which remains a largely underrepresented body of literature (Burge, 2011; Butterwick and Elfert, 2012).

One should not assume that the WI is a passive advocate on rural matters due to their governmental connections. The Institute has preserved their autonomy from government influence on many critical matters over the decades. One such case from the 1940s highlights the pioneering efforts of the mothers of the Institute to lay claim to their autonomy as a rural advisor at the federal level. For years the Canadian government had relied on the Institute's help in coordinating rural efforts to support the country's men at war. Their contribution ranged from coordinating goodie baskets for soldiers to raising funds for medical equipment and mobile hospital units. A charitable organization in one regard, the Institute was also heavily committed to their activism and did not treat their role as a rural advisor lightly. In 1942, one of many women invited to join the campaign to increase the ranks of women's enlistment in the Canadian Women's Army Corp (CWAC) was Mrs. Dunham, President of the FWIC. Mrs. Dunham would have represented about 75,000 rural women in Canada at that time (Ambrose, 2000). Instead of subscribing to the hegemonic military enlistment discourse, as a rural advisor Mrs. Dunham instead spoke out against the exploitation of rural women joining the ranks and she subsequently declined the CWAC's offer. Her critical examination of and resistance to the structures of power operating on behalf of the federal government's enlistment agenda is one of many stances that the WI took in shaping women's rights and elevating their position in the federal sector.

Activism, Feminism, and Emancipation: Quilting and Binding

The Institute has not worked in isolation all of these decades. A central tenet of their survival and success for 117 years is their ability to develop partnerships and alliances with powerful women and feminist organizations. The leaders of the Institute exhibited diverse backgrounds ranging from careers that spanned public administration to community-based roles. What follows is a selection of profiles of organizational leaders, affiliations, and partnerships that speaks to the diverse techniques used in forming their activism—an under-acknowledged field of study for Institutes (Langley, 2012).

Leading their national federation, Emily Murphy served as the first President of the Federated Women's Institute of Canada (FWIC) from 1919-1921. Murphy was one of the Famous Five, along with Nellie McClung, Irene Parlby, Louise McKinney, and Henrietta Muir Edwards, who lobbied the "Person's Case" that made women legally defined as persons and eligible to hold a seat in the Senate of Canada (Government of Canada, 2000). Murphy was revolutionary in resisting and challenging power structures that created new discourses about women's rights at the judicial level, and it was a substantial defeat to have laws for women created by the very patriarchal legal system in Canada that had previously denied these rights. The astonishing leadership of the FWIC did not end with Murphy in 1921. Nancy Adams, FWIC president until 1957, was a university academic who became an early member of the Canadian Federation of University Women (CFUW). With her ties to the CFUW and the FWIC, she was equipped to facilitate rural issues that would make their way to the Royal

Commission, thus elevating the status of rural women. Additionally, in 1927 the Institute partnered with Dr. Helen MacMurchy, Chief of the Child Welfare Division, to reduce infant mortality rates, resulting in a national campaign called "Make maternity safe for every mother in Canada" (Ambrose, 2000, p. 30). This campaign created national awareness and increased exposure for the Institute in terms of validating their stance as a trusted rural advisor. The leaders of the WI and the partnerships they developed are varied, but they all promote the same goal of preparing, educating, and informing women to attain new knowledge and to create a voice for change.

Although the WI does not self-identify as feminist, their goals and activities align with feminist and emancipatory ideologies. The Institute has advanced the interests of women through a movement based on freeing them from the very gender relations that restrict their access to opportunities, and from the gender inequalities that devalue women's work in the homeplace. From lobbying for the Marital Property Act, raising public awareness about the value of domestic work as a science and promoting women's entrance into the labour force, to pursuing political appointments and access to higher education, the Institute has always held a vested interest in protecting women's rights. These pioneering activities advanced the interests of women, though not without conflict, resistance, and perseverance. After decades during which the Institute pressed forward to effect these changes, adult educators are still writing about the necessity of recognizing the value of women's work in both spheres (e.g., Gouthro, 2007), which highlights that research must continue in this field.

It cannot be said that all WI members have experienced emancipatory learning, or that they assume a feminist identity. The members of the Institute are like the stitching that holds a quilt together. The diversity in their experiences contributes to the strength of their organization, and when one more stitch is added, the durability of the quilt is enhanced. Given the diversity of members, their motivations for joining the organization and the learning they develop as a result of membership differ for each person. Some members have had a long history of participation with other feminist groups before joining the Institute and the organization offers no more than an ability to socialise and enjoy the company of like-minded individuals; whereas others find new learning and motivation to contribute to and lead community change through collective action.

New Directions: From Locally Crafted Quilts to Competing with Mass Production

With increasing changes to the education sector in Canada marked by the country's efforts to compete in the global marketplace, non-profits that promote education for social change are quietly being swept under the rug. The Maritimes are experiencing a shift in adult education from a platform that once promoted personal, social, and political change towards a neo-liberal skills agenda (Benjamin, White, MacKeracher, and Stella, 2012). The Canadian government has shown little support for sustaining adult education programs (Nesbit, 2013). Learning is falling victim to the marketplace (Gouthro, 2002), and Canada's drive towards a knowledge economy is under pressure to conform to this highly skilled and trained workforce (Gibb and Walker, 2013). Educative organizations such as the WI are experiencing a decline in membership, are receiving considerably less government funding, and continue to be underrepresented in the public sphere. Under the nation's capitalist regime that brings fierce competition to the interactions of everyday life, community organizations are pressured to compete for resources divided among a plethora of voluntary and non-voluntary groups. The WI is under pressure to remain relevant in the midst of turbulent economic and societal changes, including the growing number of women entering the workforce who are expected to maintain their paid labour alongside unpaid familial responsibilities (Gouthro, 2009), leaving little to no time to join a community group such as the Institute.

There are provincial Women's Institutes in Canada that are robust and thriving, and there are many on the brink of disbanding. Rural regions are growing older, young adults are moving to provinces that offer steady income, and women and men are enrolling in universities in urban regions, which leaves rural communities with declining populations and little opportunity for young women to participate in community groups. New Brunswick is one of the regions facing serious decline in Institute membership. My experiences speaking with people in the community who are non-WI members and listening to government leaders speak about the New Brunswick Women's Institute are disappointing. Why has this group that has impacted so many women and families globally remained widely unknown in Canada and underrepresented in the public space? A key reason pertains to the gender inequalities in Canada that place the Institute and its feminist agenda at a disadvantage compared to favoured male-dominated organizations. The WI's issues occur in the undervalued, privatized world that we call home (see Gouthro, 2005). Child rearing, marital rights, and women's needs all become less relevant when these concerns go up against public campaigns that make us believe that investing in job creation and business startups are urgent priorities that will resolve our complex economic and social deficiencies. The WI and the issues it brings forward become less relevant when it must compete against patriarchal governmental priorities.

The powerful effects of marginalization have weakened society's knowledge of the Women's Institute and have perpetuated the masculinist worldview that overpopulates what gets documented in history, which stories are told, which heroes prevail, and which minority groups are subjugated. These subjugated discourses are the intrusive exercises of power that maintain the status quo (Foucault, 1980). Ignorance about the WI has silenced the organization, excluded women's experiences in the public world, and limited the opportunities for new knowledges to form about women's issues, thereby maintaining the very systems that privilege the masculinist worldview. In challenging the status quo, I encourage readers to get to know their local Institute and its agenda, and to observe its organization at a branch, district, or provincial convention. It is not often we have an opportunity to enact change alongside one of the longest-standing women's organizations in the world.

References

- Ambrose, L. (2000). *Women's Institutes in Canada: The First One Hundred Years 1897-1997.* Ontario: Tri-Co Printing.

- Ashcraft, K.L. (2000). Empowering "professional" relationships: Organisational communication meets feminist practice. *Management Communication Quarterly, 13*(347), 346-392. doi: 10.1177/0893318900133001.

- Belenky, M.F., Clinchy, B., Goldberger, N., and Tarule, J.M. (1986). *Women's Ways of Knowing: The Development of Self, Voice, and Mind.* New York, NY: Basic Books.

- Benjamin, A., White, M., MacKeracher, M., and Stella, K. (2012). Riding the river: Adult education in a have-not province. In S. Bringham (Ed.), *Proceedings of the Canadian Association for the Study of Adult Education 19-25.*

- British Columbia Women's Institute. (2014). Women's Institutes Helping Other Nations [Organizational website]. Retrieved from http://www.bcwi.ca/womens-institutes-helping-other-nations/.

- Burge, E. (2011). *Women Social Activists of Atlantic Canada: Phenomenal Women of Atlantic Canada*. Retrieved from http://etc.lib.unb.ca/womenactivists/phenomenal-women-atlantic-canada.

- Butterwick, S. and Elfert, M. (2012). The social movement learning of women social activists of Atlantic Canada: "What Shall We Do and How Shall We Live?" In S. Bringham (Ed.), *Proceedings of the Canadian Association for the Study of Adult Education 53-59*.

- Canadian Legal Information Institute. (2010). *Women's Institute and Institut Féminin Act, RSNB 1973, c W-11*. Retrieved from https://www.canlii.org/en/nb/laws/stat/rsnb-1973-c-w-11/latest/rsnb-1973-c-w-11.html

- Carfagna, R. (1995). A developmental core curriculum for adult women learners. New directions for adult and continuing education. In K. Taylor and C. Marienau (Eds.), *Learning Environments for Women's Adult Development: Bridges toward Change* (pp. 53-61). doi: 10.1002/ace.36719956509

- Darroch-Lozowski, V., Crawford, L.A., and Ponti-Sgargi, L. (1996). Not one but many: On the centennial of the Women's Institute (1897-1997). Ontario: Ice Lakes Press.

- English, L. (2004). *Feminine/Feminist: A Poststructural Reading of Relational Learning in Women's Social Action Organisations*. Retrieved from http://www.adulterc.org/Proceedings/2004/papers/English.PDF.

- English, L. (2005). Foucault, feminists and funders: A study of power and policy in feminist organisations. *Studies in the Education of Adults, 37*(2), 137 150.

- Fondas, N. (1997). Feminisation unveiled: Management qualities in contemporary writings. *Academy of Management Review, 22*(1), 257-292.

- Foucault, M. (1980). *Power/Knowledge: Selected Interviews and Other Writings 1972-1977*. New York, NY: Pantheon.

- Gibb, T., & Walker, J. (2013). Knowledge economy discourses and adult education in Canada: A policy analysis. In T. Nesbit., S.M. Bringham., N. Taber, & T. Gibb (Eds) *Building on Critical Traditions: Adult Education and Learning in Canada* (pp. 258-269). Toronto, ON: Thompson Educational Publishing Inc.

- Gouthro, P. (2002). Education for sale: At what cost? Lifelong learning and the marketplace. *International Journal of Lifelong Education, 21*(4), 334-346.

- Gouthro, P. (2005). A critical feminist analysis of the homeplace as learning site: Expanding the discourse of lifelong learning to consider adult women learners. *International Journal of Lifelong Education, 24*(1), 5-19.

- Gouthro, P. (2007). Active and inclusive citizenship for women: Democratic considerations for fostering lifelong education. *International Journal of Lifelong Education, 26*(2), 143-154.

- Gouthro, P. (2009). Neoliberalism, lifelong learning, and the homeplace: Problematizing the boundaries of "public" and "private" to explore women's learning experiences. *Studies in Continuing Education, 31*(2), 157-172.

- Government of Canada. (2000). Are women persons? The "Persons" case. Retrieved from http://www.collectionscanada.gc.ca/publications/002/015002-2100-e.html.

- Grey Otty, M. (1961). *Fifty Years of Women's Institute in New Brunswick, Canada 1911-1961*. New Brunswick: New Brunswick Women's Institute.

- Jordan, J., Kaplan, A., Baker Miller, J., Stiver, I., and Surrey, J. (1991). *Women's Growth in Connection: Writings from the Stone*. New York, NY: The Gulford Press.

- Kechnie, M. (2003). *Organizing Rural Women: The Federated Women's Institutes of Ontario, 1897-1919*. Montréal, QC: McGill-Queen's University Press.

- Langley, D. (2012). Women reaching women: A story of change. The role of narrative in building trust and commitment during an action research project. *Educational Action Research, 20*(1), 41-53.

- Lyons, N. (1987). Ways of knowing, learning and making moral choices. *Journal of Moral Education, 16*(3), 226-239.

- MacKeracher, D. (2009). Social change in historical perspective. *New Directions for Adult and Continuing Education, 24*, 25-35.

- Meinhard, A.G. and Foster, M.K. (2003). Differences in the response of women's voluntary organisations to shifts in Canadian public policy. *Nonprofit and Voluntary Sector Quarterly, 32*(3), 366-396. doi: 10.1177/0899764003254910.

- Nesbit, T. (2013). Canadian adult education: A critical tradition. In T. Nesbit., S.M. Bringham, N. Taber, and T. Gibb (Eds.), *Building on Critical Traditions: Adult Education and Learning in Canada* (pp. 1-15). Toronto, ON: Thompson Educational Publishing Inc.

- Perriton, L. (2009). The education of women for citizenship: The National Federation of Women's Institutes and the British Federation of Business and Professional Women 1930-1959. *Gender and Education, 21*(1), 81-95.doi: 10.1080/09540250802213156.

- Rosener, J.B. (1990). Ways women lead. *Harvard Business Review*, 1-11.

- Thompson, E.A. (1987). *Holding Fast That Which Is Good: The Centurial Third Quarter (1961-1986)*. Fredericton, NB: Fiddlehead Poetry Books and Goose Lane Editions Ltd. Fredericton: New Brunswick.

- Walby, S. (2011). *The Future of Feminism*. Malden, MA: Polity Press.

This vignette was prepared by Katherine McManus.

Florence O'Neill came from the small fishing community of Witless Bay in Newfoundland, situated not far from the capital city, St. John's. She initially seemed an unlikely candidate to become someone who would change adult education in her home province. No one paid any special attention to her as she struggled to educate herself, one year at a time, to the level of a baccalaureate degree at Dalhousie University, or as she found ways to push herself through an Ed.D degree at Columbia University. When she returned to Newfoundland with her doctoral degree, she was offered an Assistant Directorship in the provincial government's Department of Adult Education. She was the most educated woman in the government and among the educated elite of the province.

O'Neill had prior experience both as an adult educator and as an elementary education teacher, but this was not enough to prepare her for the bureaucracy inherent within the government. Her ability to bring a new and innovative approach to helping adults learn literacy, numeracy, and life skills in the thousands of small fishing communities around the island of Newfoundland was hindered by conventional practices. In particular, she found that the government provided better opportunities to those communities in less need of help, and offered almost nothing to those communities mired in poverty.

In order to develop the skills and potential of the residents of all of the small fishing villages in Newfoundland, she created regional offices throughout the island that were able to coordinate staff (outreach development workers) and other resources. She did this so that every community would have access to male and female trained adult education specialists whose job was to help each community develop in the way the residents of that community desired and required. The outreach workers would respond to the community needs as the community described them, as well as offer workshops and goal-oriented community planning.

O'Neill worked first as the Assistant Director of Adult Education and subsequently moved into the Director position. Her fourteen years (1944-1958) within the Department included some very solid victories in creating adult education regional offices and expanding the number of adult education workers in the province. These years also included some deep disappointments. She had hoped that the "Plan" for developing an island-wide cohesive program for adult education, which she had created in her doctoral dissertation, would be adopted by the government. Instead, it prompted the Minister of Education at the time to write a caustic letter to O'Neill's immediate superior. The letter was filled with complaints that she had painted Newfoundland in a bad light by identifying the endemic poverty of the inhabitants and illuminating the ill-effects of a denominational school system.

In the end, O'Neill struggled to gain acceptance for her vision and ultimately lost the battle when the Smallwood government dismantled the Department of Adult Education in 1958. O'Neill moved on to work in the education division within Indian Affairs in Ottawa, and her early work was adopted as a method of practice by Memorial University's continuing education field workers until the 1990s.

References

- O'Neill, Florence (1944). *A Plan for the Development of an Adult Education Program for Rural Newfoundland.* Unpublished Ed.D dissertation, Columbia University.

- From the Provincial Archives of Newfoundland and Labrador, specifically from Home Affairs and Education files, 1934-1958. Box #7250.

- Commissioner of Home Affairs and Education (H. A. Winter) to C. W. Carter, Director of Adult Education, St. John's. 6 December, 1945. Memo. Winter writes: ". . . I cannot consent to any publication [of dissertation] as I consider that the worst conditions found in settlements in the most depressed areas in the country. . ., and that the most damaging statements about this country, it's [sic] people, and some of it's [sic] institutions are made. . . ."

- McManus, K. (2000). *Florence O'Neill: Alone in the Wilderness.* Unpublished doctoral dissertation. University of British Columbia.

Pedagogies for Change

Alannah Young Leon, PhD, Anishnabe Midekway and Nehiy/naw Cree from Treaty One and Treaty Five territories, at the UBC convocation in 2015.

Photograph: Courtesy of Lorena Fontaine.

9

Weaving Indigenous Women's Leadership
Pedagogies, Protocols, and Practice

I have listened for many decades as the Elders told leadership stories involving their strategic engagement with colonialism. Yet historically I, like Kelm and Townsend (2006), have noticed how women's perspectives have been frequently overlooked and, as a result, I set out to explore this gendered gap in my doctoral research (e.g., Young, 2015). In that enquiry, I held multiple conversations with eighteen Indigenous knowledge holders from diverse Indigenous nations (Young, 2015). The primarily female Indigenous Elders in my research described neglected knowledge systems, the context of colonialism, and how their leadership fulfilled the wholistic health education needs of communities.

Alannah Young Leon

The focus of our conversations was in particular the place-based pedagogy they employed at a tribal Indigenous land-based health education program called the Medicine Camp in rural Manitoba. About one hundred Indigenous health educators have participated in the four-year land-based health education program. The main female Elder leaders, including myself, have Anishnabe and Nehiy/naw Cree tribal affiliations.

The Medicine Camp was developed in light of the reality that Aboriginal students are underrepresented at educational graduation levels and overrepresented in health care systems. For example, one-quarter of non-Aboriginal adults had a university degree, compared to 9% of Métis, 7% of First Nations peoples, and 4% of Inuit persons. In 2006, one-third (33%) of Aboriginal adults aged 25 to 54 had less than a high school education compared to nearly 13% of the non-Aboriginal population, a difference of 20 percentage points (see Statistics Canada, 2005, 2008).

This land-based health education program began in 1992 and demonstrates that despite colonialism, Indigenous Knowledge and leadership education endures. What I have learned is that the tribal Midewiwin matriarchs' transmission of knowledge through the land-based education program continues to provide relevant leadership and demonstrates the persistence and application of tribal women's leadership and laws, in spite of the pressures imposed by the assimilationist Canadian state narratives, illegal policies, and genocidal practices.

Land-Based Leadership

During our conversations at the Medicine Camp, the land-based leadership pedagogy of Indigenous women's leadership emerged and five key practices were identified. These practices, listed below, wove together local Indigenous pedagogies and protocols based on understanding Indigenous laws and legal traditions; these laws and traditions can inform a trans-disciplinary education practice.

- Coordinate research with local Indigenous nation's culture and stories and partner with appropriate resource people;
- Follow local protocol principles and how they are expressed and negotiate local relationships to land and modify protocol principles for each context;
- Prepare materials and information required for students to learn in class and on the land and make space for, and provide access to, Indigenous Knowledge holders;
- Apply the learning by taking people out on the land and engage respectfully with local peoples and places; and
- Share reflections and local stories about transformation and reconnection to peoples, lands, and plants/food security/sovereignty.

Throughout the chapter, I interweave examples from my own practice of leadership training as well as from the women Elders I know. I conclude this chapter with a brief discussion of how Indigenous Knowledge ethics and land-based pedagogies can guide education leadership across institutional disciplines. I weave my womanist tribal perspective into an Indigenous constitutional narrative of what I have learned so far from women leaders. A womanist tribalism means Indigenous woman perspectives based on our own understandings of territory, community, and relationship to lands where we are the original peoples. This means that my primary leadership responsibility is to demonstrate my understandings of Indigenous relationships as a fundamental law (Hunt, 2013). This involves weaving the local protocols and principles of Indigenous peoples' relational ecologies (Donald, Glanfied and Sterenberg, 2012) with the research values of respect for responsible relationships, reciprocity, and relevancy (Kirkness and Barnhardt, 1991) for both Indigenous and non-Indigenous contemporary contexts. Although site- and case-specific, there are some elements and principles common to negotiating Indigenous education leadership and adult education contexts.

The pedagogical approach practised by Indigenous Elders often stands in sharp contrast to the normative education models introduced by the settler state. These models were devastating, as schools frequently functioned simply as colonial mechanisms to destroy Aboriginal cultures, languages, knowledges, and even, physical bodies, causing irreparable damage to many generations of First Nations, Métis, and Inuit Indigenous peoples. One of the most egregious forms of systemic violence against Aboriginal youth was the forced removal of Aboriginal children from their homes and placement in residential schools, where over half the students who attended perished. Many generations of youth suffered abuse under the doctrine "kill the Indian, save the child," which included physical, emotional, psychological, and spiritual violence under the guise of education (Milloy, 1996; Schissel and Wotherspoon, 2003). In many cases, the harm inflicted by these abuses still affects current generations, as evidenced by measures of wellness and achievement in Aboriginal communities (Adelson, 2005; Kelm, 1999; Waldram, Herring, and Young, 2006). Another form of violence is the difficulty experienced by many Indigenous peoples and educators due to the public ignorance of the long history of systemic violence and widespread misinformation about Aboriginal Indigenous peoples' nation-to-nation status in Canada (Kuokkanen, 2008).

Given this colonial legacy, and my use of two terms—Indigenous and Aboriginal—at the beginning of this document, some clarification about this terminology is needed. In this chapter, the term "Indigenous" describes groups of people who have unique cultural expressions and ecologies different from those of colonial groups. Sustainable connections to the land that predate colonial contact are one of the unique features of Indigeneity. Collectivist-based expressions of diverse linguistic groups are other distinguishable features. Where appropriate, I use the term "Indigenous" as inclusive of First Peoples globally. The Constitution Act Section 35 (2), 1982 and the Royal Commission on Aboriginal Peoples (RCAP) use the term "Aboriginal" to refer inclusively to Aboriginal, Inuit, and Métis peoples in the Canadian nation state discourses. However, these terms do not reflect how the diverse groups of people refer to themselves prior to European settler contact.

Five Key Practices

The pathways of research, preparation, orality, application, and reflection have guided our pedagogical processes and these are captured in the figure below. It is important to remember that the five-step process illustrated in this figure will vary according to the resources available to the adult educator. Furthermore, while the practices are offered as a list, in reality, they are interrelated and their enactment is not linear.

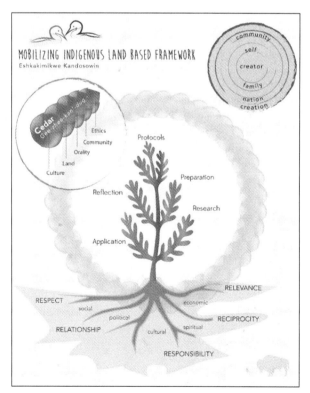

Figure 1.

Mobilizing Indigenous Land-based Framework Eshkakimikwe Kandosowin: Earth Ways of Knowing.

Source: A. Young, 2015.
Illustration: Clarissa Poernomo, 2014.

Research

For many Indigenous peoples, the purpose of adult education is to cultivate self-knowledge, foster core personal development of whole human beings using all of the senses, and enhance self-determined leadership capacities within communities (Young, 2006). Flexible leadership allows for education that makes spaces for diverse concepts such as social justice through reconciling the ongoing residential school histories of genocide and creatively connecting the socio-economic and ecocide realities and reinforcing alternative ways of being, of which Simpson gives examples below.

> A resurgence of Indigenous political cultures, governances and nation-building requires generations of Indigenous peoples to grow up intimately and strongly connected to our homelands, immersed in our languages and spiritualities, and embodying our traditions of agency, leadership, decision making and diplomacy. This requires a radical break from state education systems—systems that are primarily designed to produce communities of individuals willing to uphold settler colonialism…. (p. 1)

Rebuilding Indigenous nation-to-nation status involves a regeneration of treaty[1] relationships and natural laws such as Wahkotowin (Young, 2015; Lindberg, 2004; McAdam, 2015), a Cree word meaning "kinship" or "the state of being interrelated." This concept describes the fundamental aspect of understanding Indigenous laws. Indigenous women have continued to enact their leadership and their relational responsibilities by perpetuating grounded land literacies so the future generations will survive and counter grand master patriarchal narratives with Indigenous constitutional narratives (Vizenor, 2013). The Elders in my study modelled the recounting of our individual and collective stories as constitutional narratives. These constitutional narratives recounted the treaties as agreements for mutually beneficial relationships and suggested how we understand them from our particular regions and landscapes. Articulating these cultural expressions and restoring the spirit of the treaty relationships, as the basis for respectful relationships, illustrate how to educate learners about living out Natural Indigenous laws and respecting the land and the humans who live on it, which is a primary responsibility.

Protocols

Indigenous protocols are cultural norms specific to particular places, peoples, and contexts. They are diverse and yet share some common unifying features. Lightning suggests, "a protocol refers to any one of a number of culturally ordained actions or statements, established by ancient tradition that an individual completes in order to establish a relationship" (cited in Archibald, 2008, pp. 37–38). Archibald (2008) also speaks to the values conveyed by following protocols, which are negotiated for each context as practice principles. She indicates that knowledge must be shared in a manner that incorporates cultural respect, responsibility, reciprocity, and reverence because these teachings are cultural values, beliefs, lessons, and understandings that are passed on from generation to generation.

One of the goals of education is to empower people by providing a diversity of knowledges and including many ways of knowing and educating while balancing the ethics and protocols of protecting Indigenous knowledges from exploitative practices (Hill, 2008). This includes role modeling for students about how to convey respect for Aboriginal worldviews, changing the practices of teaching and the processes of learning by applying the protocol principles across disciplines, and shifting curricular content towards an inclusive infusion of Indigenous legal perspectives, and ways of knowing and educating for all learners. Educators can learn by researching place-based histories and comparing narratives, which lead to the development of critical thinking skills and trans-disciplinary approaches.

Preparation

Preparation involves connecting with other tribal leaders who want to pass on this rich heritage. It is an important feature of Indigenous leadership pedagogy because it allows for network building and strategizing self-determined, land-based teaching initiatives across disciplines. This process can involve the examination of local protocols to see if they can be modified for the contemporary context. I learned that connecting stories to the land and to well-being are the primary pedagogical features of many tribal societies and that the nation-to-nation agreements are often upheld through women's leadership councils (McAdam, 2012). Preparation involves research and relationship building, to make space for, and to provide access to, Indigenous Knowledge holders. The preparation of education materials can follow and can then be applied on the land in partnership with Indigenous Knowledge holders.

Application

In urban Vancouver, many Indigenous laws are mobilized and applied through a network of Indigenous women who connect and address social movements, such as *Idle No More*, regarding the protection of lands and access to food security and water (McAdam, 2015; Nason, 2014; Nadeau and Young, forthcoming; LaDuke, 2014). For example, the Medicine Collective participants provide an Indigenous advisory function to support the local water walk[2] in Vancouver. This walk was part of an initiative to end violence against women in Vancouver's Downtown Eastside. I am part of this advisory council and we looked to xʷməθkʷəy̓əm Musqueam Elder—the late Norma Rose Point— and her suggestions regarding how leadership training would include teaching how to put on an event and learning how to become a good relative by following the local territories' protocol principles. We suggested that local Indigenous female leadership should be represented in the planning stages for the water walk event and that they welcome the people to the event. Regional, intergenerational, and gender representation were other leadership considerations in planning an event. I learned to use these local Indigenous protocols as appropriately modified as principles explicitly intended to build understandings across common interests and to create healthy community relationships.

Elders taught us the importance of being a good relative and how to reflect on the ways to become a good relative and how taking people out on the land is part of our leadership development. They taught us to take the leadership learning they shared and apply it to our own contexts. While building relationships with local Indigenous health practitioners, Jeri Sparrow (xʷməθkʷəy̓əm Musqueam) and Dr. Jeanne Paul (Tla'amin Sliammon) helped to deepen our relationship with the plants and the peoples of the Coast Salish territories. We worked with the Institute of Aboriginal Health and the Faculty of Land and Food Systems' staff to develop culturally relevant medicinal gardens and we provided health education as the Medicinal Collective,[3] which modelled many of the pedagogical methods we applied from the Indigenous Elders' leadership at Medicine Camp. These examples demonstrate how we have worked together to bring the Elders' leadership pedagogies to our "adopted home" communities. The Indigenous health leadership and related pedagogies are structured by local protocol and legal principles that provided frameworks for how we develop policy and practice (Gomes, Young and Brown, 2011).

From 1995-2009 I reflected on and applied these learnings by developing a Longhouse Leadership student program (Young, 2006). The program included elective cultural components such as a tribal women's sweat lodge in order to provide leadership for students that reconnected them to the land and to Indigenous legal traditions. I trained specific women in local protocols, sweat lodge tribal practices and protocols, songs, and Wahkotowin relational laws and responsibilities. The sweat lodge (Oleman, 2010) is an Indigenous structure heated by steam by pouring water on hot stones and it is used for therapeutic sweating, and instructional leadership teachings are transmitted through mentoring processes—as appropriate for a women's teaching lodge.

Reflections

As I reflect on the Elders' leadership discussions, I learned that it is my responsibility to embody a relational approach by living by the tribal women's laws and teachings in flexible and creative ways. I learned that the way to begin to teach and learn is through their example and through providing leadership mentorship opportunities. The Elders stressed that they were taught to convey the knowledge in the ways they learned it, and to make space in the learning environments for those who are practised at teaching the tribal laws and knowledge. I also reflected on and applied the learning that Indigenous pedagogies are beneficial for all learners' leadership development. An example of partnering among learners from diverse backgrounds is a digital learning resource I helped develop at UBC for teacher educators. This resource aims to support the teaching and professional development of educators in Aboriginal/Indigenous education. This online learning tool is intended to promote the place of Indigenous knowledges, knowledge holders, and pedagogies in schools and communities that will enrich classroom experiences for all learners (Hare et al., n.d., n/p).

The topics relevant to current issues in Indigenous education are highlighted in this website and focus on Indigenous perspectives, curricular resources, multimedia, and literature that link theory to practice. The website provides educators with a variety of pedagogical tools such as stories, documentaries, and counter narrative approaches that help educators to interrogate concepts such as the "perfect stranger" (e.g., Higgins, 2013). The "perfect stranger" interrogates non-Indigenous peoples' excuses, such as "willful ignorance," and examines why there is inaction on common concerns related to social justice, such as equal access to healthy homes, food security, and clean water claims. This critical self-examination skill can help educators to ground pedagogies that facilitate relationships with Elders, Indigenous peoples, and places on Turtle Island.

The research reflections and connections with local communities helped us to learn the local protocol principles and to apply their teachings to ethical leadership. Ethical leadership was illustrated through role modeling by the Indigenous women and the health education leaders—they showed us that we begin to get ready for knowledge by using local language and, in partnership with local knowledge keepers, to develop appropriate pedagogies that include stories as teacher and land as leader, according to ethical and Natural Indigenous laws.

At the Indigenous Research Gardens at UBC we approached Larry Grant and Rose Point who are local knowledge holders and language instructors to help us name the teaching gardens; they were given the name "Our Place of Growing Together." Ethical leadership ensured that we were not siphoning knowledge out of communities but supporting the self-determined health education goals of the communities in which we are located, and working together to create sustainable and decolonizing pedagogies that aim to develop shared understanding of respect, integrity, and ethics (Ermine and Hampton, 2007). These applied examples include, through the stories shared and the interactions on the land, an analysis of how each person can address the impacts of colonialism, paternalism, and capitalism on our leadership.

The application and reflection phase is also a time to assess the students' capacity for leading their own learning, which can be a challenge for educators within a limited timeframe. Adult educators can use multimodal media, such as the growing and gathering of herbs and other wild plants, hunting, and fishing, followed by show-and-tell activities to let students tell the class what they have hunted or how they have gathered something demonstrating reciprocity gestures involving their senses. Alternatively, adult educators can encourage people to demonstrate their relationships with plants through skits that include local stories as appropriate. This can include growing small herb gardens or preparing tea, jam, or salves as follow-up activities during the application and reflection phases. Integrating decolonizing learning creatively and experientially enhances land-based Indigenous pedagogies.

Leadership Implications

Indigenous women's leadership stories provided me with critical understandings; their narratives addressed how they understand complex interconnected and interdependent relationships as legal responsibilities. They shared reflexive stories about how the Elders negotiate the ongoing context of colonialism, gendered violence, and structures of imperialism. The Indigenous women's and Elder's stories, legal traditions, and teaching methods point towards a sustainable pedagogy of direct action that addresses the dispossession experienced in both urban and land-based settings (Anderson, 2010, 2011). Their stories speak of moving away from state dependence towards the construction of Indigenous alternatives to paternalism and capitalism based on Indigenous legal principles. The Indigenous women's Elder leadership provides and encourages multiple expressions built on the love and heritage of Ancestral knowledge and legal traditions. The pedagogy they employ points to the relationship possibilities of places, and of thinking, educating, and acting according to the legal traditions. Ultimately, Indigenous leadership and laws are about nurturing and honouring the relationships that promote interdependence and that sustain the health and well-being of communities and individuals, as well as challenge people to connect more fully to the multiplicities of the places they inhabit (Battiste, 2013; Corntassel, 2014; Andreotti and Ahenakew, 2014; 2015; Coulthard and Simpson, 2014; Gruenewald, 2009). I suggest that trans-disciplinary approaches can begin with tracking our leadership stories and by understanding local Indigenous protocols and relationship to lands (Gomes, Young, and Brown, 2011).

Many of the Indigenous leadership stories I heard described a critical moment when the tellers experienced racism. The stories they shared have strategic pedagogical features that teach us about educational barriers and how people overcame them. These teaching stories are Indigenous constitutional narratives about the Canadian context and they suggest how adult educators can use narratives in their place-based teaching practice (Dua, 2008; Grande, 2004; Kimmerer, 2013; Regan, 2005; St. Denis, 2007). The Elders' stories have many possible interpretations (as indicated by the two circles and root systems shown in Figure 1), and we are left to examine the outcomes of each of the narratives. Narratives can "increase humans' cognitive adaptability and stretch our imaginative capacities so that we can generate new ways of thinking and being in the world" (Nelson, 2013, p. 229). Perhaps through the weaving of stories we can deconstruct the barriers of racism and create our own constitutional narratives beginning with local identities and our relationships with Indigenous peoples and places (Vizenor and MacKay, 2013).

Manitowabe and Simpson (2013) agree that stories and learning processes are personal, and that leadership theories and methods of teaching that use Indigenous stories can help us to learn how to embody an ethic of sustainable, mutually beneficial relationships. Story and narrative forms teach and illustrate how colonial policies are used to control and subjugate Indigenous identities. Scholarship calls for readers and adult educators to be aware of the social, political, and historical complexities that face Canadians so they may be better equipped to engage with the work of decolonization and Indigenous critical and feminist theorists.

Like Smith (2005) and McAdams (2012, 2015), Simpson (2011) challenges hetero-patriarchy and colonial practices through the use of decolonization pedagogies whereby Indigenous women-centered models are articulated, applied, and mobilized. Indigenous women and men successfully continue to assert traditional tribal values, redefinitions of clan roles, and adaptations of Indigenous Knowledges to new conditions. These alterNative knowledges still defy "outsider" representation and remind us that the university system of knowledge is not complete and that transformation can be achieved, at least in part, through pedagogical interventions (Adams, 2009). Linking to an Anishnabe-Nehiyaw Ogichita kway (tribal warrior women's leadership) and theories of the P/Bimadiziwin, the Good Life ways and practice, helped me to bridge social theories, Indigenous theories, and methods of inquiry in my graduate research to investigate and apply Indigenous pedagogy as an education leadership example (Young, 2015).

One of the ways to stop the continued exploitation and dispossession of Indigenous peoples is to feature pedagogies that build on our laws and distinct positioning. Indigenous place-based stories distinctly convey what we know and how we transfer knowledge in Indigenous land-based learning. In the UBC post-secondary context, the work of Sarah Ling and Spencer Lindsay's place-based projects weave Indigenous land learning (2014). The projects, "Knowing the land beneath our feet," provide videos that demonstrate that students are producing some exciting leadership examples. In the areas of adult education recruitment and retention of Indigenous students, staff, and scholars, community service must count towards prior learning equivalences and tenure. It must also provide specialized legal and professional mechanisms if institutions are to keep up with anti-racism, gender equity, and leadership beyond the existing corporate patriarchical models.

Thus, a trans-disciplinary approach must re-animate and re-imagine Indigenous Knowledge Systems (IKS) and tribal histories and laws, and provide opportunities to reflect on and apply the ways in which these aspects inform our present-day actions. In this intergenerational health education land-based program setting, Elders, academics, and lay people interface scientific inquiry language with Traditional Indigenous Knowledge practices. Canadian legislation, using the authority of the *Indian Act,* led to the loss of lands, and the residential school system interrupted the intergenerational transmission of IKS and led to the loss of many Indigenous languages. Despite this, knowledge is not lost. Instead, Indigenous practices are currently being transmitted from one generation to another in new ways, and communities are being mobilized through stories and the Elders' traditional laws and ways of teaching, which re-establish links to the land (Young and Nadeau, 2014, Forthcoming; McLeod, 2007; Manitowabe and Simpson, 2013, Simpson, 2011, 2015).

The next steps in our adult education leadership might involve redefining what it means to engage with a trans-disciplinary approach and potentially transformative framework, one that is rooted in places, local protocols, and legal principles and that examines our roles in Indigenous land-based relationships.

Endnotes

1   For more information on the numbered treaties in Canada see: Canada. INAC. Treaties. http://www.ainc-inac.gc.ca/al/hts/mp-eng.asp.

2   For more information on water advocacy and food security initiatives see: http://www.motherearthwaterwalk.com/?page_id=11http://www.Indigenousfoodsystems.org/tools-and-skill-building.

3   For more information about Indigenous gardens and the Medicine Collective see: http://lfs-Indigenous.sites.olt.ubc.ca/Indigenous-research-partnerships/Indigenous-education-and-research-garden-at-ubc-farm/.

References

- Adelson, N. (2005). The embodiment of inequity: Health disparities in Aboriginal Canada. *Canadian Journal of Public Health.* 96: 245-61.

- Adams-McGuire, T. (2009). *Ogichitaakwe Regeneration* (Unpublished Master's thesis). University of Victoria, Victoria, Canada. Retrieved January 15, 2013 from: http://www.collectionscanada.gc.ca/obj/thesescanada/vol2/BVIV/TC-BVIV-3111.pdf.

- Ahenakew, C., de Oliveira Andreotti, V., Cooper, G., & Hireme, H. (2014). Beyond epistemic provincialism: De-provincializing Indigenous resistance. *AlterNative: An International Journal of Indigenous Peoples*, 10(3): 216-231.

- Anderson, K. (2010). *Aboriginal Women, Water and Health: Reflections from Eleven First Nations, Inuit, and Métis Grandmothers.* Winnipeg, Manitoba. Report for the Atlantic Centre of Excellence for Women's Health & Prairie Women's Health Centre of Excellence. Retrieved March 2014 from http://www.pwhce.ca/womenAndWater.htm.

- Anderson. K. (2011). *Life Stages and Native Women: Memory Teachings and Story Medicine.* Winnipeg, University of Manitoba Press.

- Andreotti, V. and Ahenakew, C. (2015). Red skin, white masks: Rejecting the colonial politics of recognition [Book Review] [online]. *AlterNative: An International Journal of Indigenous Peoples*, Vol. 11, No. 1, 76-78. Availability: <http://search.informit.com.au/documentSummary;dn=980458130775430;res=IELIND> ISSN: 1177-1801.

- Archibald, J. (2008). *Indigenous Storywork: Educating the Heart, Mind, Body and Spirit.* Vancouver, Canada: UBC Press.

- Battiste, M. (2013). *Decolonizing Education: Nourishing the Learning Spirit.* Saskatoon, Canada: Purich.

- Canada, Royal Commission on Aboriginal Peoples. (1996). Report of the Royal Commission on Aboriginal Peoples (Vols. 1-5). Ottawa, Canada: Minister of Supply and Services.

- Canada, Statistics Canada. (2005). Projections of the Aboriginal populations, Canada, provinces and territories 2001 to 2017 (Cat. No. 91-547-XIE). Ottawa, Canada: Statistics Canada.

- Canada, Statistics Canada. (2008). *Aboriginal Peoples in Canada in 2006: Inuit, Metis and First Nations, 2006 Census* (Cat. No. 97-558-XIE). Ottawa, Canada: Statistics Canada. http://www.statcan.gc.ca/daily-quotidien/090116/dq090116a-eng.htm.

- Canadian International Development Agency. (2002). *The Human Development Division. Draft—CIDA Policy on Indigenous Knowledge and Sustainable Human Development*. Ottawa, Canada: CIDA.
- *Constitution Act*, 1982, being Schedule B to the Canada Act 1982 (UK), 1982, c 11.
- Corntassel, J. (2014). Our ways will continue: Indigenous approaches to sustainability. The Internationalization of Indigenous Rights: UNDRP in the Canadian Context Special Report. *Indigenous Centre for International Governance Innovation*, 65-71. Retrieved March 12, 2015 from: http://www.corntassel.net/Sustainability.pdf.
- Coulthard, G. and Simpson, L. (2014). Leanne Simpson and Glen Coulthard on Dechinta Bush University, Indigenous land-based education and embodied resurgence. *Decolonization: Indigeneity, Education and Society*. Retrieved on January 15, 2015 from: https://decolonization.wordpress.com/2014/11/26/leanne-simpson-and-glen-coulthard-on-dechinta-bush-university-indigenous-land-based-education-and-embodied-resurgence/.
- Donald, D., Glanfied, F., and G., Sterenberg (2012). Living Ethically within Conflicts of Colonial Authority and Relationality. *Journal of the Canadian Association for Curriculum Studies,* 10(1), 53-77.
- Dua, E. (2008). Thinking through anti-racism and Indigeneity in Canada. *The Ardent Review,* 1, 31-35.
- Earth Mother Water Walk (n.d.). Retrieved on May 1, 2015 from: http://www.motherearthwaterwalk.com/?page_id=11.
- Ermine, W. and Hampton, E. (2007). Miyo-Mahcihowin: Self-determination, social determinants, and Indigenous health. In B. Campbell and G. Marchildon (Eds.), *Medicare: Facts, Myths, Problems and Promise* (pp. 342-348). Toronto, Canada: James Lorimer & Company.
- Grande, S. (2004). *Red Pedagogy: Native American Social and Political Thought*. Lanham, MD: Roman & Littlefield.
- Gomes, T., Young Leon, A., and Brown, L. (2013). Indigenous health leadership: Protocols, policy and practice. *Pimatisiwin: A Journal of Indigenous and Aboriginal Community Health,* 11(3), 565-578.
- Gruenewald, D. (2009). Place, survivance and white remembrance: A decolonizing challenge to rural education in mobile modernity. *Journal of Research in Rural Education*, 24(10). Retrieved on December 7, 2009, from http://jrre.psu.edu/articles/24-10.pdf.
- Ling, S. and Lindsay, S. (2014). *Knowing the Land Beneath Our Feet*. [Video file]. Retrieved on May 7, 2015 from: http://fnsp.arts.ubc.ca/research-resources/knowing-the-land-beneath-our-feet/.
- Hare, J., Madden, B., Higgins, M., Young Leon, A., Wager, A., and Mashon, D. (n.d.) *Teaching for Indigenous Education* (homepage). Retrieved from: http://www.indigenouseducation.educ.ubc.ca/.
- Higgins, M. (2013). *Dr. Susan Dion: Introducing and Disrupting the "Perfect Stranger"* [video file]. Retrieved from: http://vimeo.com/59543958.
- Hill, D. M. (2008). *Traditional Medicine in Contemporary Contexts: Protecting and Respecting Indigenous Knowledge and Medicine*. Ottawa, Canada: National Aboriginal Health Organization. Retrieved on January 15, 2015 from: http://www.naho.ca/documents/naho/english/pdf/research_tradition.pdf.
- Hunt, S. (2013). *Relationships as Laws*. [Video file]. Retrieved from https://intercontinentalcry.org/name-relationships-law-sarah-hunt-tedxvictoria-2013/.
- Kelm, M. (1999). *Decolonizing Bodies: Aboriginal Health and Healing in British Columbia, 1900-50*. Vancouver: UBC Press.
- Kelm, M. and Lorna Townsend (Eds.) (2006). *In the Days of our Grandmothers: A Reader on Aboriginal Womens History*. Toronto: University of Toronto Press.
- Kirkness, V. J. and Barnhardt, R. (1991). First Nations and higher education: The four R's—Respect, Relevance, Reciprocity, Responsibility. *Journal of American Indian Education*, 30(3), 1-15.
- Kimmerer Wall, R., (2013). *Braiding Sweetgrass: Indigenous Wisdom, Scientific Knowledge, and the Teachings of Plants*. Minneapolis, Minnesota. Milkweed Editions.
- Kuokkanen, R. (2008). What is hospitality in the academy? Epistemic ignorance and the (im)possible gift. *Review of Education, Pedagogy, and Cultural Studies, 30*(1), 60-82.
- La Duke, W. (2011). *Durable and Respectable Economics*. [Video file]. Retrieved from http://tv.powwows.com/video/2015/05/04/winona-laduke-durable-and-respectable-economics/.
- Lindberg, T. (2004). Not my sister: What feminists can learn about sisterhood from Indigenous women. *Canadian Journal of Women and the Law*, 16, 342-352.
- Indian and Northern Affairs Canada 2013. Information: First Nations People of Canada. Retrieved from http://www.aadnc-aandc.gc.ca/DAM/DAM-INTER-HQ/STAGING/texte-text/ach_lr_ks_rrds_fnpc_1302786002220_eng.pdf, accessed April 27, 2015.
- McAdam, S. (2015). *Nationhood Interrupted: Revitalizing Nêhiyaw Legal Systems*. Saskatoon, Saskatchewan. Purich Publishing.
- McAdam, S. (2012). *Nehiyaw Weyeswewna (Cree Laws)—Revitalizing Okicitaw*. [video file]. Retrieved from: https://www.youtube.com/watch?v=pKJ4mW5urgU.
- McLeod, N. (2007). *Cree Narrative Memory: From Treaties to Contemporary Times*. Saskatoon, Canada: Purich.

- Milloy, J. (1999). *A National Crime: The Canadian Government and the Residential School System 1879 to 1986*. Manitoba, Canada: University of Manitoba Press.

- Nason, D. (2014). We hold our hands up: On Indigenous women's love and resistance. In the Kino-nda-niimi Collective (Eds). *The Winter We Danced: Voices from the Past, the Future and Idle No More Movement*. Winnipeg, Arbeiter Ring Publishing. pp. 186-190.

- Nelson, M. (2013). The hydromytholoy of the Anishnaabeg: Will Mishipizhu survive climate change, or is he creating it? In J. Doerfler, H. K. Stark, and N. J. Sinclair (Eds.), *Centering Anishinaabeg Studies: Understanding the World through Stories* (pp. 213–236). Winnipeg, Canada: University of Manitoba Press.

- Oleman, G. (2010). Elder. *BCIT Aboriginal Services: Traditional Sweat Lodge*. Retrieved from: https://www.youtube.com/watch?v=BqT91dKHKzg.

- Regan, P. (2011). *Unsettling the Settler Within: Indian Residential Schools, Truth Telling and Reconciliation in Canada*. Vancouver, Canada: UBC Press.

- Schissel, B. and Wotherspoon, T. (2003). *The Legacy of School for Aboriginal People*. New York, NY: Oxford University Press.

- Simpson, L. (2011). *Dancing on Our Turtle's Back: Stories of Nishnaabeg Re-Creation, Resurgence and a New Emergence*. Winnipeg, Canada: Arbeiter Ring.

- Simpson, L. and Manitowabi, E. (2013). Theorizing resurgence from within Nishnaabeg thought. In J. Doerfler, H. K. Stark, and N. J. Sinclair (Eds.), *Centering Anishinaabeg Studies: Understanding the World through Stories* (pp. 279-296). Winnipeg, Canada: University of Manitoba Press.

- Simpson, L. (2015). Land as pedagogy: Nishnaabeg intelligence and rebellious transformation. *Decolonization: Indigeneity, Education and Society*. Vol. 3, No. 3, 2014, pp. 1-25.

- Smith, A. (2005). Native American feminism, sovereignty, and social change. *Feminist Studies*, 31(1), 116-132.

- St. Denis, V. (2007). Aboriginal education and anti-racism education: Building alliances across cultural and racial identity. *Canadian Journal of Native Education,* 30(4), 1068-1092.

- Waldram, J.B., Herring, D.A., and Young, T.K. (Eds.). (2006). *Aboriginal Health in Canada*. Toronto, ON: University of Toronto Press.

- Vizenor, G. and MacKay, J. (2013). Constitutional narrative: A conversation with Gerald Vizenor. In J. Doerfler, H. K. Stark, and N. J. Sinclair (Eds.), *Centering Anishinaabeg Studies: Understanding the World Through Stories* (pp. 133-148). Winnipeg, Canada: University of Manitoba Press.

- Wotherspoon, T. and Schissel, B., (2000). Marginalization, decolonization and voice: Prospects for Aboriginal education in Canada. In Y. Lenoir, W. Hunter, D. Hodgkinson, P. de Broucker, and A. Dolbec (Eds.), *A Pan-Canadian Education Research Agenda* (pp. 193-214). Ottawa, Canada: Canadian Society for Studies in Education.

- Young, A. (2006). *Elders' Teachings on Indigenous leadership: Leadership Is a Gift* (Unpublished master's thesis). University of British Columbia, Vancouver.

- Young, A. (2015). *Indigenous Elders' Pedagogy for Land-Based Education Programs: Geeshee kan' duk Cedar Pedagogical* (Unpublished thesis). University of British Columbia, Vancouver.

- Young Leon, A. and Nadeau, D. (2014). Embodied pedagogy: All our relations. In Ritenburg, H., Young Leon, A., Linds, W., Nadeau. D., Goulet, L., Kovach, M., and Marshall, M. Embodying decolonization: Methodologies and indigenization. *AlterNative: An International Journal of Indigenous Peoples*, 10(1), 67-80.

- Young Leon, A. and Nadeau, D. (Forthcoming). Moving with water: Water relationships and responsibilities. In R. Wong and D. Christian (Eds.), *Downstream: A Water Anthology*. Wilfred Laurier University Press. Waterloo, ON, pp. 149-180.

This vignette was prepared by Mary Kostandy.

Verna Kirkness was born in 1935 in Fisher Reserve, Manitoba. She lived with her mother Gladys Grace Williams, her stepfather Fred Kirkness, her uncle Jim, and her grandmother, who instilled in her a love of the Cree language.

Kirkness had always aspired to become a teacher especially. Her dream came true at the age of 18 as she began teaching in a one-room school in Reedy Creek. Desiring wider experiences in Aboriginal schooling, she went on to teach in different residential schools. There she noticed how Aboriginal students identified with Aboriginal teachers like herself. She sought to instill pride in Aboriginal students concerning their heritage.

Verna became a high school counsellor in Winnipeg, looking after those students who were living with non-Aboriginal host families. Among her many duties were encouraging students to stay in school, helping them prepare for a job interview, showing them how to manage money, and finding suitable homes for them. She then became a supervisor of schools, overseeing more than 200 teachers. Noticing a lack of Indigenous resources, she worked on creating a supplement for social studies in Grades 1 to 3, which led to her job as a consultant of cross-cultural education at the Department of Curriculum and Instruction. She started the Manitoba Native Bilingual Program in schools to ease the transition of Aboriginal pre-school children from Native to English language using a "language shift" method that included translating nursery rhymes into Cree and Ojibway. After evaluating the bilingual program, she observed that Aboriginal students who completed it had a stronger sense of self, which confirmed her understanding that Aboriginal students thrive when rooted in their culture and identity.

In 1971, Verna headed the education section of the Manitoba Indian Brotherhood (now the Assembly of Manitoba Chiefs) to advocate for the Indian control of Indian education. She participated in writing the position paper *Wahbung: Our Tomorrows.* This paper resulted in an agreement stating that the federal government, in addition to paying tuition fees, had to pay the province an extra amount, at the request of Band Council, for each Aboriginal child who attends a public school in order to develop Native resources and to hire Native teacher aides. In 1972, Verna participated in developing and later implementing the landmark National Policy of Indian Control of Indian Education.

Verna decided to further her education in 1973 by attending the University of Manitoba, where she completed a B.A. (1974), a B.Ed. (1976), and a Master of Education (1980). She joined the University of British Columbia (UBC) in 1981 as Assistant Professor in the Administrative, Adult, and Higher Education (AAHE) Department and as the Supervisor of the Native Indian Teacher Education Program (NITEP). She also created the Ts'kel Graduate Program. Students chose the name "Ts'kel" because it means "Golden Eagle" in the Halq'eleylem language, a phrase that symbolizes soaring higher.

In her position as the first Director of UBC's First Nations House of Learning, she helped raise funds to build the First Nations Longhouse, which has served as a "home away from home" for many Indigenous students. She authored many publications, including her own autobiography. She received many awards, including the Gold Eagle feather award, the Order of Canada, and honorary degrees from the University of Manitoba, Mount St. Vincent University, the University of Western Ontario, the University of British Columbia, and St. Johns College.

References

- Kirkness, V. J. (1964-2009). Verna J. Kirkness fonds. University of British Columbia Archives. Vancouver, BC. Finding aid available at http://www.library.ubc.ca/archives/u_arch/kirkness.pdf

- Kirkness, V. J. (2013). *Creating Space: My Life and Work in Indigenous Education.* Winnipeg: University of Manitoba Press.

- Kirkness, Verna J., and Ray Barnhardt. (2001). First Nations and Higher Education: The Four R's—Respect, Relevance, Reciprocity, Responsibility. In *Education Across Cultures: A Contribution to Dialogue Among Civilizations.* Hong Kong: Comparative Education Research Centre, University of Hong Kong. Published in English and Chinese.

- Kirkness, Verna J., and Jo-ann Archibald. (2001). *The First Nations Longhouse: Our Home Away from Home.* Vancouver: UBC Press.

- Kirkness, Verna J. (Ed.), (1994). *Khot-La-Cha: The Autobiography of Chief Simon Baker.* Vancouver: Douglas and McIntyre.

- Kirkness, Verna J., and Sheena Selkirk Bowman. (1992). *First Nations and Schools: Triumphs and Struggles.* Toronto: Canadian Education Association. Published in English and French.

- Sealey, D. Bruce, and Verna J. Kirkness (Eds.), (1973). *Indians Without Tipis: A Resouce Book.* Winnipeg: W. Clare.

Photo: Verna Kirkness in 2013, as photographed by Ian McCausland. Courtesy of the University of Manitoba Press.

"Regarding the Pain of Others" by Sundus Abdul Hadi, an Iraqi-Canadian multimedia artist.

10

War, Diaspora, and Learning
Arab Iraqi Refugee Women

This chapter sets forth an analysis of Arab Iraqi refugee women's learning and work in the context of diasporic existence and the labour market in Canada. We examine Arab Iraqi refugee women's experiences of the War on Terror and how its policies of securitization, border controls, and anti-refugee sentiments have served to deny Iraqi women access to learning and labour markets. We also analyze the ways in which Canada's anti-terrorism measures and immigration, refugee, and citizenship policies in recent years contribute to creating and maintaining racialized gendered violence. Using a feminist anti-racist, anti-colonial perspective, we argue that Iraqi women's access to learning and labour force participation is essential to restore opportunities lost through war and violence in Iraq, displacement in refugee camps, and resettlement in Canada.

Sajedeh Zahraei and Shahrzad Mojab

We are two refugee women who survived and succeeded against all odds despite displacement, exile, and resettlement. We are from Iran; I, Sajedeh, am an Arab-Iranian and I, Shahrzad, belong to the dominant nation (I am Persian). We are both survivors of the brutality of the Iran-Iraq war of the 1980s, and continue to be deeply affected by its enduring political and cultural consequences. However, it was the occupation of Iraq in 2003 by the imperialist powers, led by the United States, which reconnected us to the plight of Iraqi women struggling to live amidst conditions of war, militarization, and displacement. Sajedeh has witnessed the ways in which war interrupts family ties and permanently inscribes belonging (or not) on the bodies of the living and the dead. Our past experiences have stimulated our intellectual and political curiosity to trace, interrogate, and analyze the displacement of Arab Iraqi refugee women and their difficulties in settling in Canada.

The chapter begins with an overview of Iraqi women's status and citizenship during periods of war, economic sanctions, and occupation, with a particular focus on examining the gendered impacts of these historical events in Iraq's recent history. We then trace Iraqi women's displacement as war refugees following the 2003 invasion and occupation of Iraq and review Iraqi refugee women's everyday experiences with the settlement process in Canada. Finally, we show how the study of women refugees and war migrants in the context of post-9/11 Canada presents us with new theoretical challenges, ones that require the expansion of the gendered and racialized analysis of learning and labour market participation to include the realm of state structural violence and securitization. Securitization is now a central feature of the re-organization of state policy, shifting investment priorities from public services to state security infrastructure, policing, and crime prevention; the tightening of immigration regulations and border security; and enhanced surveillance of public spaces and institutions. The crisis of national security is coupled with a more general crisis of economic and social insecurity that has further deepened social and economic inequality.

Women of Iraq: A Historical Sketch of War and Occupation

Iraqi women have been active participants in the public sphere since the late 19th century when they struggled to establish the first women's Grammar and High School in Iraq in 1899, followed by the establishment of two other schools for women in 1911 and 1913. Ironically, British occupiers in 1918 discouraged further development of schools for girls in Iraq, arguing that "the people are fanatic and do not want to send their daughters to school" (Daud, 1958, cited in Ismael and Ismael, 2000). Despite British and religious opposition, however, Iraqi women's involvement in the public sphere continued through the establishment of women's associations and this involvement expanded internationally through their participation in regional and international conferences from the 1930s onward (Ismael & Ismael, 2000).

A military-led revolution in 1958 toppled the monarchy in Iraq and was followed by the establishment of the left-oriented government of Abd Al-Karim Qasim, who instituted a major gender-egalitarian reform of family law in 1959. The personal status courts under the 1959 law replaced the Shari'a courts. Qasim's government was overthrown by a coup led by the Ba'ath Party in 1963. The new government of Abdul Salem Aref caved under religious pressure and restored the inheritance rules and a few other features of the pre-reform law. However, the key features of the 1959 family law remained operative and further reforms were added following another Ba'ath coup in 1968 (Ismael and Ismael, 2000).

Iraq's modernization campaign under the Ba'ath regime was pursued from the 1960s until the start of the Iran-Iraq war, when militarization became the central focus of the government. The Ba'ath regime also adopted a strategy to undermine Iraq's traditional kinship structure by focusing on women's involvement in the public sphere through education, work, unionization, and women's associations. In 1977-1978, female enrolment in primary education was 37.4%, with 29.6% female enrolment in secondary education, and 31% female enrolment in university and other post-secondary education. The proportion of women's participation in government bodies was 15.4% in 1977 (Ismael, 2004).

The Ba'ath party's state created a large middle class dependent on the existence of the state. Their social mobility was dependent on education and membership in the Ba'ath Party (Ismael, 2004). State control of the media and suppression of opposition parties also solidified the state's authoritarian rule, commonly referred to as the "Republic of Fear" in Iraq (Al-Khalil, 1989). As part of this program, the Ba'ath Party dismantled most independent women's organizations that had existed prior to 1968 and established the General Federation of Iraqi Women (GFIW) in 1972 to help implement state policies and legal reforms, and to lobby for further reforms in the personal status code. The Iraqi Provisional Constitution of 1970 declared all citizens equal before the law and adopted an education law making primary education mandatory for both sexes. Saddam Hussein came to power in 1979 and despite the general political repression under his rule he generally maintained a more progressive approach to women's rights, motivated by his desire to subordinate traditional tribal and religious forces (Kiddie, 2007). As a result of Iraqi women's ongoing involvement in the public sphere and these gender-egalitarian reforms, Iraqi women were among the most educated in the whole region and they were active at all levels of state institutions (Al-Ali, 2005; Zangana, 2007).

Iraqi women's social and economic conditions changed drastically during the devastating Iran-Iraq war that lasted for eight years (1980-88). With men being deployed in large numbers to fight the war, women took on the vast majority of jobs outside the home while also maintaining their households and raising their children (Al-Ali, 2007; Zangana, 2007). Although women had carried Iraqi society forward during the war years, they were encouraged to leave their jobs and return to work at home in order to free up jobs for returning soldiers when the war ended in 1988.

During the 1991 Gulf war and its UN-imposed sanctions, women again shouldered the responsibility to compensate for the lack of infrastructure and to sustain their families through the various calamities that ensued. This was particularly the case for poor and low-income women in urban and rural areas who struggled for survival in the face of malnutrition, disease, and child mortality. The economic hardships and the rise in the number of widows and female-headed households also resulted in a rise in prostitution for daily survival. Widespread unemployment, high inflation, and generalized impoverishment have contributed to increased poverty and hunger (Al-Ali, 2005).

In addition, Iraqi women were faced with shifts towards more conservative gender relations and ideologies in the social and cultural fabric of Iraqi society. Many girls and young women were pulled out of schools and there was a steady increase in illiteracy rates from 8% in 1985 to 45% in 1995. The economic crisis, high unemployment, and elimination of previously available supports, such as child care and free transportation to work, pushed many women to return to the home simply because they could no longer afford to go to work. Young women and girls also confronted increased social conservatism as demonstrated by a changing dress code that pressured them to wear the hijab or Abayyah; higher emphasis on preserving their reputation and family honour; and marriage at an earlier age (Al-Ali, 2005; Ismael, 2004). This shift towards more conservative moral values was particularly harmful to women's status as the regime began to institute more conservative patriarchal policies to appease tribal chiefs and religious leaders. As a result, we have seen a deterioration in all aspects of Iraqi women's rights and social citizenship—education, employment, income, and family and gender relations—during the eight years of the Iran-Iraq war, the 1991 post-Gulf war, and the sanctions regime in Iraq.

The Iran-Iraq war, followed by the dismantling of Iraq's basic infrastructure after the Gulf War, combined with sanctions, set the stage for the further deterioration of Iraqi women's status during the post-2003 Iraq Occupation. The general chaos and lack of security that ensued following the 2003 invasion of Iraq later extended into sectarian violence and targeted kidnappings, assaults, and killings of specific groups of people—including ethnic-religious minorities, professionals, and women. Professional working women and university students were particularly targeted and threatened with kidnappings and assaults if they did not wear the hijab or convert to Islam if they were Christian. In many cases, professional women working in hospitals, universities, and other public institutions or government ministries were actually kidnapped and killed, not just for not wearing the hijab but simply for working (Al-Ali & Pratt, 2006 and 2011). Since 2003, Iraqi women have lost many of the gains they had made since the 1960s, including being pushed out of their jobs, schools, and universities and back into their homes (Women for Women International, 2008). As indicated by a United Nations Inter-Agency Analysis (2009), net primary school enrolment decreased from 91% to 86% between 1990 and 2007, and this rate was particularly low at 70% for girls in rural areas. Similarly, illiteracy rates were much higher for women at 24% as compared to men at 11%. Employment and labour force participation show similar trends, with only 18% of women being employed or looking for employment, and just 17% of women participating in the labour force (United Nations Inter-Agency Analysis, 2009). Iraqi women are struggling to meet their basic needs on a day-to-day basis under difficult conditions, including a lack of any civil infrastructure, increased gender-based violence, Islamization and strict patriarchal tribal values, a rise in prostitution and sex-trafficking, and deteriorating health conditions, to name a few (Al-Ali, 2007 and 2013; Amnesty International, 2009; Human Rights Watch, 2011; Oxfam International, 2009; United Nations Inter-Agency Analysis, 2010).

Since the 2003 U.S.-led invasion, between 4.5 to 4.7 million Iraqis were displaced. Around 2.8 million were internally displaced and the remaining 2 million primarily became refugees in Syria and Jordan. Syria and Jordan are not signatories to the 1951 Convention, and yet they have absorbed the largest share of Iraqi asylum-seekers since 2003. Iraqi asylum-seekers in these countries are unable to work legally and are not granted permanent residency status. They live precarious lives in fear of deportation, having to survive on their own savings while awaiting resettlement to other countries. The vast majority have already exhausted their savings and live in poor neighbourhoods with limited access to health care, education, or other necessary supports. They have had to resort to a variety of means to survive, including working illegally, begging on the streets, prostitution, and child labour. Some have given up and have returned to Iraq out of desperation, bereft of any other options (Cohen, 2007; Harper, 2008; Refugees International, 2010).

Overview of Recent Canadian Immigration and Citizenship Policy Changes

To comprehend the processes of social exclusion of Arab Iraqi refugee women, we have undertaken a review of Canadian policies developed in response to the terrorist attacks in the U.S. on September 11, 2001. Canada has implemented a series of anti-terrorism measures, including the Anti-terrorism Act (Bill C-36) of 2001 (http://www.justice.gc.ca/eng/cj-jp/ns-sn/act-loi.html); the enactment of security certificates under the Immigration and Refugee Protection Act (IRPA) (http://www.publicsafety. gc.ca/cnt/ntnl-scrt/cntr-trrrsm/scrt-crtfcts-eng.aspx); Canada's Passenger Protect Program, 2007 (http://www.publicsafety.gc.ca/cnt/ntnl-scrt/cntr-trrrsm/pssngr-prtct/index-eng.aspx); and Beyond the Border Action Plan, 2011 (http://actionplan.gc.ca/en/content/beyond-border). These measures have had differential and severely detrimental effects on racialized communities, particularly Blacks, South Asians, Arabs, and Muslims in Canada. These effects have included increased racial profiling, unlawful detentions, torture, and deportations (Bahdi, 2003; CAF & CAIR-CAN, 2005). Canada's response to Iraqi refugee women's learning needs, desires, and dreams must be analyzed within the context of these policies.

The Canadian government has also taken drastic measures amounting to a complete overhaul of Canada's immigration, refugee determination, and citizenship policies over the past several years. The Immigration and Refugee Protection Act (IRPA) was introduced in 2002 to replace the Immigration Act of 1976 in providing the legal framework for Canada's federal immigration system. Since their election as a majority government in 2008, the Conservative government has introduced a series of legislative and regulatory changes to Canada's immigration system effectively aimed at increasing Canada's competitiveness in the new political economy. These changes mostly serve the needs of the market through privatization and the expansion of a temporary, precarious, racialized, and gendered migrant labour force. The historically racialized, gendered, and classed nature of Canadian immigration policy has been well documented by immigration historians (Backhouse, 1999; Iacovetta, 2006) as well as by feminist critical race scholars (Guo, 2006; Mojab, 1999, 2006; Ng, 1998; Ng and Shan, 2010; Thobani, 2007). Recent immigration and citizenship policy changes have further intensified the racialized, gendered, and classed inequalities while increasing the vulnerability of women to further structural and interpersonal violence, social exclusion, precarious immigration status, and deportation (Alboim and Cohl, 2012; Alaggia et al., 2009; Bhuyan et al., 2013; Bhuyan et al., 2014).

The recent immigration and citizenship policy changes affecting Iraqi refugees impinge on refugee determination, refugee sponsorship, settlement programming, family reunification, health care benefits, and access to permanent residency and citizenship. In 2012, the federal government significantly reduced health care benefits available to different groups of refugees through cuts to the Interim Federal Health Program.[1] Additionally, Government Assisted Refugees (GARs) and Privately Sponsored Refugees (PSRs) face increasingly limited supports, including general low social assistance rates, overall reductions to settlement services, and reductions in terms of the duration and types of assistance provided to GARs (OCASI, 2011).

Canada's Response to Iraqi Refugees

Since 2007, the government of Canada has made a commitment to increase its refugee targets in the Middle East to allow for more resettlement of Iraqi refugees. Since 2002, over 11,000 Iraqi refugees have been resettled in Canada (CIC, 2010). Between 2009 and 2011, 2,500 Iraqi refugees were accepted annually under the private sponsorship program. An additional 8,600 Iraqi refugees were to be resettled to Canada between 2011 and 2013 (CTV News, Oct. 23, 2010). However, refugee and human rights advocates have criticized Canada for not doing enough to address the Iraqi refugee crisis. The refugee resettlement process is fraught with bureaucratic delays, an inadequate refugee determination process, and backlogs within the system (CCR, 2006; Keung, June 21, 2011). In 2006, the Canadian Council for Refugees (CCR) documented a number of Iraqi private sponsorship cases refused at Damascus. The CCR undertook this analysis following a series of concerns raised by private sponsors at CCR meetings and CCR's finding that about half of Iraqis sponsored by a private group in Canada were refused by a Canadian visa officer (CCR, 2006). CCR's analysis of 11 cases found many problematic issues with respect to negative decisions, including: lack of proper reasons for rejection, lack of consideration of Iraq's context when assessing the credibility of claims, misinterpretation of the Convention refugee definition, failure to consider all relevant grounds for concluding the refugee claim decisions, and failure to consider Country of Asylum Class. CCR's analysis of the refusal decisions concluded that there was a general attitude of suspicion towards the applicants' accounts, with no sufficient objective explanations provided, calling into question the quality of decision making and the inadequate understanding of the legal requirements for refugee determination (CCR, 2006, p. 6). It is important to note that the commitment to resettle 20,000 Iraqi refugees has resulted in the resettlement of only about 12,000 mostly privately sponsored refugees at no cost to the government. The timeframe for the resettlement—which was supposed to have been completed by 2013—has now been extended to 2018.

Iraqi Refugee Women in Canada: Processes of Social Exclusion

Iraqi refugee women's resettlement experiences in Canada are closely intertwined with the everyday symbolic and cultural violence they experience in their day-to-day interactions, as well as the structural violence of immigration and refugee policies manifesting in their lives. In this section, we will discuss the different ways in which these forces have impacted Arab Iraqi women's access to learning and labour force participation.

In Sajedeh Zahraei's study of Iraqi refugee women conducted in 2011-2012 in Toronto (2014), access to employment and learning emerged as a key area that had direct implications for Arab Iraqi women's sense of belonging and community integration. Most of the women interviewed (all quotations below come from those interviews), expressed their frustration in the face of lack of access to jobs and shared experiences of racism and discrimination in their attempts to gain access to education and employment in Toronto. As a young, aspiring professionally trained engineer, the predominant metaphor in Ahlam's story is that of her "wanting to build herself" and the structural forces that have prevented her from doing so. The continuity of violence and trauma in her life is directly related to her not having a chance to procure a job and work in her chosen career:

> I get really frustrated...for instance now, my staying at home, is really frustrating me...In that...I DON'T WANT TO STAY AT HOME! ... I DON'T WANT THAT ANYMORE. I WANT TO BUILD MYSELF. When am I going to get a chance to build myself?...What we suffered in Iraq stopped us... What we went and suffered in Syria, that you had to work without the government's knowledge, this...I mean...affects you negatively...Then you come here and also ... also ...there are numerous conditions and numerous barriers that tie you down until you get a job.

Ahlam clearly articulates the continuity of structural violence and how her suffering, which began in Iraq, continued in Syria and now in Canada. Her story highlights how the structural violence of war, displacement, restrictive refugee policies, and systemic processes of social exclusion—which have travelled with her across various borders in search of safety and security—have prevented her from exercising her substantive citizenship rights of access to employment, income, and participation in public life.

All the women participating in the study shared similar stories. These stories illustrate a significant drop in their social and economic status as a result of state policies under Saddam Hussein's regime, particularly during the Iran-Iraq War, the Gulf War, the UN economic sanctions, and the more recent U.S.-led invasion and occupation of Iraq. Most of the women interviewed were university- educated and came from middle-class families that place a high importance on women's education and careers. Now, however, they were all living in conditions of poverty, unable to access jobs in their chosen careers and experiencing racism, discrimination, and social exclusion on many levels. Many of the study participants emphasized the role of the historical ideological constructions and stereotypes of Arabs and Muslims as "terrorists" in shaping their everyday lives and limiting their social participation and community integration. Iraqi refugee women shared vivid examples of experiences of racism and discrimination, which ranged from being called a terrorist and getting beaten up by classmates; to being ignored and pushed aside by their teachers at school; to being denied access to social assistance benefits and entitlements; and, finally, to being denied family reunification through stringent sponsorship policies and bureaucratic dehumanizing practices on the part of immigration officials.

Similar to Ahlam, Amani describes her exposure to the violence of racism and discrimination as being "shot down" every time she tries to get up. She describes how her experiences with racism and discrimination post 9/11 and the Iraq war impacted her work and her everyday interactions with people as follows:

> ...It kept on shooting me down ....because every time I wanted to get up and I wanted to try something, like apply for a job, I get shot down. Every time I wanted to do something, people would always come with something. And like I got to a point where I don't want to go to work, I don't want to walk outside, because it was like, Oh my God [sigh], here I am gone go now... I'm gone get attention.

Amani also describes one of the biggest challenges facing the Iraqi community in Toronto today as the experience of being excluded:

> Exclusion! Not being a part of the Canadian society. There's a lot of that. … It's not always about speaking English. Oh, if you don't speak English, there's a lot of smart people that don't speak English that still have a lot of skills and abilities but, but it's, it's getting them into the system. It's, it's including them. There's not a lot of that. You know, it's hard to get people even volunteering experience.

Amani explains further that she sees this type of exclusion and lack of opportunity as a contributing factor explaining why a lot of Iraqi people give up trying to establish themselves and remain on welfare or long-term disability; as she states, "every time they try, the door claps in their face" so they are just giving up trying:

> there is so many people I have met from my community … that are saying forget it. What's the point of working in Canada when nobody recognizes you? Even if you're given an opportunity you get shut down. You stay in a LINC school for three or four months and then you stay home because nobody wants to hire you. No one wants to give you the opportunity because of your strong accent, because of where you're from.

Another form of social exclusion that commonly cropped up in the interviews with Iraqi refugee women involved withholding information and denial of access to programs and services, as illustrated by Yesra's case. Yesra is an Iraqi refugee woman who recently came to Canada with her husband and two young children. Yesra shares her experience in which a welfare worker withholds information from her husband and denies him a training program:

> We met with the welfare worker once and we could tell that she did not like us, did not want to give us any information. My husband is an engineer and he asked her if there were any training programs he could take. She just told him no and that's it. She did not provide any other information.

Yesra had been asking her welfare worker to provide her with approval for a training program that would enable her to have her own home daycare. She described her experience with the welfare worker as extremely demoralizing. Yesra felt that the worker was denying her an opportunity to do something that could lead to employment by withholding the funding for the training program with no explanation and by not responding to her many calls requesting follow-up. Social service providers and welfare workers can exercise a great deal of power and discretion in deciding who gets access to information, training, and other resources that have the potential to facilitate more successful community integration and access to social citizenship rights. As Bhuyan (2010) has argued, "Social welfare benefits as social entitlements are crucial aspects of citizenship and a contested site of who belongs and is fully endowed with their rights and protections offered by the state" (p. 65). In the context of service provision to Iraqi refugee women, the regulation of citizenship has taken the form of withholding information and denial of access to services and resources. Service providers' decisions can be informed by their assumption that refugees are defrauding and abusing the system (Mirchandani and Chan, 2007). This is a predominant perception of refugees in contemporary Canada, shaping its neo-liberal immigration and refugee policy reforms.

War, Migration, and Learning: Implications for Adult Education Research

The experiences of Iraqi refugee women outlined in this chapter challenge notions of "freedom" and "democracy" that were used by the imperialist forces led by the United States as justifications for the invasion of Iraq. Our historical review has shown that, on the contrary, the 2003 invasion of Iraq delivered nothing but chaos and lack of security, and caused the regression of Iraqi society in all aspects of life, in particular unleashing religious and sectarian violence against women. Several Iraqi refugee women participating in the research study discussed above were young professionals from highly educated middle-class backgrounds who were forced out of the public sphere for their safety and security. In addition to gender-based violence, the women highlighted the fundamental changes in Iraqi society as a result of the general state of lawlessness that took the form of kidnappings and murders, and changing societal values with respect to religious and gender relations that ensued after the 2003 invasion.

Arab Iraqi refugee women traversed multiple national, community, and familial boundaries to resettle in Canada. However, as we have discussed above, the lives of these women have been entangled in the "War on Terror" policy directive. Canada has extensively reformed immigration policy and has introduced new policies in order to realign the social welfare services with market and security demands. This has resulted in extensive privatization and cut-backs in social services and the transfer of responsibility for public welfare onto communities and individuals. This shift has also profoundly impacted employment and resettlement services, including immigrant and refugee women's access to training programs and the labour market. Securitization and the global transformation of economic and social life in Canada can theoretically and politically be seen as a continuation of structural violence in Iraqi women's lives. The patriarchal imperialist interventions and their intimate interconnections with nationalist patriarchal institutions and tribal, traditional, and religious fundamentalist forces have militarized and securitized Iraqi society and displaced millions of its inhabitants. Ironically, these same forces interrupted the aspirations of Iraqi women even after "liberation" and in the context of the promised "freedom" and "democracy." This means that Iraqi women's lives continue to be entangled with the complex web of global capitalist patriarchal systems of oppression, dispossession, and exploitation.

This political and economic context necessitates a renewed research agenda with regard to the study of women, migration, learning, and work. As discussed above, there is a body of literature that extensively covers the gendered and racialized nature of learning and migration. However, as war-driven migrants, in particular women, are arriving in Canada, our research intention should go beyond exposing barriers to access and participation, processes of exclusion, or the limits of citizenship rights. We need to raise research questions that focus our attention on history, on the structural impediments such as patriarchy, racism, capitalism, imperialism, fundamentalism, and local and global policy enactors. Immigrant and refugee women arrive in a Canada that is mired in this (dis)order. As anti-racist and critical feminist activists and educators, how should we intervene, analyze, and explain the experience of displaced and dispossessed women? Furthermore, what are the limits in our theoretical approach and where is the place for the shift in our thinking? We are closing this chapter with these reflections and questions to point out the urgency of digging deeper in order to advance our thinking and practices on the topics of war, migration, learning, and work.

Endnote

[1] There has been a strong ongoing opposition to these cuts and a recent federal court ruled these cuts to be unconstitutional. The federal government is pursuing an appeal of this ruling and refugees continue to experience significant access barriers to health care (CCR, 2015).

References

- Al-Ali, N. (2005). Reconstructing gender: Iraqi women between dictatorship, war, sanctions and occupation. *Third World Quarterly*, 26(4-5), 739-758.

- Al-Ali, N. (2007). *Iraqi Women: Untold Stories from 1948 to the Present*. London and New York: Zed books.

- Al-Ali, N. (2013). The forgotten story: Women and gender relations 10 years after. Costs of war project, Accessed from http://costsofwar.org/article/did-wars-liberate-afghan-and-iraqi-women

- Al-Ali, N. and Pratt, N. (2006). Women in Iraq: Beyond the rhetoric. *Middle East Report (MERIP)*, 239, 18-23.

- Al-Ali, N. and Pratt, N. (2011). Conspiracy of near silence: Violence against Iraqi women. *Middle East Report (MERIP)*, 258, 34-37.

- Alaggia, R., Regher, C., and Rishchynsk, G. (2009). Intimate partner violence and immigration laws in Canada: How far have we come? *International Journal of Law and Psychiatry*, 32(6), 335-341.

- Alboim, N. and Cohl, K. (2012). *Shaping the Future: Canada's Rapidly Changing Immigration Policies*. Maytree Foundation. Retrieved from http://maytree.com/spotlight/shaping-the-future-canadas-rapidly-changing-immigration-policies.html.

- Al-Khalil, S. (1989). *Republic of Fear: The Politics of Modern Iraq*. Berkeley: University of California Press.

- Amnesty International (2009). Trapped by violence: women in Iraq. Retrieved from http://www.amnesty.org/en/library/asset/MDE14/005/2009/en/e6cda898-fa16-4944-af74-f3efc0cf6a4d/mde140052009en.pdf.

- Backhouse, C. (1999). *Colour-Coded: A Legal History of Racism in Canada, 1900-1950*. Toronto: University of Toronto Press.

- Bahdi, R. (2003). No exit: Racial profiling and Canada's war against terrorism. *Osgoode Hall Law Journal*, 41(2-3), 293-316.

- Bhuyan, R. (2010). Reconstructing citizenship in a global economy: How restricting immigrants from welfare undermines social rights for U.S. citizens. *Journal of Sociology and Social Welfare*, 37(2), 63-86.

- Bhuyan, R., Osborn, B.J., and Juanico Cruz, J.F. (2013). Unprotected and unrecognized: The ontological insecurity of migrants who are denied protection from domestic violence in their home countries and as refugee claimants in Canada. *CERIS Working Paper* No. 96. CERIS–The Ontario Metropolis Centre, Toronto. Retrieved from http://www.ceris.metropolis.net/wp-content/uploads/2013/02/CWP_96_Bhuyan_Osborne_Cruz.pdf.

- Bhuyan, R., Osborn, B.J., Zahraei, S., and Tarshis, S. (2014). *Unprotected, Unrecognized: Canadian Immigration Policy and Violence against Women, 2008-2013*. Retrieved from http://www.migrantmothersproject.com/wp-content/uploads/2012/10/MMP-Policy-Report-Final-Nov-14-2014.pdf.

- Canadian Arab Federation (CAF) and Canadian Council on American Islamic Relations (CAIR-CAN). (2005). *Brief on the Review of the Anti-Terrorism Act Justice, Human Rights, Public Safety and National Security.* Retrieved from http://www.caircan.ca/downloads/CCC-RAA.pdf.
- Canadian Council for Refugees (CCR). (2006). *Analysis of a Small Number of Iraqi Private Sponsorship Applications Refused at Damascus.* Retrieved from http://ccrweb.ca/IraqiPSRrefusals.pdf.
- Canadian Council for Refugees (CCR). (2015). *Refugee Health Survey by Province and by Category.* Retrieved from: http://ccrweb.ca/sites/ccrweb.ca/files/ccr-refugee-health-survey-public.pdf.
- Citizenship and Immigration Canada (CIC). (October 23, 2010). *News Release–Canada to Resettle More Iraqi Refugees.* Retrieved http://www.cic.gc.ca/english/department/media/releases/2010/2010-10-23.asp.
- CTV News (October 23, 2010). *Canada Extends Iraqi Refugee Program to 2013.* Retrieved from http://www.ctvnews.ca/canada-extends-iraqi-refugee-program-to-2013-1.566262.
- Cohen, R. (2007). Iraq exodus revives region's refugee trauma. *International Herald Tribune* (April 21), p. 2.
- Guo, S. (2006). Adult education in the changing context of immigration: New challenges in a new era. In Fenwick T., Tom Nesbit, and Bruce Spencer (Eds.) *Context of Adult Education: Canadian Perspectives* (pp. 198-207). Toronto: Thompson Educational Publishing Inc.
- Harper, A. (2008). Iraq's refugees: Ignored and unwanted. *International Review of the Red Cross,* 90(869), 169-190.
- Human Rights Watch. (2011). At a crossroads: Human rights in Iraq eight years after the US-led invasion. Retrieved from http://m.hrw.org/sites/default/files/reports/iraq0211W.pdf.
- Iacovetta, F. (2006). *Gatekeepers: Reshaping Immigrant Lives in Cold War Canada.* Toronto: Between the Lines.
- Ismael, J. and Ismael, S. (2000). Gender and state in Iraq. In J. Suad (Ed.), *Gender and Citizenship in the Middle East* (pp. 185-211). Syracuse, New York: Syracuse University Press.
- Ismael, S. (2004). Dismantling the Iraqi social fabric: From dictatorship through sanctions to occupation. *Journal of Comparative Family Studies,* 35(2), 333-349.
- Keung, N. (June 21, 2011). Quality of refugee decisions in question. *Toronto Star.* Retrieved from http://immlawyer.blogs.com/my_weblog/2011/06/toronto-star-article-on-overseas-refugee-decisions.html.
- Kiddie, N. (2007). *Women in the Middle East: Past and Present.* Princeton: Princeton University Press.
- Mirchandani, K. and Chan, W. (2007). *Criminalizing Race, Criminalizing Poverty: Welfare Fraud Enforcement in Canada.* Halifax: Fernwood.
- Mojab, S. (2006). Turning work and lifelong learning inside out: A Marxist-Feminist attempt. In L. Cooper and S. Walters (Eds.), *Learning/Work: Turning Work and Lifelong Learning Inside Out* (pp. 4-15). Cape Town: Human Sciences Research Council.
- Mojab, S. (1999). De-Skilling immigrant women. *Canadian Women's Studies,* 19, 123-128.
- Ng, R. and Hongxia Shan (2010). Lifelong learning as ideological practice: An analysis from the perspective of immigrant women in Canada. *International Journal of Lifelong Education,* 29(2), 169-184.
- Ng, R. (1998). Work restructuring and recolonizing third world women: An example from the garment industry. *Canadian Women Studies,* 18(1), p. 21-25.
- Ontario Council of Agencies Serving Immigrants (OCASI) (2011). Backgrounder on CIC Cuts. Retrieved from http://www.ocasi.org/sites/default/files/2011,%20OCASI%20CIC%20Cuts%20B ackgrounder.pdf.
- Oxfam International (2009). In her own words: Iraqi women talk about their greatest concerns and challenges. Retrieved from http://www.oxfam.org/sites/www.oxfam.org/files/oxfam-in-her-own-words-iraqi-women-survey-08mar2009.pdf.
- Refugees International. (2010). No way home no way to escape: The plight of Iraqi refugees and our Iraqi allies. Retrieved from http://refugeesinternational.org/policy/testimony/no-way-home-no-way-escape-plight-iraqi-refugees-and-our-iraqi-allies.
- Thobani, S. (2007). *Exalted Subjects: Studies in the Making of Race and Nation in Canada.* Toronto: University of Toronto Press.
- United Nations Inter-Agency Analysis Unit in Iraq (2009). Iraq labour force analysis 2003-2008. Retrieved from http://www.unglobalpulse.org/sites/default/files/reports/OCHAIAU%20LabourFo rceImpactsIraq.
- United Nations Inter-Agency Analysis Unit in Iraq (2010). Violence against women in Iraq fact sheet. Retrieved from http://www.peacewomen.org/assets/file/Resources/Government/vaw_vawiraq_ira q_nov252010.pdf.
- Women for Women International (2008). Stronger women, stronger nations: 2008 Iraq report—Amplifying the voices of women in Iraq. Retrieved from http://wfwmarketingimages.womenforwomen.org/news-women-for-women/assets/files/IraqReport.03.03.08.pdf.
- Zahraei, S. (2014). *Memory, Trauma, and Citizenship: Arab Iraqi Women.* Unpublished thesis, University of Toronto.
- Zangana, H. (2007). *City of Widows: An Iraqi Woman's Account of War and Resistance.* New York: Seven Stories Press.

A Take Back the Night march and candlelight vigil focused on ending violence against women.
Painting by Georgia Collins. Reproduced by permission.

11

Nonviolent Adult Education Violence and Nonviolence in the Context of Women's Adult Education in Canada

This chapter focuses on violence and nonviolence in the context of violence against women in Canada and their experience of adult education. Theories of violence and nonviolence provide the lens through which I examine educational institutions, structures, and practices; however, nonviolent education is a largely under-theorized concept. I examine violence against women, the impacts of violence on learning and Nonviolent Communication (NVC) education in order to provide insights as to how we can meet the needs of women learners who have experienced violence. I have included excerpts from interviews with women who are engaged in NVC education. There is a need to develop a theory and practice of nonviolent education, showing how NVC education in combination with feminist adult education can provide tools that support the needs of women learners.

Laurel Collins

Violence such as physical abuse, sexual assault, and systemic oppression happens around the world and can affect any individual, regardless of gender identity or sexual orientation. In other words, violence can affect women, men, or gender non-conforming/gender-queer people, whether gay, straight, bisexual, pansexual, or asexual. In this chapter, I focus on the impacts of violence against women in Canada, and in particular on the impact of this violence on adult women learners. While I believe that men need to take on responsibility for ending men's violence against women, I focus here on women's experiences and on the needs of women learners. It is also important to acknowledge that much of the systemic and instutionalized violence that women experience is a result of patriarchal structures.

Men's violence against women is an issue that affects me deeply and personally. I have experienced sexual assault, have witnessed domestic violence, and have supported close friends and family members who have been physically and/ or sexually assaulted by male partners, friends, acquaintances, and strangers. In addition, as a woman, I am continually impacted by the violence of sexism in our society, in the media, laws, institutions, cultural norms, economic policies, and representations of history. While writing this chapter, I frequently stopped to grieve the violence present in my own stories, but also to grieve the pervasiveness of women's experience of violence. Simultaneously, as a white, able-bodied, cisgendered[1] woman, I lack the direct, personal experience of how women of colour, women with disabilities, and trans women navigate the violence of these intersecting oppressions. It is impossible to do justice to all the intricacies of violence against women, and how it impacts women whose social location is made up of multiple marginalized identities. However, it is important to acknowledge the history of racism, ableism, classism, and transphobia in society and within Canadian feminism (Withers, 2012). It is especially important to avoid reinforcing the notion of a gender binary and to challenge discourses that centralize the experiences of middle-class, able-bodied, white, cisgendered women as the predominant subjects of violence.

My Theoretical Framework

Theorists such as Walter Benjamin, Jacques Derrida, Hannah Arendt, Mahatma Gandhi, Judith Butler, and Reiner Schürmann have influenced my theoretical perspective on violence and nonviolence. I have developed a conception of nonviolence, characterized by compassion, temporality, and interdependence, and a conception of violence, framed in terms of fixed hierarchies, individualism, and the violation of human integrity or dignity. My conception of nonviolence has similarities to how Gandhi describes *ahimsa*, which is "the complete absence of violence in word and even thought as well as action. This sounds negative, just as 'nonviolence' sounds passive. But like the English word 'flawless,' ahimsa denotes perfection. Ahimsa is unconditional love" (Easwaran, 2011, p. 18). I distinguish nonviolence from non-violent action, which refers to actions that do not use force to cause physical harm or damage. Non-violent action is related to but not equivalent to nonviolence. Instead, nonviolence signifies compassion and interdependence, and is not defined in binary opposition to violence. Derrida (1981) argues that Western philosophy is limited by the way in which binaries arrange the world. Thought, experience, and singularity cannot be contained in the tidy polarity of conceptual dichotomies or in their efficient resolution. Violence and nonviolence here are presented not as mutually exclusive opposites, but rather related concepts that overlap and inform one another.

The interdependence of nonviolence challenges the modernist view of the subject as either dependent or independent, and instead views the subject as always relational. Butler (2009) explains that the subject is "always outside itself, other than itself, since its relation to the other is essential to what it is" (p. 49). Relationality, marked with instability and vulnerability, becomes the necessary shifting terrain from which nonviolence can spring. In this chapter I expand the concept of violence; I recognize that it can be physical, sexual, psychological, emotional, spiritual, or economic, and it can be perpetrated by society, by institutions, or by individuals, frequently men. According to this definition, sexism is violence, as are all forms of oppression. Any structure or system that objectifies, marginalizes, or renders people invisible or inferior is thus a form of violence.

Men's Violence against Women in Canada

The prevalence of violence against women in Canada is staggering: 51% of Canadian women have experienced physical or sexual violence in their lifetime (Johnson, 1996). Therefore, it is not surprising that Canadian women have been leaders in working to end men's violence against women over the past four decades. In the 1970s, the first shelters for women fleeing domestic violence were opened in various Canadian provinces, and in 2012 there were over 600 shelters for abused women operating across the country (Mazowita and Burczycka, 2012). Women's shelters were often started by grassroots feminists working with limited funds, who, in collaboration with other women's groups, eventually convinced the government, or other funders, to support their important work (Larkin and McKenna, 2002).

Before the 1970s there was little research on gender-based violence. In addition, there was, and continues to be, widespread under-reporting of cases of both spousal abuse and sexual assault; thus, the magnitude of gender-based violence in Canada has been concealed (DeKeseredy and Dragiewicz,

2014). It was not until 1980 that the Canadian Advisory Council on the Status of Women presented the first national estimates on men's violence against women in heterosexual intimate partnerships, revealing that one in ten Canadian women who were married or in a common-law relationship experienced physical abuse from their male partner (Larkin and McKenna, 2002).

On December 6, 1989, a man killed 14 women at École Polytechnique in Québec, claiming that he was fighting feminism. This event became known as the Montréal Massacre, and December 6 has since been commemorated as the National Day of Remembrance and Action on Violence Against Women. In the decades since then, in large part due to the efforts of feminist activists and scholars, there has been considerable attention paid to the prevalence of men's violence against women. In the 1990s, the number of projects such as the Violence Against Women Survey (VAWS) and other feminist-informed research increased. In recent years, there has been an anti-feminist backlash in response to the findings of these studies. Given a conservative Canadian federal government, which is sympathetic to these anti-feminist initiatives, ending violence against women has become less and less of a priority for politicians and funding agencies (DeKeseredy and Dragiewicz, 2014). In the current neo-liberal political economic era, there has been a movement to de-gender how we think and talk about men's violence against women. Gender-blind language, such as domestic violence and intimate partner violence, works to conceal how gender shapes violence and abuse, unless it is accompanied by theories that account for how individuals' experiences are profoundly gendered (Dragiewicz, 2009).

When engaging in the important work of recognizing how violence is gendered, and how women experience men's violence, it is also essential to understand how different women's social location impacts their experience of violence. Women who are located at the interstices of converging oppressions are more likely to experience violence, and they often experience more obstacles when seeking assistance. Nonetheless, the anti-violence service sector has traditionally considered services targeted at specific populations to be specialized, "with service for middle-class, able-bodied white women experiencing violence in heterosexual relationships still centralized as the predominant experience of violence" (Scott-Dixon, 2006, p. 223).

Indigenous women are subjected to a simultaneously racist, sexist, and colonial culture, which frequently perpetuates dehumanizing stereotypes that "render all Aboriginal female persons vulnerable to physical, verbal, and sexual violence" (Larocque, 2002, p. 149). In Canada, over the past decade, Indigenous women have been three to four times more likely to experience violence compared to non-Indigenous women, and eight times more likely to be a victim of homicide (Daoud, Smylie, Urquia, and Allan, 2013). Studies on missing and murdered Indigenous women show how this violence needs to be considered in the context of discrimination, marginalization, and impoverishment, which increases vulnerability to violence (Amnesty International, 2004; Native Women's Association Canada, 2010). While Indigenous women's average socio-economic position has contributed to their greater odds of experiencing violence, controlling for this factor and other available risk factors does not fully account for the difference in the likelihood of experiencing violence. This finding is consistent with the theory that Indigenous women's elevated odds of violent victimization are linked to the impact of colonization and the loss of cultural traditions (Brownridge, 2008).

Exposure to recurrent poverty, along with racism in everyday life, puts women of colour at greater risk for domestic and other forms of violence. Approximately 20% of women of colour reported experiencing barriers to accessing the healthcare system as a result of racism, specifically in terms of cultural insensitivity, stereotypes, name-calling, and inferior quality of care (Mssaquoi, 2005). Immigrant women, especially immigrant women of colour and/or those who do not speak English or French, face compounded difficulties navigating through a frequently unaccommodating system. They encounter numerous barriers to reporting and seeking support for domestic violence or sexual assault, including barriers relating to their immigration status, sponsorship relationship, and unjust immigration laws. Further, women with disabilities are often impacted by ableist policies and social contexts in Canada, which heightens their risk of experiencing poverty, social isolation, inaccessibility of services, and the devaluation of their experience. Powers et al. (2009) describe how this social context of disability "increases women's vulnerability to abuse, duration of abuse experience, and complexity of addressing abuse" (p. 1). Implementing safety promotion for women with disabilities is important, but in order to effectively prevent violence, we need to change societal attitudes that dehumanize women who have disabilities.

Trans women in Canada experience numerous forms of violence, and yet it is nearly impossible to discuss the extent of violence against trans women because the current mechanisms for tracking the violence are scarce or inadequate (White and Goldberg, 2006). In addition, coming out as a victim of violence may mean coming out as trans. This means risking further marginalization and abuse (Scott-Dixon, 2006), since police and emergency medical services in Canada have a long history of abuse towards trans individuals, particularly against trans women who are prisoners and sex workers (White and Goldberg, 2006). In Canada, hate crimes against transgendered people are problematically subsumed under the sexual orientation category, and thus there are fewer statistics focused specifically on violence against transgendered people. In addition to direct physical violence, trans women also frequently experience the violent impacts of systemic oppression, including being denied access to services, along with legal, social, and economic opportunities, and in turn, this inequity increases their vulnerability to physical violence.

In addressing men's violence against women, there is a need to address the dehumanization of individuals in all traditionally marginalized social groups. Particularly, it is important to address how structural violence operates, and how each overlapping social context intersects to complicate and perpetuate violence against women. Structural violence against women occurs in many areas, including health care systems, educational systems, and the ways in which women are represented and impacted by dominant discourses in the media. Women experience many forms of non-physical violence, such as street harassment, stalking, and online violence, and are subjected to re-victimization discourses and practices, such as slut-shamming and victim blaming, in social environments, in the media, and in the Canadian legal system.

The Effects of Violence on Learning

The impacts of men's violence against women and the effects of patriarchal systemic violence go far beyond physical injuries and immediate emotional stresses. While there is a vast array of personal, societal, and economic costs of violence against women (Day and McKenna, 2002), in this chapter I focus on the impacts on women themselves and on their learning. For example, during or after experiencing intimate partner violence, women who develop what has been called "Battered Women's Syndrome" frequently suffer from long-term physical symptoms such as ulcers, heart disease, hypertension, vision problems, anaemia, skin allergies, and digestive disorders, as well as psychological symptoms such as extreme nervousness, extreme irritability, confusion, disassociation, insomnia, fatigue, eating disorders, memory loss, and acute anxiety (Day and McKenna, 2002). Studies show that women's exposure to interpersonal violence is linked with increased depression, Post Traumatic Stress Disorder (PTSD), and suicide (Mechanic, Weaver, and Resick, 2008; Sato-DiLorenzo and Sharps, 2007), as well as lower levels of social functioning and substance abuse (Jones, Hughes, and Unterstaller, 2001; McCaw, Golding, Farley, and Minkoff, 2007).

The aftermath of a woman's experience of violence can also create barriers that prevent her from accessing education, and if she is able to gain access, it can also impede her ability to learn. Horsman (1999) described a number of common impacts of violence on literacy learners, including spacing out; disassociation and inattention; difficulty with ambiguity; living perpetually in crisis; difficulty trusting educators, themselves, and the safety of a situation; and challenges in creating healthy boundaries. Additionally, educational settings in and of themselves can be sources of suffering and distress, as many women had traumatic elementary or high school experiences. For example, educational settings are one of the most common sites of hate crimes in Canada. For Indigenous women who survived residential schools or who had parents who survived, educational spaces may be associated with memories of sexual assault, physical and emotional abuse, humiliation, ridicule, malnutrition, and cultural genocide (Jones, 2008).

Given the pervasive nature of violence against women, particularly against those women who face intersecting oppressions, and given the potential adverse effects of women's experience of violence on their learning, it is important for adult educators and education systems to incorporate the needs of trauma survivors into curriculum and program planning. Horsman (1999) argues for normalizing the needs of learners who have experienced violence. Rather than thinking about the impacts of violence as atypical or as exceptions, adult educators need to come to terms with the reality that a large portion of adult women learners have experienced physical abuse and/or sexual assault, and all of them will have been impacted in different ways by the systemic violence of sexism.

Nonviolent Communication Education

Marshall Rosenberg (2003) developed the idea of Nonviolent Communication in the 1970s, initially as a way to address the judgmental and violent communication he witnessed in the teacher-pupil relationship in schools, and his model quickly spread around the world. The current core model has four main components: observations, feelings, needs, and requests, which can be used in three ways: naming or expressing oneself to others, receiving communication from others, and communication with oneself. In line with these three modes, the practice of Nonviolent Communication includes a commitment to determine what needs are not being fulfilled, expressing oneself honestly and without judgment, receiving feedback empathically, and practising self-compassion. Kashtan and Kashtan

(2010a) explain that needs are the general, essential conditions for human beings to live fulfilled lives, for example, autonomy, meaning, play, peace, and connection; needs are "an expression of our deepest shared humanity" (p. 4). In addition to these commitments, NVC also features a number of important concepts and intentions. These include prioritizing connection and moving beyond ideas of right and wrong; in other words, connecting to the needs of those involved before seeking immediate, potentially unsatisfying strategies and making assessments based on consideration of needs rather than on moralistic judgments (Kashtan and Kashtan, 2010b). Other key concepts in the NVC model include taking responsibility for one's own feelings and actions, increasing one's capacity for immediacy and interdependence, and holding everyone's needs as equally valuable (Kashtan and Kashtan, 2010b). In Canada, women who have promoted and expanded Nonviolent Communication include educators, authors, and researchers such as Ingrid Bauer, Marcelle Bélanger, Gina Cenciose, Raj Gill, Rachelle Lamb, Lucy Leu, Marion Little, Judi Morin, Sarah Peyton, Penny Wassman and Lesley Williamson.

The Nonviolent Communication model has evolved over the past four decades from a means to restructure the teacher-pupil relationship to encompass the broadened purpose of transforming all hierarchical relationships (Little, 2008; Rosenberg, 2005). Given this aim, when I was developing compassionate communication workshops for women who had experienced abuse, I was surprised that I was not able to find Nonviolent Communication material on men's violence against women, and little or no material on Nonviolent Communication and sexism. Traditionally, Nonviolent Communication has been framed in terms of effectively working towards a power-with (partnership) paradigm verses a power-over (domination) paradigm. Despite this attention to power, the vast majority of studies on Nonviolent Communication focus on the micro-level issues of personal and interpersonal nonviolence and empathy development, and make no mention of macro-level issues of systemic oppression or privilege (e.g., Blake, 2002; Branscomb, 2011; Jones, 2009; Little, 2008; Riemer and Corwith, 2007). Kashtan (2015) is among the few authors writing about Nonviolent Communication who tackle issues of oppression and privilege, including how Nonviolent Communication can assist with internalized oppression. Conversely, in their book *Connecting across Differences,* Connor and Killian (2012) focus only on either institutional hierarchies, such as that of students and teachers or employers and employees, or interpersonal power-with or power-over behaviour. There is a need to develop a theory and practice of Nonviolent Communication education in order to engage with systemic power dynamics that are structured based on gender, race, class, ability, sexual orientation, age, or other social categories.

Exploring NVC

In exploring the possibility of an expanded theory and practice of nonviolent education, I conducted interviews and groups with students who were engaged in Nonviolent Communication education, as part of a larger research project on the theory and practice of embodied, nonviolent education and social activism. These students had taken part in a transformative clowning course and in an annual Nonviolent Leadership for Social Justice Retreat in California, which focuses on race, class, and ethnicity. In this chapter I focus only on the retreat, which brought together people from diverse racial, ethnic, and class backgrounds, and was unique in being one of the only trainings with a specific focus on combining Nonviolent Communication education with education for addressing systemic oppression and privilege.

Participants in the research repeatedly expressed gratitude and appreciation for a space to explore issues of race, class, and ethnicity within the context of the principles of nonviolence. One participant explained the power of using Nonviolent Communication in social justice work as:

> this nonviolent capacity to hold everyone's needs, and to invite us to go beyond our walls and sense of separation, and stay together no matter what ... it is easy to stigmatize or to feel better than: I'm more progressive or I'm more open-minded, or I wouldn't do that ever in my life. And, with the application of Nonviolent Communication ... you don't have to agree, but at least take your time to understand what's going on there; there is a space for everyone's expression.

The principles of nonviolence, particularly those of interdependence and compassion, provide an alternative to traditional moralistic approaches to conversations about systemic oppression. At the Nonviolent Leadership for Social Justice Retreat, rather than dividing actions and beliefs into binary categories of right and wrong, social justice activists and educators using the principles of nonviolence attempt to understand the human needs behind all judgments and actions. It is important to note that this is not to say that condemning oppression is wrong, but rather that it is one possible strategy among many that attempts to meet needs such as equality, understanding, and justice. Strategies in line with nonviolence also attempt to meet similar or sometimes identical needs, but rather than using moralist judgments, strategies are evaluated using needs-based assessments.

While sexism was not a focus of the Nonviolent Leadership for Social Justice Retreat, which perhaps speaks to a problem here, a number of participants expressed a desire to apply the principles they were learning and practising at the retreat to address other kinds of systemic oppression, including sexism. Most of these participants also spoke about the value of maintaining a specific focus on race, class, and ethnicity at the retreat, and some wanted to create other spaces where they could explore gender oppression, and/or a space to explore the intersectionality of various types of oppression. One participant in the research explicitly linked the impacts of gender-based violence in her own life to her struggles in certain educational contexts: "I think the reason presenting is so scary for me, is because my experience tells me that when I put myself in vulnerable spaces that people will cross my boundaries and I will get hurt." She also explained that NVC education assisted her in feeling more comfortable entering vulnerable spaces. Another participant described how "having NVC tools ... supports me in feeling confident in entering learning situations with compassion for myself and compassion for others, when I may not have been able to enter into those situations and hold a level of clarity without them."

Women learners who are dealing with the impacts of violence can use NVC to develop self-compassion and to express their needs and limits. For feminist adult educators, adopting a needs-based assessment approach based on principles of nonviolence, rather than a moralistic approach based in a binary conception of right and wrong, can open up compassion and understanding for women who have been impacted by violence, as well as for learners who may be unwittingly perpetuating systemic violence.

Systemic Violence and Collaborative Change

Adult educators can use NVC in combination with attention to social inequality, oppression, and privilege to address structural aspects of violence in their learning spaces. This means, as feminist adult educators have argued for decades, maintaining an awareness of the power relations present within a class or learning environment, and instigating conversations around the way institutional hierarchies and social locations impact learners' experiences. Using NVC, adult educators and learners can connect to the shared humanity of all parties involved, while communicating about how specific things need to change, and they can instigate collaboration for change in a classroom.

As an example of a facilitator-instigated initiative, imagine that a woman learner who had experienced domestic abuse enters a course, and one of the men makes derogatory comments about his ex-wife. She may feel threatened or re-stimulated in the classroom, and the facilitator has the opportunity to address this dynamic using NVC. This would involve a one-on-one meeting with each learner to discuss their experience, listening to their needs, and developing strategies that would work for everyone. In certain situations, if both parties are willing and if there is a place that would be appropriate, the facilitator could mediate a dialogue either between the two individuals or with the class as a whole.

Alternatively, suppose there were a culture of misogyny at an educational institution, and the administration has failed to address it despite attempts to foster dialogue around the issue. NVC can be used in mass mobilizations of non-violent resistance. The non-violent action taken—sit-ins, art exhibitions, and so forth—is used to create the conditions where dialogue is possible, and it involves an appeal to the humanity of the people in power. Learners could also use NVC as a self-empathizing tool to cultivate the internal resources that can counterbalance the absence of structural power (Kashtan, 2015). Collaborating for change involves empathic listening, creating concrete proposals grounded in needs and observations, and a commitment to ensuring everyone's needs matter.

Concluding Thoughts

Given the prevalence of gender-based violence in Canada and its impact on women learners, it is essential to develop and encourage new practices, strategies, and frameworks. What I have shown in this chapter is how NVC education can be adopted. It is a theory and practice that I would argue needs to be developed more fully, but it can expand ideas for how we deal with the needs of women learners who have experienced violence, and, like feminist adult education, it helps us to uncover and confront the systemic and intuitional violence affecting both learners and feminist adult educators. I recognize that to date, no prominent NVC initiatives focus on gender-violence, although I would argue that NVC offers valuable principles and tools with the potential to support women impacted by violence. Furthermore, there are gaps in the NVC education literature in terms of how it addresses systemic violence, and there is a need to link non-violent principles with feminist adult education and issues of social justice, since education that fails to confront the effects of systemic and institutional violence risks perpetuating violent educational and social structures. Despite these gaps, NVC education encourages the recognition of interdependence and commitment in creating compassionate learning spaces using needs-based assessments, and thus has great potential to support adult women learners.

Endnote

[1] Cisgendered refers to people whose experience of their own gender identity conforms with societal norms around their corresponding sex; i.e. women who were assigned the sex female or men who were assigned the sex male at birth.

References

- Amnesty International. (2004). *Stolen Sisters: A Human Rights Response to Discrimination and Violence against Indigenous Women in Canada.* Amnesty International Publications. Retrieved from: http://amnesty.org/en/library/info/ AMR20/003/2004/en.

- Blake, S. M. (2002). *A Step toward Violence Prevention: Nonviolent Communication as Part of a College Curriculum* (MA Thesis). Florida Atlantic University, Boca Raton, FL. Retrieved from https://www.cnvc.org/sites/cnvc.org/files/NVC_ Research_Files/Training%20Assessments/Blake2002-MAThesis.pdf.

- Block, S. and Galabuzi, G.-E. (2011). Canada's Colour Coded Labour Market: The Gap for Racialized Workers. Ottawa: Centre for Policy Alternatives. Retrieved from: https://www.policyalternatives.ca/publications/reports/canadas-colour-coded-labour-market.

- Branscomb, J. (2011). *Summative Evaluation of a Workshop in Collaborative Communication* (MA thesis). Rollins School of Public Health of Emory University.

- Brownridge, D. A. (2008). Understanding the elevated risk of partner violence against aboriginal women: A comparison of two nationally representative surveys of Canada. *Journal of Family Violence*, 23(5), 353.

- Brownridge, D. A. (2009). *Violence against Women: Vulnerable Populations* (1st edition.). New York: Routledge.

- Butler, J. (2009). *Frames of War: When Is Life Grievable?*. New York: Verso.

- Connor, J. M. and Killian, D. (2012). *Connecting across Differences: Finding Common Ground with Anyone, Anywhere, Anytime* (Second Edition). Encinitas, CA: Puddledancer Press.

- Daoud, N., Smylie, J., Urquia, M., and Allan, B. (2013). The contribution of socio-economic position to the excesses of violence and intimate partner violence among aboriginal versus non-aboriginal women in Canada. *Canadian Journal of Public Health*, 104(4), 278.

- Day, T., & McKenna, K. (2002). The health-related economic costs of violence against women. In K. McKenna & J. Larkin (Eds.), *Violence Against Women: New Canadian Perspectives.* Toronto: Inanna Publications and Education.

- DeKeseredy, W. S. and Dragiewicz, M. (2014). Woman abuse in Canada: Sociological reflections on the past, suggestions for the future. *Violence Against Women*, 20(2), 228.

- Derrida, J. (1981). *Positions.* (A. Bass, Trans.). Chicago, IL: University of Chicago Press.

- Dragiewicz, M. (2009). Why sex and gender matter in domestic violence research and advocacy. In E. Stark & E. Buzawa (Eds.), *Violence against Women in Families and Relationships: Making and Breaking Connections.* Praeger, Santa Barbara, California, pp. 201-215.

- Easwaran, E. (2011). *Gandhi the Man: How One Man Changed Himself to Change the World.* Tomales, CA: Nilgiri Press. Retrieved from http://www.goodreads.com/work/best_book/108614-gandhi-the-man-the-story-of-his-transformation.

- Horsman, J. (1999). *Too Scared to Learn: Women, Violence and Education.* Toronto, ON: McGilligan Books.

- Johnson, H. (1996). *Dangerous Domains: Violence against Women in Canada.* Scarborough, ON: Nelson Canada.

- Jones, C. (2008). Balancing the impact of residential schools on second and third generations. In E. Battell et al., *Moving Research about Addressing the Impacts of Violence on Learning into Practice.* Edmonton, AB: Windsound Learning Society.

- Jones, L., Hughes, M., and Unterstaller, U. (2001). Post-traumatic stress disorder (PTSD) in victims of domestic violence: A review of the research. *Trauma, Violence, & Abuse: A Review Journal*, 2(2), 99.

- Jones, R. (2005). *Understanding the Nature of Empathy: A Personal Perspective* (MA thesis). University of East London, London.

- Jones, S. (2009). *Traditional Education or Partnership Education: Which Educational Approach Might Best Prepare Students for the Future?* (MA thesis). San Diego University, San Diego, CA.

- Kashtan, M. (2015). *Reweaving our Human Fabric: Working Together to Create a Nonviolent Future.* Oakland, CA: Fearless Heart Publications.

- Kashtan, M. and Kashtan, I. (2010a). A Deeper Look at the Building Blocks of NVC. Unpublished hand-out provided through the NVC Academy. (Contact via website: www.nvcacademy.com).

- Kashtan, M. and Kashtan, I. (2010b). NVC Intentions and Assumptions. Unpublished hand-out provided through the NVC Academy. (Contact via website: www.nvcacademy.com).

- Larkin, J., & McKenna, K. M. J. (2002). *Violence against Women.* Toronto: Inanna Publications and Education.

- Larocque, E. (2002). Violence in Aboriginal communities. In K. McKenna & J. Larkin (Eds.), *Violence Against Women: New Canadian Perspectives*, pp. 147-162. Toronto: Inanna Publications and Education.

- Little, Marion. (2008). *Total Honesty/Total Heart: Fostering Empathy Development and Conflict Resolution Skills. A Violence Prevention Strategy.* A thesis submitted in partial fulfillment of the requirements for the Degree of Master of Arts in dispute resolution. University of Victoria, 2002.

- Mazowita, B. and Burczycka, M. (2012). *Shelters for Abused Women in Canada, 2012.* Ottawa, ON: Statistics Canada. Retrieved from: http://www.statcan.gc.ca/pub/85-002-x/2014001/article/11906-eng.htm.

- McCaw, B., Golding, J. M., Farley, M., & Minkoff, J. R. (2007). Domestic violence and abuse, health status, and social functioning. *Women & Health, 45*(2), 1.

- Mechanic, M. B., Weaver, T. L., & Resick, P. A. (2008). Mental health consequences of intimate partner abuse: A multidimensional assessment of four different forms of abuse. *Violence Against Women, 14*(6), 634.

- Mssaquoi, N. (2005). Think globally act appropriately: A community health centres response to violence against women. In S. Harding (Ed.), *Surviving in the Hour of Darkness: A Look at Women of Colour, Indigenous Women and Healing.* University of Calgary Press.

- Native Women of Canada. (2010). *What Their Stories Tell Us: Research Findings from the Sisters in Spirit Initiative.* Retrieved from: http://www.nwac.ca.

- Palmer, P. J. (2009). *A Hidden Wholeness: The Journey toward an Undivided Life.* San Francisco, CA: Jossey-Bass.

- Powers, L. E., Renker, P., Robinson-Whelen, S., Oschwald, M., Hughes, R., Swank, P., and Curry, M. A. (2009). Interpersonal violence and women with disabilities: Analysis of safety promoting behaviors. *Violence against Women, 15*(9), 1040.

- Riemer, D. and Corwith, C. (2007). Application of core strategies: Reducing seclusion and restraint use. *On The Edge, 13*(3), 7.

- Rosenberg, M. B. (2003). *Nonviolent Communication: A Language of Life,* 2nd edition. Encinitas, CA: Puddledancer Press.

- Rosenberg, M. B. (2005). *Speak Peace in a World of Conflict: What You Say Next Will Change Your World.* Encinitas, CA: Puddledancer Press.

- Sato-DiLorenzo, A. and Sharps, P. (2007). Dangerous intimate partner relationships and women's mental health and health behaviors. *Issues Mental Health Nursing, 28*(8), 837-48.

- Scott-Dixon, K. (Ed.). (2006). *Trans/forming Feminisms: Trans/Feminist Voices Speak Out.* Toronto, ON: Sumach Press.

- White, C., & Goldberg, J. (2006). Expanding our understanding of gendered violence: Violence against trans people and their loved ones. *Canadian Woman Studies, 25*(1/2), 1240.

- Withers, A. J. (2012). *Disability Politics and Theory.* Halifax, NS: Fernwood Publishing.

UNITE HERE Local 75 union activists Andrai Babbington and Zeleda Davis take part in the Good Jobs for All rally in Toronto on June 13, 2009.

Photo: Courtesy of John Maclennan.

12

Building Solidarity for All Voices of Women of Colour, Anti-Racism Leaders, and Labour Educators

> Moving from silence into speech is for the oppressed, the colonized, the exploited, and those who stand and struggle side by side a gesture of defiance that heals, that makes new life and new growth possible. It is that act of speech, of "talking back," that is no mere gesture of empty words; that is the expression of our movement from object to subject—the liberated voice.
> —bell hooks, 1989, p. 9.

The act of "talking back," in the poignantly inspiring vision of bell hooks, is to my mind exactly what labour education in Canada is all about. When workers come together to share, to reflect critically, and to support one another, it is an act of "making whole," a term that is often used by unions when filing grievances and seeking redress.

Winnie Ng

When workers self-organize into a cohesive force to challenge hegemony, I believe this is in fact a "gesture of defiance that heals." The ongoing process of creating and reclaiming space for that "liberated voice" within us is where both the magic and challenge of worker education lies. It lies in acts ranging from organizing garment workers in the late 1970s to building leadership among downtown hotel workers in the 1990s; in organizing English classes in workplaces and in integrating anti-racism and equity training within the labour movement. There is nothing more inspiring and empowering to me than to hear a union member switch from using "I" to saying "We." This is strength of solidarity, the power of the union movement.

From an anti-racism and gender equity perspective, the question is how labour education can help build the space for such transformative change and expand its reach among workers from the racialized and equity-seeking groups. This chapter provides a critical reflection on the existing practices and strategies of anti-racism education within the labour movement from the perspective of women of colour.

The Current Context of the Anti-Racism and Equity Agenda within Labour

I begin by situating the anti-racism and equity agenda in the broader political and economic context of the labour movement. In section two I draw on the voices of a group of racialized women activists and educators who participated in my doctoral research titled *Race-ing Solidarity, Remaking Labour* (2010), which examined how race impacts and intersects with gender and class in the building and fracturing of worker solidarity. The final section is a re-imagining of labour education in Canada as part of the necessary conditions for solidarity building and labour renewal. This chapter is, therefore, a collective weaving and re-imagining of a working-class movement for this country that would not leave anyone behind.

Over the last 30 years, and the past eight in particular, the neo-liberal agenda has tightened its grip globally and deep labour market restructuring has devastated workers and their families and weakened organized labour as a whole. Women and people of colour, who frequently have lesser seniority, have borne much of the brunt of job losses and plant closures in the name of profit. Across the board, growing precariousness in employment has become the new norm. *Still Working on the Edge*, a recent report by the Workers Action Centre (2015), showed that in comparison to its 2007 study, the employment situation in Ontario has worsened. Not only has the number of part-time jobs risen much faster than that of full-time jobs, but also workers are increasingly working longer hours, and are subjected to more exploitative working conditions as they juggle work and family responsibilities. While many are affected, women are disproportionately affected in all these areas (Briskin, 2009).

Yet for workers of colour and Aboriginal workers, and particularly the women in these categories, the sense of membership disaffection in unions today is real. Therefore, in responding to the challenge of declining union membership, values, and density, feminist and anti-racist labour scholars and unions are giving priority to organizing to the unorganized, particularly the growing rank of marginalized, contingent workers who, again, are predominantly women, as well as workers of colour and Aboriginal workers (Fairbrother and Yates, 2003; Kumar and Schenk, 2006; Fudge and Vosko, 2001). This divide was well expressed in the Canadian Labour Congress (CLC) National Anti-Racism Task Force Report (1997), *Challenging Racism*, which argues

> the impact of racism weakens our solidarity and robs the labour movement of the energies, ideas and skills of union members from Aboriginal Peoples and People of Colour communities.... In particular, after years of passing policy statements and resolutions, writing reports, and giving speeches about the need to fight racism, there is a huge gap between union principles and the actions of union members and leaders. (p. 7)

But for a number of years now, feminist and anti-racism labour educators have emphasized the centrality of the equity agenda as a prerequisite to labour renewal in Canada (Foley and Barker, 2009; DasGupta, 2009; Briskin, 2009). However, a study by Briskin, Genge, McPhail, and Pollack (2013) reveals that equality issues have still not moved into the mainstream of union culture. In fact, there is now a decline in women's participation in leadership, fewer resources for equity organizing, and in some cases, outright attacks on advocates. This means that the road to equality within the labour movement for workers of colour and, more recently, Aboriginal workers, continues to be too long with far too many detours (Wall, 2009).

Eighteen years after the publication of the Task Force Report, some dramatic labour movement leadership changes have unfolded over the past year. In May 2014, Hassan Yussuff, a longtime anti-racism and human rights activist from Unifor and a former Secretary Treasurer of the Canadian Labour Congress (CLC), ran in a contested election and won the position as its President. It was a historic moment and represented the potential for a bold, inclusive, and progressive working-class movement. However, the election of a racialized person as president does not translate automatically into a "post-racial" era where racism or inequity no longer exists.

Like traditional organizing, the traditional union education approach to anti-racism and equity issues has been problematic on two counts. One is the overrepresentation of workers of colour and Aboriginal workers in human rights and anti-racism courses. The second is their underrepresentation in regular, core courses offered in union education. While such educational opportunities have been invaluable for racialized workers in terms of sharing and networking, embedded in the action of the leadership is a very clear message that anti-racism and human rights are issues solely for a worker of colour or an Aboriginal worker.

Solidarity in Practice: Voices of Racialized Women Leaders

> For immigrant workers, workers of colour, the system doesn't receive us as equals, not as warriors, not as the heart of the movement ... the members stop caring in order to protect themselves. Once the union gets the contract, the education stops, the mobilizing stops. They just want us as numbers, not as thinking people.

One of the major realities I discovered in my doctoral research, as the above quotation suggests, is that once a contract has been obtained, women workers and workers of colour often return to invisibility within the union ranks. In other words, the intensity of attention and education during an organizing drive will suddenly evaporate once the vote is won. This led one Black woman activist I interviewed to ask:

> Are you in it for the same reason as I'm? The labour movement is not a campaign; it's my life! How do we better the movement when people you work with treat you like crap? If we're supposed to walk side by side, why am I being left behind? Should I just walk away and feel like a loser?

Experiencing a perpetual sense of otherness, racialized women activists find themselves in in-between spaces with little control or choice. The notion of prescribed space, invisible as it may be, seems highly palpable in the narrative of the following racialized activist who works as a staff representative in a public sector union. She asks:

> Have we been "pigeon-holed" as equity activists so much that they don't see me for my strength... Just because we are involved in equity issues, we're seen as lightweight! But where else can I start? When are people going to see beyond my colour? They train us to come up through the rank, and yet when we are ready to move forward, there is no place for us. They already have their succession plan and it does not include people who are in equity positions ... I watch my friend who is an

outright fearless and smart activist who got promoted to be an equity officer within the local. She is being seen as a one-trick pony! That means she can only talk equity.

The notion of being "pigeon-holed" and the questioning of whether we have "ghettoized" ourselves reflect the predicament in which Aboriginal women activists and women of colour frequently find themselves. Once a union has promoted an equity activist into a staff position, the leadership is applauded for doing equity hiring. Simultaneously, the activist is now removed from her base and is devoid of her influence and power.

Sometimes the boundaries are internalized—there is an invisible line that separates and weakens the potential of worker solidarity and power. Indeed, solidarity and equity become only optics, that is, opportunities to be seen as doing the right thing rather than doing what is right as long as the elected leadership will not offend anyone or lose their traditional base of support. As one of the participants in my study noted, "Equity issues get twisted. Underlying support is not in place ... the structure of the union has not changed. The sense of entitlement is very much present. Workers of colour have a difficult time getting elected. Power is very much guarded." This illustrates a widening rift between what union solidarity could be and how it is practised. This inconsistency between the rhetoric and the action on the equity agenda is a source of frustration among leaders who are women of colour. Briskin et al. (2013) spoke of a similar pattern, described as "closing the circle," an act on the part of male leaders within many unions to both actively or inadvertently exclude women and members of other equality-seeking groups as an attempt to consolidate power and decision making.

The Latina sister who earlier declared there was no labour movement—just union organizations—argued that without fundamental change—including embracing an anti-racism and equity agenda—labour renewal strategies are akin to "pouring new wine into a barrel of old wine." They do not work. She continued by providing a metaphor of childbirth to describe the transformation needed:

> We need to start a new phenomenon...there is no new life without pain and bleeding; continue to push for labour community actions. Different dynamics give different strategies ... workers will create, resist, and break away from years of torture in the labour movement. We are not the ones who make the policies within our unions. Questions on who leads will be threatening to them... having some "success stories" does not translate into power for men and women in the workplace and the community.

This deep sense of frustration has also prompted younger woman activists to question whether it is worth their while to invest their energy and get on this train called the labour movement, which is seen as "going in a wrong direction—there is going to be a train wreck!"

Among this new generation of racialized women activists, there is a shared desire for meaningful engagement in a labour movement that reflects and looks like them. They also want to see a movement that will embrace the needs of diverse communities of precarious workers, not for pragmatic or political expediency, but based on a shared commitment to dismantle the systemic barriers of race, gender, class, abilities, sexual orientation, and other forms of discrimination.

Solidarity as "Collective Consciousness-in-Association"

What is clear is that despite their profound disappointment, women activists of colour and Aboriginal activists keep going and refuse to be cast as victims. They continue to engage and experience deeply the power of solidarity on the picket line, across the bargaining table, when handling grievances, and while standing up for each other in workplaces. The quotation below by another women leader in the hospitality sector union speaks volume to this incredible sense of solidarity:

> When we had the lockout … a few workers were picketing that particular day. CUPE was having their convention and it was arranged that they would come by. When the time came, they were delayed…. I remember all of a sudden hearing the echo way down the street as the group came marching up. At that moment, I cried. It was seeing the faces of the workers from different parts of Canada and knowing that they are there as one to support my union and the strikers. At that moment, you feel you belong to something bigger. It is different unions but we are unions.

Fantasia (1988) characterizes this expression of unity as "consciousness-in-association…and the metaphysic of labour, representing a potent mythic theme that carries remarkably transcendent qualities" (p. 10). In the context of unequal social relations of power, these moments of collective agency and solidarity carry a deeper sense of bonding and knowing that has the capacity to heal the soul, the spirit, and the communities to which we belong (Dei and Kempf, 2006). The challenge then lies in extending such an invigorating sense of solidarity into everything that we do in the workplace, at the local level and in the community, and above all, to inspire rank and file members into becoming activists for the long haul. This is where re-imagining the immense possibility of labour education becomes such a critical endeavour.

Photo: Courtesy of John Maclennan.

UNITE HERE Local 75 members from the Delta Chelsea hotel greet marchers demonstrating for jobs and justice.

From Union Education to Labour Education for All Workers

In the context of growing inequalities and the emergence of divisive politics based on fear and insecurity, we as labour educators need to develop a new repertoire of practices to overcome the fragility of worker power that has been fractured by new norms in workplaces. Examples of these norms include workers who are doing the same job but with different precarious work arrangements, classifications, pay rates, unions, and immigration status. In his study on the organizing efforts of workers in precarious employment in four East Asian countries, Dae Oup Chang (2012) envisions a shift in re-conceptualizing and broadening the traditional frame of a labour movement into building a "movement of labour." To my mind, this is a much more liberating concept of building a mass workers' movement in which workers—regardless of status, workplace, or union affiliation—can come together and where worker power is built from the bottom up. The potential transformation into a united force to counter the hegemony of the elites will require political will and courage, and a deliberate strategy to insert labour education into community space and capture the public's attention.

It will also require a re-imagining of how such educational programs need to be done. The traditional framework of delivering a union-specific education program—in terms of who gets in, who teaches it, and where it is held—can therefore be made more innovative and more accessible to workers who are non-unionized and precariously employed. Such classes can be moved out of the union hall and into community centres. Another possibility will be to transform union halls into community hubs for workers and their families. The format and content can be multi-faceted, ranging from labour rights information sessions to study circle/book clubs that enable community members to come together and engage in "the act of talking back" (hooks, 1989). The act of reclaiming voice is very much grounded in Paulo Friere's (1970) idea of consciousness raising, in which workers participate as subjects in their own education and in their own lives. To maximize such potential, my ideal vision of worker education would be to fully embrace four core elements. The first element is that labour education must become a space for radical re-imagination. The second element is that it must be an ongoing political project of decolonization and environmental justice. Third, labour education needs to deepen interracial working-class consciousness and, in particular, worker solidarity. And fourth, labour education must be a site for courageous and honest conversation about gender, power, and privilege within the ranks of workers.

Labour Education as a Space for "Poetic Knowledge"

In *Freedom Dreams* (2002), Kelley traces the importance of the radical imagination, the capacity to dream in each juncture that enables people to rise up against the daily emotional toll, and move beyond the marches and protests.

Progressive social movements do not simply produce statistics and narratives of oppression; rather, the best ones do what great poetry always does: transport us to another space, compel us to relieve horrors and, more importantly, enable us to imagine a new society … it is that imagination, that effort to see the future in the present that I shall call poetry or poetic knowledge (p. 9). As an anti-racism educator, I am deeply moved by the notion of poetic knowledge in which the re-imagination of the labour movement resides. The freedom to dream, to have a different way of seeing and even feeling is part of the organic process of political engagement. For Aboriginal and racialized women workers, labour education should be that unleashing of the mind as Kelley implores, and to open up a space for exploring possibilities. When asked what solidarity looks like, an Asian Canadian activist visualizes solidarity as a solar system with different planets revolving around and protecting each other, while another women leader offers the following imagery:

> My visual image of solidarity is a DNA strand because it's full of diverse codes, diverse messages and components that serve different functions; and put together, they create a strong, vibrant, alive, and healthy being! It moves in a spiral … when something is not healthy, the DNA will try to fix it. We all have a purpose, a different role in fixing. Even though each is different, they are of equal value.

It is from such optimism and love for the movement, as reflected in the above imageries, that feminist and anti-racism educators and activists draw their strength to keep going. It is in such space for radical re-imagination that we can replenish our soul, fuel our passion, and thereby sharpen the purpose of our actions.

Labour Education as a Project of Decolonization and Environmental Justice

Over the past decade, the Truth and Reconciliation Commission, the Idle No More movement (begun by a group of Aboriginal women adult educators), the hunger strike of Chief Theresa Spence, the ongoing blockades and marches against mining and oil companies' environmental degradation, and the push for a national inquiry into more than 1000 murdered and missing Aboriginal women have thrust into the forefront of the public mindset the ongoing colonization and systemic discrimination of Aboriginal peoples on their own land. If the labour movement is to make a commitment to an anti-racism and equity agenda, relearning the history of Canada from the perspectives of Aboriginal peoples is a mandatory first step to un-learn all the misinformation that has been fed throughout the public schools. As Justice Murray Sinclair of the Truth and Reconciliation Commission stated in an interview with the *Ottawa Citizen* (2015), "This is not an Aboriginal problem. This is a Canadian problem" (n.p.). Grounding anti-racism education in an anti-colonial discursive framework involves a recognition that trade unions, like other social institutions, are deeply entrenched in the "nation building" of Canada through its ongoing colonization of the Aboriginal peoples. The challenge then is for us to find new ways to forge new relations with Aboriginal peoples to order to subvert and dismantle the entrenched power structures.

Furthermore, there is an urgent conversation that needs to take place about the links between environment, employment, and equality. The Alberta Tar Sands project is but one of the prime examples of how the federal government has callously disregarded their own Treaty obligation to their Aboriginal Treaty partners, causing irreversible and irrefutable damage to the well-being, health, and environment of Aboriginal communities. Pam Palmmater, an Aboriginal scholar and a spokesperson for the Idle No More movement, has passionately reminded us that as Canadians, we are also "Treaty people" because of the historical Treaty agreements signed between the Crown and the Aboriginal nations.

In addition, there is a relative muteness among organized labour with regard to engaging members in real conversations acknowledging the fact that a large number of jobs, particularly in resource and energy sectors, have been created as a result of the destruction of Aboriginal communities. Corporations are exploiting the vulnerability of workers by using employment as bait and as a means of silence and complicity. Additionally, the necessity of a just transition strategy to reverse or slow down the pace of climate change cannot be suffciently underscored. What will such a transition plan for action and solidarity with Aboriginal peoples look like beyond words, and how can it be accelerated before it is too late?

Probing and critical reflection such as this needs to take place within the labour education program. To begin this journey, labour education needs to be grounded in the notion of solidarity based on the Aboriginal worldview, represented in this quotation by an Anishnaabe Nation sister working in a public sector union representing social services agencies:

> There is no specific word for "solidarity" as it is defined in the English language; however, there is a term that means "all things together, everything in existence" (kaawin piiwitekaataken kitanishinaapemowin). For Anishnaabe, solidarity is not limited to people, which makes perfect sense when you think about it. Everything and everyone is interconnected, each affecting one another. Therefore Anishnaabe's view of "self" ultimately includes all of creation.

The universality implicit in extending the same type of care and compassion to the Earth, water, and creatures around us is an expression of solidarity. The nurturing of a renewed sense of humility and collectivity will be instrumental in countering the individualistic and monolithic culture and practices of the neo-liberal agenda.

Caregivers rally against federal policies making it harder to get permanent residency in Canada (November 22, 2014).

Photo: Courtesy of the Caregivers' Action Centre.

Labour Education to Deepen Inter-Racial Working-Class Consciousness and Solidarity

In workplaces, for workers to break away from silence and alienation to engage in collective activities against capitalism is itself an act of class resistance, and such action "though short of the will or capability to make revolution, represents a transformative associational bonding that can shape class relations in significant ways" (Fantasia, 1988, p. 11). Such action creates the space where ordinary people can experience the power of transformation that propels them to take extraordinary actions, as illustrated in this narrative by a courageous woman of colour leader in the hospitality sector:

> I was at [name of company] for 17 years. For a long while, I didn't even understand or feel that there's a union in the place.... It's not okay to do work, getting disrespect from the management, getting crap on and going home feeling crappy ... during the time, we had a problem with vacation; management was stealing our vacation money. Talking to the people, mobilizing them to fight for that money, I see people's respect for me, and for the union. It got me thinking that it might make sense to get involved.... There shouldn't be a day that I'd allow management to disrespect the workers. The silence was broken in the hotel. We started standing up for our rights. (Ng, 2010)

While union leaders proclaim "a worker is a worker is a worker" as their mantra in the hope of a unified movement, many have failed to make the links and to perceive the complexities and ambiguities of capitalism, a system that engenders competition and that promotes and absorbs division along race and gender as a means of maintaining social control (Fletcher and Gapasin, 2008).

Labour Education as a Site for Courageous Conversation about Privilege and Power

Q: "Winnie, can you give me an example of White privilege ... what are you talking about?

A: "I can't because I'm not White!" I responded without even thinking.

The above exchange took place in a women's activist training class where I was facilitating a session on privilege. In a class of 21 women participants, only three, including myself, were women of colour. I wrote this question on the board: "Can you recount a personal experience that makes you aware of your White privilege?" I asked participants to take a couple of moments to reflect on this question, when suddenly one of them raised her hand and asked me the question above. My spontaneous response in some way startled the participants and jolted them out of their own sense of comfort and everday normalcy as White unionists. What followed was a profoundly honest conversation about the unpacking of privileges and how race, gender, and class intersect in the meaning making of sisterhood. We turned this brief episode into a teachable moment. However, the stakes are often high for racialized women in talking about racism and sexism when confronting the White male-dominated labour leadership. Sara Ahmed (2012) used the metaphor of a brick wall, invisible to the dominant class/culture, as something that makes "you" the "problem" for pointing out that there is a wall:

> To use the language of racism is to risk not being heard ... but to keep on using the language does not mean you get the message through. No wonder anti-racism work can feel like banging your

head against a brick wall. The wall keeps its place, so it is you who gets sore. Embodying diversity can be a sore point, but the soreness of that point is either hidden from their view, if we go along with the happiness of the image, which sometimes we "do do," or attributed to us (as if we talk about walls because we are sore). (p. 156)

For many of us as anti-racism educators, it is not uncommon in labour education settings to observe that when race and gender are in the foreground of a discussion, someone will bring up the issue of class as a corrective measure or as a way to reinsert their own voice as the centre of attention. There is often an attitude of dismissiveness when such equity issues are viewed as distractions from the more pertinent material conditions of class. I share Ahmed's stance (2012) that the positioning of gender and race as merely aspects of culture and identity is "a denial of the material and systematic aspect of racial experiences" (p. 211). Personally speaking, it is exhausting to have to remind others that race, gender, and class are inextricably linked and that talking about racism does not negate class, but rather complicates and sharpens the discussion and emphasizes the meaning of the effects of capitalism. For as Stuart Hall (1983) once argued so eloquently, "Race is one of the most important keys, not into the margins of the society, but into its dynamic centre" (p.273).

It is critical that we learn to talk about race. It is even more critical for White brothers and sisters to have honest conversations about race without anger, remorse, guilt, or defensiveness and to take personal responsibility for combatting racism and oppression. Derald Wing Sue (2015) refers to the resistance to racism as ignoring "the elephant in the room" and provides clarity in discussing the cycle of denial:

> The denial of colour is a denial of differences. The denial of difference is really a denial of power and privilege. The denial of power and privilege is really a denial of personal benefits that accrue to Whites by virtue of racial inequities. The denial that they profit from racism is really a denial of responsibility for their racism. Lastly, the denial of racism is really a denial of the necessity to take action against racism. (p.34)

We cannot afford to deny the ongoing colonization project concerning the Aboriginal communities in Canada, nor can we be silent about the injustices experienced by migrant workers and others due to the systemic racism in Canadian Immigration and Refugee programs. Additionally, we need to acknowledge the brutality of anti-Black racism and heed the call for justice by the emerging Black Lives Matter movement. The intersectionality of race, gender, class, disability, sexual orientation, and Islamophobia requires all of us to reflect critically and to work across differences. Recognizing our mutuality and taking responsibility to build a different world and a different labour movement requires that we be willing to step outside our own comfort zone and destroy the mask of benevolence. In the remaking of our labour movement, it is imperative to engage in courageous conversations about privilege, power, gender, and race-ing. Only then will we reach solidarity for "all."

Labour education in Canada, grounded in the notion of equity and solidarity, is an intensely political project that embraces hopefulness. I believe we must be bold and innovative in creating a space, a gathering place, a circle where workers can truly wrestle with issues, unlearn and relearn, and above all, develop strategies of resistance based on a collective vision of building a strong interracial working-class movement.

References

- Ahmad, S. (2012). *On Being Included: Racism and Diversity in Institutional Life*. Durham, NC: Duke University Press.

- Briskin, L. Genge, S., McPhail, M., & Pollack, M. (2013). Making time for equality: Women as leaders in the Canadian labour movement. *Our Times*. Retrieved one June 2015 from: http://womenunions.apps01.yorku.ca/wp- content/uploads/2012/10/OT1-pdf.pdf.

- Briskin, L (2009). Cross-constituency organizing: A vehicle for union renewal. In J. Foley and P. Baker (Eds.), *Unions, Equity, and the Path to Renewal* (pp. 137-156). Vancouver, British Columbia, Canada: UBC Press.

- Canadian Labour Congress (1997). *Challenging Racism: Going Beyond Recommendations*. Report of the CLC National Anti-Racism Task Force. Ottawa: Canadian Labour Congress.

- Chang, D. (2012). The neo-liberal rise of East Asia and social movements of labour: Four moments and a challenge. *Interface: A Journal for and about Social Movements* 4(2), 22-51.

- Das Gupta, T. (2009). *Real Nurses and Others: Racism in Nursing*. Halifax, Nova Scotia: Fernwood.

- Dei, G. J. S. and Kempf, A. (Eds.). (2006). *Anti-Colonialism and Education: The Politics of Resistance*. Rotterdam: Sense Publishing.

- Fairbrother, P. and Yates, C. (Eds.) (2003) *Trade Unions in Renewal: A Comparative Study*. London: Routledge.

- Fantasia, R. (1988). *Cultures of Solidarity: Consciousness, Action, and Contemporary American Workers*. Berkeley, CA: University of California Press.

- Fletcher, B., Jr. and Gapasin, F. (2008). *Solidarity Divided: The Crisis in Organized Labor and A New Path toward Social Justice*. Berkeley: University of California Press.

- Foley, J. R. and Baker, P. (2009). *Unions, Equity, and the Path to Renewal*. Vancouver: UBC Press.

- Freire, P. (1970) *Pedagogy of the Oppressed*. New York, NY: Seabury Press.

- Fudge, J. and Vosko, L. (2001) By whose standards? Re-regulating the Canadian labour market. *Economic and Industrial Democracy* 22 (3): 327-356.

- Gellatly, M. (2015) Still working on the edge: Building decent jobs from the ground up. Toronto: Workers Action Centre. Retrieved from: http://www.workersactioncentre.org/press-room/policy-papers/.

- Hall, S. (1983). Teaching Race. *Early Child Development and Care*, 10, 239-274.

- hooks, b. (1989). *Talking Back: Thinking Feminist, Thinking Black*. Toronto: Between the Lines.

- Kelley, R. (2002). *Freedom Dreams: The Black Radical Imagination*. Boston: Beacon Press.

- Kumar, P. and Schenk, C. (Eds.) (2006). *Paths to Union Renewal: Canadian Experiences*. Peterborough, ON: Broadview Press.

- Ng, W. W. (2010) Race-ing solidarity and remaking labour: Labour renewal from a decolonizing and anti-racism perspective. PhD thesis, University of Toronto.

- Palmater, P. (2013) Why Idle No More matters to us all. *NOW Magazine*. Retrieved on June 2015 from: http://www.nowtoronto.com/news/story.cfm?content=190705.

- Sinclair, M. (2015). Interview with *Ottawa Citizen*. Retrieved on June, 2015 from: http://ottawacitizen.com/news/politics/teachings-about-aboriginals-simply-wrong-says-murray-sinclair.

- Sue, D. W. (2015). *Race Talk and the Conspiracy of Silence: Understanding and Facilitating Difficult Dialogues on Race*. Hoberken, New Jersey: John Wiley & Sons, Inc.

- Wall, C. (2009). Equity in unions: Political correctness or necessity for survival? In J.R. Foley and P. L. Barker (Eds.), *Unions, Equity, and the Path to Renewal* (pp. 78- 83). Vancouver and Toronto: UBC Press.

The Canadian Congress for Learning Opportunities for Women (CCLOW) was a national feminist organization that grew out of an ad hoc committee formed by the Canadian Association for Adult Education (CAAE). The committee first met in 1973 to consider the continuing education of women and it made several recommendations to the executive of CAAE, including the creation of the Canadian Committee for the Continuing Education of Women (CCCEW). At that time there existed no Canadian organization concerned with the education and training needs of women. In 1976, the committee sought and secured funding from the Secretary of State Women's Program (that had developed as a result of the Royal Commission on the Status of Women) to support the hiring of staff to look for creative models and conduct research on the status of women's learning opportunities. Janet Willis, the first Executive Director, wrote a series of essays about successful programs for women and she prepared longer policy briefs based on research with adult educators in advance of a workshop held on October 16-18, 1976 in Winnipeg. The CCCEW committee reported the results of that workshop back to CAAE; it was subsequently decided that a separate organization devoted to the continuing education of women was needed.

Another successful proposal to the Secretary of State Women's Program in 1977 led to the opening of a national office in Toronto. That year's activities focused on the development of a purpose statement and a structure that included regional networks. In 1978, Dorothy Smith was invited by CCLOW to give a public lecture in March on the topic of the women's movement. That same year a newsletter was developed to maintain communication and several skills workshops were held in Toronto. A second Congress was held in 1978; as part of the preparations for it, Dorothy MacKeracher was invited to submit a report titled "Roadblocks to Women's Learning: Issues for Advocacy." This led to CCLOW's first of many advocacy initiatives; in 1979, CCLOW presented reports on cutbacks in training allowances and outreach programs to three federal political parties. In April of 1979, another Congress was held in Banff, where women's learning opportunities were further defined and a national coordinating committee was created.

The 1980s saw the creation of many regional networks (e.g., in British Columbia, Saskatchewan, and Newfoundland), from which emerged several successful models for women's programs (e.g,. The Bridging Program and Women Interested in Successful Employment—WISE). The BC network published two issues of the *Back to School Survival Guide for Women*. In 1982 the first issue of the CCLOW magazine *Women's Education des Femmes* was released. The national office and regional networks worked somewhat independently of each other, but there was much integration of their concerns. Between 1978 and 2000, CCLOW produced many other reports, including studies on systemic and institutional barriers to women's learning, child care, pay equity, paid educational leave, women's learning styles, violence against women, the impact of violence on women's learning, and women's literacy programs. [For a full list of these documents, visit the National Adult Literacy Data Base (NALB) in the NALB website (www.nald.ca).] As well, frequent conferences often included skills training workshops. After decades of survival despite ongoing budget cuts to women's programs, CCLOW finally ceased operating as an organization in 2001. It left behind more than two decades of strong advocacy, backed by original research and network building.

References

- Canadian Women's Health Network (n.d). Canadian Congress for Learning Opportunities for Women. Retrieved August 7, 2015 from http://www.cwhn.ca/en/node/15087

- Smith, E. (1996). *Convergences and Divergences in Feminist Theorizing and Organizing Practices during the Second Wave Women's Movement: A Case Study of the Canadian Congress for Learning Opportunities for Women*. Unpublished PhD dissertation, Carleton University.

Vignette: Canadian Congress for Learning Opportunities for Women

Members of the Emanuel African Methodist Episcopal Church congregation in Edmonton, Alberta in the 1920s.
Glenbow Archives ND 3-1199.

13

African-Canadian Women, Leadership, and Adult Education Reclaiming a Past

Little has been written specifically about how African-Canadian women have been constituted in relation to early twentieth century Alberta or, more specifically, in relation to their engagement in different forms of education across their communities. Traditional adult education texts have only recently begun to include the experiences of minoritized women. This chapter seeks to restore some of that important history.

Jennifer Kelly and Thashika Pillay

At the Centre

Today doves flew from my head
and my hair grew
the longing is gone from my body
and I'm filled with peace, perfect peace
No longer shall I speak of electrocuted poets
or the ones who inhaled gas until
they danced in the dizziness of death
But of brown women
who turn the soil with their hands
making vegetable gardens and tending fruit trees
Today I went into my storehouse
selected the choicest oil and anointed my body
wrapped myself in the rarest cloth
of a deep wine red
stood at my front gate
and words poured from my mouth in flaming chants
Today the craftsman has come
to make a design for me
of a woman sitting in deep repose
with doves flying from her head
He has made all the pieces and they fit
well together
I shall hang it at my window for all the world to see
    — Afua Cooper, 1996

Researching African-Canadians in Edmonton and Alberta

We are engaged in scholarship related to African-Canadian women and race and are actively involved with African-Canadian communities in Edmonton.[1] Jennifer is African-Canadian and of Caribbean descent; Thashika is an Indo-African Canadian, born in South Africa. This chapter draws on research funded by the Social Sciences and Humanities Research Council (SSHRC). It examines the socio-historical representation of educational activities undertaken by African-Canadian women living in early 1920s communities in and around Edmonton, Alberta.

Through an analysis of the newspaper column, *Our Negro Citizens* (*ONC*), written by Reverend George W. Slater, Jr.,[2] and published in the *Edmonton Bulletin* and *Edmonton Journal* between 1921 and 1924, we explore the socio-historical representation of African-Canadian women as engaged in what we would argue are important forms of public adult education. We illustrate the ways in which newspapers act as sites of public adult education and learning while also acting as brokers of power, playing a critical role in the creation of social and discursive realities. This chapter further explores this site of education and leadership in relation to the ways in which the newspapers serve as critical power brokers in their representation of African-Canadian women living in Edmonton, thereby both negotiating and navigating the discourses created, constructed, and produced through the newspaper.

Between 1905 and 1912, immigration authorities employed various strategies to discourage African Americans from moving to Canada. In Edmonton, official organizations "such as the Board of Trade and the Imperial Order Daughters of the Empire gathered petitions of protest to send to Ottawa" (Kelly, 1998, p. 38), and resolutions were passed in 1910 asking for the immigration of African Americans to cease (Abdi, 2005). Although much recognition has been given recently to late nineteenth and early twentieth century pioneer women racialized as white (Chilton, 2007; Kitossa, 2002; Perry, 2003; Valverde, 2008;) or in relation to Aboriginal women in Western Canada (Carter, 2006), and their role in the construction of national myths, little emphasis has been given to women of African descent. Furthermore, several researchers have identified the erasure of Black women and communities from established historical narratives (Calliste, 1993, 1994; Carter and Akili, 1981; Cooper, 2007; hooks, 1997).

Thirty percent of African immigrants arriving by 1911 settled in urban areas; others were located in isolated rural communities, with 208 in Edmonton and 72 in Calgary. By 1921, the census information for Calgary recorded 66 under the "Negro" column, while the Edmonton population had grown to 277 (Cui and Kelly, 2010). Although Edmonton was the hub for the *ONC* column, the comings and goings among rural communities were also highlighted.

It is to the *ONC* newspaper column that we turn in order to tease out and understand the role of African-Canadian women in educating their communities. While women and men are discussed in the column, it is the constitution of women's experiences that we highlight through the narratives of the creator of the column, Reverend Slater.

Newspapers as Sites of Education and Learning

Newspapers are one site through which the "learning society" is operationalized. Welton (2005) defined the learning society as "a collective achievement, something created intentionally in time and space by human actors deliberating with each other" (p. 21), and as an objective fact and social project. With regards to the African-Canadian population of Alberta in the early 1920s, the *ONC* column showcased a group of people coming together to create a stronger, more engaged, better educated, and economically successful community. Citing a study by the British government, Welton (2005) contends that adult education

> reveals the reasons that underlie [men and women's] daily work, the way in which
> that work ha[d] come to be arranged as it is, and … its place in the economics of the nation
> and the world. (p. 23)

We contend that the *ONC* column depicted the ways in which adult education occurred within the African-Canadian community. The *ONC* column thus acted as a site of learning and as a tool through which collective community achievement could be showcased.

Educating through Newspapers

Newspapers are educational tools, informing a newspaper's readership about issues at local, regional, national, and international levels (Campbell, Smith, and Siesmaa, 2011; Voisey, 2004). However, the educative nature of newspapers is impacted by economic, socio-cultural, and political factors; newspapers are, therefore, more useful in educating certain segments of the population compared to others (Campbell et al., 2011). Barnhurst and Wartella (1991) contend that newspapers largely tell the story of white, middle-class males, thus normalizing the acts, behaviours, and ways of living of one specific group of the population to its readership.

The *ONC* column purposefully attempts to disrupt this hegemonic purpose attributed to newspapers by telling the stories and thereby normalizing the experiences of African-Canadians. This leads us to question the educative purpose of the *ONC* column; which segment of the larger Edmonton population is being educated through the newspaper column? As exemplified by the *ONC*, newspapers go beyond merely depicting the facts; they allow readers to further their understanding of specific topics (Campbell et al., 2011), and they constitute symbols and social objects that affect our daily and societal rituals, such as voting (Barnhurst and Wartella, 1991).

Writing about weekly newspapers, Voisey (2004) contends that a rural weekly newspaper often provided its readership with a plethora of information regarding goings-on in the community that was rarely news to readers "in rural communities where 'everyone knows everyone' [and] word of mouth effectively relayed recent events" (Voisey, 2004, p. xxi). The inclusion of information already known to the community is an occurrence mirrored in the *ONC* column. This raises questions regarding the reasons behind choosing to include information or "news" of which the community has already been made aware and the purpose of this act.

Newspapers as Tools of Power

Newspapers can act as brokers of power, negotiating who is to be empowered and who is not (Olien, Donohue and Tichenor, 1995). By highlighting the distinctive roles played by various community actors, newspapers can serve to recognize the strengths of particular groups within the community while simultaneously disenfranchising other groups. Barnhurst and Wartella (1991) refer to the newspaper as a contradiction, as a lowly object that confers status and which readers experience "in three ways: as a ritual, as a symbol, and as a tool" (p. 206). Through these experiences, the newspaper both reveals and creates power relationships and dynamics. Community newspapers and local journalists' framing of issues often reflect traditional power structures (Cohen, 2000; Sakamoto, 1999). Therefore, newspapers can act either to illustrate the positive points of a community or to marginalize already oppressed peoples (Mosco, 1998). Campbell et al. (2011) contend that newspapers may not consciously work to disenfranchise groups, but the decisions concerning what issues to cover and how to depict news stories play a role in deciding and negotiating who is empowered and who is not (Olien et al., 1995). Furthermore, decisions about which groups to support and disenfranchise often has an economic element (Voisey, 2004).

We can look at the decision by the *Edmonton Journal* and the *Edmonton Bulletin* to publish the newspaper column by Slater through this lens. Do these newspapers "in fact favour this local organization" (Campbell et al., 2011, p. 291) over others? How can the *ONC* column, then, be considered the primary source of credible information and knowledge about the African-Canadian community? How does this influence the way the community views the members of the Emanuel African Methodist Episcopal (EAME) Church or African-Canadian women in Edmonton, thereby reflecting local power structures?

Newspapers and the Creation of a Discursive and Social Reality

The research data as analyzed through a critical discourse framework demonstrates that Edmonton society in 1900-1925 was both "knowledge based" and "knowledge driven" (Fairclough, 2004). According to Jager and Maier (2009), knowledge refers to the ways in which people interpret and shape their environment through meanings; this knowledge is derived from discursive surroundings. "Knowledge is therefore conditional [and dependent] on people's location in history, geography, class relations" (p. 39). What is considered knowledge is not part of an "objective truth" but rather a subjective reality. Therefore, what is knowledge, what constitutes knowledge and the transmission of knowledge are discourses embedded within the relations and structures of power. As Fairclough and Wodak (1997, p. 258) remind us:

> Discursive practices … can help produce and reproduce unequal power relations between … social classes, women and men, and ethnic/cultural majorities and minorities through the ways in which they represent things and position people.

Newspapers are tools through which particular discursive and social realities are produced. Campbell et al. (2011) assert that the content of newspapers reflects a social reality, what is actually happening within the society in which the newspaper is constructed. For many community and local newspapers, the social reality produced and constructed not only avoided allusion to conflict but actively promoted a sense of social cohesion within the community "by acting as cheerleader for the community, encouraging, supporting, and praising every local event, activity, and organization" (Voisey, 2004, p. xxviii). Did Reverend Slater use the *ONC* column to also attempt to create a similarly cohesive community and to ensure the promotion of women within it?

There is limited research that considers the role of newspapers within particular racialized environments. Chari's (2014) research on the Zimbabwean diasporic community is relevant as Chari found that newspapers can create a sense of community by enabling a group of people to experience a collective memory and identity. By serving as an arena for civic engagement, dissent, and status production, the newspaper becomes a site to build collective experiences and histories. Writing of a context more similar to that of African-Canadians, Yingling (2013) contends that Black newspapers used local, national, and international events during the 1800s and early 1900s to construct new ideas of citizenship, community solidarity, liberation, inclusion, and rights among the African-American community of New York. Newspapers, therefore, confer status on both readers and non-readers through their power to create, construct, and re-imagine the discursive and social realities of particular populations.

The creation and construction of particular social and discursive realities by newspapers is the result of an ideology that views the readership of newspapers as a commodity, with readers "shift[ing] from being the *consumers* of a product, to being the *product themselves* (Richardson, 2007, p. 79). Newspapers tend to represent the working classes as either invisible or hyper-visible (Moon and Rolison, 1998). One could contend that once newspaper readers become the product as opposed to the consumers of the product, it would more specifically be the middle class or the aspiring middle class who become the targets of newspapers. Is this the purpose of the *ONC*?

Reverend George W. Slater Jr., A Promoter of Education and Women's Leadership

From 1921 until 1924, Reverend George W. Slater, Jr. compiled the community's narratives into a newspaper column; thus, he had control over which activities were included and which were excluded. Slater's narratives constitute him as having a sense of presence and active involvement as a community leader (Cui and Kelly, 2010). The *ONC* column reveals a flurry of different social and political activities organized around the Emanuel African Methodist Episcopal (EAME) Church, some of which gave social and economic solace that would certainly challenge the status quo. However, "for all that these churches—Baptist, Methodist, and other—did give the Negro in succor and inspiration, on the whole they were ineffective in meeting the major problems" (Winks, 2000). In terms of everyday life, the women depicted took up education and leadership roles through the church to challenge and engage broader issues.

Slater's *ONC* newspaper column offers a rare glimpse into the lives of African-Canadian women from 1921-1924. During this period, Slater used the *ONC* column to paint a specific depiction of the African-Canadian community living in Alberta: as fairly tight-knit, homogenous, exhibiting middle-class sensibilities, and sharing similar interests and desires as White Canadians. The *ONC* showcased a socially and economically mobile community that exhibited a strong sense of political consciousness and involvement. Of particular interest to the authors is the depiction of women within the *ONC* wherein African-Canadian women are central figures engaged in leadership and education. Four specific themes emerged: 1) knowledge is power; 2) women as entrepreneurs; 3) women as community leaders; 4) women as nurturers.

Knowledge Is Power for Community

Slater placed high value on formal education, for both men and women. Although he did not express his thoughts openly, he highlighted and privileged the experiences of women as educators and as crucial contributors to the growth of the community. Slater once presented the case of Mrs. O. A. Brooks, who was taking a "modiste" [sic] course at the technical school as well as studying typewriting and bookkeeping at the McTavish Business College. He used the example of Mrs. Brooks to state that such educational attainments "will pay the colored (sic) people big dividends if many more would do likewise" as "Knowledge is Power" [14 Oct 1921]. Reverend Slater continued to reiterate this message concerning the importance of education, asserting in his April 11, 1922 column "Go to school! Go to school! Go to school!—Go both night and day. It will pay you in happiness, health and prosperity." He propagated this message by exemplifying the actions of African-Canadian women such as Mrs. C. Hinds who attended Alberta College South (13 March, 1922) and Mrs. E. O. Anderson who attended McTavish Business School (22 July, 1922). The *ONC* column depicts a community that values education for all of its people, viewing formal learning as a route to success, power, and happiness as more women and men in school showed that "a trained, head, heart and hand makes for the greatest success and worthiness" (21 Oct 1922).

Women in Positions of Leadership

The EAME Church was a space in which it was socially and culturally acceptable for women to seek out positions of leadership. In 1923, for example, Mrs. Oliver was the only woman chosen to be one of nine church trustees (27 January, 1923). Slater also gave women the opportunity to present sermons and lectures and thus provide leadership to the church community. For example, Mrs. Golden initially gave lectures at the church; this eventually became a weekly event that was extended to preaching at the church in Junkins, Alberta. On occasions when Slater was away, women such as Evangeline Estelle Proctor delivered sermons in his place (8 December, 1923). These examples demonstrate the opening up of leadership positions for African-Canadian women at the EAME Church and in the public sphere and highlight the significance of influential men such as Slater. It is not evident in the newspaper how women were active in creating opportunities for themselves, but it is clear that women could be represented as educational leaders within the community.

Women as Entrepreneurs

Through the *ONC* column and the example of numerous African-Canadian businesswomen, Slater emphasized the importance of economic success to individuals and to the community, even stating "we are glad to see more of our people going into business" (28 March, 1922). He continually praised the entrepreneurial skills of Mrs. Richard Proctor, who opened her own needlework shop, Mrs. Anna Bell, who had a dressmaking store, Mrs. Russell and Mrs. McCathrone, who owned a hand laundry, cleaning, and pressing business, Mrs. Shirley Oliver, who ran a dressmaking store, and Mrs. J. H. Whaley, who invented toiletry articles. This praise illustrates the importance placed on the economic success of the community. It is interesting to note that Slater's praise for community members' entrepreneurial spirit is limited to a relatively large number of women in the African-Canadian community and does not include African-Canadian men. We have pondered the reasons for this and wonder if women were having greater success opening their own businesses because they sold goods and services that the rest of the community could purchase, as opposed to relying on support from the larger White community. This conclusion garners some support through Slater's statement that Mrs. Proctor and Mrs. Bell "will succeed and get the patronage of their friends as they are skilled in their work."

Women as Nurturers

Scholarly literature on the role of women historically and in contemporary times tends to focus on women as nurturers, mothers, and caregivers. This nurturing theme is increasingly evident in the *ONC* column. Slater took care to highlight a number of issues that the women of the EAME Church supported, such as: 1) a stop smoking campaign by Mrs. Noble, who "told of the great destruction that the cigarette smoking of young people … was bringing upon the minds, spirits and bodies of the nation" (13 March, 1922); 2) clothing drives in order to find warm clothes for women and children in need; and 3) the focus on temperance, which continued throughout the existence of the *ONC* column. Not only did Slater announce the various meetings being held by the different temperance societies in the area, but he also took time and space to praise various supporters of the temperance movement, such as Madame Lora Lamance, National Organizer for the WCTU (8 October, 1921) and Mrs. Nellie McClung who spoke on the "Temperance Question of Alberta" (13 January, 1923). The presence of these two women, both racialized as White, appears to illustrate the extent to which the issue of temperance was seen as a societal issue, and the inclusion of predominantly African-Canadian WCTU chapters demonstrates temperance as a unifying discourse across different social groups.

The issue of racial uplift is identified most explicitly in terms of the discourse and social practices of women's organizations, a situation that has been recorded in other parts of Canada (Walker, 1980). Indeed, racial uplift through education joins with other discourses around temperance to create a larger discursive formation. For example, in the February 1922 issue, the column published its regular report on the meeting of the Phylis Wheatley Woman's Christian Temperance Union (WCTU).[3]

> Mrs. H. Brooks and Mrs. Shirley Oliver read well-written papers on the life of Miss Williard, and Madame Pinkey Hunt read one of Dunbar's poems on Frederick Douglas. Mrs. Edna Anderson recited a beautiful poem. After several very interesting remarks the ladies took up the discussion of heredity and environment.

The reference to discussions of heredity and environment indicate how this particular chapter of the WCTU was concerned with broader social issues that were topics of the day in a public sphere often dominated by men. As well, the relationship between heredity and environment, and possibilities for social change, were important topics among those racialized as Negro during the turn of the century.

The WCTU provided an educative space for these churchwomen to demonstrate leadership around these issues.[4]

According to Valverde (2008),

> The WCTU was largely a small town organization particularly in the West. While drawing on women who already worked in Protestant churches to maintain the cross-gender social bonds of congregations, its exclusively female membership gave many Protestant women their first glimpse of autonomous organization. (p. 58)

The Phylis Wheatley WCTU was a gendered and raced organization that existed in parallel to other mainstream WCTU chapters.[5] That it bore the name of Phylis Wheatley, regarded as the founder and representative of African-American literature in the United States, is symbolic in terms of identification, and this organization provided women of the African-Canadian community with a spiritual and intellectual place for consciousness-raising. Two prominent leaders of the mainstream WCTU—Nellie McClung and Emily Murphy—were referenced in the *ONC* columns. In referencing the speeches and homilies of "Mrs. Magistrate Murphy," better known as Emily Murphy, the column linked these new Canadians of African descent to existing dominant discourses concerning social change and prohibition in 1920s Edmonton. Slater discursively reproduced, introduced, and linked women within his church community to mainstream White women's discourses on moral regulation. Embedded in these discourses were perceptions of women as responsible for saving the sanctity of the home and the patriarchal rule within it. Emily Murphy—a well-known women's rights activist and the first woman magistrate in Canada—represented mainstream Canadian feminism at that time. By consistently making positive references to Murphy, the column emphasizes the key role that Slater played in mediating between ideas of the racialized White and Black communities. It demonstrates the role of African-Canadian women's organizations in trying to upgrade their knowledge, and through uplift and leadership to be on par with mainstream White women. In other words, the subtext is that African-Canadian women held similar ideas regarding temperance compared to their White counterparts and that through reading and consciousness-raising they had the potential to be equal to white middle-class women. Furthermore, the columns indicated that the Phylis Wheatley WCTU members were active women who associated with the mainstream WCTU and attended meetings alongside other women representing rural and urban unions.

Nellie McClung, a prominent Member of the Legislative Assembly, is often praised in the column for her various political activities as well as for her ecumenical and Methodist work in Canada and England. McClung was credited by Slater for giving a presentation at the Wesley Methodist Church that was a "rich feast filled with fact, reason and soul." While McClung's interaction with the EAME Church and with Slater seemed to revolve amicably around Methodism and temperance, in contrast, Valverde (2008) argues that "feminism, Christianity, chauvinism, and ethnocentrism were for McClung and her fellow feminists a unified whole" (p, 120). Ideas espoused by McClung, Murphy, and other women involved with the WCTU on the importance of mothers and families were linked to a wider social concern for racial purity at that time. Questions are raised here as to how the women of the Phylis Wheatley WCTU were related to the dominant discourse of moral regulation that was infused with issues of racial degeneration, Whiteness, nation, and woman's mission as mother of the race (Valverde, 2008). Were these African-Canadian women aware of this disjuncture? The *ONC* columns do not include any mention of how this WCTU reacted to the racist narratives of their temperance allies. However, we can conclude that the activities described demonstrated an educative space both through the initiatives undertaken by the women in this WTCU as well as the leadership they demonstrated within the textual construction of the *ONC*.

Concluding Discussion

The *ONC* column became a tool through which Reverend Slater attempted to disrupt societal expectations of the African-Canadian community. The main audience of the column was both African-Canadians living in Alberta as well as the wider White community. In regards to the latter, Slater attempted to provide a portrayal of the community that echoed their own understanding of themselves. In a similar vein to Barnhurst and Wartella's (1991) assertion that newspapers largely tell the story of White, middle-class males, which thereby normalizes the acts, behaviours, and ways of living of the White, middle-class male population, the *ONC* column depicted the African-Canadian community as markedly similar to this segment of the readership. However, the *ONC* column also depicted an African-Canadian community that viewed education as emancipatory and which valued the education of both males and females equally. This admiration for formal education illustrates the ways in which this particular newspaper column acted as a broker of power, negotiating who was to be empowered and how—through education. However, the focus on the issue of temperance also portrayed African-Canadian women as sharing fears over consumption of alcohol similar to those of White women. Through the *ONC* column, Slater promoted prohibition and the WCTU, thus producing and constructing a social reality that both avoided the allusion of conflict and actively worked to promote a sense of social cohesion within the African-Canadian and White communities (Campbell et al., 2011).

Slater was instrumental in using the newspaper column as a tool to disrupt societal expectations while also reinforcing particular gendered discourses within the African-Canadian community. The *ONC* column showcased various women as leaders within the EAME Church and, therefore, the broader community. The church was positioned as the space through which women could gain and wield power; however, these leadership opportunities were only available for women because men allowed them to occupy that space. The discourse of the *ONC* column regarding the opening up of leadership positions for women in the church reflected traditional power structures (Cohen, 2000; Sakamoto, 1999). Nevertheless, African-Canadian women appeared to not only take up these positions of leadership but they continued to push for greater control. This can be seen by the example of Mrs. Golden, who was not content with giving lectures at only the EAME Church but went on to give sermons at the Church in Junkins, as well as Mrs. Charleston, who is positioned in the community as a "Canadian heroine" (21 August, 1922) for taking a "homestead and improv[ing] upon it doing the work herself just as a man would" (13 February, 1922). However, like the other women mentioned in the *ONC* column, Mrs. Charleston is congratulated not only for building her own home without the help of a man but also because "she finds time to do much work in the church, Sunday school and the Order of Eastern Star" (21 August, 1922).

As did the *High Level Times*, Slater also often defended and promoted the economic interests of self-employed groups (Voisey, 2004). Those whom he promoted most often tended to be women from within the African-Canadian community who were embracing entrepreneurship, such as operating women's dressmaking and needlework shops. According to Richardson (2007), this promotion reflects a shift away from readers as consumers of a product (the newspaper) to readers as the product themselves. Furthermore, as the readership of the *ONC* column became the product, it became important in the column to focus on the middle class or the aspiring middle class. This focus enabled the producing and reproducing of specific social realities through the transformation of social beliefs. The valorization of African-Canadian women as leaders and adult educators allowed the greater Edmonton public to witness a racialized community that was progressive and in the process of transformation while still adhering to common goals. This was a community that discursively produced women as integral to the success of the community. Given the attention paid at this time to women getting the vote, the authors contend that this valorization of African-Canadian women helped to depict African-Canadians as leaders within their own as well as the larger community.

Endnotes

1 According to a Wikipedia entry on African-Canadians, the population of the African-Canadian population in 1921 was approximately 18,300 (http://en.wikipedia.org/wiki/Black_Canadians).

2 According to Foner (1977), Reverend George W. Slater Jr. began his career as a newspaper columnist in 1908, writing for the *Chicago Daily Socialist*. Slater wrote for the *Chicago Daily Socialist* from September 8, 1908 until March 27, 1909. Slater re-embarked on his writing endeavours again in 1912, and from 1912 to 1919, Slater distributed a pro-socialist monthly, the Western Evangel (Foner, 1977). Slater moved to Edmonton and became pastor of the Emanuel African Methodist Episcopal (EAME) church of Edmonton.

3 The Woman's Christian Temperance Union (WCTU) was organized in 1874 by women primarily racialized as white and who were concerned about the problems alcohol was causing their families and society. The members chose total abstinence from all alcohol as their life style and protection of the home as their watchword (http://www.wctu.org/).

4 The following section on the Phylis Wheatley WCTU draws directly on analysis presented in Cui and Kelly, 2010.

5 There were several other Edmonton branches/unions of the Alberta Women's Christian Temperance Union. The Phyllis Wheatley union sent at least two delegates to the Annual Convention in 1916.

References

• Abdi, A. A. (2005). Reflections on the long struggle for inclusion: The experience of people of African origin. In W. J. Tettey and K. P Puplampu (Eds.), *The African Diaspora in Canada: Negotiating Identity and Belonging* (pp. 49-60). Calgary: University of Calgary Press.

• Barnhurst, K. G., & Wartella, E. (1991) Newspapers and citizenship: Young adults' subjective experience of newspapers, *Critical Studies in Mass Communication*, 8(2), 195-209, doi: 10.1080/15295039109366791

• Berelson, B. (1954). What missing the newspaper means. In D. Katz, D. Cartwright, S. Eldersveld, and A. M. Lee (Eds.), *Public Opinion and Propaganda* (pp. 263-271). New York: Holt, Rinehart & Winston.

• Bernal, V. (2006). Diaspora, cyberspace and political imagination: The Eritrean diaspora online. *Global Networks*, 6(2), 169-75.

• Calliste, A. (1993-4). Race, gender and Canadian immigration policy: Blacks from the Caribbean, 1900-1932. *Journal of Canadian Studies* 28(4): 131-48.

• Campbell, C., Smith, E., and Siesmaa, E. (2011). The educative role of a regional newspaper: Learning to be drier. *Australian Journal of Adult Learning*, 51(2), 269-301.

• Carter, S. (2006). "Britishness, 'Foreignness,' Women and Land in Western Canada 1890s-1920s." *Humanities Research* 13(1): 43-60.

• Carter, V., and Akili, Leffler W. (1981). *Windows of Our Memories*. 2 vols. St. Albert: BCR Society of Alberta.

• Chari, T. (2014). Performing patriotic citizenship: Zimbabwean diaspora and their online newspaper reading practices. *Journal of African Media Studies*, 6(1), 91-109.

• Chilton, L. (2007). *Agents of Empire: British Female Migration to Canada and Australia, 1860s-1930*. Toronto: University of Toronto Press.

- Cohen, J. (2000). Group identity: The case of synagogue pamphlets. *Rhetoric and Public Affairs*, 32, 247-275.
- Cooper, A. (2007). *The Hanging of Angelique*. Athens: University of Georgia Press.
- Cooper, A. (1996). At the centre. In T. Nanavati (Ed.), *Understatement: An Anthology of 12 Toronto Poets*. Toronto: Seraphim Editions.
- Cui, D. and Kelly, J. R. (2010). "Our Negro citizens": An example of everyday citizenship practices. In A. Finkel, S. Carter, and P. Fortna (Eds.), *The West and Beyond: New Perspectives on An Imagined Region* (pp. 253-277). Edmonton: Athabasca University Press.
- Cowling, L. (2014). Building a nation: The Sowetan and the creation of a Black public. *Journal of Southern African Studies*, 40(2), 325-341. doi:10.1080/03057070.2014.901639
- Ehrenreich, B. (1995). The silenced majority: Why the average working person has disappeared from American media and culture. In G. Dines and J. M. Humez (Eds.), *Gender, Race and Class in Media: A Test-Reader* (pp. 40-42). London: Sage.
- Fairclough, N. (2009). A dialectic-relational approach to critical discourse analysis in social research. In R. Wodak and M. Meyer (Eds.), *Methods of Critical Discourse Analysis* (pp. 162-186) (2nd ed.). Los Angeles: Sage.
- Fairclough, N. and Wodak, R. (1997). Critical discourse analysis. In T. van Dijk (Ed.), *Discourse as Social Interaction* (pp. 258-284). London: Sage Publications.
- Foner, P. S. (1977). *American Socialism and Black Americans: From the Age of Jackson to World War II*. Westport: Greenwood Press.
- Jager, S., & Maier, F. (2009). Theoretical and methodological aspects of Foucauldian critical discourse analysis and dispositive analysis. In R. Wodak and M. Meyer (Eds.), *Methods of Critical Discourse Analysis* (pp. 34-61) (2nd ed.). Los Angeles: Sage.
- Kelly, J. R. (1998). *Under the Gaze: Learning to be Black in White Society*. Halifax: Fernwood.
- Kitossa, T. (2003). Criticism, reconstruction and African-centred feminist historiography. In N. Nathani Wane, K. Deliovsky, and E. Lawson, (Eds.) *Back to the Drawing Board: African-Canadian Feminisms* (pp. 85-116). Toronto: Sumach.
- Moon, D. G. and Rolison, G. L. (1998). Communication of classism. In M. L. Hecht (Ed.), *Communicating Prejudice* (pp. 122-135). Thousand Oaks: Sage.
- Olien, C. N., Donohue, G. A., and Tichenor, P. J. (1995). Conflict, consensus and public opinion. In T. L. Glaser and C. T. Salmon (Eds.), *Public Opinion and the Communication of Consent* (pp. 301–322). New York: Guilford.
- Perry, A. (2003). From "The hot-bed of vice" to the "good and well-ordered Christian home": First Nations housing and reform in nineteenth-century British Columbia." *Ethnohistory* 50(4): 587-610.
- Richardson, J. E. (2007). *Analyzing Newspapers: An Approach from Critical Discourse Analysis*. Palgrave Macmillan: New York.
- Sakamoto, K. (1999). Reading Japanese women's magazines: The construction of new identities in the 1970s and 1980s. *Media, Culture and Society*, 21, 173–193.
- Valverde, M. (2008). *The Age of Light, Soap, and Water*. Toronto: University of Toronto Press.
- van Dijk, T. A. (2009). Critical discourse studies: A sociocognitive approach. In R. Wodak and M. Meyer (Eds.), *Methods of Critical Discourse Analysis* (pp. 62-86) (2nd ed.). Los Angeles: Sage.
- Voisey, P. (2004). *High River and the Times: An Albertan Community and Its Weekly Newspaper, 1905-1966*. Edmonton: University of Alberta Press.
- Walker, J. W. (1980). *A History of Blacks in Canada*. Ottawa: Supply and Services.
- Welton, M. (2012). *Unearthing Canada's Hidden Past: A Short History of Adult Education*. Ontario: Thompson Publishing.
- Welton, M. (2005). *Designing The Just Learning Society: A Critical Inquiry*. NIACE, UK.
- Winks, R. (2000). *The Blacks in Canada*. Montréal: McGill-Queen's University Press.
- Wodak, R., and Meyer, M. (2009). Critical discourse analysis: History, agenda, theory and methodology. In R. Wodak and M. Meyer (Eds.), *Methods of Critical Discourse Analysis* (pp. 1-33) (2nd ed.). Los Angeles: Sage.
- Yingling, C. W. (2013). No one who reads the history of Hayti can doubt the capacity of colored men: Racial formation and Atlantic rehabilitation in New York City's early Black press, 1827-1841. *Early American Studies*, 11(2), 314-348.

This vignette was prepared by Thashika Pillay.

Jeannette Austin-Odina has been a teacher and educator for most of her life; in fact, it has been her life mission: "That's how I see education—if you are not sharing it, it has no value." She was born in 1949 in Trinidad-Tobago. At the age of 12, she was charged with tutoring and mentoring other young children in her community. Her expertise as an educator at such a young age led to her being hired as a teacher when she finished high school at the age of 16. At 17, she immigrated to Canada with her spouse but was unable to pursue her passion for teaching, so she worked as a dishwasher. However, her dedication to being an educator was an innate part of her being and while working as a dishwasher, she encouraged other employees to pursue further educational opportunities and she helped them with their homework. Jeannette was also able to return to university, and she received a Bachelor of Education degree from the University of Alberta.

In those early days of living in Edmonton, the African-Caribbean-Canadian community was very small and according to Jeannette, almost every member of the community spent time in her home. It was a community space in many ways, and it was the home from which a significant number of people married and embarked on a new life.

Regardless of where life has taken her, Jeannette has continuously engaged in helping people learn. In 1979, while living in Belize, she helped local women set up a cooperative in order to ensure that they could sell their produce, and together they created an organization that canned and sold fruit. The cooperative afforded the women in the community a way to come together to achieve economic and social stability. After moving back to Edmonton, Austin-Odina created the Afro-Quiz in 1991 as a way to educate the community about the history and experiences of peoples of African and Caribbean heritage. The Afro-Quiz brought together a large group of African-Canadian women who helped create the quiz, thus opening up a space in which African-Caribbean-Canadian women could highlight their knowledge and transfer it to the larger community. The Afro-Quiz, which Austin-Odina initiated, is now an established annual event in Edmonton.

Giving back to her community is an integral part of who Jeannette is, and her identity as a teacher and adult educator is the medium through which she engages with the community. In 2003, Jeannette helped organize a youth homework and tutoring service. However, she was not content simply to help youth achieve better grades at school. Instead, she was keen to ensure that this tutoring service was an opportunity for young African-Caribbean-Canadian men and women to receive professional work experience where they could apply the knowledge they were gaining at college and university, thus showcasing these young women and men as leaders in the community and as mentors for youth. This mentorship allowed a new generation to take up the work that Austin-Odina had begun, thus cementing her legacy as a leader and life-long educator in the community.

Photo: Courtesy of Godwin Onu Odina.

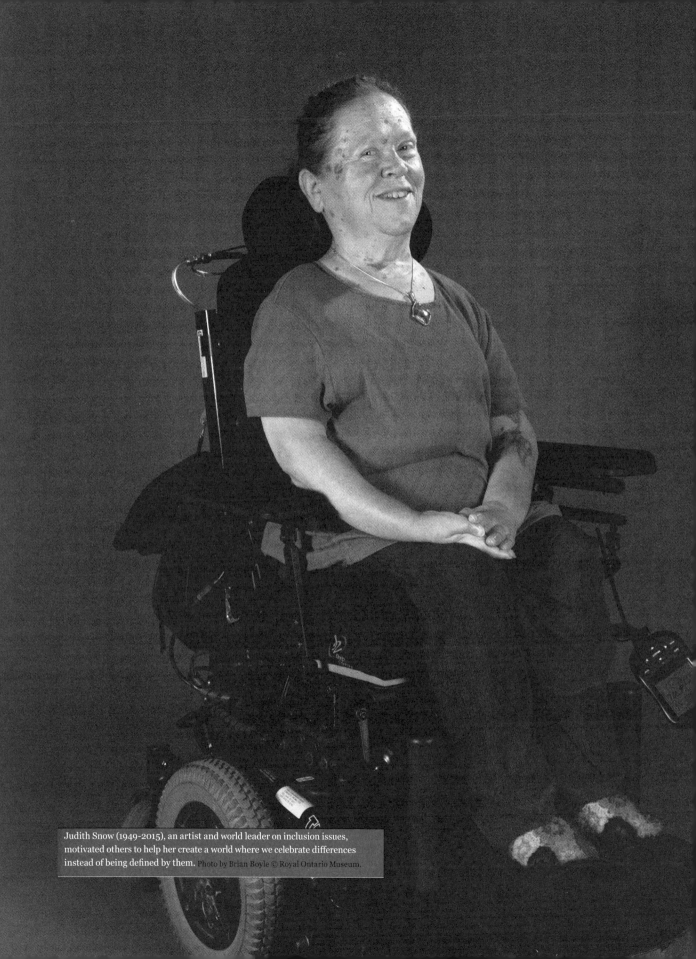

Judith Snow (1949-2015), an artist and world leader on inclusion issues, motivated others to help her create a world where we celebrate differences instead of being defined by them. Photo by Brian Boyle © Royal Ontario Museum.

14

Dialogue as Interdependence
Disability, Gender, and Learning across Difference

> If you can't get out of your chair or lift your hand higher than your waist, you can't do the physical games I'd been taught to think essential to theater (sic) practice … I wasn't that good at those body warm-ups myself. This group would never miss them, and what did it matter anyway? I said, "Why don't we just read some of these scripts aloud." Even as I said it I realized that half the people in the workshop couldn't speak above a whisper or didn't have the strength or physical skill to hold the scripts or the cognitive skill to read at all. It brought me up short. I floundered a bit, shuffled through my bag, and then said, "You want to just talk?"
>
> —Terry Galloway, *Mean Little Deaf Queer* (2009, pp. 150-151)

Ashley Taylor

This chapter discusses the benefits and pitfalls in efforts to "just talk" across differences of ability in adult education. Scholars of adult learning often describe dialogue as critical to crossing differences. However, participants in adult learning are always socially positioned relative to gendered norms of ability such that their experiences of dialogue differ greatly. These gendered norms of ability shape not only how testimony is given within dialogue across differences, but also how listening takes place—that is, what stories or experiences are acknowledged or intelligible. However, the relative invisibility of these dimensions of communicative practice means that they often go unacknowledged, frequently rendering educational dialogue complicit in ableist structures. Drawing upon the experiences of women and girls labelled as having disabilities and upon feminist theory and feminist disability studies research, I focus in this chapter on how dialogue, and listening within dialogue, is complicated and constrained by communicative and conceptual norms that govern not only who is heard but also how they are heard.[1]

Beyond making visible the problems encountered in dialogue across differences of ability, this chapter lays out a proposal for how feminist adult educators can facilitate students' engagement in dialogue that is more consistent with social justice goals. I argue that this engagement requires students' acknowledgement of their roles in constructing meanings within dialogue, meanings that can further entrench but also challenge assumptions and expectations about disability. The chapter looks, therefore, to reframe and reorient dialogic exchange as developing cross-positional *interdependence*, more so than cross-positional understanding. Such a view acknowledges participants' social connections and their dependence on one another for the construction of narratives. Furthermore, it acknowledges participants' embeddedness in abled and gendered webs of political, economic, and cultural meanings and social power.

Dialogue, Power, and Interdependence

In the first section of this chapter, I describe how dialogue and the related activities of deliberation have been trumpeted within the field of adult education as enabling cross-cultural understanding and the learning of civic practices and dispositions. I explore important critiques of dialogue and deliberation, notably how these pedagogical practices can reinforce existing inequalities and relations of power. In the second section, I describe how dialogic practice is built on gendered norms of ability that disadvantage and marginalize women with disabilities in particular ways. Finally, I describe how meaning is constructed through relationships of cross-positional interdependence and that acknowledgement of these relationships requires recognition of our responsibility to one another and to systems of power.

In *Pedagogy of the Oppressed*, Paulo Freire (1970) described dialogue as a process of empowerment that fundamentally humanizes its participants, treating them as sources of knowledge rather than as "empty vessels to be filled" (p. 88-91). Dialogue as a pedagogical and interpersonal mode of communication has played a central role in conceptions of adult education from higher education contexts to community activism (Burbules, 1993; Kaufmann, 2010; McGregor, 2004). Scholars of adult learning tout the significance of cross-cultural and cross-positional dialogue among students in the development of valuable civic and interpersonal skills in adult learning contexts, such as post-secondary institutions, employment preparation and training programs, and community-based or continuing education. Dialogue promises to allow for mutual exchange of knowledge, persuasive discussion, and unifying of ideas, and to empower students and community members who otherwise find their voices and perspectives marginalized or ignored. In dialogic pedagogy, teaching and learning are often understood as shared and dynamic processes in which students participate in learning that is transformative and empowering and in which personal and political awareness is conjoined with critical thinking about the social world.

In many ways, this educational focus on dialogue reflects broader democratic and social justice goals of adult education. Much as deliberation is seen as a fundamental activity of democracy, dialogue is seen as a fundamental activity of democratic education in which civic virtues and moral responsibility are developed and nurtured (Houston, 2005). Like democratic deliberation, dialogue promises to redress social injustices through its practice of critical reflection, the sharing of ideas, and understanding across social, political, cultural, and economic differences (e.g., Jones, 2005). Students share how the world looks from their particular position and their experience of belonging or marginalization. In this way, differences can be reconciled and shared democratic goals identified. The vision here is that of "a revitalized public sphere characterized by citizens capable of confronting public issues critically through ongoing forms of public debate and social action" (Ellsworth, 1989, p. 300). The goals of dialogue are multiple and various: it can be seen as fostering understanding, tolerance, and solidarity; empowering marginalized groups by allowing them to share their stories and experience; expanding knowledge through a sharing of ideas; teaching specific values and virtues for democratic life; or providing a space for emotional expression or rational debate, or both. Furthermore, dialogue is regarded as providing an opportunity for students to develop certain communicative and social virtues—of tolerance, of empathy, and of inclusivity (e.g., Burbules 1993).

Dialogue perhaps also presents an opportunity for students to learn about the ways that "social power"—I define this as a relational system in which social practices form and enforce the ways in which people are situated with respect to one another, and that governs social meanings and possibilities for expression—marginalizes some voices and stories and privileges others.

However, dialogue is a pedagogical activity characterized by differential relations of power that influence the nature of participation and possibilities for understanding (Berlak, 2005; Ellsworth, 1989; Jones, 2005; Taylor, 2010). It is always influenced by the social dynamics among participants, by their relation to one another, by their vested interests, emotions, and expectations, and by their place within social, political, cultural, and economic structures (e.g., Burbules 1993; Jones 2005). As a *communicative* activity in particular, dialogue is also influenced by the complex relationship between listening and speaking, silence and silencing, and speaking and hearing. Certainly, for dialogue to be successful, participants must be able to share their experiences, cultural knowledge, and perspectives, but also to listen to others sharing theirs. Yet social dynamics shape these potentialities: that participants will listen to one another is not guaranteed and the silence or ignorance that results can have very different meanings, marking a refusal to share, a failure to listen, or a refusal to hear (Li Li, 2005).

Many educational scholars have addressed these concerns in their work on dialogue and listening, some suggesting that the goals of dialogue are misguided and even dangerous in their emphasis on modernist ideals of equality, mutual understanding, and unity (Ellsworth, 1989; Jones, 2005; Leach, 1992). These critics have described how dialogue can actually reinforce existing and oppressive relations of power, especially when it takes place across racial, gender, sexuality, class, and ability groups. Viewing dialogue in an idealized way, these critics say, ignores the important ways in which social power and privilege work against such ideals, even obscuring the persistence of inequalities and injustices. In fact, dialogic pedagogy often appears to require that its participants act rationally and autonomously and that they be "capable of agreeing on universalizable 'fundamental moral principles' and 'quality of human life'" (Ellsworth, 1989, p. 316). Such requirements underestimate individuals' connections to broader social and political groups through which their experiences are shaped, as well as how the meanings that participants impart to particular values differ according to their different experiences and relationships (Ellsworth, 1989; Levinson, 2003). Furthermore, proponents of dialogue frequently assume that participants in dialogue are or can be *equally heard*, despite the obvious social backgrounds of racism, sexism, ableism, and other forms of oppression. In fact, educational institutions are frequently complicit in this oppression and are therefore compromised in their ability to provide a dialogic space in which all individuals are granted authority in sharing their experiences. Educators cannot fairly expect oppressed people to be willing to share their experiences and assert their interests within this context. Many students are unable or unwilling to participate in dialogue, and others who find it an alienating and objectifying process choose silence as an explicit refusal to take part in an exercise that further oppresses them (Blackwell, 2010; Jones, 1999). Simply put, not everyone is regarded as able or is enabled to participate equally in dialogue. I believe specific challenges can arise within dialogic pedagogy because of the diverse and often unrecognized communicative and behavioural modes of participants, and because norms and standards of communication, behaviour, and cognition privilege the able-bodied and able-minded.

While some adult educators reject the educational potential of dialogue altogether, others argue that if dialogue is designed to engage dominant and marginalized groups in sharing their experiences and perspectives, then it must account for the unequal social locations of its participants. As I am inclined towards transforming rather than rejecting dialogue, I will explore how the explicit recognition of the social and epistemic positioning of participants, their knowledge of social relations and norms, and their role in the production of social meanings can help guide us towards envisioning more transformative pedagogies of learning across difference.

Dialogue and the Disabled "Voice"

> ...What kinds of knowledge might be produced through having a body radically marked by its own
> particularity, a body that materializes at the ends of the curve of human variation?
> —Garland-Thomson, 2006, p. 267

People with disabilities are frequently perceived as voiceless or as lacking the ability to understand and share their lived experiences. This is especially true of those labelled with intellectual and developmental disabilities, those who experience difficulty with verbal communication, and those who have significant physical disabilities. These perceptions arise because such individuals are perceived as lacking independence, rationality, or the capacity for effective communication, qualities central to what feminists have described as the disembodied—and mythological—subject, a mind somehow detached from bodily needs and limitations (Kittay, 1999; Lanoix, 2007). These expectations of ability are gendered in ways particularly detrimental to women with disabilities. While all people with disabilities are devalued by such norms and expectations, women who have disabilities experience this oppression in unique and compounded ways because they are marked by an intersectional vulnerability and dependency (Fine and Asch, 1988; Erevelles and Minear, 2010; Garland-Thomson, 2006; Wendell, 1996). This intersectionality not only affects the degree to which they are vulnerable to gendered forms of violence, but also the degree to which they are vulnerable to the violence of societal erasure or dismissal.

The power relations created by these gendered norms of ability shape opportunities for effective and transformative dialogue. Some participants experience the privilege of being regarded as able-bodied or able-minded and this privilege protects their social and epistemic position as credible and competent contributors to dialogue. In contrast, perceptions of disabled women's vulnerability and inferiority can complicate and even prevent dialogue. People with disabilities occupy epistemic positions within a social structure framed by overwhelmingly negative expectations and perceptions of individuals with disabilities, especially with regard to their competence and credibility (Taylor, 2010). Similarly, women and non-normatively gendered people often find their credibility in question because of their perceived gender (Alcoff, 2001). These assumptions and expectations about cognitive and communicative competence shape not only how testimony is given within dialogue across difference, but also how testimony is understood, challenged, or dismissed.

Let us consider, for example, how "voice" is constructed in relation to women with disabilities. The notion of "voice" has been broadly contested within feminist literature that acknowledges it as a privileged space of access and power (Leach, 1992; Lugones and Spelman, 1983). The problem of access is, of course, a central concern in considerations of disability. Many disability theorists point out that "voice" is a privileged ability because spoken language is assumed and normalized as a primary mode of communication, thus neglecting those who type to communicate, those who sign, or those who engage in slurred, stuttered, or truncated speech. Even for those whose mode of communication is spoken language, their speech might, through its difference, encode particular stereotypes of disability: stuttering, slurred, or truncated speech have all been associated with lower intelligence, thus presuming a connection between an individual's voice and their cognitive or expressive abilities (McArdle, 2001). For others who do not communicate verbally, the ability to contribute to dialogue in which the primary mode of communication is spoken language is dependent on access to interpreters, facilitators, and/or other forms of assistance. Indeed, it is often due to a perceived *absence* of communicative ability that people with intellectual disabilities are perceived as voiceless and as lacking the ability to understand and share their lived experience (Cushing and Lewis, 2002). Within a dialogue across differences of ability, then, voice will need to be construed as far broader than spoken language and we must come to understand how expectations of voice express values of ability and gender that disadvantage disabled women.

Consider the following example from the popular American television show *The West Wing*:

> Main character Josh encounters Joey Lucas, a woman campaign manager who is deaf. Accompanying Joey is her sign language interpreter, a man. Joey signs quickly and angrily while the interpreter translates with the same intensity. A confused Josh asks, "What is happening right now?," to which Joey responds, "I'm Joey Lucas." Importantly, Josh is looking at the interpreter who speaks this aloud, translating for Joey. Josh then replies to the interpreter, "You're Joey Lucas?" The interpreter, again speaking for Joey, who is signing, says "No, *I'm* Joey Lucas" (and the camera pans to Joey). Josh, still confused, says to the interpreter, "Help me, cuz (sic) I don't ... " and Joey, this time verbally, says "You idiot, I'm Joey Lucas!" (*The West Wing*, 2000).

While acknowledging the ableist language in the term "idiot," I want to focus on the confusion that Josh experiences in his exchange with Joey. The initial process of speaking through an interpreter disrupts Josh's easy understanding of voice and of authority; he is, quite simply, confused about whose voice he is listening to and he is challenged by an unconscious privileging of the spoken voice. Indeed, it is only when Joey speaks (rather than signs) that Josh finally understands. In this example, we see how the expectation of spoken language along with gendered norms of authority operates to structure what is made intelligible within the exchange. The confusion that the well-intended Josh experiences is a product of the unconscious privileging of spoken voice, as well as the expectation of professional authority as being male.

This example demonstrates how listening is constrained by the communicative and conceptual impediments formed by societal norms and expectations surrounding ability and gender. This is a relatively benign enactment of these norms, but such impediments can come in far more insidious forms. Importantly, the misunderstanding, ignorance, or dismissal of testimony of people with disabilities can occur even in the presence of well-intended interlocutors, especially because the tendency to intervene and speak for people with disabilities is often encouraged. This helping stance can function to re-inscribe disabled people's assumed dependency and can excuse able-bodied interlocutors from doing the work of listening in ways that are unfamiliar to them.

Power and Testimony

Just as perceived differences of ability play a role in who is perceived as a competent and credible communicator and communicative authority (who is given "voice"), so, too, do such perceptions play a role in how testimony is evaluated (Alcoff, 2001; Fricker, 2007). Social and political culture position certain voices and stories as unrecognizable and illegitimate and grant epistemic authority to some and not others. This claim can shed more light on why and how unequal relations of power complicate educational dialogue across differences of ability and constrain the epistemic growth that is assumed to result from dialogic encounters.

It is a common experience of individuals with disabilities that by virtue of their often visible differences they are marked by uncritical social and epistemological assumptions regarding their capabilities and worth. Measured against implicit norms of able-bodiedness and able-mindedness, people with disabilities fall outside what Graham and Slee (2008) call "a man-made grid of intelligibility" that privileges particular ways of being and obscures or pathologizes others (p. 86). Individuals with intellectual disabilities are frequently seen as globally incompetent; people with physical disabilities as pitiful and suffering; people with mental health disabilities as dangerous; and people with autism as "in their own world."

Amelia Baggs is an autism rights activist. In a now popular YouTube video (2007) titled *In My Language*, Baggs, who is autistic, is featured making sounds and interacting with the objects in her room. Later in the video we are introduced to a computerized spoken voice reading out the words that Baggs (2007) types:

> The way I naturally think and respond to things looks and feels so different from standard concepts or even visualization that some people do not consider it thought at all, but it is a way of thinking in its own right.... The thinking of people like me is only taken seriously if we learn your language.... *It is only when I type something in your language that you refer to me as having communication* (my emphasis).

Baggs' own language is characterized by physical interaction with her environment; her voice is not, to use her own words, "standard." Baggs says that her movement and active engagement with her environment (feeling and smelling books, playing with water from the tap, flapping her hands) are mistakenly perceived as evidence of her "being in a world of [her] own"; rather, she says, "It is about being in constant conversation with my environment." Although Baggs' personal testimony challenges the assumption of her absence, it is testimony conveyed in a normalized communicative mode—spoken (albeit computerized) voice. This example illustrates how those individuals on the margins of normative experience are intimately familiar with dominant ways of being and knowing, while the reverse is not true (Jones 1999). Baggs knows my language intimately. I have no fluency in her language. Baggs' suggestion that she must use written text to provoke a listening response illustrates her awareness of the language of power: the call to be heard is a call made in the communicative mode of power.

This example makes plain that *what* one expects to hear and how one expects to hear it bear heavily on the outcome of the dialogic encounter. Some voices and some stories are excluded or more profoundly distorted in the process of exchange because of their outsider status or unrecognizability.

Disability scholar Susan Wendell (2006) describes how these narrative exclusions arise in part out of the medicalization of disability experience, which often leads to a disconnect between one's personal experience and the prescripts of medical authority. In the face of the invalidating power of this medical authority, an individual is likely to question her personal experience and to alter or silence herself in the process of recounting that experience (Wendell, 2006). In cases in which medical or educational professionals are situated as the authorities, this can mean that people with disabilities— especially young people—are reluctant or unable to speak up (Danforth, 2000). Cowley and Bacon (2013) point out that such learned acquiescence is also a result of special educational practices that promote young disabled women's compliance through learned character traits like politeness and good behaviour. Such a climate makes it difficult for women with disabilities to develop personal narratives that they can claim as truly their own.

Because so much of the experience of disablement is inscribed from the outside, Wendell's caution speaks to the challenge of fluid exchange within dialogue that is propelled by narrative exchange. Importantly, though, these cautions do not necessitate an abandonment of dialogue, but rather the recognition "that our conversation will never be innocent" (Bingham, 2002, p. 367). In continuing the dialogue, we must become far more aware of the scripts and narratives that are available to people with disabilities in describing their experience, as well as those that remain at bay. Furthermore, able-bodied and able-minded interlocutors have a particular responsibility to recognize their role in limiting opportunities for the social and epistemic development of people with disabilities.

Responsibilities in Listening

> I learn to help my heart by all the people listening.
> —"Woman with intellectual disability," quoted in Cushing and Lewis, 2002, p. 173.

Megan Boler (1999) wrote that the listener "plays a tremendous role in the production of truth" (p. 168). As a listener, one is a co-producer of the story because of the role that each of us plays in shaping one another's stories. Rather than thinking of dialogue as a fluid exchange between listener and testifier, wherein the listener is seen as a passive receptacle for the testifier's story, dialogic exchange can better be understood as an active co-construction of narrative. As discussed, listening takes place within unequal relations of power, not only in relation to the positioning of its participants but also in relation to the interpretive resources available to its participants (Fricker, 2007). In dialogue across difference, wherein listening requires tuning into what is perhaps unintelligible to us, listening to another's story involves being open to hearing and attending to difference, all the while recognizing one's own role in contemplating, relating, and producing that story for oneself through the interpretive scripts that are available to us.

Importantly, we all form our narratives and conceptions of ourselves in relation to cultural and social scripts that govern who and what is intelligible (e.g., Berlak, 2005). For example, my identification as a woman goes relatively unnoticed if I embody culturally accepted attributes of femininity. On the other hand, women who maintain obvious facial hair have their identities not only questioned but actually dismissed (Miller, 2008; see also Dowl, 2005). Moreover, because of the construction woman = not bearded, I am dependent on that negative construction to remain securely intelligible as a woman. The dominant social meanings that shape what forms of bodily, cognitive, or communicative expressions are intelligible are also those upon which dominant groups depend for their recognition. In other words, dominant groups require the marginalization of non-dominant groups in order to perpetuate the notion that they are normal and good. This narrative dependency shows us the challenge *as well as* the potential promise of dialogue.

The role of listener calls for the listener's recognition of her (albeit unequal) social positioning in structures of power and of her responsibility as a co-producer of the social scripts that are available as narrative resources in dialogue. This epistemic mutuality is promising because testimony and its meanings are transformed through the process of narration and interpretation itself (Burbules, 1993). However, the process of listening and transformation privileges dominant interlocutors. These individuals therefore have a responsibility to attend to how their social positioning gives them an unequal share in the constructive process.

In their study of caring relations within a L'Arche[2] community in Canada, Pamela Cushing and Tanya Lewis (2002) describe what they call "relational mutuality" between caregivers and the people they care for. In doing so, they illustrate the interdependence involved in learning across differences. Lisa, a caregiver, describes this mutuality in her commitment to understanding and honouring the life-world complexities of Donna, a woman with intellectual disabilities:

> I really identify with Donna in that she doesn't let people get close to her quickly and has layers of protection that keep her somewhat distant. Since she is also essentially non-verbal, this means that you often aren't sure what is going on with her and I struggle to interpret her movements without imposing my own perceptions on her world. (p. 184)

This example illustrates both the challenges and promises posed by cross-positional understanding. Lisa's own understanding of her responsibility to Donna involves both the recognition of her potential power to ignore and even erase Donna's experiences, as well as her commitment to seeing Donna as a competent and complex person whose expressive engagement is shaped by a very understandable—and, we might imagine, experientially based—sense of self-protectiveness. Because Lisa and Donna are socially positioned unequally relative to norms of ability, they both negotiate the risks of their engagement. This places a special burden on Lisa to exercise deep care and vigilance so as not to silence and further marginalize Donna, even as Lisa recognizes that her own epistemic identity is intimately bound up with Donna's.

Berlak (2005, p. 193) argues that being an "empathetic listener" requires confronting the way one has been socialized into a particular institutional order, and how each of us is commonly arrested by such a system of social ordering. We must learn to recognize that none of us is outside of, and thus unaffected by, this system of social inequality. To listen to another—and therefore, for Berlak, to bear witness to them—one must become conscious of and mourn one's own experience of normalization or socialization into a privileged social order. At stake is the ability "to recognize oneself as implicated in the social forces that create the climate of obstacles the other must confront" (Boler, 1999, p. 159). Thus, shared responsibility is cultivated in one's learning to listen and to attend to the testimony of others who are unfamiliar to us in ways that require discomfort and risk. The marginalized person risks how she will be heard, understood, and assimilated. The privileged interlocutor risks her own solid ground of meaning, risks provoked changes in consciousness, and, finally, risks the safety of her own knowing.

What, then, does this caring mutuality tell us about the role of dialogue in adult learning? I believe it shows us that the cultivation of students' recognition of narrative and social interdependence is a necessary pre-condition for responsible learning across differences; that is, without acknowledging our narrative interdependence, we cannot satisfy our goals of transformation through dialogue. There are two reasons that I choose to highlight interdependence rather than understanding as both a precondition and a goal of dialogue. First, interdependence expresses a more accurate understanding of social relations: no person exists independently of a social, domestic, economic connection to any other person (Erevelles and Minear, 2010; Kittay, 1999). Second, interdependence highlights how participants within dialogue are dependent on one another in the construction of narratives, albeit within a context of unequal social power. Just as the narratives of Baggs, Donna, and the fictional Joey—as disabled women—are always constructed in relation to and dependently on the social meanings of dominant groups, so, too, are able-bodied and able-minded women also dependent on the devaluation of women with disabilities to avoid social erasure. So, while the women whose experiences I have described do want to "just talk," they know that talk is not always *just*. And for just conditions of dialogue to be realized, those in positions of social and epistemic power have a lot of work to do.

Acknowledgements

- I am grateful to editors Darlene Clover, Shauna Butterwick, Donna Chovanec, and Laurel Collins for their imagination and labour, and for their generous invitation to be part of this volume. My work on this chapter was generously supported by a National Academy of Education/Spencer Dissertation Fellowship.

Endnotes

[1] The use of "heard" here does preference individuals who are hearing even as it imparts meaning about receipt of information and understanding. Our language is fraught with references to and implicit messages about disability. Making explicit those instances in which ableism is reinforced through language helps to disrupt these implicit messages.

[2] L'Arche is an international organization of faith-based communities that is home to people with intellectual and developmental disabilities and their non-familial caregivers. See http://www.larche.ca.

References

- Alcoff, L. M. (2001). On judging epistemic credibility: Is social identity relevant? In N. Tuana and S. Morgen (Eds.), *Engendering Rationalities* (pp. 53-80). Albany: SUNY Press.

- Baggs, A. [silentmiaow] (2007). *In My Language*. [Video file]. Retrieved from https://www.youtube.com/watch?v=JnylM1hI2jc

- Basile, N. [booya9d] (2007, November 20). *American Carny Jennifer Miller*. [Video File]. Retrieved from http://www.youtube.com/watch?v=uoschCAdpjs.

- Berlak, A. C. (2005). Confrontation and pedagogy: Cultural secrets, trauma, and emotion in antioppressive pedagogies. In M. Boler (Ed.), *Democratic Dialogue in Education: Troubling Speech, Disturbing Silence* (pp. 123-144). New York: Peter Lang.

- Bingham, C. (2002). A dangerous benefit: Dialogue, discourse, and Michel Foucault's critique of representation. *Interchange* 33(4), 351-369.

- Blackwell, D. (2010). Sidelines and separate spaces: Making education anti-racist for students of color. *Race, Ethnicity and Education,* 13(4), 473-494.

- Boler, M. (1999). *Feeling Power: Emotions and Education*. New York: Routledge.

- Burbules, N. (1993). *Dialogue in Teaching: Theory and Practice*. New York: Teachers College Press.

- Cowley, D. M. and Bacon, J. K. (2013). Self-determination in schools: Reconstructing the concept through a disability studies framework. *PowerPlay,* 5(1), 463-489.

- Cushing, P. and Lewis, T. (2002). Negotiating mutuality and agency in care-giving relationships with women with intellectual disabilities. *Hypatia* 17(3), 173-193.

- Danforth, S. (2000). What can the field of developmental disabilities learn from Michel Foucault? *Mental Retardation*, 38(4), 364-369.

- Dowl, A. (2005, Spring). Beyond the bearded lady: Outgrowing the shame of female facial hair. *Bitch 28*, 54-59.

- Ellsworth, E. (1989). Why doesn't this feel empowering? Working through the repressive myths of critical pedagogy. *Harvard Educational Review*, 59(3), 297-325.

- Erevelles, N. and Minear A. (2010). Unspeakable offenses: Untangling race and disability in discourses of intersectionality. *Journal of Literary & Cultural Disability Studies,* 4(2), 127-145.

- Fine, M. and Asch A. (Eds.) (1988). *Women with Disabilities: Essays in Psychology, Culture, and Politics*. Philadelphia, PA: Temple University Press.

- Freire, P. (1993 [1970]). *Pedagogy of the Oppressed*. New York: Continuum.

- Fricker, M. (2007). *Epistemic Injustice: Power and the Ethics of Knowing*. Oxford: Oxford University Press.

- Galloway, T. (2009). *Mean Little Deaf Queer: A Memoir*. Boston, MA: Beacon Press.

- Garland-Thomson, R. (2006). Integrating disability, transforming feminist theory. In L. J. Davis (Ed.), *The Disability Studies Reader* (2nd Edition). (pp. 257-274). New York: Routledge.

- Graham, L. J. and Slee, R. (2008). Inclusion? In S. L. Gabel and S. Danforth (Eds.), *Disability and the Politics of Education* (pp. 81-100). New York: Peter Lang.

- Houston, B. (2005). Democratic dialogue: Who takes responsibility? In M. Boler (Ed.), *Democratic Dialogue in Education: Troubling Speech, Disturbing Silence* (pp. 105-129). New York: Peter Lang.

- Jones, A. (1999). The limits of cross-cultural dialogue: Pedagogy, desire, and absolution in the classroom. *Educational Theory,* 49(3), 299-316.

- Jones, A. (2005). Talking cure: The desire for dialogue. In M. Boler (Ed.), *Democratic Dialogue in Education: Troubling Speech, Disturbing Silence* (pp. 57-68). New York: Peter Lang.

- Leach, M. (1992). Can we talk? A response to Burbules and Rice. *Harvard Educational Review*, 62(2), 257-64.

- Kaufmann, J. J. (2010). The practice of dialogue in critical pedagogy. *Adult Education Quarterly*, 60(5), 456-476.

- Kittay, E. F. (1999). *Love's Labor: Essays on Women, Equality, and Dependency*. New York: Routledge.

- Lanoix, M. (2007). The citizen in question. *Hypatia*, 22(4), 113-129.

- Levinson, M. (2003). Challenging deliberation. *Theory and Research in Education,* 1(1), 23-49.

- Li Li, H. (2005). Rethinking silencing silences. In M. Boler (Ed.), *Democratic Dialogue in Education: Troubling Speech, Disturbing Silence* (pp. 69-88). New York: Peter Lang.

- Lugones, M. C. and Spelman, E. V. (1983). Have I got a theory for you! Feminist theory, cultural imperialism and the demand for "the woman's voice." *Women's Studies International Forum*, 6(6), 573-581.

- McArdle, E. (2001). Communication impairment and stigma. In C. Carlisle, T. Mason, C. Watkins, and E. Whitehead (Ed.), *Stigma and Social Exclusion in Healthcare* (pp. 92-103). London: Routledge.

- McGregor, C. (2004). Care(full) deliberation: A pedagogy for citizenship. *Journal of Transformative Education*, 2(2), 90-106.

- Sorkin, A. (Writer) and Schlamme, T. (Director). (2000). Take this Sabbath Day. [Television series episode]. In A. Sorkin (Executive Producer), *The West Wing*. Los Angeles: John Wells Productions, Warner Bros.

- Taylor, A. (2010). "Can You Hear Me?" Questioning dialogue across differences of ability. In G. Biesta (Ed.), *Philosophy of Education 2010* (pp. 45-53). Urbana, IL: University of Illinois Press.

- Wendell, S. (1996). *The Rejected Body: Feminist Philosophical Reflections on Disability*. New York: Routledge.

Pedagogy and
the Imagination

One of 1,808 pairs of moccasin vamps in an art installation remembering the lives of missing and murdered Indigenous women and girls in Canada.
Courtesy of Sarah Schmidt/Walking With Our Sisters.

15

Imagining the Possible
Feminist Arts-Based Adult Education and Leadership

> The radical shift in the structure of the world begs for creativity; it asks us to rethink who we are as human beings.... It may be that writers, painters, and musicians have an unprecedented opportunity to be co-creators with society's leaders in setting a path. For art, after all, is about rearranging us, creating surprising juxtapositions, emotional openings, startling presences.
> —Nancy Adler, 2006

Artists have a long history of responding to upheavals and change, interpreting and representing these in visual, poetic, narrative and performative forms. Kidd and Selman (1978) reminded us that the partnership between the arts and adult education and learning too has a long history. This chapter focuses on how feminist adult educators, artists, and researchers harness the power of art to investigate, invoke, re-negotiate, critique, build, and re-imagine the world with and for women today.

Darlene E. Clover and Laurie McGauley

The work of feminist adult educators, artists, and researchers is contextualized in Haiven and Khasnabish's (2014, p. 3) depiction of contemporary Canada as a slow-motion apocalypse, a cascade of inter-connected social, cultural, and ecological crises brought about by a capitalist system determined to impoverish, undermine, and deny our capacities to act, think, and engage "the creative possibilities in human life" (Williamson, 2004, p. 36).

We would add the need to recognize the current gender crisis in Canada, characterized by an escalation of violence and harassment on university campuses, the street, in social media, and beyond. We argue this crisis demands greater "feminist," political, and creative praxis to develop a more *gendered*, radical imagination, defined, to borrow from Havien and Khasnabish, as "the capacity to think critically, reflexively and innovatively about [gender] and the ability to imagine [male-female relationships] not as they are, but as they might otherwise be" (Haiven & Khasnabish, 2014, p. 3). For as Wyman (2004, p. 10) contends, it is this imagination, "liberated by engagement with cultural expression," that will enable all we hope for in Canadian society.

This chapter focuses on how women are combining the intellectual, the activist, the investigative, the aesthetic, the imaginative, and/or the expressive to address gender injustices pedagogically through critical-creative consciousness, analysis, and action in the pursuit of positive gender change. We illustrate how, through sign and symbol, performance and realism, the pursuit of dignity, and provocation, feminists' cultural practices stretch discourses of community arts, adult education, and enquiry, and cultivate aesthetic knowledge and action to challenge the neo-conservative terrain of Canada today. We begin with a discussion of the community arts discourses that have informed feminist cultural practice in Canada and bring to life their various aspects through five stories about feminist adult education and research work in Ontario and British Columbia. We conclude with a discussion of other key elements of feminist cultural projects that, motivated by the pursuit of positive gender change, help women to re-imagine and re-make the world.

Community Arts, Arts-Based Adult Education, and Arts-Based Research/Enquiry

Community arts is one discourse that informs current feminist cultural practice in Canada. It has it antecedents in counter-culture debates about art's function in politics and society. Herbert Marcuse (1978) laid out one of the foundational challenges. He articulated the idea of "high culture," a problematically reified, socially constructed positioning of the arts that, both literally and figuratively, took them beyond the reach of the majority of people by placing them in elitist cultural houses such as galleries. This reification can in fact be traced back to Aristotle, whose hierarchy of knowledge and art separated the "useful and necessary" from the "beautiful and ephemeral." For Aristotle, the world was governed by competing interests and was thus unstable, messy, and unreliable. The pursuit of beauty/art, therefore, needed to occur within the realm of "pure thought," an ideal space untainted by politics and society. While justified on the one hand—art, for example, had been employed as a tool of fascist "propaganda" and instrumentalized to bring about social compliance and conformity—this positioning neglected how easily notions of idealism, beauty, and truth could align with privilege and delegitimize the "untrue" "popular arts" and daily struggle for existence of hundreds of people in the "material" world (McGauley, 2006).

Contemporary community arts in Canada is a practice that recognizes creative expression as "a powerful element of the social, economic and political landscape" and active participation in cultural life as an essential goal of democracy (Lee & Fernandez, 1988, p. 7). The Ontario Arts Council defines community arts as "a collaborative creative process [or art-making] between a professional, practising artists and a [self-defined] community.... It is as much about process as it is about the artistic product or outcome" (p. 7).

Inherent in community arts discourse are a number of inter-related understandings. The first is that cultural practice is a crucible for personal as well as social transformation that is less polarizing and thereby able to create deeper connections than other social-engaged practices (Adams & Goldband, 2006). Another is that the arts are effective healing agents that can be very therapeutic for people from disadvantaged groups. A third is the notion of cultural democracy, articulated as participation in the "co-creation" of artistic works to move beyond mere individual expression. People involved in cultural projects are creators, actors, and meaning makers, and not merely the passive viewers or consumers of others' artworks. A fourth key understanding of community arts is that the process of engagement is equally as important as the product. This understanding responds to the over-emphasis in aesthetic discourses on the product (artwork) as it recognizes that "to consciously execute something with less skill than one actually commands on the grounds that this is good enough for community work—surely the insult inherent in such a decision cancels any democratic intention that might motivate it" (Adams & Goldard, 2006, p. 23). This means that artists play a dual role as "as agents of transformation" as well as teachers and guides around artistry (Adams & Goldband, 2006, p. 16). Finally, all community arts projects must be relevant to community and they must revolve around notions of mutual respect, safety, inclusivity, and consensus decision making (Amadahy, 2004; Lee & Fernandez, 1998).

There are, however, equally important inter-related critiques of community arts. One is the over-emphasis often placed on "healing." While healing can be framed around ideas of reconciliation between social divisions, this emphasis can reduce community arts projects to platitudes that deny any systemic cause for pain, such as racism or misogyny, and simply offer a quick aesthetic fix to an "individual" problem (McGauley, 2006). This leads to a second critique: community art's tendency to focus on the purely expressive nature of art. Problematically, this can inadvertently reinforce a liberal idea that "any point of view proposed for agreement is simply the expression of one's particular disposition" (Pelletier, 2002, p. 12) and, therefore, all points of view are equally valid due to subjectivity. But not all points of view are valid, particularly if they are racist or misogynist, and there are always power dimensions that are hidden "consensus." Free expression and subjectivity are crucial and consensus is an ideal, but so too are active debate, dissent, and challenging assumptions. Problematically, however, community artists do not necessarily have the types of experiences or backgrounds required to enable them to address complex social or gender issues and, therefore, they tend to shy away from conflict and confrontation. A third critique is around the emphasis on social cohesion. While bringing people together to share their commonalities is an important goal, community arts projects can unconsciously—or consciously, if we think about the above point—gloss over power and other important unbalanced socio-cultural and, particularly, gender relations within a "community." This brings us to arts-based adult education, a discourse that has emerged in Canada over the past decade.

Arts-based adult education draws on many of the understandings of community arts, but places more emphasis on pedagogical and political intentionality. In essence, arts-based adult education is a balance of aesthetics through a pedagogical lens and pedagogy through an aesthetic lens, bringing together key elements of critical and feminist adult education with the human aesthetic dimensions of imagination and creativity as the means to work towards politically progressive change. The arts and the process are used actively to critique and challenge the present world, but equally to imagine a world beyond what now exists. Expressive freedom happens within a dialogical context against horizons of significance and power struggles, but not as an affirmation of them nor as an escape from them. Rather, expressive freedom, in a pedagogical and aesthetic sense, is necessarily part of a creative dialogue that implies a responsibility to use art to become conscious of, and learn to challenge, horizons, not to idealize or deny them (McGauley, 2006). Aesthetic forms—quilts, photography, metissage, murals, theatre—encapsulate what Beyer (2000) calls a "structure of feeling," allowing us to see and respond to our own and others' circumstances in both realistic as well as symbolic and metaphoric ways that contribute to new, radical forms of consciousness.

Arts-based adult education also places creativity and the imagination within the realm of social activism. To borrow from Allman (1994), injustices cannot be simply thought, talked, or visualized away; they have to be eradicated through effecting change. Claiming and developing people's creativity is, therefore, integral to their sense of agency to reclaim control over lives, institutions, and political structures, and to re-assert social constructs and representations. Feminists refer to this as "activist art" (e.g., Mullins, 2003), art that collectively explores political and social topics. Of particular importance is presenting the work publicly in order to provoke dialogue and new understandings of complex and persistent social, political, cultural, and gender issues both beyond and within the formal art world.

Arts-based research/enquiry is another important discourse that shapes women's cultural practice. Butterwick (2002) reminded us that arts-based research in Canada emerged as an important challenge to the "limitations and oppressive features of traditional scientific research, opening spaces for experimentation of alternative approaches" (p. 243). Ball (2002) described the practice as "writing outside of the lines, transgressing the rules, while staying within the lines of dominant discursive practices... [and is one of the] few ways we have left to disrupt the dominant discourses in society that silence and marginalize" (p. 2). The primary goal of arts-based research/enquiry is intentionally to weave "aesthetic sensibilities and post-positivistic forms of expression" (Butterwick, 2002, p. 243) in order to, among other things, allow "us to hear silences and see absences and invisibilities" in ways we could not necessarily before (Ball, 2002, p. 2). The art, be it visual, narrative, or performative, functions as a vehicle to respond to a research question and to collect, represent, and disseminate the data. Depending upon the context and nature of the study, the artwork is often curated for public display or exhibition in order to engage people in dialogue and interpretation around the findings and their implications study (Clover & Craig, 2009; Cole & McIntyre, 2006; Cahnmann-Taylor & Siegesmund, 2008).

The Feminist, Arts-Based Pedagogical Imagination in Motion

We turn now to our stories of five feminist cultural practices and their creative energies and possibilities. Although these are but a few of the many initiatives across this country, we have chosen them because they illustrate the breadth, depth, and scope of creativity and imagination in feminist pedagogical research, the diversity of genres employed, the range of issues, and the social or site-specific contexts.

Knitting Connections

In talking about how to build community among disadvantaged social groups, Nina Montmann (2009) called for "art works that have practical value and which make a political impact" (p. 14). *In the Hood* was such a response. This one-year, arts-based project was facilitated by a small group of feminist artists who lived in an economically deprived yet culturally rich neighbourhood in central Toronto. It is described by one of the group like this:

> The boarded up shop front windows in the neighbourhood are an interesting metaphor for the community itself. What normally is wide open and designed to facilitate seeing is instead covered, hidden, and neglected. The richness, diversity, and colour of the Hood are unseen, ignored, and invisible, except as stereotypes in the media.

The project began with the women artist-educators going door-to-door to speak with residents about their lives and the neighbourhood. They discovered many women created crafts but kept these in the private domain of household and family. The also discovered, paradoxically, that despite an ever more globalizing, urbanizing, and inter-connected world, many women expressed a fear of the "other" and felt alienated and isolated. Over 100 women were brought together weekly through a series of workshops at the local library to talk, interact, and knit "fantasy" slippers that reflected their individual stories and dreams for the future. A collaborative aspect central to the project was the sewing of a giant slipper, representative of the "gathering," the collective story of their community. The feminist artist-educators then lobbied shop owners to display the slippers in the windows to transform the drab and soulless streetscape, and they also organized a street festival to bring more people out of their homes to meet and celebrate. Running parallel to these events was a collective, experimental process using paint and poetry to transform one local Laundromat from its present unsightly state to a place of colour and poetry that was no longer frightening to the women. In a second Laundromat, a group of women came together weekly to talk about their lives and to create beautiful, re-usable "Designer Laundry Bags." As they were completed, the bags were placed on display where, serendipitously, they found a local market keen to buy them.

Fabricating a Voice

The aging demographic of Canada is often characterized as a "burden" to society in economic terms. Ageism has also lead to diminished understandings of the knowledge and value of seniors and, particularly, of elderly women (Roy, 2013). In the hands of some feminist seniors, however, aging has been re-politicized and activated through art. *Crying the Blues* was a collective quilt project conceived by a small group of feminist members—some from the Raging Grannies, a radical group of comedic activists—from the progressive branch of the provincial Seniors Association of British Columbia known as the Old Age Pensioners (OAP). The project sprang from mounting concerns by these women about the draconian social funding cuts by a newly elected provincial government. *Crying the Blues* was conceived as a creative means to provide an opportunity for other concerns— raised by seniors across the province, many of whom felt voiceless—to experiment and imaginatively represent their views on the social impacts of the cuts.

Letters went out from the women OAPs across the province, explaining the idea of the quilt but with no specifications save quilt square size and colour (it had to be blue). Once the numerous individual squares/stories were returned, themes that represented a diversity of views and expressions were identified and the sewing to weave them together began. The collective story of the finished quilt represents a re-imagining of the fraying social fabric of the province. In some cases, it uses symbolic images, such as a pair of scissors to illustrate the cuts being introduced or a set of scales tipped towards inequity. In others, images were more overt, such as images of hospital closure, or rising housing and tuition costs. Through a mix of metaphor and realism, the quilt characterizes what Stecker called "beautify, grace, vibrancy, expressive power and vividness in representation" (cited in Mullins, 2003, p. 190). The quilt was displayed at the provincial Legislature Building and at other protests to engage the public and attract media attention. It has also been borrowed by other local seniors' organizations to encourage their members to link creatively with politics and establish a voice in the future of their province.

(Re)framing Power

A primary aim of feminist adult education is to reposition how women's power and leadership in society are viewed, and this was a primary goal of *According to Us*. This was a multi-year project by a group of ethnically diverse women from the women's program in Central Neighbourhood House, a social service agency in Toronto.

This group collectively decided to do something substantive with their time and, as they all shared an interest in photography, they chose this medium to begin a project. Lacking the photographic "skill" that they felt was required, the group advertised for, and then chose, a professional feminist photographer. Through experimentation, the feminist photographer taught skills such as using depth of focus, subject and photographer positioning, and light and shadow to capture, figuratively and metaphorically, things concrete (such as a face) and things abstract (such as power).

Behind the lens, the women explored issues of poverty, isolation, and disempowerment. But equally importantly, as they became more confident in their identifies as photographic artists, they talked about feeling able to take part in women's marches and protests in Ottawa and New York, spaces from which they had previously felt excluded. They also designed a research project to identify and capture images and stories of women role models in their lives. The images were assembled into a collective calendar displaying the women "who inspire us, who challenge us," and exhibitions were mounted under the title *Portraits of Resistance: Celebrating Women's Lives* in community centres, art galleries, and art shows across the city. Similar to the quilt, there are images that are relatively more metaphoric, such as the one in which lightness, darkness, and subject positioning portray the complexity of "coming out" sexuality.

Enacting Feminist Coalitions

The feminist movement in Canada can be characterized as both a series of setbacks and backlashes, as well as progress made and optimism at work. This ebb and flow was at the heart of a multi-year participatory theatre-based research project in Vancouver. Conceived by feminist adult educator Butterwick (2002), the project collectively explored, through performative activities, past and emerging experiences and challenges of working as feminists in various community-based and institutional contexts.

The process included interviews in which two women shared dangerous and exciting moments, alternating listening, recording, and probing for deeper understandings, followed by metaphoric and impressionistic representations of events, themes, and emotions through body sculptures of "frozen pictures," which included interpretations and further discussions of meaning. Butterwick cautions about dangers in this type of work, "in revealing our limitations as listeners; in revealing what was important to us as narrators; in finding words, gestures, images that attempted to capture and reflect what we thought we had understood as listeners. The process meant that we were vulnerable and accountable to others" (n/p). She argues that projects like this are most effective when they include trust-building, listening, learning the skills and principles of popular theatre techniques, and attention to individual and group subjectivities and creativity.

Beading Remembrance

Over the past 30 years, more than 1200 Indigenous women and girls have gone missing or have been murdered in Canada. Many have simply vanished without a trace, including from the eyes of the media, politicians, and even law enforcement. "This is a travesty of justice," argues Indigenous artist-educator Christi Belcourt, the curator of the collaborative travelling art installation entitled *Walking With Our Sisters* that is being exhibited in communities and art galleries across Canada and the United States. With the aim of honouring grandmothers, sisters, and women, this installation focuses on the power of art to remember and honour the lives of the missing and murdered Indigenous women and girls in Canada. *Walking With Our Sisters* is a massive, commemorative art installation comprising more than 1808 pairs of moccasin vamps (tops) plus 118 pairs of children's vamps that were created by artists or donated by hundreds of caring and concerned individuals to draw attention to this injustice. The vamps are arranged in a winding path formation on fabric and include local medicines, such as cedar or sage. Viewers remove their shoes to walk on a path of cloth alongside the vamps. This work illustrates the power of the collective as well as the pain of many who have lost or been lost. The unfinished lives of murdered or missing Indigenous women and girls are exhibited in way that represents a path or journey that ended abruptly and prematurely. As a collective work, like many of the others above, this project is about cultural democracy. Exhibiting it in art galleries, however, also makes it a democratization of culture project—bringing art to the people—albeit with a very feminist and political positioning that unflinchingly takes on one of Canada's most important gender issues.

A Feminist Pedagogy of Activism and Aesthetics

> The ultimate test of democracy lies in the quality of the artistic and intellectual life it
> creates and supports.
> —Maeve Moore, 1978

Collectively, the stories we have shared in this chapter demonstrate the breadth of differing purposes and needs, processes of engagement and genres, audience engagement, sites, and issues. They attend to individual and collective agency or identity, to the importance of connecting, of being heard, of remembering, of building strength and rendering visible that which is hidden. We believe they are feminist projects because, in their own ways, they "focus on sex and gender and work toward politically progressive change" (Mullins, 2003, p. 192). And yet, feminist cultural praxis is not a single pathway or route, but rather a potpourri of visuals, skills, narratives and conversations, performances, techniques, and exhibitions that encapsulate complexity and variation and that work to disrupt, affirm, remember, oppose, or build. We conclude this chapter with a discussion of other important features of feminist cultural practices as outlined above.

All of the projects take place against and within a backdrop of diverse and contending social forces, which are named and exposed through the practice of what Lippard (1996) calls "empowered, democratic art" (p. 244). These processes of naming and exposing give attention to two often competing narratives about the power and potential of art. Jenick (2013) challenges "realism" in arts products and in collective-activist projects, arguing they reduce art/practice to an ineffective

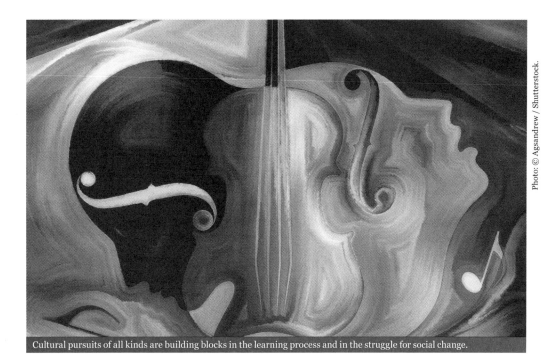

Cultural pursuits of all kinds are building blocks in the learning process and in the struggle for social change.

pedantic or didactic. She argues the power of art lies in single-authored stories that are ambiguous and nuanced. There is evidence in feminist arts-based practices that much attention is given to women's individual creativity and sense of artistic self and, equally, to teaching and learning techniques that enable the ability to use story, metaphor, and other types of techniques—light and shadow in a photograph as suggestive of "coming out," for example—in ways that demonstrate a comfort with ambiguity. The role taken by the artist-educator is to transmit or encourage particular arts-related skills that value indistinctness, representation, and, equally often, "the maintenance of the aesthetic quality of art" (Kelley, 1995, p. 223; see also Clover, 2012).

The artist-educator thus assists women to develop critical and metaphoric thinking and establish a link between the two capabilities. The artworks produced through feminist aesthetic praxis are not simply visual or dramatic translations of what might otherwise simply be said, but rather are visual or dramatic transformations of a certain awareness of the world. They are not simply assertions of the world but rather what Leppert (1996) calls "interrogatives, enquires and explorations. [They] do not so much tell us anything, as they make available—by making visible in a certain way—a realm of possibilities and probabilities, some of which are difficult to state in words" (p. 6). Yet, within this commitment to art, and to individual and self-deliberation, agency, and ambiguity, we also find a commitment to the creative, pedagogical power of collective generative artworks and activities, a sense of "truth," and their public ability to disrupt the present order of things. Narratives that dismiss realism are what feminist Mullins (2003) calls "misguided theories about the nature of art and the nature of politics" (p. 189). Feminist imagination, as these projects illustrate, is simultaneously artistic and political. It is neither "controlled by a predefined political agenda nor as floating disconnected from the political engagements and aspirations of those who create and respond to works of art" (p. 190). Lippard (1985) suggests there are many limitations to individual artistic endeavours, situating collective production as both an "organizing tool as well as a source of aesthetic expression and provocation" (p. 243). Advocacy and change mean taking a stand, and this must by necessity include the open and actual naming and exposing of an issue this affords. Feminist arts-based adult education actively encourages collective cultural negotiations around knowledge, power, and agency, attending to difference as it brings out the commonalities that marginalize, oppress and silence.

The collective emphasis on the human aesthetic dimension politicizes arts practice and the women involved in such practice by altering systems of participation, de-centring power, and binding the work to larger social, cultural, and political realities. Culture becomes the building block in cultural learning and the struggle for change. What we are arguing here is that feminist arts-based practices bring balance to product and process, because of their different yet mutually supporting roles and purposes. Pedagogical process, as understood in feminist adult education practice, revolves most often around conversations, dialogue, and debates that are always and ever dynamic, spontaneous, and inter-subjective (Butterwick, 2002). These necessarily involve active and often vocal interpretations and re-interpretations as people engage with each to make sense of experiences and realities. But process is never a final or finished product. Art is the embodiment of ways of seeing, of interpretations and re-interpretations. Art is also not a "finished or final product" because viewers are in fact active participants in the making and re-making of the images and stories. To realize a radical imagination, we need words but we need more than words. We need stories of reality but, equally, we need inventiveness. We need intimate activity, but also disobedient public works. In other words, we need the varied knowledges, actions, and ways of seeing that come when art and process convene.

Feminist cultural practices are situated within or, perhaps better said, combine two other aspects which Rogoff (2012) in fact separates: "emergency" and "urgency." He defines emergency as a "reactive" state to a set of imperatives or circumstances that produce an endless chain of crises. Feminist cultural practice is, and of course must be, reactive in a highly disobedient form to patriarchy, which is itself an endless chain of crises for women enacted through what Thompson (1983) defined as the "all-encompassing power that men have as a group over women, the systemic exclusion of women, and the systemic devaluation of all roles and traits which society has assigned to women" (p. 9). It is equally reactive to the "slow motion" but constantly emerging imperatives and crises brought about by neo-conservatism. For something to be truly affirmative of another world, it must be ultimately reactive and oppositional. But feminist cultural practice is also about "urgency," characterized by Rogoff as the possibility of producing new, creative understandings and imaginings of the crucial issues of society. Urgency, manifest through feminist art practice, is the driving force for gender change that alters ways of seeing, disrupts the order of things, or makes a new sense of place and time. This combination of "emergency" and "urgency," therefore, is about responding across pluralities of problems and working with and through the localized (e.g., the need for the beautification of a Laundromat to help women feel safe) and the globalized (e.g., a public canvas that interrogates actions that would affect the life-support systems of the planet). Together, they represent a release of creative energies in terms of what we need to oppose, what can be imagined, and the knowledge or action-creating negotiations that come from the two.

The Final Curtain

Nancy Adler (2006) asks: if community arts have paved the way for us to do anything, what will we do? What feminist artist-educators and researchers in Canada do, as illustrated in our examples, is enact extraordinary senses of hope, remembrance, inspiration, resistance, and imagination. Creative images and metaphors are realistic and critical, but they are equally playful and uplifting, choreographed to rekindle energy and activism or strengthen knowledge learning. Integrating individual art-making and collective practice is to personify how we need to relate creatively to each other, as well a sense of relationships, aesthetic agency(ies), and identity(ies) that serve and expand how we enact and negotiate culture and education. The feminist poet and writer M. Nourbese Phillip once argued that culture should never be seen as an insignificant site of struggle, although its power often lies in masking that very fact. This is perhaps most apparent in this story we use to conclude our chapter.

On the front page of England's *Guardian* newspaper, Tory Chancellor (the equivalent to Canada's Finance Minister) George Osborne was quoted as urging a group of business leaders "to raise their heads above the parapet ... to defend the economy" against unions and other pressure groups (Allen & Mason, 2014, p. 1). He argued that these groups were turning people against business and capitalism through their dangerous counter-views and actions. He suggested that they (metaphorically of course) "stick to their knitting" (p. 1). We suggest he be careful what he wishes for.

References

- Adler, N. (2006). The arts and leadership: Now that we can do anything, what will we do? Accessed on 11/11/14 from http://amle.aom.org/content/5/4/486.short.
- Allen, K. and Mason, R. (2014). Outcry as Osborne rails against "anti-business" charities. *The Guardian*, News, p. 1.
- Amadahy, Z. (2004). *Leading Community Arts into the Future*. Toronto, ON: Community Arts Ontario.
- Ball, H. K. (2002). Subversive materials: Quilts as social text. *Alberta Journal of Educational Research*, 60(3), 1-27.
- Butterwick, S. (2002). Your story/my story/our story: Performing interpretation in participatory theatre. Accessed on 8/8/14 from http://search.proquest.com.ezproxy.library.uvic.ca/docview/228619390?pq-origsite=summon.
- Cahnmann-Taylor, M. and Siegesmund, R. (Eds.) (2008). *Arts-Based Research in Education*. New York and London: Routledge.
- Clover, D. E. and Dogus, F. (2014). In case of emergency, break convention: A case study of a Human Library project in an art gallery. *Canadian Journal for the Study of Adult Education*, 26(3), 75-91.
- Clover, D. E. (2012). Feminist artists and popular education: The creative turn. In L. Manicom and S. Walters (Eds.), *Feminist Popular Education: Creating Pedagogies of Possibility* (pp. 193-208). New York, NY: Palgrave.
- Clover D. E. and Craig, C. (2009). Street-life's creative turn: An exploration of arts-based adult education and knowledge mobilization with homeless/street-involved women in Victoria. *Canadian Journal for the Study of Adult Education*, 21(2), 21-36.
- Clover, D. E. and Stalker, J. (2007). *The Arts and Social Justice: Re-Crafting Adult Education and Community Cultural Leadership*. Leicester: NIACE.
- Cole, A. and Knowles (2008). Arts-informed research. In J. Knowles and A. Cole (Eds.). *Handbook of the Arts in Qualitative Research* (pp. 55-70). Thousand Oaks, CA: Sage.
- Fegan, T. (2003). *Learning and Community Arts*. Leicester: NIACE.
- Haiven, M. and Khasnabish, A. (2014). *The Radical Imagination*. London: Zed Books.
- Hyland-Russell, T. and Groen, J. (2013). Crossing a cultural divide: Transgressing the margins into public spaces fosters adult learning. In D.E. Clover & K. Sanford (Eds.), *Lifelong Learning, the Arts and Contemporary Universities: International Perspectives*. Manchester: Manchester University Press.
- Kidd, J.R. and Selman, G. (1978). *Coming of Age: Canadian Adult Education in the 1960s*. Toronto: CAAE.
- Klein, N. (2014). *This Changes Everything: Capitalism vs. the Climate*. Toronto: Penguin Books.

- · Lee, A. and Fernandez, M. (1998). *Community Arts Workbook*. Toronto: Ontario Arts Council.
- Leppert, R. (1996). *Art and the Committed Eye: The Cultural Functions of Imagery*. Oxford: Westview Press.
- Marcuse, H. (1978). *The Aesthetic Dimension: Toward a Critique of Marxist Aesthetics*. Boston: Beacon Press.
- McGauley, L. (2006). *Utopian Longings: Romanticism, Subversion and Democracy in Community Arts*. Laurentian University, Unpublished thesis.
- McNiff, S. (2008). Arts-based research. In J.Knowles and A. Cole (Eds) *Handbook of the Arts in Qualitative Research* (pp.29-40). Thousand Oaks, California: Sage.
- Montmann, N. (Ed.) (2006). *New Communities*. Toronto: Public Books.
- Moore, M. (1978). Report on the performing arts. In J.R. Kidd and G. Selman (Eds.), *Coming of Age: Canadian Adult Education in the 1960s* (pp.272-276). Toronto: CAAE.
- Mullin, A. (2003). Feminist art and the political imagination. *Hypatia*, 18(4), 190-213.
- Pelletier, L. (2002). *A War of Believers*. University of Sudbury. Unpublished thesis.
- Rogoff, I. (2013). Turning. In D. Sherman and I. Rogoff (Eds), *Museum Culture: Histories, Discourses, Spectacles* (pp.32-46). London: Routledge.
- Thompson, J. (1983). *Learning Liberation: Women's Responses to Men's Education*. London: Croom Helm.
- Walking with Our Sisters (2014). Accessed on 11/10/14 from http://walkingwithoursisters.ca/about/.
- Williamson, B. (2004). *Lifeworlds and Learning*. Leicester: NIACE.
- Wyman, M. (2004). *The Defiant Imagination*. Vancouver: Douglas & MacIntyre.

This vignette was prepared by Mary Kostandy and Michel Clague.

Barbara Clague made many contributions to adult education and to women's rights. She was born in Ontario in 1940 and, in 1961, she earned her Bachelor of Arts from Queens University in Kingston. She married Michael Clague and had two daughters, Ellen and Lindsay (and then five grandchildren). Barbara's work life began as secretary for the United Nations Association of Canada, Toronto Branch, and then as Program Coordinator for the Student Christian Movement of Canada. After the family's move to Vancouver in 1970, she worked part-time with the Pacific Association for Continuing Education (PACE) and later became a board member. In 1988, she became Acting Executive Director of the BC Association of Colleges (BCAC) and, in 1992, she was appointed Administrative Assistant for the Minister of Advanced Education and subsequenctly to the Minister of Aboriginal Affairs in Victoria. In 2000, Barbara became Executive Secretary of the BC Council on Admissions and Transfer, from which she retired in 2005.

Barbara also worked with the Telecollege at Vancouver Community College, the Adult Special Education Association, and the UBC Centre for Continuing Education (seniors and human rights programs). Along with her partner Michael Clague, she created a manual titled *Chautauqua Is Back!* that describes how to organize community education festivals. The scope of her influence went beyond Canada and included the public program for the World Council of Churches gathering in Vancouver in 1983, the International Council for Distance Education, and the educators' recruitment program of the BC Centre for International Education for the Higher Colleges of Technology in the United Arab Emirates.

For almost half a century, Barbara was a supporter of women's reproductive rights. She was a founder and coordinator of Ottawa's first birth control clinic (just before birth control had been legalized in 1968). She was the founding member and President of Planned Parenthood Vancouver and a board member of the Planned Parenthood Federation of Canada.

Barbara was passionate about music and especially enjoyed musical theatre. She was a choir member of the Brock House/Kerrisdale Choir, involved with the Pantages Theatre Arts Society and the Amy Ferguson Summer Choral Festival, and she performed at Vancouver's Theatre Under the Stars. She was a board member of the Greater Vancouver Operatic Society and of the Vancouver International Song Institute. In her honour, the Vancouver Academy of Music has created The Barbara Clague Festival of Song Awards for young, talented vocalists.

For Barbara's multiple activities and commitments, she was awarded numerous awards including PACE's Outstanding Adult Education Project Award with President Bill Day of Douglas College. She was awarded the Dorothy Shaw Award for Leadership from the Planned Parenthood Association of BC. She was also recognized for her service to the Planned Parenthood Federation of Canada.

Barbara passed away in March of 2012. She lived her life as a warm and deeply loving parent, grandparent, and partner. She was an outstanding humanitarian and a passionate advocate for learning, for the arts, and for social justice.

References

- An eloquent voice for reproductive rights has been stilled. (2012, March 23). Retrieved April 16, 2015, from https://www.optionsforsexualhealth.org/news/an-eloquent-voice-for-reproductive-rights-has-been-stilled

- Barbara Elizabeth Clague. (2012, March 22). Retrieved April 16, 2015, from http://v1.theglobeandmail.com/servlet/story/Deaths.20120322.93289502/BDAStory/BDA/deaths

- Barbara Clague Festival of Song. (n.d.). Retrieved April 16, 2015, from http://www.vancouveracademyofmusic.com/wp-content/uploads/2012/08/VAM-Calendar-of-Events-2012_final-draft-1-1.pdf

Publications
- Clague, B., and Clague, M. (1985). *Chautauqua Is Back! How to Organize a Community Education Festival*. Retrieved from http://eric.ed.gov/?id=ED26

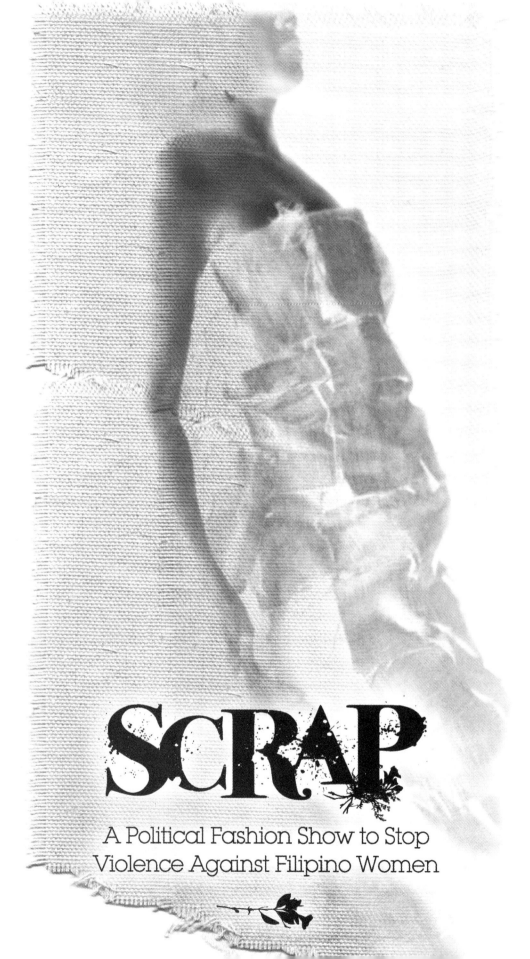

SCRAP

A Political Fashion Show to Stop
Violence Against Filipino Women

16

The Political Fashion Shows of Filipina Activists
Creating Defiant Imagination through Creative Processes

This chapter brings attention to the power of arts-based activities in feminist movements for social justice. Arts-based and creative expression can create a space of engagement where injustices are given voice, where these truths have an audience, and where alternatives can be imagined. As Maxine Greene (1995) observed, artistic expression is central to "making community and becoming wide awake" (p. 4). Art can tap into our unconscious biases, offer creative solutions to problems, and also provoke, generate outrage, challenge biases, and show us things we might not want to see (Clover & Markle, 2003).

Shauna Butterwick and Kim Villagante
with the Philippine Women Centre of British Columbia

Photo: The Philippine Women Centre of British Columbia has staged political fashion shows that tell stories of Filipino colonization and the ongoing resistance of Filipino workers. (Courtesy of Carl Sayo)

One feminist organization that has been using, to great effect, various forms of creative expression, including visual art, theatre, and quilt making, is the Philippine Women Centre in Vancouver, British Columbia (PWCBC). One particular creative format used by the PWCBC captured our attention. In 2003, 2004, and 2008 respectively, the PWCBC put on three political fashion shows. While fashion shows are not usually associated with feminist expression or seen as an activist space, the PWCBC successfully tapped into its performative potential to tell stories of Filipino colonization, the ongoing exploitation of Filipino workers, and the continuous history of Filipino resistance to these injustices. The shows proved to be powerful forms of education and community building and created alternative pathways for many to become more politically involved.

This chapter is based on the author's study of these fashion shows, conducted in partnership with the PWCBC and in collaboration with Kim Villagante, the community-based researcher the PWCBC identified for this project (Butterwick, Carrillo & Villagante, 2015). Kim is a second-generation Filipina and an artist. Our inquiries involved reviewing archival material, including videos and photographs, and interviews and focus groups with participants. We position these fashion shows as forms of feminist popular education; this research thereby makes a contribution to Manicom and Walters' (2012) call for better understanding of "the pedagogical dimensions of feminist practice, the intentional and facilitated processes of collective learning and knowledge production that enable and provoke self- and social transformation towards the realization of contextually determined feminist goals." (p. 2)

The Exploitation and Resistance of Filipino Women

Researchers have conducted studies on the activist engagement of Filipino women (Stasilius & Bakan, 1997; Lindio-McGovern, 1999; Lindio-McGovern & Wassiman, 2009), drawing attention to the development of their political consciousness, identities, and forms of resistance. The PWCBC in many respects has carried on this tradition and commitment to feminist social praxis. It began in 1989 "to empower Filipino women to understand the roots of their challenges as migrants, immigrants, women of colour and low-income earners, and to collectively assert their struggle for their rights and welfare" (http://pwc.bc.ca). When the PWCBC was formed, the position of Filipino domestic migrant workers arriving in Canada through the Live-in Caregiver Program (LCP) was a central concern. The policies of the LCP in many ways illustrate what Cohen (1991), Khan (2009), and Fraser (2005) have observed regarding how migrant workers are caught up in globalized labour practices of twenty-first-century capitalism and how racialized groups, such as Filipino nannies, are overrepresented in the circulation and exploitation of migrant labour but are misrecognized and not considered citizens. Through its advocacy for LCP workers, the PWCBC was intimately familiar with how domestic migrant workers encounter "social exclusion, abysmal working conditions, sub-standard living accommodations, sexual and racial discrimination, and exploitation on the part of employers, labour brokers, and employment agencies" (Kahn, 2009, p. 23).

In the absence of any national policy, the LCP was created as a private solution to Canadians' need for child and elder care. Filipino women are much sought after, given their education and English language skills. As Go and Casipullai (2015) point out, "given the lack of a national child care strategy, and poor investment in home care for those that need it, Canadians will continue to rely on migrant workers for child care and elder care for the foreseeable future" (p. 21). This global demand for Filipino caregivers has led to the construction of a "singular feminized identity [of Filipino women] as obedient, nurturing, complacent" (Khan, 2009, p. 29). Through their self-abnegation and self-sacrifice, a process of "re-feudalization" (Rosca, 2010, p. 6) has occurred, one that is closely associated with what Sassen (2002) calls the feminization of survival. Because the LCP workers were often the main income-earners of their families, the PWCBC found that these women often faced multiple and at times competing loyalties. Challenging employers' exploitative practices and exercising their social, cultural, and political rights were not positions easily taken (Lister, 2003; Young, 2000; Yuval-Davis, 1997, 2002).

The LCP required these women to live with their employer (although this policy has recently changed); many had no other contacts and thus experienced isolation and were vulnerable to exploitation and abuse. The PWCBC helped these women escape from these abusive situations and know their rights. As more and more Filipino women wanted to stay in Canada and bring their families over from the Philippines, the PWCBC expanded its advocacy work to include critical analysis of Canada's migrant worker and immigration policies. To better understand the issues facing these women, the PWCBC conducted its own research, often in partnership with academics. The PWCBC research documented, often for the first time, the lived experience of Filipino nannies (e.g., PWCBC, 1997a; 1997c; Pratt 2005). As Filipino domestic workers sought permanent residency and brought their families over, studies were conducted on the traumatic outcomes of family separation (e.g., Pratt, 2005, 2009, 2012b). As families were reunited and more Filipino migrant workers stayed in Canada, attention was turned to the racism and marginalization of first- and second-generation Filipino youth (e.g., PWCBC, 1997b; Pratt, 1999, 2003). Research was also done on housing (PWCBC, 1996) and on how Canada's migrant worker policies have directly contributed to the de-skilling of Filipino women (Moors 2003) and how Filipino women who entered Canada as domestic migrant workers, even after becoming permanent residents, cannot escape the low-waged service sector (Zaman, 2006; Zaman, Diocson, and West 2007; Zaman, 2012).

In addition to undertaking research, the PWCBC was organizing and building a movement (Carrillo, 2009), often through community gatherings which were intergenerational and where food and music figured prominently. Their activities often involved aesthetic and creative expression, and so the political fashion shows became a natural extension of this community building. As Davidson (2003) notes, "art can create ... the emotional urgency resulting from the encounter with strangeness, with knowledge we do not know we know" (pp. 164-165).

The Political Fashion Shows—Arts as Provocation

The idea of using the genre of a fashion show for political education was borrowed from GABRIELA (General Assembly Binding Women for Reform, Integrity, Equality, and Action), a national feminist coalition in the Philippines, which had launched their first show in 1985 to raise political awareness among the masses prior to an election. Other fashion shows followed.

Cecilia, a founding director of the PWCBC, brought the idea to the PWCBC. "I picked up the idea when I saw their [GABRIELA] video and brought it to Vancouver. I thought that we could learn from it and make it a model for our education and empowering process at the PWC." PWCBC members agreed this would be a good way of educating and empowering their community. While the PWCBC had employed a variety of successful fundraising initiatives, such as catering, walkathons, and raffles, as well as direct political action, Cecilia observed how the fashion shows proved to be a powerful cultural medium for delivering their message:

> People love to see costumes, and they get the political message in a subtle manner and it is not forced upon them and this becomes more acceptable to many people. In other words, the politics is embedded in the production process and the show itself and people did not even notice that they had been politicized.

The posters for each of the PWCBC's political fashion shows (see page 204) were created by Carlo Sayo and Reva Diana. The shows involved close collaboration between members of the PWCBC and others involved with the Kalayaan Centre on Powell Street in Vancouver. The Kalayaan Centre (*kalayaan* means "freedom") was a meeting place for various Filipino groups, including the PWCBC, youth groups, and Sinag Bayan, the cultural arm of the Kalayaan Centre. Marilou, a longstanding PWCBC member, spoke of this communal and collaborative approach and how all aspects of the production, including the stories and themes of the fashion shows, emerged from participatory and grassroots discussions of issues:

> Designing the dresses as well as directing was a collaborative effort. I remember chuckles about learning how to walk the catwalk. Everyone was involved in the art of script writing and text and dramatic staging. Stories—especially those in the third show—were transferred from stories shared in discussion groups.

The first two fashion shows focused on the history of colonization of the Philippines and migration, issues the PWCBC and the Kalayaan Centre had been exploring for several years. The third and last show shifted to current concerns regarding violence against women and the struggles with settlement and integration of Filipinos living in Canada. This shift was noted by Cecilia, who commented:

> The show's contents were now grounded in Canada and would constitute a rupture from the past and a confrontation with present reality in Canada and as part of the transnational working class demonstrating the continuity of the struggle and resistance against marginalization and the negative impacts of globalization.

The First Fashion Show—"Product of the Philippines: Made in Canada"

The first PWCBC fashion show, *Product of the Philippines: Made in Canada*, was held in Vancouver in March 2004 at the Capri Hall, a local venue that could accommodate 200 people. Preparation for the show involved work-study groups examining pre-colonial times as well as Spanish and American colonization. Many artists got involved, bringing their respective skills, as well as community members, board members, family members, and friends. A writing committee was formed. For most participants, creating a fashion show was a new experience.

Jill, a fashion design student at the time, aided in the creation of garments, the designs of which had been collectively generated. She said the first fashion show was her "doorway to organizing with the Kalayaan Centre." And she recalled how the shows also created pathways for many others, in particular, Filipino youth:

> Youth were all involved with every part ... the logistics, scriptwriting, making the stuff and everything. We would have members from every single group. Everyone had a hand or a say in how things were done, so it was cool.

Carlo, involved in all three shows, remembered the huge self-education initiative of the first show. He noted how they were "finding as many resources as we could for each other ... we adopted film history work, previous theatre material about our history."

The first show's theme followed a historical linear path, starting with pre-colonization followed by Spanish colonization. The opening began with a group of women dressed in colourful malongs (traditional Filipina cloth tied and draped from their waists) who formed a circle and beat the kulintang (small drum). Other Indigenous dances were performed, choreographed by members of Sinag Bayan, and these dances were interspersed with models wearing various Indigenous costumes.

The first few scenes were very musical, showing much pride in Filipino dances and songs. Then the sense of celebration shifted, with the following scene in which oppression of Indigenous peoples through Spanish colonization was performed.

Indigenous Dress

In this scene, Marilou entered the stage wearing Indigenous garb, followed by two soldiers; each carrying what looked like wooden crosses. Behind them stood another model wearing a long robe, also painted with a cross. As Marilou walked forward, the two soldiers, who flipped over their crosses so they now resembled swords, seized her. Several other women came on stage and removed Marilou's Indigenous garments, dressing her in a Spanish Maria Clara dress and handing her a bible and a rosary. Marilou recalls vividly the impact this had on her and the audience.

> I stood there on the stage ... a couple of the women removed the beads around my hair, the dress, the skirt, and then they sort of stood around me. I was in my longish underwear, and then they put the lace, the embroidered long dress. And then the clincher was then they put a crucifix necklace around me. So it was really, really powerful. And then they give me a rosary, a little bible, prayer book, and there I stood. I felt so vulnerable ... [and] I felt more part of the history of the whole thing.

This scene was also transformative for an audience member named Christina. Born in Canada to parents who had left the Philippines looking for a better life, Christina spoke about how this scene helped her understand her parents and her own struggles with identity. Witnessing this scene opened the doors to many years of involvement with the PWCBC.

> I started bawling ... I get emotional thinking about it still ... It was Marilou, dressed in Indigenous [Filipina] clothing. [She] comes out and she's undressed and put in the Maria Clara. I was like, "Oh my God!" I felt that they were telling my story ... to see other people say that the American and Spanish influence on the Philippines was not all positive, and these are the things that happened to us. That history is playing into our current situation. I just said to myself, "Wow. I need to talk to these people because this is what I've been feeling for so long."

Part of the first show also focused on resistance movements during the 300 years of Spanish colonization. Models in this scene symbolized the story of the Katipunan, the Filipino revolutionary group led by Andres Bonifacio who fought against the Spanish for independence. They wore white T-shirts with iron-on symbols of the letter "K" written in alibata script, the pre-colonial writing of the Philippines. While the narrator tells the story of resistance, the models acted out movements akin to fighter stances. Carlo explains: "This was a scene of some of the casualties of fighting against Spain but the resistance against the colonisation."

The Second Fashion Show—"Philippine Independence Re-Veiled"

Building on the success and momentum of the first show, in 2005 the second fashion show was launched. *Philippine Independence Re-veiled: A Political Fashion Show* continued to explore colonization but shifted to current struggles in the Philippines. As Jill observes, the organizers decided to "delve more into details," particularly globalization, capitalism, imperialism, and commercialism. "We covered a lot of the same topics [as the first show], but instead of focusing on pre-Spanish colonization we focused more just on colonization of our land [and] our people."

The venue was the Russian Hall, a larger space than the one for the first fashion show. Many of the same core members who participated in the first show were involved, and there was no problem getting additional help from enthusiastic volunteers. Denise, a member of the organizing committee, noted how this show built on valuable skills and experience from the first project but was more ambitious and participants were more confident. There was also more time to prepare, which allowed more thought and creativity. Some garments from the first show were reused and new ones were developed. As Denise noted, every aspect was bigger and bolder. "This was the year after and we told ourselves … that we're going to spend more time on making individual pieces. I think that was the biggest thing, we're going to spend more time."

The Rice Terrace Dress

The first series of dresses illustrated the abundance of natural resources in the Philippines, such as the rice terraces. Carlo and Denise recalled the labour and collaboration, as well as the workshops, involved in the creation of the Rice Terrace Dress. As Denise noted, "We actually put each green thing individually into the dress." Jill had designed the structure of the dress and then it was created over time as people came in and out of the centre working on different pieces.

As with the first show, this show included Indigenous dances, but in the second show more emphasis was placed on using the genre of the fashion show. As Jill commented: "It focused more on the fashion aspect instead [and we weren't] going to do everything we did last time … we just wanted to present it differently than the first one." At the time of the show, a dance troupe from the Cordillera region in the Philippines were visiting the city to attend an Indigenous youth conference, and they also participated in the show. As with the first fashion show, the Indigenous costumes used for these dances were donations from Sinag Bayan.

In one scene, an older male model wears a barong made out of burlap. The barong is an embroidered shirt worn mostly by men and is often made out of piña (pineapple leaf fibres), which makes them very lightweight. As Carlo explains, this shirt was symbolic of Spanish control of the Philippines. "The piña [is] naturally see-through, but they were originally given to peasants so that they couldn't hide anything under their shirts." Denise describes the thinking behind creating a burlap shirt: "We wanted it to look like piña fabric because piña fabric is really expensive and highly regarded but we actually made it out of burlap; we just kind of juxtaposed the idea that burlap is so cheap and uncomfortable." Carlo explained how the shirt made of burlap symbolized current forms of colonization, and therefore, that "they were supposed to be uncomfortable because it's something that's not natural."

The Third Fashion Show—"Scrap: A Political Fashion Show to Stop Violence against Filipino Women"

In 2008, several years later, the third fashion show was held. *Scrap: A Political Fashion Show to Stop Violence against Filipino Women* focused on violence against women, including the experiences of mail-order brides and migrant domestic workers. There were two shows presented in one day at Centre A, the Vancouver International Centre for Contemporary Asian Art. A press release speaks to the desire to raise Canadian awareness:

> Through this fashion show, we hope to provoke Canadians into thinking about these women's stories and their daily struggles against the violence of modern-day slavery. Too often, Canadians are lulled into thinking that these programs are signs of Canada's humanitarian immigration policy. But from the stories of the live-in caregivers themselves, we know that the LCP is an exploitative and racist policy that stifles these women's dignity.

As with the previous shows, planning included workshops, storytelling, script writing, and creating the fashion pieces. Ayex described the process like this:

> We'd all meet up, and have a meeting, like a focus group and then we'd share the story and then when we were starting to talk about the pieces and how they should look like, and when people were describing it, they were describing it with really what they felt, or what they wanted people to feel, you know?

Carlo reflected on the development and growth between the first, second, and third shows. In the first show, he says: "We didn't know anything about fashion so we tried on theatre to carry things," but by the final show, working with fashion, garments, and dresses was more fully employed. Like previous shows, the dresses were designed collectively, with Jill guiding the final production. This time, however, all the dresses were made of the same material—unbleached muslin—which helped create a coherence linking the stories together. Using unbleached cloth was also chosen to symbolize exploitation and oppression. For Niki, this show deepened her understanding of violence against LCP workers.

> I think that [the fashion show process] really solidified my knowledge about what women were really facing because I was hearing it directly from their mouths and some of the stories were so disgusting, so … you can't even put it into words how intense their stories were….

Another feature of the final show the absence of an elevated stage or catwalk. The audience was arranged in a U shape surrounding an aisle down the middle where the models walked; this brought audience members and models together on the same level. Rain, an audience member, remembered the impact of this arrangement. "There was a lot of silence … it was very solemn as the subject matter was not joyful at all; it was very political and very dark and heavy."

The Burden Dress

Throughout all the shows, Kalayaan Centre members were the models. In the final show, many of the dresses were modelled by the very women whose stories were being portrayed. One such dress was called the "Burden Dress," a floor-length garment with long ties at the back that were attached to a "balikbayan box," which Filipinos use to send goods back to their families.

Cora, who modelled the dress, recalled how it symbolized her experiences as an LCP worker and how wearing the dress and being involved in its creation led to a long-term commitment to the PWCBC.

> I wanted to be a part of the change … to change the system … eliminating violence against women, eliminating oppression and exploitation … Many people asked me how heavy was the balikbayan box. I said the box itself is not heavy but if you connect to our issues, so many issues impacting women's lives, it's so heavy. Very heavy.

As with previous shows, the third show included scenes and images of resilience and resistance. In one scene, four models walked out and broke various symbols of bondage. One woman untied her roped wrists, another took off her mouth guard, another freed herself from her rope bouquet, and another unzipped a cape that, when zipped up, had covered most of her face. For the finale, a model is wearing the "Empowerment Dress," a long formal gown with a purple sash[1] covered in script. As Ayex recalled, words that symbolized liberation were brainstormed and then participants wrote them "on scrap on the fabric [which was] transferred onto the sash."

Arts and Feminist Social Praxis

These political fashion shows were a powerful site of arts-based feminist social praxis, which explicated both injustices and forms of resistance. Other studies have illustrated how creative expression can facilitate the expression of defiant imagination and how these creative forms of expression speak to alternative realities (Greene, 1995; Clover & Stalker, 2007; Butterwick & Lawrence, 2009). This study affirms what is known and also brings attention to several aspects of collective and performative processes (Kilgore, 1999).

Using the genre of a fashion show meant that colonization as an embodied practice and form of knowledge became more conscious and public. The embodied and performative elements of a fashion show tapped into participants' and audience members' senses (Lawrence, 2012). As Yakhlef (2010) reminds us, the body is "an active producer of culture, at the same time being a product thereof" (p. 411). In this respect, these political fashion shows offered both a language of critique as well as possibility (Allman, 1999; Manicom and Walters, 2012) and enabled what Freire (2004) called a pedagogy of freedom, liberation, and hope. Learning the history of the Philippines through the genre of the fashion show aided in a process of decolonization (Tejeda, 2008). The embodied and performative character of these activities, because they were felt in the body, proved to be a powerful medium for praxis (Freire, 1970), which, for some, was also deeply transformative (Willis, 2012). The shows enabled a politics of recognition (Fraser, 1997). Creating the shows, through study circles and other forms of engagement, facilitated a dialectical encounter between inner sensibilities and outer social action (Sandoval, 2000). What were once considered private and personal troubles were moved into the light and recognized as part of a collective struggle.

For many who would not have joined an advocacy or activist group, the fashion shows and the intergenerational activity associated with each show created a pathway for political engagement and action (Ollis, 2008). While the final productions were powerful and significant to the PWCBC and all participants involved, what was equally important was the collective and creative process, which we regard as an example of Ellsworth's (2005) idea of knowledge in the making.

This approach, in many ways, illustrates what Sandoval (2000) calls a "methodology of the oppressed" which she describes as a dialectic between identity construction and social action. This leads to the development of a differential consciousness, one that is flexible and diasporic. The research and advocacy of the PWCBC has creatively engaged in both inner sensibilities as well as outer forms of social praxis. Fraser's (1997) notion of the "subaltern counter-public"—that is, spaces for dialogue and the construction of oppositional discourse—are well illustrated in the work of the PWCBC, particularly its creative and innovative activities.

In conclusion, the political fashion shows of the PWCBC were community-based, collaborative, and creative processes that proved to be powerful avenues for building community, educating and politicizing, and speaking truth to power. Such creative initiatives, while requiring much labour and energy on the part of participants, can also foster processes of renewal. Fashion shows, often linked to a world of excess and consumerism, can offer a format with which to imagine a more just world.

Acknowledgements

- We thank the Philippine Women Centre of British Columbia (PWCBC) for its partnership on this project and those specific individuals who gave us their time and wisdom to document this important moment in the history of the PWCBC. Some elements of this chapter can be found in *Feminist Fashion Shows as Feminist Trans-formation*, published in 2015 in the *Canadian Journal for the Study of Adult Education*, 2015, volume 27, number 2. This partnership project was funded by the Social Sciences and Humanities Research Council of Canada.

Endnote

1 The purple sash was chosen to link with The Purple Rose Campaign, which was initiated by GABRIELA and taken up by the PWCBC to raise awareness about the trafficking of Filipino women.

References

- Allman, P. (1999). *Revolutionary Social Transformation: Democratic Hopes, Political Possibilities and Critical Education*. Westport, CN: Praeger.

- Butterwick, S. and Lawrence, R. L. (2009). Creating alternative realities. Arts-based approaches to transformative learning. In Mezirow, J. and Taylor, E. W. (Eds.). *Transformative Learning in Practice. Insights from Community, Workplace, and Higher Education* (pp. 35-45). San Francisco, CA: Jossey-Bass.

- Butterwick, S., Carrillo, M., and Villagante, K. (with the Philippine Women Centre of BC) (2015). Women's fashion shows as feminist trans-formation. *Canadian Journal for the Study of Adult Education*, 27(2), 79-99.

- Carrillo, M. (2009). *Socially Transformative Transnational Feminism: Filipino Women Activists at Home and Abroad*. Unpublished PhD dissertation, University of British Columbia.

- Clover, D. and Markle, G. (2003). Feminist arts practices of popular education: Imagination, counter-narratives and activism on Vancouver Island and Gabriola Island. *New Zealand Journal of Adult Education*, 31(2), 36-52.

- Clover, D. and Stalker, J. (Eds.) (2007). *The Arts and Social Justice—Re-Drafting Adult Education and Community Cultural Leadership*. Leicester: NIACE.

- Cohen, R. (1991). Women of colour in white households: Coping strategies of live-in domestic workers. *Qualitative Sociology*, 14, 197-215.

- Davidson, H. (2003). Poetry, witness, feminism. In. A. Douglass & T. A. Vogler (Eds.), *Witness and Memory: The Discourse of Trauma* (pp. 153-172). New York and London: Routledge.

- Ellsworth, E. (2005). *Places of Learning: Media, Architecture, and Pedagogy*. New York: Routledge.

- Fraser, N. (1997). *Justice Interruptus: Critical Reflections on the Postsocialist Condition*. New York, NY: Routledge.

- Fraser, N. (2005). Reframing justice in a globalizing world. *New Left Review*, 36, 69-88.

- Freire, P. (1970). *Pedagogy of the Oppressed*. New York: Seabury Press.

- Freire, P. (2004). *Pedagogy of Hope: Reliving Pedagogy of the Oppressed*. New York: The Continuum Publishing Company.

- Go, A. and Casipullai, A. (2015). A land of unequal opportunity. *Monitor*, May-June, 20-21.

- Greene, M. (1995). *Releasing the Imagination: Essays on Education, the Arts, and Social Change*. San Francisco, CA: Jossey Bass.

- Kahn, S.A. (2009). From labour of love to decent work: Protecting the human rights of migrant caregivers in Canada. *Canadian Journal of Law and Society*, 24(1), 23-45.

- Kilgore, D.W. (1999). Understanding learning in social movements: a theory of collective learning. *International Journal of Lifelong Education*, 18(3), 191-202.

- Lawrence, R. (2012). Bodies of knowledge: Embodied learning in adult education. *New Directions for Adult and Continuing Education*, 134. San Francisco, CA: Jossey-Bass.

- Lindio-McGovern, L. (1999). Political consciousness, identity, and social movements: Peasant women in the Philippines and Filipino immigrant activists in Chicago. *Social Movements, Conflict and Change*, 21, 271-292.

- Lindio-McGovern, L. and Wassiman, I. (2009). *Globalization and Third World Women: Exploitation, Coping and Resistance*. Burlington, VT: Ashgate.

- Lister, R. (2003). *Citizenship: Feminist Perspectives*. New York: New York University Press.

- Manicom, L. and Walters, S. (Eds.) (2012). *Feminist Popular Education in Transnational Debates: Building Pedagogies of Possibility*. New York: Palgrave Macmillan.

- Moors, A. (2003). Unskilled labour: Canada's Live-in Caregiver Program. *Comparative Studies in Society and History*, 45, 386-394.

- Ollis, T. (2008). The "accidental activist": Learning, embodiment and action. *Australian Journal of Adult Learning*, 48(2), 317-334.

- Philippine Women Centre of BC (1996). Housing needs: Assessment of Filipina domestic workers. http://pwc.bc.tripod.com/research.html.
- _____ (1997a). Is this Canada? Domestic workers experience in Vancouver, BC. http://pwc.bc.tripod.com/research.html.
- _____ (1997b). Bridging the gap: The legal needs of Filipino youth. http://pwc.bc.tripod.com/research.html.
- _____ (1997c). Trapped! Holding onto the knife's edge: Economic violence against Filipino migrant/immigrant women. http://pwc.bc.tripod.com/research.html.
- Pratt, G. (1999). From registered nurse to registered nanny: Discursive geographies of Filipina domestic workers in Vancouver, BC. *Economic Geographer*, 75 (3), 215-236.
- _____ in Collaboration with the Ugnayan Ng Kabataang Pilipino Sa Canada/Filipino-Canadian Youth Alliance (2003). Between homes: Displacement and belonging for second generation Filipino-Canadian youths. *BC Studies*, 140, 41-68.
- _____ (2005). Abandoned women and spaces of the exception. *Antipode*, 27(5), 1053-1078.
- _____ in collaboration with the Philippine Women Centre of BC (2009). Circulating sadness: Witnessing Filipino mothers' stories of family separation. *Gender Place and Culture*, 16, 3-22.
- _____ (2012b). *Families Apart: Migrant Mothers and the Conflicts of Labor and Love*. Minneapolis: University of Minnesota Press.
- Rosca, N. (2010). Transnational is a noun: Break the pattern, change the narrative! Paper given at the Kapit-Bisig conference, Montréal, Canada, April 30 to May 2, 2010.
- Sandoval, C. (2000). *Methodology of the Oppressed*. Minneapolis, MN: University of Minnesota Press.
- Sassen, S. (2002). Countergeographies of globalization: The feminization of survival. Paper presented to Gender Budgets, Financial Markets, Financing for Development, February 19th and 20th, Heinrich-Boell Foundation in Berlin.
- Stasiulis, D.K. and Bakan, A.B. (1997). Regulation and resistance: Strategies of migrant domestic workers in Canada and internationally. *Asian and Pacific Migration Journal*, 6, 31-57.
- Tejeda, C. (2008). Dancing with the dilemmas of a decolonizing pedagogy. *Radical History Review*, 102, 27-31.
- Willis, P. (2012). An existential approach to transformative learning. In E. Taylor and P. Cranton (Eds.), *The Handbook of Transformative Learning—Theory, Research, and Practice* (pp. 212-227). SanFrancisco, CA: Jossey-Bass.
- Yakhlef, A. (2010). The corporeality of practice-based learning. *Organizational Studies* 31(4), 409-430.
- Young, I.M. (2000). *Inclusion and Democracy*. New York: Oxford University Press.
- Yuval-Davis, N. (1997). *Gender and Nation*. London: Sage.
- Yuval-Davis, N. (2002). Some reflections on the questions of citizenship and anti-racism. In F. Anthias and C. Lloyd (Eds.), *Rethinking Anti-Racism: From Theory to Oractice*. New York: Routledge.
- Zaman, H. (2006). *Breaking the Iron Wall: Decommodification and Immigrant Women's Labour in Canada*. Oxford: Lexington Books.
- Zaman, H., Diocson, C., and West, R. (2007). Workplace rights for immigrants in BC: The case of Filipino workers. Canadian Centre for Policy Alternatives. Downloaded April 14, 2009 from http://www.policyalternatives.ca/reports/2007/12/reportsstudies1775/?pa=A2286B2A.
- Zaman, J. (2012). *Asian Immigrants in "Two Canadas": Racialization, Marginalization and Deregulated Work*. Halifax: Fernwood.

Two students in the Marie Michael Library, which supports the programs of the Coady International Institute in Antigonish, Nova Scotia.
Photo: Courtesy of Catherine J. Irving.

17

Women Working for Libraries
Learning and Social Change

The development of both libraries and adult education over the decades has run parallel paths (Imel and Duckett, 2009). Libraries grew alongside evening schools and Workers' Education Institutes to support learning for the working classes. The history of women adds a third parallel path. Librarianship, like teaching, is one of the professions widely identified with women. Importantly, librarians in Canada have been active in well-known education and social action programs throughout this shared history, such as the Antigonish Movement (Irving, 2013).

Catherine J. Irving

My own love of libraries began as a child enthralled with McGill University's bookmobile, the outreach program that served my small, rural community in Québec. For over two decades, I have worked at Coady International Institute's Marie Michael Library in Antigonish, Nova Scotia. Coady program participants include development leaders and social activists from Africa, South Asia, Latin America, the Caribbean, and Canada's First Nations. From our participants, we have learned much about both inclusive and exclusionary library procedures and practices. My mentor, Sue Adams, has taught me to bring adult education into the heart of library practice, and she has also taught me about the history of librarian Sister Marie Michael MacKinnon's philosophy of creating safe and welcoming places to create knowledge. She has added her own feminist ways of librarianship and her insights on "when to know what rules to break." We share an interest in ferreting out women's stories from the archives—women librarians who travelled these paths.

Returning to thoughts expressed above, I speak of parallels between adult education and libraries, but there are many intersections on the pathways of women, adult education, and libraries although, as noted, they are not well documented in this country. In fact, little is known of women librarians' stories, since library history generally is not a strong field of research in Canada. In the United States, the documentation of women's librarianship primarily features biographies of accomplished professionals who have contributed to the specialized discipline of library and information science rather than an "educational" analysis. This reflects a shift within library scholarship from social engagement to the professionalization of practice, something familiar to adult educators. The past decade has brought a renewed focus on the role of libraries and librarians in adult education, including in Canada (e.g., Adams, 2005, 2009, 2015; English, 2011; Irving, 2010; Irving and Adams, 2012; Sanford, Clover, and Dogus, 2013; Taylor, Parrish, and Banz, 2010).

In this chapter, I highlight some of the women who have worked to promote libraries and adult education in Canada in the past and the present. My aim is for these historical and contemporary sketches to provide openings to explore commonalities in issues such as safety, inclusion, people's knowledge, power, and resistance—areas that feminist adult educators know well. Moreover, they are illustrative of women's library leadership in the cause of social justice and learning and I hope they will inspire others to think about this important area of feminist work and skill.

Helen Gordon Stewart: Promoting Rural Libraries

Helen Gordon Stewart is most widely known among adult educators for her leadership in library development in British Columbia (BC). Charles Keith Morison's (1952, 1967) accounts paint a formidable portrait of Stewart as a force charged with a pioneering spirit. As a young teacher in Manitoba, Stewart became interested in library work and pursued library training. In 1910, she secured employment at the Victoria Public Library, which she modernized before travelling to Europe in 1916 to assist in the war effort. Following the war, she was instrumental in the creation of provincial library legislation in 1919 for BC. Her growing interest in the importance of adult education led her to pursue further studies in the 1920s, earning a PhD at Columbia University (Gilroy and Rothstein, 1970). Since Stewart's doctoral research focused on rural libraries, she was invited to lead a Carnegie-funded library demonstration project in BC's Fraser Valley from 1930-1934 to encourage the creation of a regionally coordinated rural library system (Obee, 2011). The Carnegie Corporation was known at this time for its investments in libraries in the British Commonwealth (Rochester, 1995). The demonstration project process involved considerable political savvy on Stewart's part to introduce library services to the populace, negotiate with local levels of governments, and secure a plebiscite approving taxation to sustain the new libraries. Morison (1967) marvels at this accomplishment: "It is doubtful whether anyone else could at that time, in the depth of the depression, have persuaded the hard-bitten farmers and city fathers of the Fraser Valley to take over the demonstration library as a tax-supported institution" (p. 2). Stewart later led a similar process in Trinidad and Tobago with another Carnegie-funded library scheme from 1940-1948, though her leadership style was not universally appreciated there (Hill, 2007).

A more traditional female presence also emerges as Morison (1967) extolls Stewart's hospitality and domestic skills:

> Indeed Dr. Stewart started a new vogue in depression décor for many a home in the Fraser Valley. The big windows of her old frame house were draped with curtains made of wide-mesh onion sacking, which, with the addition of a few spots of applique made interior and exterior views very presentable. The ladies of the women's institutes, universally strong supporters of the library, spread the good news of onion sacking from end to end of the valley (p. 3).

This anecdote of Stewart's thrifty decorating sense also reveals the importance of women's groups as allies in library formation—in this case, the Women's Institutes. Dennison (1987) notes the central role of these groups to promote publicly funded infrastructure and services, and adds, "The acquisition of library facilities, whether travelling or permanent, was a priority of all Institutes" (p. 60).

By the mid-twentieth century, the professionalization of librarianship, as in other fields, led to a perceived distancing from community development and adult education. Even in Helen Gordon Stewart's day, this was becoming a prickly issue. Stewart expressed pride that her community awareness was enhanced by her practical library training in a community-linked program that was scorned by the elite schools (Gilroy and Rothstein, 1970). She herself implemented a library apprentice training program to develop expertise among the local population (Gilroy and Rothstein, 1970). This program appears to have been an important initial stepping stone for women in the region who later took on leadership roles, including Margaret Clay, who succeeded Stewart to run the Victoria Public Library, and Jeannette Sargent, who began the library in Prince George, BC (Obee, 2011). Stewart later replicated this training method in the Caribbean.

Feeding the Antigonish Movement on the East Coast

The story of the Antigonish Movement is well known in the history and folklore of adult education in Canada. While Helen Gordon Stewart and her cadre were bringing libraries to the Fraser Valley, new libraries were also emerging in Nova Scotia (NS) and Prince Edward Island (PEI) to support the growing hunger for knowledge in the Maritimes.

Sister Marie Michael MacKinnon was a driving force within St. Francis Xavier University's Extension Department as a fieldworker and librarian. In 1933, Reverend Dr. Moses Coady approached the Sisters of St. Martha in Antigonish to identify someone to direct the Women and Work program. Recruited for the task was Sr. Marie Michael, who had studied household sciences at Macdonald College in Québec and later earned a degree at St. FX. In her first year, she supported the creation of over 300 women's study clubs and took on the task of maintaining the Department's growing book collection. The library received a boost in 1936 when St. FX obtained a grant from the Carnegie Corporation—one third of which was earmarked for the library (Irving and Adams, 2012). This grant allowed library services to expand to smaller locations, including credit union branches. As the women's program wound down by the 1940s, Sister Marie Michael devoted her energies fully to the library.

In the late 1940s, Sister Marie Michael hosted a local radio program entitled "This Is Your Library" during which she described books that were available and encouraged people to write in to request any books of interest. These books were then posted out on one-month loans and could be returned by post at no cost to the borrowers. Sister Marie Michael's early programs tended to reflect the practical interests of study clubs, such as sustainable small-scale agriculture, crafts, and co-operatives. She soon expanded themes to nurture broader interests in literature and to feature books addressing growing concerns in the lives of her listeners, such as the spectres of unfettered capitalism and nuclear war (MacKinnon, 1951). Sister Marie Michael was also aware of the Canadian Association for Adult Education's (CAAE) Citizens' Forum radio broadcasts (Irving and Adams, 2012). For example, in response to the October 27, 1949 broadcast "Is there a teenage problem today?" (CBC, 1949/2015), she featured a book encouraging youth development and maturity (MacKinnon, 1949).

Sister Marie Michael shared the Antigonish Movement's philosophy of promoting community ownership. The Extension Department's initiatives were intended to be taken over by the organizations created by the people themselves. Sister Marie Michael hoped this too would happen with library service (e.g., Irving and Adams, 2012). In 1964, the Extension Department Library was closed. Sister Marie Michael acknowledged they were duplicating services provided by the public library system that was now established across the region. She continued her library work at the Coady International Institute until 1971, moving to the library of St. Augustine's seminary in Toronto until her retirement, where for many years she entertained students with her stories of her life in Antigonish. Sister Marie Michael believed libraries should be friendly, welcoming places where discussion is encouraged (Adams, 1991). If people are fearful or intimidated, they will stay away. All of Sister Marie Michael's work—the library and the radio programs—can be understood as a form of feminist adult education in that they open a space to raise difficult issues and critique social structures, but ensure that the learning space is accessible, comfortable, and welcoming.

The Antigonish Movement was also supported by the work of Nora Bateson. who led PEI's rural library demonstration project. Throughout her life, Bateson was a key leader in public library development in Canada and around the world (e.g., Adams, 2009, 2015). Her formative years near Manchester, England, occurred during the blossoming of the co-operative movement, workers' education, and the women's suffrage movement in the region. Upon graduation from university, she followed in the footsteps of many adventurous, educated Englishwomen of the day. She travelled abroad in 1920 to teach, ending up in a girls' school in Québec. However, her interest quickly shifted to libraries. She gained experience and training across the continent over the next decade, including a stint in 1930 with Stewart's library demonstration project in BC's Fraser Valley, which made a lasting impression on Bateson (Adams, 2009, 2015). In 1933, Bateson was recruited to lead a Carnegie-funded library demonstration project in PEI. Adams' archival research on Bateson's times in PEI documents her voluminous correspondence responding to library patrons' requests and lobbying government officials for support. Bateson reached out to make personal connections with local organizations, including Women's Institutes, promoting the value of libraries for the well-being of communities and of society at large. Bateson's libraries provided life to the study clubs on the Island (Rochester, 1995).

During her time in PEI, Bateson met Dr. J. J. (Father Jimmy) Tompkins, a leader of the Antigonish Movement, and they became co-conspirators advocating for public libraries in support of the civic education of adults, co-authoring a concise manifesto entitled *Why Not a Co-operative Library?* in 1936. Seeing the growth of urban libraries, they called for a rural regional library system, such as those made possible by the two demonstration projects in Fraser Valley and PEI.

Bateson was particularly respected among the people, but frequently found herself on the opposite side of politicians. Like Stewart, Bateson developed a reputation as no push-over. This lack of deference to the male-dominated political leadership likely contributed later to her losing her post in Nova Scotia, where she had been contracted to replicate the successes of PEI (Adams, 2009). She found greener pastures elsewhere, leading library programs in Jamaica and New Zealand. Adams (2015) notes Bateson's scholarly writing advocating the importance of libraries shifted from library journals to adult education in the 1940s, through her contributions to CAAE's *Food for Thought.*

Sister Francis Dolores Donnelly worked with Father Jimmy Tompkins to support the reading interests of people in industrial Cape Breton through "The People's Library." Shortly after arriving in Reserve Mines, Cape Breton, in 1935, Father Jimmy set up a small lending library in the parish rectory. By 1941, this People's Library was a critical space that required the services of a full-time librarian. Father Tompkins called on the Sisters of Charity for assistance, and Sister Francis Dolores was dispatched to fill the position. Rusty Neal's (1998) account describes a bright, strong-willed woman who initially resented the thwarting of her promising academic career at Mount Saint Vincent University for what she viewed as exile. But it took her little time to see the potential of the People's Library, and the vital role it would and could play in adult education and social change. Sister Francis Dolores' (Donnelly, 1945) own article in CAAE's *Food for Thought* sparkles with the passion she felt for the library and the people of Reserve Mines. She describes the programs organized through the library that fostered study clubs, reading support for the miners, women's discussion groups, and the Citizens' Forum groups that would meet at the library. Rusty Neal (1998) documents the many opportunities Sister Francis Dolores had to speak at conferences, initially on behalf of Father Tompkins, but then in her own right as her abilities were recognized.

These are but three of the dynamic women who ensured libraries were at the forefront of the Antigonish movement and regional adult education programs of their day. Leona English's (2011; 2014) archival research on women in Canada's adult education past sheds light on a number of others whose paths crossed through the fields of adult education and libraries, such as Jessie Mifflen, who led library development in Newfoundland. Other women who were trained as librarians went on to make their mark as writers and editors with CAAE (English, 2011; 2014). There is a zeal in the work and writings of these women that is inspiring, for they promoted the potential of adult education and saw the centrality of libraries to that mission. Moreover, they breathed life into the libraries they developed, whether located in a rectory or scattered throughout the numerous farming settlements.

As I document these histories, I am mindful that, as unmarried women or nuns, they did reflect the stereotype of spinster librarians—women who worked in normative, service-oriented, and relatively care-giving roles, which were seen as suitable jobs for women—that is, unless they married and were obliged to resign (Obee, 2011). I am equally mindful of Myers' (2002) caution that in our attempts to balance the scales of women's representation, we risk replicating privileging bias by singling out a few "women worthies" (p. 10). And yet, in so many other ways, the women I have profiled are important because they dared to break gender stereotypes by taking on leadership and community roles and, often, the politicians who got in their way. Bateson and Gordon left their early jobs teaching children. Sister Marie Michael and Francis Dolores realized their academic and career goals through religious congregations, side-stepping the conventions of marriage. But, as always, the successes of these individual women also relied on the support of many other women with whom they worked, so we must never under-estimate women's collective power.

Women and Libraries Today

Those early women library leaders in Canada retired in an era when libraries had achieved a secure place in our society. They may be surprised to see their old battles with politicians returning amidst government cutbacks and closures today. Neo-liberalism is seeping into librarianship, which is apparent in business terms such as "customers" (Maret and Eagle, 2013). Those who are pushing back against this trend today are reasserting the raison d'etre of libraries as free places to share information and to foster learning and democratic citizenship. And in a "results-based" neo-liberal economic age, we need to document and advocate for those who challenge this framing.

The International Federation of Library Associations and Institutions' (IFLA) manifesto on freedom of information highlights the library's social democratic role to help people gain access to public information (IFLA, 2014). Just as Dennison (1987) notes the historical role of women's organizations in providing the training ground for women to learn about laws and statutes that discriminated against them, library workers today advocate for access to information and provide education to make that information understandable as a necessary condition for democracy—even though access to information alone does not equal knowledge (Lor and Britz, 2010). Badawi (2007) is forthright in describing the importance of libraries in supporting women's political awareness and participation, both in terms of the learning function for women's self-empowerment and also as a community hub where women can participate.

There is a small but lively group of researchers promoting the linkages between libraries and social justice that draw on education theory in sync with their politics. Riedler and Eryaman (2010) see how critical pedagogy can mobilize libraries for community action, proposing a model they call a "transformative and community-based library" (p. 92). Feminist pedagogy has also been embraced and adapted for library practice and instruction. Maria Accardi (2013) wants her teaching practice to promote critical thinking among her students to uncover biases in the ways information is organized. She relates to feminist pedagogical principles valuing voice, experience, reflection, and empowerment. Suzanne Hildenbrand (2000) draws on feminism to chart the representation of women leaders in library history. She also follows the implications of the gendering of library work as women's work, which some use to highlight the nurturing, collaborative leadership style of women in the field while others use it to reveal gender-based discrimination. Hildenbrand sees that integrating analyses of race, class, and gender identity can only strengthen feminist theorizing of librarianship. Katherine Adams (2000) describes a number of groups and bloggers who play with librarian identity. She reflects, "Parodying the librarian stereotype gives me the opportunity to act on my feminist and intellectual convictions while, at the same time, experiencing pride as a librarian and as a member of a feminized profession" (p. 295). There is quiet subversion at work here.

Library Spaces for Social Change

Libraries were valuable spaces for learning in our adult education past (Irving, 2013). The work of many women, in particular, brought library services to remote regions and economically excluded groups. Today, libraries are just as important for reaching out to populations that remain marginalized by the mainstream, providing them with access, safety, and opportunities to create.

Opening spaces: Lang and Sacuta (2014) document the efforts of Fireweed Library within the women's prison in Alberta. Central to the program is the trust and community building that is developed between the librarians and women inmates, and among the women themselves. Book club meetings provide a welcome diversion or may offer an entry point for women to share their stories. Creative writing workshops encourage women to write poetry and make zines. The library also provides access to practical legal information and preparation for community re-entry. The volunteer staff works to raise public awareness of the lives of incarcerated women and the importance of access to information and the ability to learn. Sacuta reflects: "Before going into the prison, I understood that the women in prison had lost the liberty to move around and be free in the world. I could not comprehend the limitation of their freedom to learn, know, and even think" (p. 98).

Kelly (2010) describes the importance of developing libraries that represent the lives of Aboriginal women. Kelly notes that often libraries are seen as "anglo" or "settler" places that implicitly or overtly do not appear welcoming to Aboriginal peoples. Biases can be evident in such things as membership policies or hiring practices, or through collections that present outdated or narrow perspectives of the lives of Aboriginal women—such as focusing only on social problems and not including the creative works of Aboriginal women. The language used in library catalogues can be culturally insensitive. Kelly describes how an alternative Aboriginal classification system has been developed among band libraries.

Spaces of safety, identity, and resistance: Internationally, library programs are working to break barriers based on gender identity. Mehra and Gray's (2014) study in the US shows the efforts of libraries "to serve as virtual spaces of resistance and protectors of human rights of LGBTQ people" (p. 1) amidst an environment that instills fear and reluctance to resist. Hope and practical strategies appear through small but visible acts, such as a school library website providing space for a gay youth alliance or including information on legal rights. When the political space does open up, as in Brazil's anti-homophobia policy implementation, libraries are ensuring that LGBTQ communities are represented fully as part of the nation's culture. NGOs are providing staff training and library materials to promote the goals of a more inclusive culture as a whole (Silva Alentejo, 2014).

Spaces for preservation and creation: The BiblioFemina panel (Kowal and Ultan in Kelly, 2010) outlines the negative impact of collection development policies and processes that funnel purchasing through mainstream publishers and distributors, thereby excluding the small, marginal presses who are dedicated to representing non-mainstream voices. Kelly stresses that, for library collection development, the act of seeking out the works of Indigenous women not only makes their work available to others but enables publishers to continue to support women's work. Elise Chenier (2009) emphasizes the need to preserve the primary data that have been collected by those researching recent struggles for social justice, such as the oral histories of lesbian activists that were collected during the 1980s and 1990s.

There is growing emphasis on the roles of librarians going beyond content curation to foster content creation in the community, such as gathering local histories. Engaging the community with more creative forms, in turn, opens the library staff to more creative ways as well (Marjanen and Roisko, 2014). There is a need for greater emphasis on archiving the work of women's organizations (Irving and English, 2011) in order to preserve the stories of activists. For, as Myers (2002) argued, "when history is not recognized in the present, it will never exist in the past" (p. 6).

Women's Leadership and Legacies

While the practices and forms of access have evolved over the years, the underlying philosophy of libraries remains to ensure people have access to the information they seek to further their interests and learning goals. Identifying excluded populations of people who are rural or Aboriginal or gay has led to a wide range of creative efforts to make libraries relevant to the populations they serve. The women who have contributed to these goals have exhibited leadership in ways that may not be easily visible. They have seen exclusion or other forms of injustice and responded with more inclusive libraries and services. This work is often done in the background, so their leadership may not always be visible.

Playing With Stereotypes of Librarians and Leaders

The popular enthusiasm for Susan Cain's (2012) book *Quiet*, which critiques the mainstream leadership models peddled by elite business schools, gives pause for thought when considering the attributes that make effective leaders. Putting librarians and leadership in the same sentence may seem anathema to both the stereotypes of the quiet introverts in the library stacks, but also to the informal and non-formal educational and support roles that library workers play. For librarians in communities, leadership is often subtle, such as providing information and a communal space for activists to become informed and engaged participants and leaders in their own right. Leadership has many guises.

The gendering of librarianship as a profession has existed for over a century, and it is rife with stereotypes (Adams, 2000). While these impressions may be sources of amusement in the movies, they can form real barriers for many people, particularly people who are socially marginalized. People may perceive librarians as gatekeepers and rule enforcers. The assumed hushed, church-like atmosphere of a well-appointed library can further intimidate those who do not feel welcome or do not believe that the library represents them. Exclusion can take on many forms: ethnicity, sexual orientation, ability, class, and other hidden or explicit barriers. How knowledge is classified and organized reproduces certain worldviews and determines what information is worth keeping. Pervading stereotypes continue to remind those of us who work in libraries of barriers, both real and perceived, that we need to continue breaking down.

Whose History?

I conclude this chapter with a challenge, returning to an important point I touched on earlier. Anyone conducting archival research is haunted by thoughts of the material that is not there, finding only clues to an intriguing mention of a person who lies just out of reach. When one leader is singled out, whose voices are not heard? Whose stories are not told? Whose trails go cold because their work was not noticed or seemed not important at the time? There are still many stories to discover about the role of libraries, and library workers, in supporting community learning and action.

References

- Accardi, M.T. (2013). *Feminist Pedagogy for Library Instruction*. Sacramento, CA: Library Juice.

- Adams, K.C. (2000). Loveless frump as hip and sexy party girl: A re-evaluation of the old-maid stereotype. *The Library Quarterly*, 70(3), 287-301.

- Adams, S. (1991). Coady International Institute. *APLA Bulletin*, 54(6), 1.

- Adams, S. (2005). Libraries. In L.M. English (Ed.), *International Encyclopedia of Adult Education* (pp. 367-369). Basingstoke, England: Palgrave.

- Adams, S. (2009). Our activist past: Nora Bateson, champion of regional libraries. *Partnership: The Canadian Journal of Library and Information Practice and Research*, 4(1), 1-13.

- Adams, S. (2015). Don't shush me: Nora Bateson—activist librarian. In S. Imel and G. Bersch (Eds.), *No Small Lives: Handbook of North American Early Women Contributors to Adult Education, 1925-1950*. Charlotte, NC: Information Age Publishing.

- Badawi, G. (2007). Libraries and women's participation in Nigerian politics. *IFLA Journal*, 33(2), 168-175.

- Cain, S. (2012). *Quiet: The Power of Introverts in a World that Can't Stop Talking*. New York, NY: Crown.

- Canadian Broadcasting Corporation (CBC). (1949/2015). Citizens' Forum: "Is there a teenage problem today?" [audio file]. Toronto, ON: CBC Digital Archives. Retrieved from: http://www.cbc.ca/player/Digital+Archives/CBC+Programmes/Radio/ID/1846418328/.

- Chenier, E. (2009). Hidden from historians: Preserving lesbian oral history in Canada. *Archivaria*, 68, 247-269.

- Dennison, C. J. (1987). "Housekeepers of the community": The British Columbia Women's Institutes. In M.R. Welton (Ed.), *Knowledge for the People: The Struggle for Adult Learning in English-Speaking Canada, 1828-1973* (pp. 52-72). Toronto, ON: OISE Press.

- Donnelly, Sr. F. D. (1945). The People's Library. *Food for Thought*, 5(8), 12-17.

- English, L. (2011). Adult education on the Newfoundland coast: Adventure and opportunity for women in the 1930s and 1940s. *Newfoundland and Labrador Studies*, 26(1), 1719-1726.

- English, L.M. (2014). Ruth I. McKenzie: The intellectual force of Farm Forum. *Proceedings of the 33rd Annual National Conference of the Canadian Association for the Study of Adult Education* (pp. 75-79). London, ON: Brock University.

- Gilroy, M. and Rothstein, S. (1970). *As We Remember It: Interviews with Pioneering Librarians of British Columbia*. Vancouver, BC: University of British Columbia School of Librarianship.

- Hildenbrand, S. (2000). Library Feminism and Library Women's History: Activism and Scholarship, Equity and Culture. *Libraries and Culture*, 35(1), 51-65.

- Hill, C. (2007). Early days of the Central Library and the book van in Trinidad and Tobago. *Libraries and The Cultural Record*, 42(2), 180-191.

- IFLA. (2014). IFLA Manifesto on Transparency, Good Governance and Freedom from Corruption. Retrieved from: http://www.ifla.org/publications/ifla-manifesto-on-transparency-good-governance-and-freedom-from-corruption.

- Imel, S. and Duckett, K. (2009). Libraries and lifelong learning. In P. Jarvis (Ed.), *The Routledge International Handbook of Lifelong Learning* (pp. 183-193). London: Routledge.

- Irving, C.J. (2010). Reviving a community's adult education past: A case study of the library's role in learning. *Journal of Adult and Continuing Education*, 16(2), 21-35.

- Irving, C.J. (2013). People's educational spaces: Antigonish and Highlander as institutional cases supporting learning in social movements. In C. Kawalilak and J. Groen (Eds.), *Proceedings of the 32nd Annual Conference of the Canadian Association for the Study of Adult Education* (pp. 239-245). Victoria, BC: University of Victoria.

- Irving, C.J. and Adams, S. (2012). Not so quiet after all: Two outspoken librarians of the Antigonish Movement. In S. Brigham (Ed.), *Proceedings of the 31st Annual Conference of the Canadian Association for the Study of Adult Education* (pp. 173-179). Wilfrid Laurier University, Waterloo, ON.

- Irving, C.J. and English, L.M. (2011). Community in cyberspace: Gender, social movement learning and the Internet. *Adult Education Quarterly*, 61(3), 262-278.

- Kelly, B. (2010). Reflecting the lives of Aboriginal women in Canadian public library collection development. *Partnership*, 5(2). Retrieved from: https://journal.lib.uoguelph.ca/index.php/perj/article/view/1245.

- Lang, M. and Sacuta, G. (2014). Library programmes and information access for incarcerated women: A Canadian perspective. In M. Morrone (Ed.), *Informed Agitation: Library and Information Skills in Social Justice Movements and Beyond* (pp. 87-102). Sacramento, CA: Library Juice.

- Lor, P.J. and Britz, J. (2010). To access is not to know: A critical reflection on A2K and the role of libraries with special reference to sub-Saharan Africa. *Journal of Information Science*, 36(5), 655-667.

- MacKinnon, M.M. (1949). This is your library, November 15, 1949 [transcript]. St. Francis Xavier University Archives, (RG30-3/29/103-104).

- MacKinnon, M.M. (1951). This is your library, January 11, 1951 [transcript]. St. Francis Xavier University Archives, (RG30-3/29/266).

- Maret, S. and Eagle, B. (2013). Situating the customer: The genealogy of customer language in libraries. *Progressive Librarian*, 41, 18-38.

- Marjanen, I. and Roisko, H. (2014). Let library loose: teens and young adults as content creators at Hattula Public Library. *Proceedings of IFLA World Library and Information Congress, Lyon, France*. Retrieved from: http://library.ifla.org/id/eprint/825.

- Mehra, B. and Gray, L. (2014). "Don't say gay" in the State of Tennessee: Libraries as virtual spaces of resistance and protectors of human rights of lesbian, gay, bisexual, transgender, and queer (LGBTQ) people. *Proceedings of IFLA World Library and Information Congress, Lyon, France*. Retrieved from: http://library.ifla.org/id/eprint/1011.

- Morison, C.K. (1952). Helen Gordon Stewart. In H. Rouillard (Ed.), *Pioneers in Adult Education in Canada* (pp. 49-54). Toronto, ON: Thomas Nelson & Sons.

- Morison, C.K. (1967, Dec.). Helen Gordon Stewart. Marion Gilroy Fonds (File 2-24). University of British Columbia Archives.

- Myers, P.A. (2002). *Preserving Women's History: An Introductory Guide to Preserving the Records of Women's Lives*. Edmonton, AB: Alberta Women's Archives Association.

- Neal, R. (1998). *Brotherhood Economics: Women and Co-operatives in Nova Scotia*. Sydney, NS: UCCB Press.

- Obee, D. (2011). *The Library Book: A History of Service to British Columbia*. Vancouver, BC: British Columbia Library Association.

- Riedler, M. and Eryaman, M.Y. (2010). Transformative library pedagogy and community-based libraries: A Freirean perspective. In G. J. Leckie, Given, L. M., and Buschman, J.E. (Eds.), *Critical Theory for Library and Information Science* (pp. 89-99). Santa Barbara, CA: Libraries Unlimited.

- Rochester, M. (1995). Bringing librarianship to rural Canada in the 1930s: Demonstrations by Carnegie Corporation of New York. *Libraries and Culture*, 30(4), 366-390.

- Sanford, K., Clover, D., and Dogus, F. (2013). An international study of the adult education philosophies and practices in public librarians in Canada and the United Kingdom. In C. Kawalilak and J. Groen (Eds.), *Proceedings of the 32nd Annual Conference of the Canadian Association for the Study of Adult Education* (pp. 535-541), Victoria, BC: University of Victoria.

- Silva Alentejo, E. (2014). Power and community: organizational and cultural LGBT responses against homophobia and promotion of inclusion values. *Proceedings of IFLA World Library and Information Congress, Lyon, France*. Retrieved from: http://library.ifla.org/id/eprint/1010.

- Taylor, E.W., Parrish, M.M., and Banz, R. (2010). Adult education in cultural institutions: Libraries, museums, parks and zoos. In C.E. Kasworm, A.D. Rose, J.M. Ross-Gordon (Eds.) *Handbook of Adult and Continuing Education*, 2010 edition. Thousand Oaks, CA: Sage.

- Tompkins, J.J. and Bateson, N. (1936). *Why Not a Co-operative Library?* Antigonish, NS: Extension Department, St. Francis Xavier University.

This vignette was prepared by Catherine Irving.

The Antigonish Movement is recognized in Canada and beyond for it initiatives in bringing together adult education and co-operative economic development. The Movement was supported through the adult education program of St. Francis Xavier University's (St. FX) Extension Department, founded in 1928.

In historical accounts of the Antigonish Movement, the women who worked in the Extension Department are named from time to time, but often with mere hints as to their contributions as fieldworkers, writers, organizers, secretaries, and editors. These women were well educated and had vast knowledge and expertise. They provided literature to feed the hungry minds of the study clubs, and documented the work and lessons of the Movement. If they could not find materials, they wrote them, generating hundreds of pamphlets and newsletters on a wide range of topics. Most of their work was done anonymously. But here are the names of some of those women and a short profile of each one.

Kay Thompson (1907-1997) was the first woman to join the Antigonish Movement. Kay was a recent teachers' college graduate who had been invited by Dr. Moses Coady to join St. FX Extension in 1931 as the secretary. In addition to handling clerical work, she wrote educational materials and reported on labour news. Her study club booklet *Maritime Techniques in Consumer Cooperation* was used extensively. By 1933, there was a growing need to share the ideas bubbling up through the Movement and *The Extension Bulletin* was born. Kay worked for many years on this newspaper in addition to writing study club booklets, and she continued with the newspaper when it was taken over by co-operatives themselves and rebranded as *The Maritime Co-operator* (the newspaper was later renamed *The Atlantic Co-operator* and is now called *The Canadian Co-operator*). In 1947, she became the publication's editor, a post she held for 23 years.

Sr. Marie Michael MacKinnon (1905-1991) completed her arts degree from St. FX in 1933 and was brought on board to run the women's program (see Irving's chapter in this volume). She was the first Sister of St. Martha of Antigonish to join St. FX Extension. The Sisters of St. Martha (called "the Marthas") was a young congregation formed to provide domestic services to the St. FX campus. Dr. Coady encouraged the Marthas to become involved in education. In addition to coordinating hundreds of women's study clubs, Sr. Marie Michael took care of the Department's library. She also contributed to *The Extension Bulletin*. She went on to pursue a library science degree and a Master of Social Work, after which she was recruited to work with the Coady International Institute. She received an honorary doctorate degree from St. FX in 1971.

Sr. Irene Doyle (1913-2008), also a Sister of St. Martha, was recruited in 1935 to organize the handicrafts program for women. Sr. Irene had just graduated with a Bachelor of Science degree in Home Economics and had studied art. In addition to working to promote the handicrafts, her talents could also be seen in booklet illustrations and an impressive mural presented to the Vatican that artistically represents the Antigonish Movement. Sr. Irene continued with fieldwork off and on until 1952. Within the congregation, she was well known for contributing to the process of renewal in the late 1960s. She received an honorary doctorate degree from St. FX in 1982. In her later years, she collected oral histories of the sisters.

Zita O'Hearn Cameron (1910-1999), who earned a Master of Arts degree from St. FX in 1937, worked with Dr. Coady as his secretary, and contributed substantially to the book, M*asters of Their Own Destiny* (Coady, 1939). A graduate of English literature, she was an accomplished journalist and poet. She was editor of the *Atlantic Co-operator* from 1970-77, and a regular columnist for Antigonish's weekly newspaper, *The Casket*, until her death. Sr. Irene Doyle remarked on Zita's sharp analytical wit. She won numerous press awards for her writing, and received an honorary doctorate from St. FX.

Ida Gallant Delaney (1907-1997) joined the Extension Department as a fieldworker in 1934. Sr. Irene Doyle described her as an inspirational orator. She promoted consumer education, as evidenced by her booklet *Shopping Basket Economics*. In 1982, a group of women from the Extension Department reunited to reminisce. They were the people who knew the story of the Department as they were the ones who had written the booklets and articles about co-operative principles and adult education methods. Ida Delaney took on the task of writing *By Their Own Hands: A Fieldworker's Account of the Antigonish Movement* (Delaney, 1985). In this book, she describes their work, but also highlights the role of women in co-operative and credit union development in the region, including not only their achievements but also the barriers that denied them leadership positions in co-op boards.

Mary Arnold and **Mabel Reed**, companions since childhood, were intrigued by the Antigonish Movement and moved to Cape Breton in 1937. As experienced co-operators, they quickly got involved in the work of St. FX Extension. Mary Arnold worked with the miners who wanted to create co-operative housing, and encouraged women to participate in the design and building process. This work is described in Arnold's book, *The Story of Tompkinsville*. She also developed curriculum to help spread co-operative housing education. She even turned her hand to writing a play—*The Miner's Wife*. Mabel Reed was also involved in the housing co-operative and worked with the local women's groups. They subsequently moved to Newfoundland in 1940, and then across the U.S. and Latin America to continue the development of co-operative housing.

Ellen McNeill Arsenault (1908-2005) was secretary to Dr. Coady for 15 years until he passed away in 1959. She then became the secretary to Msgr. Smyth, the first Director of the Coady International Institute. Originally from Prince Edward Island, she had received teacher training at Normal School. She handled the correspondence from around the world. Fr. Tophsee quipped, "Give Ellen a single word and she develops it into a good full-page letter." Correspondence between Ellen and Coady reveal the volumes of information that they gathered and shared to spread the word and secure funds for their programs. The little booklets not only supported the study clubs, but helped others learn of their work. The correspondence also reveals the amount of research and writing she did to support her directors—the hidden work behind the "secretary" job title.

Other women survive in the archival record of the Antigonish Movement. For example, **Catherine "Tat" Sears** was a fieldworker and contributor to *The Extension Bulletin* and **Margie (MacKinnon) MacDougall** worked with women in fishing communities in the 1940s. **Mary (McIntyre) MacNeil** was a writer and poet who wrote for the *Maritime Co-operator*, one of a group Coady once called "four of the smartest women in Canada."

Further Reading

- Cameron, J.D. (2000). *And Martha Served.* Halifax, NS: Nimbus.

- Delaney, I. (1985). *By Their Own Hands: A Fieldworker's Account of the Antigonish Movement.* Hantsport, NS: Lancelot Press.

- Neal, R. (1999). *Brotherhood Economics: Women and Co-operatives in Nova Scotia.* Sydney, NS: UCCB Press.

Photo 1: Left to right: Sr. Marie Michael MacKinnon and Coady Institute diploma participant Gertie Ruiz from the Philippines, 1990. Photo courtesy of the Coady International Institute.

Photo 2: Left to right: Ellen Arsenault, Zita Cameron, Sr. Irene Doyle, Kay Desjardins. Extension Department reunion, 1994. Photo courtesy of the Sisters of St. Martha, Antigonish, Congregational Archives.

Wearing their typically outrageous attire, including flamboyant hats, the Raging Grannies stage public protests for many social justice causes.

Photo: © Koozma Tarasoff.

18

More than Laughter
Raging Grannies and Creative Leadership

Since the birth of their movement in 1987 in Victoria, British Columbia, the Raging Grannies have established their presence across Canada and other countries. Their leadership is unconventional, but it is an important example of practices identified by Preskill and Brookfield (2009) as *Learning as a Way of Leading.* As leaders, the Raging Grannies see themselves as lifelong learners and educators, dedicated to social justice and encouraging active citizen participation. Furthermore, in response to the destructive threats of the United States nuclear warships that frequently visited the local Victoria military base in the 1980s, the Grannies created an engaging form of protest, using humour, that challenges the discourse of aging as decline and opens possibilities for older women interested in social and political issues.

Carole Roy

Through an approach that may seem deceptively simple, the Raging Grannies provide an example of dynamic, flexible, and socially orientated feminist leadership that has found relevance across regional differences and national borders. Their demonstrations of the "positive transformation of rage and anger" (Roy, 2004, p. 186) are also widely respected by other social and environmental leaders and activists.

In this chapter, I look at the Raging Grannies through the framework of Preskill and Brookfield: analysis of experience (creation of the Raging Grannies); critical reflection (satirical songs); creating community and fostering collective leadership (effective network and flexible leadership); and living democracy (diversity of issues and actions).

> Hey, look us over,
> Grannies proud and strong
> Time to hear our voices,
> Time to hear our song
> Silent for too long,
> Speaking up at last
> Cause now the earth
> Is crying out
> . . . Hear the Grannies' voices sing!
> —Tune: *Hey, Look Them Over* (Roy, 2004, p. 3)

Making Space for Older Women to Speak Out

Preskill and Brookfield (2009) suggest that an important aspect of leadership is analyzing experience, and this is exactly how the Raging Grannies started in Victoria. Their initial concern, as alluded to above, was visits by U.S. nuclear warships to Victoria waters, potentially endangering the health of their families and of the environment (a possibility made more real by the disaster of Chernobyl not long before). Second, they were motivated by the unresponsiveness of all levels of government to this potential threat, especially the absence of an emergency plan in case of a nuclear accident in their city. Third, as older women activists involved in a local peace group, they were also reacting to being dismissed in these discussions and being relegated to making coffee and stuffing envelopes. During a theatre workshop, they named their experience and identified their common ambition of expressing their views publicly and imaginatively. Their collective analysis resulted in the creation of the Raging Grannies, a distinctive persona with an easily identified "uniform" that allows individual creativity and public recognition.

Along with disarming smiles, they wear outrageous *accoutrements* that include ostentatious hats, ostrich feathers, vintage shawls and frilly aprons, flamboyant clothing, purple running shoes, long gloves, leather purses, and even pearls—all used to flaunt their matronly dignity. These are "warriors in sensible shoes" (Roy, 2004, p. 190). They believe the time for playing dress-up is not over and there is nothing like colour and visibility to dispel the invisibility that many older women experience. It is obvious by the outlandish clothes they wear that these women are in play mode; their choice of clothing denotes impishness while inviting passersby or audiences to enter the realm of playfulness. This costume worn by women who, at times, also sport wrinkles, canes, or walkers conveys many messages: age is no deterrent for relevant commentary on current issues, fun is important at all ages, and imagination is always elegant. The Raging Grannies embrace the physical reality of older women with a mischievous attitude and no apology, as their musical scores satirically render visible stereotypes associated with older women:

> Wrinkle, wrinkle aging star,
> Who cares just how old you are?
> Your hair is grey, your dentures click
> Your bosom sags, your ankle's thick
> Your joints all creak, your arthritis plagues
> You've got all the symptoms of Raging Age
> . . .
> Hurrah for Age, Age, to Hell with being beige
> We won't stay cooped up in a cage
> Our eyes are dim but our tongues are sharp
> We go out on a limb, our wits are sharp
> Yes we've got years, years and you'd better get it clear
> A raging gran's a force to fear
> —Tune: *Twinkle Twinkle Little Star* (Roy, 2004, p.155)

However, the Grannies also embrace a wide range of concerns that go well beyond aging, including environmental, peace-related, social, and political issues.

Reaching Out Using Humour

To add to the playfulness, the Raging Grannies write satirical songs that offer thought-provoking commentaries on current issues. Satire requires sophisticated critical reflection skills, an important aspect of the *learning as leadership* model (Preskill & Brookfield, 2009). Despite the laughs that follow them, they are deadly serious. While their singing aims to educate audiences on current issues, at times it has also become an act of protest given the context in which they perform their songs. They take on the role of storytellers embracing a certain resistance. The active ingredient in their performance is humour, which allows them to say what they want without ranting. Humour is recognized as a "[L]ubricant to smooth social interactions and as a means of expressing hostility and aggression" (Apte, 1985, p. 261). In his work on satire, Leonard Feinberg (1967) suggested that while institutions are not likely to be influenced by satire, individuals are.

An important feature of the Grannies' songs is their research. While they take liberty with lyrics, they make sure they have their facts right and they take great pride in their accuracy. Indeed, learning and research are very important to their ability to write songs. Collectively, they have written thousands of songs in which they analyzed many different experiences and pieces of information. A rap written by the original Victoria Grannies deserves mention as it informs audiences about a difficult subject:

> Po-ly-chlor-i-na-ted bi-phe-ee-nals
> Will fry your brain and rot your adre-ee-nals.
> Concentrating in our fatty ti-ish-ue
> It's not a very glamorous i-ish-ue.
> But maybe if they bury it deeper in the ground,
> By the time it kills somebody, we won't be around!
> Chlor-o-fluor-o-car-bon production
> Is causing ozone layer reduction.
> When ultraviolet rays have seared us to the bone,
> We won't get much relief from using coppertone!
> Disposables pursue us no matter where we roam,
> Who could contemplate a life devoid of styro-foam?
> We all want our comfort and convenience,
> Which leaves us sitting squarely right on the fence.
> These things are very difficult to believe,
> It's not the way that life's portrayed on our TV.
> Our kids might all get cancer, and have defective genes,
> But they will be the best-dressed mutants that you've ever seen!
> Oh! Po-ly-chlor-i-na-ted bi-phe-ee-nals
> La la la la, la la la la la la la. . .
>   —Victoria Raging Grannies (Roy, 2004, p. 51)

For Barreca (2014), humour is about power, as "humour can help women recognize new sources of power within themselves" (p. 6). Moreover, "a joke is never just a joke; it's all about power and voice... [it] allows you to be heard more clearly than before, with the fabulous, fierce triumph of the last laugh" (p. 6). Humour is sophisticated, as it relies on ambiguity and paradox; this edge gives "women a chance to criticize without pain, express our anger without injury and deflate someone's pretensions while allowing them their dignity" (p. 6). According to Barreca, women humourists "know humour is the shortest and most electric line between two—or more—points" (p. 7). While the Raging Grannies are not humourists per se, they use humour very effectively to question assumptions, governmental policies, or corporations' actions. Barreca expresses a fear that, despite women's gains, younger women may still believe "that they have to imitate men in order to be considered funny" (p. 7).

The Raging Grannies, then, provide a much needed example of women's effective use of humour as a political tool. When interviewed a few years before her 100th birthday, legendary adult educator, activist, and Halifax Raging Granny Muriel Duckworth said that humour "is a way to teach" (personal communication, March 14, 2002). While humour makes it easier for the audience to take in difficult information, Doran Doyle of the original Victoria Grannies says it also protects the Grannies themselves, who are constantly confronted with devastating information. Humour is a life-affirming response to seemingly hopeless problems; Toronto Granny Dorothy Fletcher sees humour as a way out of the despair caused by the many problems of the world. Humour reflects "an assertive orientation . . . and perhaps an impatience with negative affects such as anxiety and depression" (Lefcourt, 2001, p. 78). Granny Kathleen Dunphy, who worked as a nurse, recalls humour as a resource that helped people through pain; while it does not change the gravity of a situation, it provides some relief and a way of expressing concerns without focusing only on the difficulties that can be paralyzing. Some Grannies suggest there is a sustaining quality to humour as Granny Pearl Rice, who survived World War II in England, notes:

> It gives [you] a break…. During the war [World War II in England] lots of sad things happened during bombings…. Quite often during something really serious happening, something that was getting you down, somebody would make some remark and it might have been silly…. And you had a laugh and it lightened things up during a very serious time, you know, so I think humour is quite important. (Personal communication, June 10, 2002)

For 25 years, the Raging Grannies have used the power of humour to carve a space for themselves on the public political landscape and as the primary means to comment on socio-cultural and political concerns. While they use songs, however, they object to being called entertainment; being a pesky nuisance is more of a compliment to them. They live up to Margaret Lawrence's words that as women grow older they should become more radical, not less—words that inspired some members of the original Victoria group. The Grannies make "people laugh at the right targets; the corrupt, the powerful, giving stupidity its proper place way, way down at the bottom of our consideration, broadcasting it as a means of bringing them down," said Granny Rose DeShaw (2002, p. 26).

Sparking a Wild Network, Fostering Flexible Leadership

> To Granny means always working with other stubborn, difficult women who won't shut up, running with our shared ideas, finding something genuinely funny in the bleakest moments. Grannying is the opposite of self-pity and depression. The women who Granny have toughness I don't find elsewhere. (Granny Rose DeShaw, 2002, p. 26)

One of the remarkable successes of the Raging Grannies was to encourage older women to take a stand and publicly express their views, creating a sense of community locally but also across Canada and across borders. Creating community is an aspect of Preskill and Brookfield's (2009) leadership model for social justice. Through personal contacts as well as through media reports of the Victoria Raging Grannies' flamboyant and colourful protests, women in other places heard about them and decided to start their own group.

The Victoria Grannies were generous and willing to share their ideas, experience, and songs with any women interested in similar issues. Within a decade, there were gaggles in many cities in Canada—Vancouver, Edmonton, Calgary, Regina, Toronto, Ottawa, Montréal, Fredericton, and Halifax—as well as in smaller towns. An analysis of songs from gaggles across the country showed their remarkable consistency in perspective on various issues despite the lack of direct contact the groups had with each other in the first years. The Grannies seem to hold similar values and they wrote songs that were easily exchanged, despite not having met one another. Not only do they encourage members of their local group to participate in decision making, they also encourage connections to other gaggles, as each group remains autonomous.

Aside from the sense of community at the local level, every second year a gaggle hosts the Un-convention, a large organizational effort during which more than one hundred Grannies from across North America spend a few days together. Un-conventions are opportunities to discuss song writing, prop design, actions, group dynamics, media work, civil disobedience, and much more, as it often results in "hats competing" for attention, friendship, and much laughter! Interestingly, the emergence of this coherent movement in the mid-nineties took place at a time when Canada faced increasing regionalization in terms of formal federal politics with the election of members of the Bloc Québecois and of the Reform Party to the House of Commons in 1993. By the mid- to late 1990s, the growing use of the Internet resulted in a web presence for the Raging Grannies and this technology made it easier to communicate between Un-conventions.

The Raging Grannies' example has not only sparked the establishment of a unique, non-hierarchical, decentred but coherent network of gaggles, but also the development of innovative and flexible leadership that fits the collective leadership mentioned by Preskill and Brookfield (2009), who suggest that being open to others' contributions and a willingness to engage are cornerstones of leadership required for social justice:

> Collective leadership flows from a culture in which engagement in, and sharing of, learning is an expectation and a priority. As people learn new skills, dispositions, and epistemologies, they inevitably become aware of how individual learning is both premised upon, and contributes to, the learning of others. We cannot learn to be critically reflective, analyze experience, question ourselves, practice democracy, sustain hope, or create community without the necessary involvement of others. Once we start to see that the collective is the source of so much of our learning, our strength, and our identity, it is a short step to realizing that leadership also resides in the collective. (pp. 15-16)

A gaggle of Raging Grannies is usually made up of women from different backgrounds, each of whom brings a wide range of experiences: the labour movement; women's groups; religious organizations; groups working on environmental, poverty, racial, or Indigenous issues; or community organizations. Individual Grannies have decades-long involvement within some circles, which means the Raging

Grannies are remarkably well connected, with a vast system of social networks and learning from each other's issues. The Grannies are an example of collective leadership, as they tend not to have official "leaders" but rotating leadership, depending on the task. As they deal with current affairs and need to stay well informed on a wide range of issues, different Grannies assume a leadership role based on their knowledge of specific issues. Such dynamic leadership requires the flexibility of all involved. Like any group, the Raging Grannies have members that bring a diversity of interests and skills. Those interested in writing songs do so, while others work more closely with the media, create props and actions, write letters to government officials and to their local newspapers, network with other groups dedicated to social and ecological justice, or take on coordination of activities. Leadership is not a position, but rather a practice of activism and change.

Despite the biennial Un-convention and communication through the Internet, this remains a movement of small groups consisting of four to twenty active Grannies dispersed mostly across North America. Each group is independent and totally autonomous and can decide on which issues they wish to focus. The result is that individual Grannies have a lot of freedom in expressing their views, something a formal organization does not often permit individual members. Through their flamboyant approach and sharing of the recognizable persona of the Raging Granny, individuals benefit from a group identity and get the attention of media, citizens, and government officials not usually available to individuals or even small groups. As an organization they have no structure, except a website maintained by a few volunteer Grannies. They have no president, secretary, or director, and they don't follow Robert's Rules of Order. But what they have is highly motivated members who analyze experiences and issues in concert with others, knowledge derived from the variety of their individual interests and backgrounds, and a diversity of gifts that they are free and welcomed to use. They make decisions through discussions, at times slowly in order to include everyone's views; however, not all groups work in the same way. Some rely on consensus decision making while others may vote. Individual groups are not perfect democracies, as some Grannies have more influence through personality or abilities, yet each Granny can exert influence if she chooses to do so. Some groups predominantly sing while others court more trouble, and some even engage in civil disobedience.

Living Democracy

As they crashed commissions and politicians' carefully timed over-planned visits, the Raging Grannies "rattle the bars, rattle the cage, practice democracy ... It's ... our obligation as citizens," said Granny Barbara Siefred (Roy, 2004, p. 134). This again supports what Preskill and Brookfield (2009) suggest is another relevant task of learning and practising democracy:

> To live democratically one must learn to honour diversity, live with the partial functioning of the democratic ideal, avoid the trap of false antithesis (where we are always forced to choose between either-or, mutually exclusive options), accept the compatibility of ends and means (where we avoid the temptation to bypass the democratic process in the interests of speedily reaching a decision regarded as obviously right and necessary), correlate the functioning of social institutions (health, education, and social services) with democratic purposes, develop collective forms of social and economic planning, live with contrary decisions, and appreciate the comedy inherent in democracy's contradictions. (p. 17)

While all the factors are meaningful in relation to the Raging Grannies, the last one concerning comedy is especially significant. By using humour in their songs and actions, the Grannies help others see new aspects of a situation, including absurdity. In identifying humour, at times in bleak situations, they lead others to expand their minds and see other perspectives. However, despite their use of humour, it is not just about laughs: they also take risks. The Raging Grannies provide a form of leadership at public protests and demonstrations by ensuring that the media cannot paint a picture of protesters as young, wild, and unruly; they prove "false the theory that radicalism is synonymous only with youth" (Howard, 1992, p. D7).

While they receive invitations to sing, they also "invite" themselves to many events, using their matronly credibility to gain entrance without being noticed until they get into action. They have crashed a Lieutenant-Governor's reception, disrupted official meetings and gatherings, and interrupted governmental commissions or hearings with their songs. Their spunky actions are legendary and include offering a clothesline with their "briefs" to a British Columbia provincial commission looking into lifting the moratorium on uranium mining. The Montréal Grannies crashed the Federal Environment Assessment Review hearing on a proposal by Atomic Energy of Canada (AECL) to put highly radioactive nuclear waste in the Canadian Shield and they offered their own recipe for Radioactive Road Resurfacing:

> Take a pinch of plutonium (holding your breath because 1 microgram will give you lung cancer). Add a half a cup of strontium (fast before the cup melts). Mix well and spread evenly on road surface. The formula, which only needs to be applied once a millennium . . . comes with the following guarantee: It will glow in the dark and is self-defrosting for at least 1,000 years. (Granny Joan Hadrill in "Raging Grannies propose solution for nuclear waste," *The Montréal Downtowner*, 1990, pp. 1-2)

They also paddled canoes from Ottawa to Montebello, Québec, for the Summit of the Three Amigos (Prime Minister Stephen Harper, Canada; President George W. Bush, the United States; and President Felipe Calderon, Mexico).

Over the years, some Raging Grannies have been arrested in civil disobedience actions. In 1988, four Raging Grannies were arrested in a civil disobedience action called the Grandmother Peace Action. This took place at the Canadian Forces Maritime Experimental Test Range (CFMETR) on Winchelsea Island, located in the Georgia Strait near Nanaimo, BC. The CFMETR "has been operating since 1967, testing torpedoes, sonar, sono-buoys and other maritime warfare equipment. Ottawa allows foreign governments—principally the U.S. Navy—to use the facilities" (www.globalsecurity.org/ military/facility/nanoose). The U.S. military was testing weapons that could later be fitted with nuclear weapons. While charges were later dropped, Granny Doran Doyle felt she had "crossed out of the range of respectability" (in K. Howard, 1989, p. 14), which echoed Martha Ackelsberg when: "Those who cross the boundaries of what is considered appropriate behaviour do so in the context of a supportive group; they can become empowered and come to question the appropriateness of those boundaries in the first place" (1991, p. 165).

Granny Jean McLaren was arrested in the same action and found that arresting officers "have a hard time arresting older women, especially when you're nice to them" (Personal communication, May 10, 2002). In fact, McLaren was arrested nine times for civil disobedience, which includes being in jail for two days for participating in a peace walk in Israel. She was also arrested for taking part in a march at the Nevada nuclear test site. Other Grannies were arrested for forestry issues. Granny Alison Acker and two other Raging Grannies were arrested and convicted along with the 800-plus protesters during the largest mass arrests at Clayoquot Sound, BC, and spent two weeks in jail: "It was really important to show that it's not just young people who are concerned about the future of the planet. Us old birds care too" (Acker in Birch, 2001, p. 109). From Acker's perspective, the Grannies challenge the stereotype that environmental activists are "only a load of crazy young kids" protesting the logging (Birch, 2001, p. 109).

Some Raging Grannies have taken risks in defence of the young. The London (ON) Raging Grannies courted arrest for disobeying the new provincial law against squeegeeing. The next day, on February 13, 2000, the headlines of the local newspaper read, "Raging Grannies Take a Swipe at Squeegee Law" (Fenlon, 2000, p. A1). The article continued: To "mess with squeegee kids" in that Ontario town is to "mess with the Grannies." And,

> That's the lesson London motorists learned . . . as eight Raging Grannies staged an act of civil disobedience on a busy street corner to protest homelessness and raise money for London's food bank. The guerrilla action took place just after 10 a.m. . . . where the rabble-rousers sang, squeegeed, distributed pamphlets and asked for donations from stopped motorists. After an hour of panhandling, the Grannies . . . had already raised $158, which they celebrated by singing in front of the closed office of the MPP [PC London West]. "People have to become more aware of the homeless," said 86-year-old Florence Boyd-Graham, who blasted the province's crack-down on squeegee kids and noted that at her age, she doesn't "give a hell" about what people think of her politics. A police officer did stop to question a Grannie after the action, but no charges were laid under a new law banning soliciting on public roadways that went into effect Jan. 31. "We thought we were going to get locked up," said Boyd-Graham, laughing. Michelle LeBoutillier . . . said the Grannies were "concerned" they might get charged, but were compelled to disobey the law because they "felt so strongly that poverty isn't being addressed in the way it should be." (p. A1)

In their defiance of the new law, the London Raging Grannies strongly opposed the provincial government, using their credibility as older women and visibility as Raging Grannies to support the struggle against poverty and to expose the fact that the law was made against a specific group of people, not an action. One may ask what it means that in our society women in their 80s feel obliged to risk arrest to raise awareness about the plight of youth in poverty. But by defying the law, Grannies courageously take a stand as leaders to express their dissenting voices, a fundamental right in a democratic society.

One Granny action, during the escalation of threats related to the first Gulf War, inspired copycats across Canada. Then, more than a decade later in the United States, during the war in Iraq, the protest became a civil disobedience action. In November 1990, the Victoria Grannies dressed up in military uniforms (real for those Grannies who are veterans and made-up uniforms for others) and presented themselves at the Canadian Army Recruitment Centre to volunteer for a tour of duty in the Gulf to relieve their grandchildren of this chore. The next day their picture was on the front page of the local newspaper with this caption: "Unable by law to ask the Grannies their age, the baffled recruiters ploughed through the necessary paperwork straight-faced; one Granny was even invited back for a math test!" (Raging Grannies ready for war, 1990, p. A1). Fifteen years later, in August 2005, BBC News reported that the Raging Grannies in Tucson, Arizona, were arrested and charged with criminal trespass for having walked into their local U.S. Army Recruiting Centre to volunteer for a tour of duty in Iraq. While the charges were later dropped, the news inspired a group of 18 Raging Grannies and other grandmothers to repeat the action at New York Times Square U.S. Army Recruitment Centre, an action they called "We insist we enlist." They dared read a text that disagreed with the U.S. government's stance on the war in Iraq. After the soldiers securely locked the door and went into hiding, the Grannies were arrested, put in a paddy wagon, and taken to a police detachment for processing; among them was a 90-year-old Granny who was blind and using a walker. Their three-day trial at the Manhattan Criminal Court a few months later surprisingly revealed that the Grannies had blocked no door, but the police had! In fact, the Grannies were victims of an unlawful arrest. This shows the inability, or unwillingness, of authorities to exercise judgment in the identification of threats. It also shows that the responses were very different in Canada, where no one was arrested as they could not be discriminated against on the basis of age, whereas in the U.S. they were arrested for trespassing or supposedly blocking a door.

Reports on Canadian Grannies' actions took a more serious, or ludicrous, turn at an enquiry into the RCMP's actions towards protesters at the Asia-Pacific Economic Cooperation (APEC) summit in Vancouver in November 1997. Secret military documents showed that the RCMP had kept an eye on the Grannies as a potential threat! ("Are the Raging Grannies 'anti-Canadian',?" 1999, [np]). In an earlier article titled "Are Raging Grannies a public enemy?," this fact was also exposed:

> Military documents marked "secret" and "Canadian eyes only" contain assessments of the threat posed during the last year's APEC summit by a host of terrorist groups—as well as the Anglican Church and the singing group, the Raging Grannies. Documents made public by the RCMP Public Complaint Commission [say] . . . "the Raging Grannies, while considered a low risk, were assessed as 'anti-Canadian forces' in the military documents." (Thompson, 1998, p. A1)

The Raging Grannies further exploited this incident in one of their songs to let the RCMP and CSIS know that intimidation will not deter them from speaking out:

> CSIS
> These grandmothers still squawk/We don't sit on the shelf
> In spite of the RCMP!
> Democratic dissent / Civil disobedience
> Are supposed to be a / Canadian guarantee
> The cops and CSIS of course / Show no remorse
> As they target old ladies such as we
> While they snitch
> We will bitch / Rage and roar even more
> Till they learn 'bout democracy!
> —Tune: *Grandfather's Clock* (Roy, 2004, p. 149)

Conclusion

Remarkable creativity, daring, and most noticeably humour ensure that the Raging Grannies attract many different kinds of attention. The Raging Grannies demonstrate imaginative thinking and daring in their songs and actions and their deliberate protests and civil disobedience are empowering. Their superb use of satirical songs and humorous actions juxtapose colliding frameworks, which is at the heart of humour as well as at the very heart of the Raging Grannies' identity and purpose. Their brilliance is to embody a paradox within their name as it links grannies, usually portrayed as sweet and harmless, to an un-motherly public rage.

Old age is often portrayed as the negative experience of "dependency, disease, disability, and depression" regardless of personalities or conditions (Scheidt et al., 1999, p. 278). While the process of aging may bring gains or losses, with ageism all that is counted is loss. In their own identity and in humour Raging Grannies found empowerment, which led to the creation of an attractive form of protest, a robust identity, an effective network, and an example of flexible leadership. In the process, they dispel the passivity often expected of older women and instead provide an image of older women as leaders who are informed, smart, caring, daring, and funny, and who live life with pizazz!

Finally, now that the Raging Grannies is 25 years old as a movement, they have been around long enough for me to "catch up" to the level of "senior" and some of them are even younger than I am now! We showed the film about the Grannies on which I assisted at our film festival. To our great surprise, the local Grannies showed up with a hat made for me, and a song. I have not yet joined them in their "performance" as I feel more comfortable in the writing than the doing—at least right now. But who knows? One day I might just have to join "my subject" in real life, not just on a page.

References

- Ackelsberg, M.A. (1991). *Free Women of Spain: Anarchism and the Struggle for the Emancipation of Women*. Indianapolis: Indiana University Press.
- Apte, M. L. (1985). *Humor and Laughter: An Anthropological Approach*. London: Cornell University Press.
- Are the Raging Grannies "anti-Canadian"? (1999, January). *The Canadian Unitarian*, 40(1), [np].
- Barreca, G. (2014). The power of women's humor: From Supreme Court justices to comedy stars. *Rain and Thunder: A Radical Feminist Journal of Discussion and Activism*, 58, 6-7.
- Birch, S. (2001). Where middle age is all the rage. *SAGA*, September.
- DeSHaw, R. (2002). *Granny Grapevine* (Spring), p. 26.
- Feinberg, L. (1967). *Introduction to Satire*. Ames, Iowa: Iowa State University Press.
- Fenlon, B. (2000). Raging Grannies take a swipe at squeegee law. *The London Free Press*, February 13.
- Howard, C. (1992). Raging against the night. *The Vancouver Sun*, October 10.
- Howard, K. (1989). Those comic Raging Grannies. *The United Church Observer*, 53, 3. Retrieved from: http://www.globalsecurity.org/military/facility/nanoose.htm.
- Lefcourt, H. M. (2001). *Humor: The Psychology of Living Buoyantly*. New York: Kluwer Academic/Plenum Publishers.
- Preskill, S. & Brookfield, S. D. (2009). *Learning as a Way of Leading: Lessons from the Struggle for Social Justice*. San Francisco, CA: Jossey-Bass.
- Raging Grannies ready for war (1990). *Times Colonist*, 2 November, p. A1.
- Raging Grannies propose solution. (1990, November 21). *The Montreal Downtowner*, pp. 1-2. Roy, C. (2004). *The Raging Grannies: Wild Hats, Cheeky Songs, and Witty Actions for a Better World*. Montréal, QC: Black Rose Books.
- Scheidt, R. J., Humpherys, D. R., & Yorgason, J. B. (1999). Successful aging: What's not to like. *Journal of Applied Gerontology: The Official Journal of the Southern Gerontological Society*, 18(3), 277-282.
- Thompson, A. (1998). Are Raging Grannies a public enemy? *The Toronto Star*, October 11.

Photos: *Courtesy of the archives of the Montréal Raging Grannies.*

This vignette was prepared by Darlene E. Clover.

The Raging Grannies is an activist organization that began in the winter of 1987 in Victoria, British Columbia. As discussed in Chapter 18, Grannies groups can now be found in many cities and towns across Canada and worldwide. These women are social justice activists (in sensible shoes), most old enough to be grandmothers. They dress in clothing that mocks stereotypes of older women, sing songs at protests, and take on some of the world's most difficult problems, such as nuclear disarmament. The Grannies write the lyrics themselves (particularly Alison Acker, see below), conveying their own political messages to the tunes of well-known songs. Their activism includes peace and environmental issues but they also work for affordable housing and other causes. Although there are and have been many Grannies, we profile four of the most active ones living in Victoria today.

Fran Thoburn was born and raised in Cleveland, Ohio, on the shores of Lake Huron. Being outdoors has always been an important part of her life; hence her distress concerning the state of planet Earth and global warming. Fran married and went to Germany to be with a husband in the military who, as a private, was not allowed to have his wife with him. "I went anyway, lived as a tourist in a small room in bomb-wrecked Munich, close to the army base. I saw my husband whenever he could get a pass from the base; fairly often because the army officers were amazed a private's wife would come to Germany on her own ticket." Fran moved to Toronto in 1970, where she joined other women and a doctor to start a women's health clinic to treat street women. After her divorce, Fran spent some years in the wilds of Ontario with a writer. Coming to Victoria, she produced a radio show about peace and the environment and started engaging in street theatre with ten other women, which evolved into the Raging Grannies in 1987.

Freda Knot was born in 1936 in Vancouver into a progressive secular Jewish family. She is a widow of Erni, mother of David and Ayala, and grandmother of Madison and Reide. Freda was a founding member of the Greater Victoria Disarmament Group (GVDG), a large and influential peace organization in Greater Victoria in the 1980s and she helped to organize the annual Peace (now Earth) Walk, which has taken place in conjunction with Earth Day for 35 years now. She is also a former board member of the Victoria chapter of the Council of Canadians and a member of Independent Jewish Voices and If Not Now When, organizations of Jewish people working to promote a socially just solution to the Israeli-Palestinian dispute. Freda joined the Raging Grannies in 1992. "It was time to bring some humour into my activism." For her, the Ragging Grannies have "become very dear.... They are my friends and confidantes. They have helped to make my life meaningful and enjoyable."

Alison Acker worked as a reporter on the *Daily Express* in London before emigrating to Canada in 1955, where she worked for newspapers in Winnipeg, Vancouver, and Toronto. With a family to support, she switched to teaching, earned her Master of Arts at the University of Toronto, taught high school, and then joined the faculty at Ryerson University for 25 years. She also helped organize anti-war protests, travelled to war zones in Latin America with money to support the peoples' causes, wrote many articles about government terror attacks on the people in Chile and Central America, and then published *Children of the Volcano*. This book sold widely in Canada, the U.S., and the U.K. and was translated into German and Spanish. Upon retirement in 1989, she moved to Victoria, quickly joined the Victoria Raging Grannies, and became their chief songwriter. With Betty Brightwell, she wrote their history, *Off Our Rockers and Into Trouble*. Alison volunteered for years with therapeutic riding for the disabled, the local helpline, the Royal BC museum, and Our Place kitchen; she also sat on the Victoria Library Board. Recently, she has worked as secretary to the Committee to End Homelessness and is now working to create a micro-housing village (tiny houses that can be put almost anywhere and provide shelter for the homeless)—and get it funded by the city! She believes strongly in positive action for change and refuses to slow down.

Daphne M. Taylor was eleven years old when World War II began in 1939 and she was sent to a boarding school in North Wales. Her hometown of Liverpool was not safe as it was a port city on the northwest coast of England. She had a strange and fervent belief that if the Germans invaded England, "We'd convert them all to Christianity and all would be well." Daphne learned German so she could get a job in Germany after the war to discover why the English had fought the Germans over two generations. Daphne's mother's fiancé was killed in World War I and the family was never allowed to forget this. "My dear father was not my mother's first choice for a husband, and I as a child knew this." Daphne got a job in Germany through the British Foreign Office as a secretary with their Visa Control Office in Dusseldorf, and was very thankful to get to know a real German family. "We were, of course, not meant to fraternize with the Germans. Eva would invite me over for lunch on a Saturday with her family. Her father had been a major in the pre-Hitler German Army, but fought in the Nazi army. Her mother spoke no English, so my German came in very handy." Pete, Eva's older brother, had been in the Hitlerjugend, the Hitler Youth (Brown Shirts as they were called). Daphne of course asked "How come?" He replied, "If I hadn't joined, my family wouldn't have got ration books," which meant no food. "Pete was the first pacifist I met at the age of 23 or so, and of course it formed a great impression and an identity that has endured all my life."

Alison MacLeod is a Canadian/British fiction writer committed to beautiful and novel forms of expression while penetrating to the heart of human truth. Photo courtesy of Kate MacLeod.

19

Feminism and Femininities
Learning about Gender and Women's Leadership through Fiction

"A dried up cougar? Is that a step up from a bitch or a step down?" I wondered.
—Paretsky, 2011, p. 328

We are Canadian women and scholars who have always been avid readers of fiction. Patricia in particular has an interest in writing fiction and for the past decade has been doing research related to lifelong learning and crime fiction. Susan began her academic career with a PhD in English, has a background in Canadian literature, and teaches pre-service and graduate students about teaching English in secondary schools. As mothers, we have spent time thinking about how to introduce our children (and in the case of Patricia, now grandchildren) to reading. For a number of years, we have worked as collaborators on SSHRC-funded research projects on lifelong learning and fiction.

Patricia A. Gouthro and Susan M. Holloway

In this chapter we draw upon our research on fiction writing and our experiences as educators to explore how fiction can help us understand issues around gender and leadership. We are interested in how writers explain their creative learning processes so as to gain insights into our understanding of adult learning experiences. Our work is informed by feminist scholarship that values storytelling and arts-based approaches to research and teaching.

This chapter considers how the concept of gender is taught through fiction, from the vantage point of the reader and the perspectives of women writers. We illustrate how, by looking at understandings of feminisms and femininity, insights can be gained into how learning connected to fiction may have an impact on the development of female identity and understandings of leadership, by both reinforcing and critiquing gendered assumptions regarding behaviour. We draw upon interviews with fiction writers, bring in excerpts from their books, and weave an analysis that connects to the literature on adult learning.

Most of our examples are of Canadian women writers, but we do bring in an outside example—Sara Paretsky, the author whose quotation sets the stage for this chapter. It was listening to Sara at a Bouchercon (crime fiction writing) conference that first spurred Patricia into thinking about how fiction is an important aspect of learning about many topics, including gender. A strong and outspoken feminist, Sara Paretsky has been credited with ground-breaking work through her own writing and her involvement in establishing Sisters in Crime, an organization to combat discrimination against female mystery writers. Patricia began her research on fiction writing by looking at Sisters in Crime as a unique women's learning organization (see Gouthro, 2012). The other authors we interviewed are known for their writing in literary, crime fiction, or children's stories areas, although many of these writers cross boundaries to also write in other areas such as poetry or non-fiction. Our participants range from well-known established writers to emerging authors. The ones we have chosen to discuss in this chapter are significant in the way they draw attention to gender and inclusion issues in their fiction writing.

Learning about Gender through Fiction

> Mabel Murple's house was purple. So was Mabel's hair.
> —Fitch, 1995, p. 1

Most researchers would agree that gender involves learning social traits. It begins at infancy and continues through adulthood. Boeren (2011) explains that "the 'gender' concept refers to roles, relationships and expectations determined by socio-cultural, political and economic factors and goes beyond biology (UNESCO, 2003)" (p. 334). As Boeren points out, learning can occur in a range of different contexts. The formal realm encompasses organized schooling or educational systems. Non-formal learning occurs in structured but not necessarily certified environments, such as professional development courses or cooking classes. Informal learning is part of everyday experiences, such as reading a novel or chatting about it with a friend, but it may be just as important as other kinds of learning in shaping perceptions and beliefs about issues such as gender. Jubas and Knutson (2013) believe it is often difficult to disentangle different categories of learning, since informal learning spaces that co-exist within formal educational programs, such as medical school, can have a significant impact on how and what individuals learn.

Many factors influence how we learn about gender, including culture, class, race, ability, and sexual orientation. Our response to this learning, as women or as feminists, may include multiple ways of assessing, analyzing, debating, or refuting different assumptions, beliefs, and ideals. Most learning that girls and women engage in about gender is not taught as part of a formalized curriculum, such as when children are first exposed to fiction through picture books read to them by their parents. These storybooks can reinforce or challenge existing gender stereotypes. Often, as Benhabib (1996) argues, women develop a sense of "double vision" in understanding both masculine and feminist perspectives. The masculine point of view is represented as a universalistic perspective but, through their own experiences, girls and women may come to see the world quite differently. Fenwick (2003) explains that in these kinds of learning situations, "experience is not simply a situation being apprehended but also a positioning of self within that situation, entailing contradictory emotional responses and intuitive perceptions" (p. 82).

Both literary and popular fiction offer means for critically exploring how gender is portrayed and how women may learn about their socially acceptable roles or imagine alternative ways of being. In considering the impact of women and visible minority writers in expanding the range of books studied in higher education, hooks (2003) argues that "the critique of [literary] canons allowed the voices of visionary intellectuals to be heard" (p. 7). Similarly, popular fiction now embraces a diverse range of stories, and people learn about these through a variety of non-formal or informal means. In a study on *Canada Reads*, a radio program that profiles Canadian novels, Rehberg Sedo (2008) points out how "book clubs" created through the media have become one way individuals have chosen to engage with fictional texts. Reflecting back on her home life, children's writer Sheree Fitch stated:

> My mother had a thing, and probably a lot of women back then did, that you could only read once all the housework was done, once all the ironing was done. So you didn't see my mother sort of lying around reading during the day, except maybe on the beach in the summer and of course once she got older I would see her reading for leisure more.

As this comment suggests, learning that we see as falling into the informal realm, such as reading a novel, is dismissed as a leisure activity, and thus receives less attention and value. Moreover, since gender divisions in labour consistently accord women less leisure time than men, they frequently have less time, particularly when they are younger, to engage with fiction. Yet we feel that, through fiction, important opportunities for adult learning about gender and leadership may occur.

Femininity and Its Contradictions

> She sighed so hard Gamache expected to see the petals of the dying flowers flutter away.
> —Penny, 2008, p. 281

Femininity is taught to girls and women in multiple ways: through the media, within the homeplace, the workplace, and in our educational sector. In an examination of how brochures advertising private elite schools for young girls depict their scholastic settings, Wardman, Gottschall, Drew, Hutchinson, and Saltmarsh (2013) noted that "poetic descriptions translate 'natural femininity' as romantic, wistful, emotive and sensual" (p. 289). Drawing upon Judith Butler's work (see Butler, 1999), they argue that femininity is linked with nature and emotion, in contrast to masculinity, which is connected to reason or rationality. Femininity is also expressed through beauty, grace, goodness, and virtue, qualities valued highly under the patriarchal gaze.

In a study that examines young girls playing video games, Walkerdine (2006) notes how "Contemporary femininity demands practices and performances which bring together heroics, rationality, etc., with the need to maintain a femininity which displays care, co-operation, concern and sensitivity" (p. 520). As a social construct, femininity—in contradiction to masculinity—ensures that women and young girls receive constant messages that they need to consider how others view them, so that they can then self-censor their representation of self to meet these images of what they think are appropriate behaviours.

Christine Jarvis (2014) examines the American trilogy *Twilight*, which focuses on teens and vampires. She suggests that the reason why a book series that reinforces female powerlessness might have become so popular is that "girls are still expected to conform to rigid stereotypes of femininity even though they are now also expected to succeed at school and in careers" (p. 102). She argues that the appeal of the series is linked to a fantasy in which the female protagonist, Bella, manipulates patriarchal norms to ultimately get everything she wants by engaging in self-destructive behaviour and by being a victim.

As writers, women authors may encounter situations that reinforce traditional notions of femininity. Alison MacLeod, a writer born and raised in Canada but who has lived much of her adult life in England, shared this example from her UK experience:

> At my first literary party years ago all the women writers were being taken into a room to be photographed together, and all the male writers were photographed separately. We all had to hold up a glass of champagne... while the men were all photographed in a sort of brooding way. The narrative behind that, I think, is that female writers are more decorative than substantial, while male writers naturally exude individual genius.

Women may learn gender expectations in behaviour that prescribe acceptable roles for them in their particular social situation as a part of femininity in adult fiction as well, as is seen in this excerpt from Louise Penny's *The Murder Stone*:

> Julia Martin sat at the vanity and took off her single string of pearls. Simple, elegant, a gift from her father for her eighteenth birthday.
>
> "A lady is always understated, Julia," he'd said. "A lady never shows off. She always puts others at ease. Remember that."
>
> And she had. As soon as he'd said it she knew the truth of it. And all the stumbling and bumbling she'd done, all the uncertainties and solitude of her teen years, had fallen away. Ahead of her stretched a clear path. Narrow, yes, but clear. The relief she felt was absolute. She had a purpose, a direction. She knew who she was and what she had to do. Put others at ease (2008, p. 51).

This passage demonstrates a number of things. First, it illustrates how the word "lady" encapsulates a classed notion of femininity that includes how a woman should look physically and behave socially. This means women need to constantly think about how they present themselves, both visually and in terms of their behaviour, so that they are met with male approval.

Second, when women are socialized into accepting that their role is to be supportive, to put others "at ease," they are less likely to be seen by others, or more importantly envision themselves, in leadership roles. In Patricia's research on Canadian women as active citizens (see Gouthro, 2008), many of the women interviewed indicated that unlike their male colleagues, they never sought a political career. Similarly, in their research on Canadian and Indian women in politics, Clover, McGregor, Farrell, and Pant (2011) found none of their "women participants interviewed in either country aspired to be politicians; almost all expressed surprise at being asked to run" (p. 26). It appears that it is not just a matter of personal ambition among individual women that determines women's leadership aspirations, but also social structural factors that need to be examined from a critical feminist lens. We need to consider how gender is being learned in such a way that it continues to inhibit active participation in the political sphere.

At the same time, femininity also encompasses traits associated with women that should be respected. In a scene from *The Splendour Falls*, Susannah Kearsley captures this idea in a brief exchange between an older Frenchwoman and her protagonist: "My hostess looked in silence from my face to the book, and back again, pressed my shoulder with a gentle hand and rose with the grace of a dancer, leaving me alone in the quiet bar" (p. 303). Elegance, compassion, and kindness are also aspects of femininity that authors can capture in their writing that do not diminish female characters or represent them in ways that imply that they are subordinate to males.

Fiction and Feminism

> I talked long and hard. Nearly two hours later, Lindsay began to imagine the possibility of life without the man who could stub his cigarette on the soft skin of her belly after they'd made love.
> —Maffini, 2001, p. 2

So how is it that we can use fiction to learn about gender issues that may have an impact upon women and leadership? Sara Paretsky is widely regarded as a ground-breaking author in crime fiction. Her protagonist, V.I. Warshawski, is a female Private Investigator (PI) who through the series over the last couple of decades has helped crack the façade of the normative, hard-boiled detective story as an all-male domain. In her interview she raises this concern: "I think women have lost so much ground over the last decade in ways that you think it's an uncomfortable-making thing to call yourself a feminist." She recalls:

> When second wave feminism really began to sweep the country (the United States) in the late 60s, it really spoke to me and gave me a way of understanding the things about myself that I thought were second tier and not worthwhile. I realized that it was really nothing to do with me, and everything to do with the cultural expectations of women.
>
> So I began reading crime fiction through a feminist lens, and began seeing that women who existed in crime fiction were defined by how they used their sexuality. If they were virginal and chaste, they were heroines who were unable to act. If they were sexually active they were wicked, or at least venial. So you had women who were unmarried and sexually active—they were going to be villains. Women who were widowed or divorced were tainted and sexually available.
>
> It's interesting that widows both within British and American crime fiction are considered morally suspect; they've made themselves sexually available. You see that often with Agatha Christie and Dorothy Sayers, that the widow and divorced woman is not ever going to be the main villain but is not a moral agent for good. So I wanted to change that; I wanted to create a woman who was like me, and my friends. She was doing a job that didn't exist when she started school, she had a sex life that didn't determine her morality, and she had to solve problems on her own, as women always have.

Just as Paretsky has no hesitation in claiming the identity of feminist in real life, neither does her protagonist, V.I. Warshawski. In this scene, Paretsky's character has a sharp exchange with a young female police officer:

> "I may be a woman and a junior detective. But I know how to take a statement."
> I felt my eyes turn hot. "I am one of the old-fashioned feminists who helped open this door for you, Officer Milkova, so don't get on your high horse with me" (2011, p. 396).

Czarniawska (2006) reminds us never to overlook the "subversive role of popular culture" (p. 251). She notes how fictional characters in detective novels such as V.I. Warshawski provides insights into both the gendered realities of women's lives and ways in which women can choose to redefine women's roles to contest normatives such as patriarchal behaviour.

Yet mystery writers still find that there are limitations imposed by publishers with respect to what they can write from a feminist stance. For example, Canadian mystery author Mary Jane Maffini writes four different traditional mystery series. Two of these series are published in Canada and two (one she co-writes with her daughter) are published by a larger publisher in the U.S. Reflecting upon the differences in publishing in the two different countries, she says:

> I probably couldn't write the kinds of books that deal with battered women and things like that, and set them as amateur sleuth books in the USA. There's much more freedom for amateur sleuths in Canada—you can have political viewpoints and make strong social statements, but the market for amateur sleuth books is limited.

These comments point to the need to sustain a Canadian publishing industry that supports genre fiction, such as mysteries as well as literary books. Female Canadian crime fiction writers address many issues of importance to our country, such as R.J. Harlick's (2011) book *A Green Place for Dying*, which looks at the issue of missing Aboriginal women. A country such as Canada needs to provide opportunities for these kinds of books to be published, even though genre fiction is often designated as "popular" rather than literary fiction. There is often an assumption that publishers and writers should not be given any financial support for "popular" fiction since it is expected to make a profit. However, since we have a small population, the only way that most writers can publish "popular" fiction addressing Canadian issues or set in Canadian society is if there are government financial supports for the publishing houses. This is critical if adult educators are to have popular or genre fiction novels as well as literary texts that might address political and gender issues.

Fiction and Real Life

> Umbilically corded. Ne m'oublie pas.
> —Nixon, 2011, p. 242 (English translation: *Do not forget me*).

Learning as it relates to fiction is complicated by the relationships between readers and books, and writers and the books they create. Different aspects of writers' lives, beliefs, and circumstances may influence the types of stories that they develop, adding another layer of interpretation that can affect understanding and analysis. An intriguing aspect about doing biographical research on writers is that, in addition to the life history interviews, the fictional works the authors create can inform the research. These two data sources provide insight into issues that are important within different writers' lives.

A unique gender experience for many women is being a mother. Having a child die is one of the most profoundly difficult experiences that most mothers could ever envisage going through. Rosemary Nixon explained:

> My first child was conceived in Africa … we finished our three-year stint and came home; and she was born a few months later deathly ill. She lived for six months and died in an operation, but she had many things wrong with her …. It was incredibly hard.
> My book … deals with the baby and neonatal care, and it took me years to write it and years of grieving … the book got turned down numerous times saying, Beautiful writing, we don't deal with the baby dying.
> So it seems really wonderful to me. It's like her story's out there. It's like I'm giving something to her by getting it out there. So this book probably means the most any book will ever mean to me to be published. It's fiction; I wrote it as fiction. It's drawn from that.

Although Nixon's book, *Kalila*, is a work of fiction, the poignant descriptions from the mother's perspective were informed by her real-life experiences.

> Unmother. I spilled my blood onto the birthing table, then someone whisked away the baby: nineteen hours and I haven't seen her. The first fourteen strapped to my bed by two intravenous needles, one in each hand, to stop the bleeding …. There are the mothers, and then there's me. Nothing dislodges their identity (2011, p. 53).

There is a social script for how to be a mother in our society, but not one on how to be a mother who loses a child. Our gender norms around proper feminine behaviour fail to cover this.

Conversations in the novel reflect the discomfort and unwillingness, even among professionals, to address a mother's grief. "I long for emotion from them [the doctors]; what they want from me is none. This is a research hospital. My baby is useful" (p. 72). Or:

> My body a river: mucus and blood and breast milk. The social worker scrambling through her daybook.
> A week from Friday—get yourself together—here, this tissue, no—of course, we know it's hard. "Lady. You have no fucking idea" (p. 28).

At the same time, just because a fiction writer creates a character, or writes about a topic from a particular perspective, does not mean that she is necessarily mirroring her own life or personal beliefs about a subject. Nixon reflects on the gendered tensions created when people analyze connections between authors and their works of fiction:

> Think of Joan Barfoot, who has a story, *Abra*, where the woman looks one evening and sees her husband making cookies with the kids, and she thinks I'm not even part of this family, and she leaves them. And I just think, how could I ever write a story where the mum wants to leave her kids or leave them? I'm afraid my kids would think down deep I wanted to leave them, and I want to censor myself. But a powerful writer doesn't censor him or herself…. Imagine if you wrote this book that you think is great, but suddenly imagine what your mother or somebody close to you would think about it and they'd be hurt. There's no powerful book that wouldn't hurt somebody because it deals with our complications in how we hurt people and how people hurt, and how life isn't the way we wish it would be, and how we don't understand life….

Photo: Courtesy of Tonya Callaghan.

Suzette Mayr is a Canadian poet and novelist whose writing and teaching are often focused on issues of race and ethnicity.

Fiction is, after all, fiction. Stories are driven by conflict that may have nothing to do with the writer's own personal perspectives or experiences, so readers (and researchers) have to be careful not to make connections that do not exist.

As Nixon notes, some women authors may be reluctant to write about certain topics because a part of femininity is this notion that women are responsible for taking care of the people around them. Authors are aware that connections may be made between their writing and their personal lives. Just as femininity causes women to self-censor how they present themselves to the world in real life, it may also affect what stories they choose to tell and how they will tell them.

Leadership, Gender, and Fiction

> I knew too well the vice-grip of a love-hate relationship with a man who worked on all your insecurities to keep you grovelling at his feet.
> —Harlick, 2004, p. 75

Using fiction to explore gender relationships and issues provides us with many insights into why there are still challenges around women assuming leadership roles. When we teach educators—whether they work in community, health care, or other leadership roles, such as principals or department heads—to develop critical literacies around fiction, we challenge them to critique power relations and identity issues. Difficult questions are often raised in fictional stories, such as why it is that hegemony and the status quo keep being reproduced? From this, we as educators can challenge learners to think more deeply about how institutional practices and systemic discrimination play a role in normalizing inequities such as sexism and misogyny in Canadian society, making these practices at times invisible.

Through engaging with fictional novels, such as those written by some of the authors we have interviewed as a part of our research, we can challenge learners to shift their thinking from a more individual to a societal critique of power and citizenry. As leaders themselves, educators need to think theoretically about the rationalization for why it is important for them to choose curriculum material that deeply engages in larger social issues, such as feminism, power, identity, and citizenship. For example, Nicole Markotić questions traditional gender roles tied to religious beliefs in her novel *Scrapbook*. Suzette Mayr challenges gender stereotypes through the fabulous drag queen Crêpe Suzette in *Monoceros* (2011) or the white woman protagonist turned black in the mythical *Moon Honey* (1995). Illuminating Haisla culture in the contemporary world, Eden Robinson's *Monkey Beach* (2000), told through the eyes of the female teenage protagonist Lisa, shows a large continuum of gendered behaviours and attitudes through the family and friends in her life.

Fiction can be used to help women identify and consider how to react to patriarchal behaviours. In a scene from A *Trick of the Light*, the character Clara Moreau realizes that her husband is poisonously envious of her unanticipated artistic acclaim, which outshines his own commercially successful work. She is appalled by his reaction and says: "I actually thought deep down you were happy for me. You just needed time to adjust. But this is really who you are, isn't it?" (Penny, 2011, p. 180).

In her interview, Louise Penny talked about how some people make belittling remarks about crime fiction, insinuating that it is inferior to literary fiction. She remarks, "It's a little bit like being a woman and coming across misogyny every now and then. It doesn't change who I am and what I am; it doesn't change how I feel about myself, but it sure changes how I feel about that person." In the same way, Penny shows through her novel that patriarchal behaviours diminish the person who enacts them, rather than the individual that they are directed towards. The relationships between characters in her novels provide useful insights into the ways in which gender, as well as variables such as culture, class, race, and sexual orientation, shape how individuals perceive and interact with one another.

Czarniawska (2006) argues that insights into gender practices that discriminate against women within workplace organizations could be obtained by examining detective fiction novels with female protagonists, such as Sara Paretsky's V.I. Warshaski series. She argues that popular culture provides us with a means to radically question how we should "do gender," and that "understanding fiction is necessary to understand contemporary society" (p. 250).

Rosemary Nixon discusses how her fictional novel could be used for teaching learners in medical workplaces:

> In my book ... it's the young mother, how ostracized and alienated she feels by the doctors ... there's a lot of doctors in my family and they'll say, A parent or even a patient does not hear what you're saying sometimes. If you have a baby who is dying and you're just devastated and you're beside yourself, the doctor can tell you something and you'll later say He didn't tell you, or She didn't tell you. And I know that's true. But ... my dream would be to have my novel taught to medical students so they would understand the need for compassion (p. 34).

In her interview, Nicole Markotić says, "it's a little bit dangerous to think that a book, which in this context represents art, leads to some sort of improved, ethical awareness. Because we all know horrible people who read...." While acknowledging the common sense of this point, we still believe that fiction can play an important role in challenging people to think beyond their comfort zones and grapple with issues that are not their own. Leaders, both male and female, whether in politics, the community, or the workplace, should have an awareness of the experiences of social groups in society other than their own. Fiction can potentially be a window into diverse social and historical contexts.

As Canadians and as feminists, we believe that it is important for educators to engage with the fiction created by our writers to explore how gender is learned and enacted in various contexts. To do so may provide us with insights into why gender discrimination and inequities still exist. It may also help us to explore strategies to support women's learning so that they may become active leaders in the workplace and homeplace, and in our communities and our government.

References

- Benhabib, S. (1996). *Democracy and Difference: Contesting the Boundaries of the Political.* Princeton, NJ: Princeton University Press.
- Boeren, E. (2011). Gender differences in formal, non-formal and informal adult learning. *Studies in Continuing Education, 33*(3), 333-346.
- Butler, J. (1999 [1990]). *Gender Trouble: Feminism and the Subversion of Identity.* New York, NY: Routledge.
- Clover, D., McGregor, C, Farrell, M., and Pant, M. (2011). Women learning politics and the politics of learning: A feminist study of Canada and India. *Studies in the Education of Adults, 43*(1), 18-33.

- Czarniawska, B. (2006). Doing gender unto the other: Fiction as a mode of studying gender discrimination in organizations. *Gender, Work and Organization,* 13(3), 234-253.

- Fenwick, T.J. (2003). *Learning Through Experience: Troubling Orthodoxies and Intersecting Questions.* Malabar, FL: Krieger Publishing.

- Fitch, S. (1995). *Mabel Murple.* Halifax, NS: Nimbus Publishing.

- Gouthro, P.A. (2009) Life histories of Canadian women as active citizens: Implications for policies and practices in adult education. *The Canadian Journal for the Study of Adult Education,* 21(2), 19-35.

- Gouthro, P.A. (2012). Learning your way into a life of crime (fiction): Assessing Sisters in Crime as a grassroots learning organization. *The Canadian Journal for the Study of Adult Education,* 24(2), 34-50.

- Harlick, R.J. (2004). *Death's Golden Whisper.* Toronto, ON: RendezVous Crime.

- Harlick, R.J. (2011). *A Green Place for Dying.* Toronto, ON: Dundurn Press.

- Hogan, E.J. (2004). When art does not represent life: Nogami Yaeko and the marriage question. *Women Studies,* 33, 381-398.

- hooks, b. (2003). *Teaching Community: A Pedagogy of Hope.* New York: Routledge.

- Jarvis, C. (2014). The twilight of feminism? Stephanie Meyer's saga and the contradictions of contemporary girlhood. *Children's Literature in Education,* 45, 101-115.

- Jubas, K. and Knutson, P. (2013). Fictions of work-related learning: How a hit television show portrays internship, and how medical students relate to those portrayals. *Studies in Continuing Education,* 35(2), 224-240.

- Markotić, N. (2008). *Scrapbook of My Years as a Zealot.* Vancouver, BC: Arsenal Press.

- Mayr, S. (2011). *Monoceros.* Toronto, ON: Coach House Books.

- Maffini, M.J. (2001). *The Icing on the Corpse.* Toronto, ON: RendezVous Press.

- Nixon, R. (2011). *Kalila.* Fredericton, NB: Goose Lane Editions.

- Paretsky, S. (2011). *Body Work.* New York, NY: Penguin Books.

- Penny, L. (2008). *The Murder Stone.* London: Headline Publishing Group.

- Penny, L. (2011). *A Trick of the Light.* New York: Minotaur Books.

- Rehberg, Sedo, D. (2008). Richard & Judy's Book Club and 'Canada Reads': Readers, books and programming in a digital era. *Information, Communication and Society,* 11(2), 188-206.

- UNESCO (2003). *UNESCO's Gender Mainstreaming Implementation Framework (GMIF) for 2002-2007.* Paris: UNESCO.

- Walkerdine, V. (2006). Playing the Game: Young girls performing femininity in video game play. *Feminist Media Studies,* 6(4), 519-537.

- Wardman, N., Gottschall, K., Drew, C., Hutchesson, R., and Saltmarsh, S. (2013). Picturing natural girlhoods: Nature, space and femininity in girls' school promotions. *Gender and Education,* 25(3), 284-294.

SSHRC Grants

- Gouthro, P.A. and Holloway, S.M., "Stories of Learning": Creative Literacies and Lifelong Learning: Exploring Learning Sites and Creative Educational Opportunities around Reading and Writing Fiction.

- Gouthro, P.A. and Holloway, S.M., Creating a Canadian "Voice": Lifelong Learning, the Craft of Fiction Writing, and Citizenship.

The Art Gallery of Greater Victoria has the largest public collection in British Columbia and is a vibrant and active part of Victoria's artist community.
Photo: © Joe Mabel.

20

Women and Adult Education in Public Museums and Art Galleries
Women in the Cultural Sphere

A focus on women within museums requires tracing the challenges and contradictions that have shaped their experiences and practices. We begin this chapter with a brief discussion of the historical and socio-pedagogical terrain of public art galleries and museums in Canada. This provides a context in which to understand the early contributions and struggles of women in public museums and galleries. Following this, we discuss how contemporary women adult educators in these institutions understand and take up issues of gender. We conclude with a discussion of changes in museum adult education and examples of new, socially engaged, critical, and creative practices of women adult educators in these institutions. Our argument is that, although still problematic, the work of these women provides energy, hope, and creativity in neo-liberal times.

Lorraine Bell, Darlene E. Clover, and Kathy Sanford

Public galleries and museums are ubiquitous in Canada, with several national and provincial institutions and hundreds of regional and community museums and galleries. As dominant features of both rural and urban landscapes, these institutions have become integral to our social, cultural, political, aesthetic, and educational infrastructures. Although public museums and art galleries are often positioned as one-dimensional and neutral, encased in an aura of "detachment from real world politics" (Phillips, 2012, p. 8), critical museum scholars, such as Ashley (2007), Phillips (2012), and MacDonald and Alsford (1995), remind us that the manner in which these institutions include and represent some stories to the exclusion of others has created hegemonic and exclusive visions of Canadian culture, history, and society.

Although we tend to think of their primary function as the collection and conservation of artworks and material culture, public museums and galleries are "first and foremost learning spaces" which host a variety of adult "informal individual learning as well as structured learning activities for groups of learners" (UNESCO, 1997, pp. 3-4). This emphasis on adult education is reflected in Canadian federal public policy documents dating back to the Massey report of 1951, which recommended that museums "redefine their role from collecting and research to vehicles of adult education" (Ashley, 2007, p. 489).

In spite of this, there are few accounts of public museums in the adult education literature (Clover, Sanford, and Oliviera de Jayme, 2010). Moreover, a frequently overlooked aspect is that women have been instrumental in their founding, fundraising, education, and conservation work (e.g., McTavish, 2008; Tippett, 1990; Whitelaw, 2012a). Even less common is the more recent activist-oriented adult education in these museums and galleries (e.g., Clover, Sanford, & Dogus, 2013b). This chapter begins to address this oversight by rendering visible women's engagement with museums and art galleries, and particularly, some of the pedagogical contributions they have made in the past, and are making today.

258

Background and Context

This chapter focuses on the work of women adult educators and curators in Canadian public museums and galleries. We, the three authors, came to this area through different trajectories.

I (Lorraine) became interested in museums as an extension of my interest in community-based adult education and my fascination with art and other forms of material culture—the visual, beautiful, horrifying, tactile, noisy, even smelly things in museums waiting to surprise and intrigue us. I also firmly believe that society needs spaces where adults of diverse backgrounds can come together and learn about one another and our social and environmental challenges. Museums do not always fit this bill, but they do have great potential and this is what we, as adult educators, must recognize. Our study also revealed that a great deal of the critically engaged and innovative adult education work in museums is done by women. Yet, as in many other sectors, they are often in low paid, insecure positions and rarely receive the accolades they deserve.

I (Darlene) came to museums somewhat grudgingly, or perhaps better said, with skepticism. My academic research had been with women artists who used dance, drama, poetry, music, or craft to provide energy, hope, or critiques, or simply to be engagingly disobedient. These women suggested I also look to the formal cultural sector for creative and critical cultural practices, but I characterized this as simply elitist, exclusionary, static, and dusty showcases for the spoils of war and triumphs of great "men." However, a young woman I met at the National Gallery in Ottawa changed all that. She had worked over a summer with a group of young adults, taking them through the museum to contemplate the artworks, and facilitating workshops to create collages that spoke to neo-conservatism, imperialism, colonization, war as a "tool of democracy," and the fear-mongering and surveillance practices of the post-911 world.

I (Kathy) came to this work because of my lifelong love affair with learning. For over three decades I have attempted to understand how learning can be supported and fostered for everyone. Much of my work has been in formal school settings, but museums have offered me alternative conceptions and sites of education and learning. Engaging in conversations with the women in our research study offered new insights into ways in which we can engage more deeply in issues that matter in our lives, at whatever age, and how, through action, we can all effect change. The programs that women museum educators and curators create and support show ways to understand and intertwine education with learning, so that individual needs are met in collective ways.

The Socio-Pedagogical Terrain

Public museums and art galleries in Canada began to take shape in the nineteenth century, against a backdrop of colonization and industrialization. Several large institutions in important urban centres such as Toronto and Ottawa were established in the early 1900s (Whitelaw, 2010) and the following decades saw an expansion to other sites such as Winnipeg and Vancouver as well as to less populous areas. Government support was not consistent, according to Whitelaw, and many arts and cultural institutions resulted from volunteer work and elite patronage. They were part of a cultural sector in the first half of the twentieth century that was largely informal (Tippett, 1990) and that often functioned as sites for society's elites to pursue social advancement, intellectual improvement, and entertainment. There was not much support overall from governments that presumed to represent the educational and cultural interests of the entire population (Tippett, 1990; Whitelaw, 2010) but that in reality emphasized economic development over what they deemed as "the frivolous pursuit of art" (Whitelaw, p. 7).

However, things began to change in public museums around the mid-twentieth century, with movements towards the formalization and nationalization of arts and culture. The Massey Commission of 1951 started a process to make significant federal funds available to develop arts and culture across Canada (Litt, 1992; Wright, 2000), and governments at the federal, provincial/ territorial, and municipal levels were encouraged to play a strong role in developing, funding, and providing policy and direction for these institutions (Foote, 2003). By the 1960s, there was an explosion of public art galleries and museums (Key, 1973) as well as a re-contextualization of their purpose and pedagogical orientation towards nationalist identity formation (Foote, 2003; Terry, 2013). One result was that public museums became entwined in state-based formulations of nationalism and in elitist, colonial, and masculinist visions of Canadian history, culture, and identity (Ashley, 2007; McKenna, 2005; Terry, 2013). Somewhat paradoxically, they were also situated as part of the "extra-political" sphere—a public, pedagogical space to encourage the free exchange of ideas; a space of knowledge creation and civic debate about art, culture, democracy, and society (Ashley, 2007; Foss et al., 2010). Problematically represented, or simply missing, in both these formulations were the stories of large segments of the population, including Indigenous peoples, ethnic minorities, the poor and working classes, and women (Ashley, 2007; McTavish, 2008; Phillips, 2012).

Women in the Public, Cultural Sphere

Feminist theory brings a philosophical stance with which to consider the role of gender in our society, but it is often slow to be taken up by institutional organizations or reflected in public attitudes. Nevertheless, it provides a framework through which gender inequality can be recognized and addressed, and through which we can better understand how social roles are constructed in a variety of fields, including arts and culture (Bakhtin, 1981). And as noted by Hein (1993), experience is always gendered. Yet according to feminist museum scholar Lianne McTavish (2008), "the articulation of gender within museums has at best been considered a secondary concern" (p. 93). By re-examining the dynamics of gender and the activities of women in museums, she suggests, we can better understand the wider roles of these institutions in our society. "Instead of appearing as discrete spaces in which objects are amassed and arranged, museums begin to emerge as contested discursive mechanisms that enable as well as erase gendered identities" (p. 94).

In spite of their absence from official museum histories, "women have been central to the founding and maintenance of museums and art galleries for the past 150 years" (Whitelaw, 2012a, p. 76). In her study of museum archives in New Brunswick, McTavish was initially surprised to find that women's participation through the Ladies Auxiliary of the Natural History Society was mentioned only briefly in meeting minutes from 1862-1932 in order to thank them for providing refreshments. Her review also found reports of "events such as the annual *conversazioni* to which the general public as well as dignitaries were invited to hear talks given *by male members of the society*" (McTavish, 2008,

p. 95, our emphasis). But McTavish cautions us not to underestimate the value of "both cake and housekeeping skills," which in essence "funded the educational and social activities of the Natural History Society while providing the public face of the institution" (p. 95). In addition, she draws attention to "the more substantial presence of these women" (p. 95), revealed through accession records detailing donations and in records of a lecture series sponsored and delivered by women.

Both Whitelaw (2012a, 2012b) and McTavish (2008) conclude that a good bulk of women's contributions to museums and galleries was both collective and anonymous yet constituted a key contribution to the success of these institutions. The lack of documentation, they argue, as well as the way women's roles in these cultural organizations was framed, has served to understate the significance of women's financial, scholarly, and pedagogical contributions. A few studies do, however, highlight women with more central roles in museums and galleries. For example, at the Dundurn Castle heritage site in the first half of the twentieth century "a host of women worked as curators and administrators to establish the site as a house museum" (Terry, 2013, p. 47). Whitelaw (2012a, p. 76) also recounts the leadership of Maud Bowman, who founded and managed the Edmonton Art Gallery.

In spite of the contributions of women as both individual leaders and collective volunteers, the professionalization of museums and galleries starting from the 1930s saw a concurrent masculinization of the field (Whitelaw, 2012a, p. 78). Women, while seen as suitable for museum education and interpretation, "were not seen as potential directors of institutions of any size or influence" (Whitelaw, 2012a, p. 78). When Dundurn Castle became a national heritage site in 1967, a male director was voted in by a 10-9 margin to relieve the leadership/curatorial duties of a Mrs. Metcalfe, even though she had fulfilled these roles for several years. An article written in the local Hamilton newspaper at the time of the elections suggested that:

> … men "needed" to supervise business-related affairs to maintain Dundurn's high standards as a museum and historical monument so that women might look after the historical research, tours, displays and other items associated with the domestic—and therefore more suitable—realm of the house itself (discussed in Terry, 2013, p. 56).

These studies illustrate that the history of women's scholarly work and voluntary contributions to the formal arts and cultural sector became increasingly domesticated and sidelined once museums and art galleries gained in stature. In another example, Young has argued that in the McCord Museum in Montréal from 1921 to 1975 women were only "able to manage the collections with a degree of freedom because of McGill University's ambivalence about the value of the museum" (Young, 2000, cited in McTavish, 2008, p. 93). McTavish reminds us that:

> … when the women recognized male authority, conducted bake sales, or participated in collecting and labelling natural history specimens, they were welcomed by what they sometimes called their "parent organization." When the "ladies" attempted, however, to become full members or to thwart male supervision, their position on the margins of the organization was reaffirmed (p. 99).

Interestingly, although perhaps not surprisingly, archival reports of the minutes of meetings kept by men portrayed the women associate members "as modest, hardworking, and even servile," yet women's own minutes oftentimes demonstrate a group "impatient, ambitious, and longing to pursue goals not entirely in keeping with the original aims" (p. 100). Some feminist museum historians also note strong connections between women's struggles for institutional equity in museums and art galleries, and their greater involvement in the public sphere and in struggles for social reform (e.g., McTavish, 2008; Terry, 2013). For example, a member of the Women's Auxiliary named Emma Fiske also served as the President of the Women's Enfranchisement Association from 1898 to 1914 (McTavish, 2008, p. 107). Having said this, it must be acknowledged that the women involved in the museum sector, at least in English-speaking Canada, were usually white, Anglo, and middle to upper class. As well, critiques that addressed the troublesome colonial heritage and exclusionary practices of museums and galleries would not come until decades later (e.g., Ashley, 2007; Phillips, 2012).

Given this historical perspective, it is perhaps not surprising that historical studies of women and public museums and art galleries include little discussion of their public engagement and pedagogical work. Tippett (1990) briefly acknowledges that women involved in the museum sector fought for a broader, cultural education for both children and the general public because they did not want to see it left to chance or privilege. In the next section, we explore how women today take up discourses of gender or feminism in their institutions and in their adult pedagogy.

The Contemporary "Gender" Context

Our current research with museum educators in Canada, which included a review of museum staff directories on websites, revealed that women compose the majority of staff in education and learning departments. However, the strongest emphasis in these departments tended to be on children and schools, presumably, as some interviewees suggested, because there was seen to be a "natural" association between women, education, and school-aged learners. There is, however, a cadre of women in museums who align themselves, and their work, with adult education. We asked these women about the clear predominance of women in educational roles. A common explanation was that it was due to the enduring perception that education is a woman's domain. Many also suggested that women are drawn to the part-time/freelance nature of the work that often characterizes these institutions today. Unfortunately, this freelance work, while flexible, also lacks security and tends to be lower paid. In other words, women adult educators in public museums and galleries have similar workplace challenges as many women workers elsewhere.

Perhaps not surprisingly, when women try to explain gender differences within their institutions, they draw from taken-for-granted differences regarding the strengths and requirements of different genders. Many focus on the communication and social skills they believe women have and bring to the job, which they view as a strength in engaging with the public. Yet these observations of gender differences lacked deep understandings of gender inequity and as, one educator who had worked in a large art museum in eastern Canada confirmed, educational work in museums is seldom "actually situate[d] within feminism or within a feminist trajectory." This shying away from feminism was notable in comments by a number of interviewees, including one who said: "I certainly [recognize] that it is female oriented ... [but] I am not necessarily coming from a feminist perspective." One of the women museum educators suggested that moving away from feminism was in fact a change from the 1970s when "some women entered the field ... as a feminist radical project ... to take on the sexist nature of the gallery and to extend a critique within our educational processes."

In contrast, however, other women adult educators frame their work within feminist theory and this manifests itself in their practice. For example, an important part of one adult educator's work was to use the historical presence of painter Emily Carr to talk about the invisibility of women in history:

> One of the main things I want to get across to students is that no woman was doing [what she did], not even men were going north in a canoe by themselves, and as a woman, in 1920, are you kidding me? No way women were allowed to do things like that ... I want [people] to get a sense ... that she was blazing a trail for women, but that she was not, however, supported.

There are other examples of women adult educators working with museums to enhance women's learning experiences but also to expand the stories these institutions tell. For example, in her study in Sydney, Nova Scotia, Seana Kozar (2001) describes a women's adult literacy project connected with the Whitney Pier Museum. The project sought to include the people and voices "who might otherwise have little to do with museums" (p. 100) in order to improve the museum's service to diverse communities. Kozar explains how "within an expressive framework of women's folklore and culture centred on crafts, foodways and belief, these women engaged in learning that was at once guided and self-directed" (p. 97). Moving well beyond traditional didactic modes of museum education, the participants as researchers and learners uncovered and celebrated women's knowledge in the context of local history and culture, and also explored the area's multi-cultural heritage. As Kozar explains, exploring women's traditional folklore in the manner of these women learners re-worked the concept of "tradition" from patriarchal social practices to those that challenge divisions between private and public domains. The museum site was powerful because it incorporated oral, visual, and tactile modes of learning into the literacy work using archival photographs and cultural objects. The project offered benefits to the participants in the development of literacy skills and their confidence levels. The museum and the wider community also benefited from the contributions the participants made to the documentation of local history, the valuing of women's folklore, and the critical examination of traditionally gendered domains.

Critical Practices of Social Engagement from Coast to Coast

Within the last few decades there has been a remarkable change in the discourse around public museums and art galleries, of which many women scholars and practitioners are at the forefront. Emphasis has shifted from collections and scholarship to education and public engagement, in particular, "non-authoritative representation and inclusive participation" (Ashley, 2007, p. 489; see also MacDonald & Alsford, 1995). Among other things, this shifting discourse in Canada, and internationally, includes notions of equality, human rights, and cultural diversity rather than elitism, marginalization, and cultural hegemony (MacDonald & Alsford, 1995; Phillips, 2012).

Having said this, it is important to acknowledge that discourses of "social engagement" are far from straightforward. Museum and adult education scholars and practitioners worldwide, as well as in wider administrative and policy environments, have interpreted them in divergent ways. Cuno (1997), for example, suspects that social engagement and inclusion is a shift towards state-mandated social work, including programs such as educational and therapeutic activities for seniors, dementia patients, and people with disabilities. While this may be interpreted by some as museums and galleries becoming more relevant and responsive to their communities (e.g., Silverman, 2010), others view it as a cynical moment in which museums are compelled to prove their worth with quantified metrics of social outcomes, while neo-conservative governments abdicate social responsibility and allow corporations to gain undue influence over this public, pedagogical, cultural, and scholarly milieu.

Yet other museum and adult education scholars, and we would include ourselves in this, recognize this shift towards social engagement through culture as a remarkable opportunity that allows for new ways of teaching, engaging, exhibiting, and acting with and in communities (e.g., Barr, 2005; Clover, 2015; Mayo, 2013; Nightingale & Sandell, 2012; Steedman, 2012). As Giroux (2004, p. 60) has cautioned, we must never lose sight of the fact that "the primacy of culture's role as an educational site where identities are being continually transformed, power is enacted, and learning assumes a political dynamic as it becomes not only the condition for the acquisition of agency but also the sphere for imagining oppositional social change." Rather than simply dismissing public arts and culture institutions as mere reflections of larger economic forces, we need to re-conceptualize and understand them as sites of emerging contestation and of possibility, spaces in which an emancipatory, pedagogical politics can be made possible, particularly in the hands of women.

To capture how women are re-shaping and working with and in museums as a response to new notions of greater social responsiveness and responsibility in Canada, we share three examples of how women educators in these institutions navigate these contradictions, tensions, and opportunities. These are but two of a growing number of examples, but they illustrate the range of possibilities of contemporary, critical, and creative adult practice aimed at challenging the boundaries of these institutions and addressing issues to promote social and environmental justice and change.

Unmasking Hetero-Normativity in Vancouver

An example of working with controversial issues and ideologies comes from the Museum of Vancouver and the work of Viviane Gosselin. Although Canada was one of the first countries to legalize both abortion and same-sex marriage, debates on these issues are still very active. The Museum of Vancouver hosted an exhibition and series of educational events entitled Sex Talk in the City. The purpose was to promote a comprehensive and inclusive understanding of sexual education, and to use the museum's cultural position in the city to normalize diverse expressions of sexuality. It sought to emphasize political and cultural understandings rather than the biological and moralistic aspects that usually prevail in discussions of sexuality.

Gosselin (2013) notes that the strategy used to develop this project involved an unusually large advisory committee and a "shared authority" comprised of sexual health workers, sexologists, youth, sex trade workers, historians, artists, education scholars, and members of the LGBTQ community. This group "determined the target audiences and developed a new interpretive approach that would communicate the complexity and multi-dimensionality of human sexuality" (p. 23). Using three frames, "The Classroom," "The Bedroom," and "The Street," the exhibition explored the educational, private, and public dimensions that inform sexual beliefs, attitudes, and behaviours.

Gosselin defines this work as "civic museography," a performative pedagogy designed to collectively identify and explore issues of public concern. The exhibition and educational events provoked lively debate around the disruptive and often humorous re-framings of gender, sex, and sexuality in individual lives and in the city.

Troubling "The Other" in Ottawa and Victoria

"Othering" is the practice of differentiation that humans use to distance themselves from each other and to create distinctions composed of problematic, hierarchical values. It essentializes and creates "blatant misrepresentations which can have serious, negative consequences on individuals and groups" (James and Shadd, 2006, p. 6).

As a response to this form of intolerance, the women educators and curators at the Canadian War Museum in Ottawa (CWM) and the Art Gallery of Greater Victoria (AGGV) separately organized a "Human Library," an idea first conceived in Denmark which has since proliferated around the world to address intolerance and prejudice of many varieties (e.g., Kudo, Motohashi, Enomoto, Kataoka & Yajima, 2011). The events in the AGGV and the CWM brought together people from different walks of life who had agreed to be "books" and to speak with "readers" about their lives or work. Examples of these human "books" included a graffiti artist, a Muslim woman, a conscientious objector, a sex trade worker, an anti-poverty worker, a soldier, a peace activist, and a community police officer. The Human Library provided an opportunity to explore stereotypes through conversations between people who would not normally come into contact with each other. Although the events were mostly calm and well received in both venues, the women did not shy away from controversy—which erupted around "religion" and "graffiti" in two cases—but rather saw this as a valuable aspect of learning.

This Changes Everything: Small Museums Tackling Big Issues

The environmental crisis challenges adult educators in all sectors to develop our capacity to embrace what authors such as Klein (2014) describe as radical yet necessary changes to dominant ideologies and political systems. Canadian museum scholar Janes (2009) suggests that museums can and should play a much stronger role in promoting this kind of social and epistemological change.

An example of how museums can respond with their communities to environmental threats can be seen in the recent *Thanks, but No Tanks* exhibition in the Haida Gwaii Museum. The exhibition explored how expanded tanker traffic might affect natural, social, psychological, and spiritual spaces. It brought together the work of twenty artists that explored a proposed oil pipeline and increased numbers of oil tankers on the Pacific coast of British Columbia (Richard, 2013). It featured works such as Gwaii Edenshaw's haunting *Hollow Promises: Two Hundred Years of Pain and Exploitation*, and an animated video with the rap song *Haida Raid 2: A Message to Stephen Harper* performed by JA$E El-Nino. Displayed in the window were juxtapositions of statements by Haida elders and from pipeline proponents (Noyes Platt, 2013) inviting viewers to draw their own conclusions.

More than putting art on walls, the goal of the exhibition, as the interim director of the museum suggested, was "to create a space where critical thought and dialogue are inspired [and to highlight] quandaries, contradictions and emphatic positions" (Richard, 2013, p. 14). By encouraging critical dialogue around dominant government-industry narratives and enactments, the exhibition attracted some criticism and controversy, including accusations of hypocrisy and bias. The exhibition's curator welcomed the lively debate: "I feel we brought a quality of critical inquiry to this subject that is still generating a lot of consideration about our use of oil and how we are implicated in that relationship" (quoted in Richard, 2013, p. 14). Similar to the Human Library, this project exemplifies how women museum educators employ "cultural activism in a time of crisis" (Noyes-Platt, 2013, n.p.) towards increasing awareness of crucial issues and facilitating principled dialogue between divergent views.

Final Thoughts

Historically, women have been foundational to the work of public museums and art galleries in Canada. However, the gendered hierarchies at these sites have often excluded women, minimized their contributions, and marginalized their work. And yet, as women have participated in the shaping of trajectories for museums and galleries, they have inserted their perspectives and made important contributions, including a reconsideration of the purposes of these institutions and the need for cultural education. We must also acknowledge in looking at these institutions historically that they have, despite women's presence and work, continued to marginalize the stories and voices of others. This is aspect of museums is being challenged today through the critical pedagogical practices of some curators and educators.

We believe public museums potentially have a crucial pedagogical role to play in our society in the future. And despite the fact that women frequently lack institutional power or job security, they are making museums important sites of feminist and social struggle and learning. Coinciding with the goals of critical and feminist adult education, these women are developing creative activities and exhibitions that address some of Canada's most pressing social and environmental issues, and as such contribute to discourses of justice and change. But in order to challenge existing and pervasive gender inequities, and the near invisibility of the adult education work of these women in museums, much more needs to be done. This chapter is presented as one step in that direction.

References

- Ashley, S. (2007). State authority and the public sphere—Ideas on the changing role of the museum as a Canadian institution. *Museum and Society*, 3(1), 5-17.

- Bakhtin, M. (1981). Epic and novel. In M. Holquist (Ed.), *The Dialogic Imagination: Four Essays* (pp. 3-40). Austin, TX: University of Texas Press.

- Barr, J. (2005). Dumbing down intellectual culture. *Museum and Society*, 3(2), 98-114.

- Clover, D.E. (2015). Adult education for social and environmental change in contemporary public art galleries and museums in Canada, Scotland and England. *International Journal of Lifelong Education*, 1(1), 1-16.

- Clover, D.E., Sanford, K., and Dogus, F. (2013b). A study of women, adult education and community development work in art galleries and museums in Canada and the United Kingdom (UK). In C. Kawaliak and G. Groen (Eds.), *Proceedings of the 32nd Annual Canadian Association for the Study of Adult Education* (pp. 90-96). Victoria, BC: University of Victoria.

- Clover, D.E, Sanford, K., and Oliviera de Jayme, B. (2010). Adult education, museums and libraries: A content analysis of journals and proceedings in the field. *Journal of Adult and Continuing Education*, 16(2), 5-19.

- Cuno, J. (1997). Whose money? Whose art? Whose art history? *The Art Bulletin*, 79(1), 6-9.

- Foote, J. (2003). Federal cultural policy in Canada. Paper prepared for the Council of Europe/ERICarts. Retrieved on October 10, 2014 from http://www.oas.org/oipc/english/documentos/pol%C3%ADticasculturalescanada.pdf.

- Giroux, H. (2004). Cultural studies, public pedagogy, and the responsibility of intellectuals. *Communication and Critical/ Cultural Studies*, 1(1), 59-79.

- Gosselin, V. (2013). *Embracing a New Understanding of the City: The Museum of Vancouver's Vision in Action*. Vancouver, BC: Museum of Vancouver.

- Hein, H. (1993). Refining feminist theory: Lessons from aesthetics. In Hein, H. and Korsmeyer, C. (Eds.), *Aesthetics in Feminist Perspective* (pp. 3-18). Bloomington, ID: Indiana University Press.

- James, C.E. and Shadd, A. (Eds.) (2006). *Talking about Identity*. Toronto, ON: Between the Lines.

- Janes, R. (2009). *Museums in a Troubled World*. Milton Park, Abingdon, USA: Routledge.

- Klein, N. (2014). *This Changes Everything*. Toronto and London: Penguin Group.

- Kozar, S. (2001). Beyond the coke ovens: Women's literacy in Whitney Pier, Nova Scotia. *Convergence*, 34(1), 97-117.

- Key, A. F. (1973). *Beyond Four Walls: The Origins and Development of Canadian Museums*. Toronto: McClelland and Stewart.

- Kudo, K., Motohashi, Y., Enomoto, Y., Kataoka, and Yajima, Y. (2011). Bridging Differences through Dialogue: Preliminary Findings of the Outcomes of the Human Library in a University Setting. Accessed 10/5/14 from http://humanlibrary.org/paper-from-dokkyo-university-japan.html.

- Litt, P. (1992). *The Muses, the Masses, and the Massey Commission*. Toronto, ON: University of Toronto Press.

- MacDonald, G. F. and Alsford, S. (1995). Canadian museums and the representation of culture in a multicultural nation. *Cultural Dynamics*, 7(1), 15-36.

- Mayo, P. (2013). Museums as sites of critical pedagogical practice. *Review of Education, Pedagogy, and Cultural Studies*, 35(2), 144-153.

- McKenna, K. M. (2005). Women's history, gender politics and the interpretation of Canadian historic sites: Some examples from Ontario. *Atlantis*, 30(1), 21-30.

- McTavish, L. (2008). Strategic donations: Women and museums in New Brunswick, 1862–1930. *Journal of Canadian Studies/Revue d'Études Canadiennes*, 42(2), 93-116.

- Nightingale, E. and Sandell, R. (Eds.) (2012). *Museums, Equality and Social Justice*. London: Routledge.

- Noyes-Platt, S. (2103). Art and Politics Now: Part Two: Thanks, But No Tanks. Retrieved on November 1, 2014 from http://www.artandpoliticsnow.com/2013/08/part-ii-haida-gwaii-thanks-but-no-tanks/.

- Phillips, R. B. (2012). *Museum Pieces: Towards the Indigenization of Canadian Museums*. Montréal and Kingston: McGill-Queen's University Press.

- Richard, G. (2013). Thanks, but no tanks—An art exhibition. *Haida Laas-Newsletter of the Council of the Haida Nation*, 14. Accessed on 01/10/15 http://www.haidanation.ca/Pages/haida_laas/pdfs/newsletters/2013/sep.13.pdf.

- Silverman, L. (2010). *The Social Work of Museums*. London: Routledge.

- Steedman, M. (Ed.) (2012). *Gallery as Community: Art, Education, Politics*. London: Whitechapel Gallery.

- Terry, A. (2013). Gender, Canadian nationhood and "keeping house:" The cultural bureaucratization of Dundurn Castle in Hamilton, Ontario, 1900–1960s. *Gender and History*, 25(1), 47-64.

- Tippett, M. (1990). *Making Culture: English-Canadian Institutions and the Arts before the Massey Commission*. Toronto, ON: University of Toronto Press.

- UNESCO (1997). *Museums, Libraries and Cultural Heritage: Democratising Culture, Creating Knowledge and Building Bridges*. Hamburg, Germany: IEU.

- Weil, S. E. (2002). *Making Museums Matter*. Washington, DC: Smithsonian Institution Press.

- Whitelaw, A. (2012a). Women, museums and the problem of biography. In K. Hill (Ed.), *Museums and Biographies: Stories, Objects, Identities* (pp.75-86). Woodbridge, UK: Boydell Press.

- Whitelaw, A. (2012b). Professional/volunteer: Women at the Edmonton Art Gallery, 1923-1970. In K. Huneault and J. Anderson (Eds.), *Rethinking Professionalism: Women and Art in Canada, 1850-1970* (pp. 357-379). Montréal and Kingston: McGill-Queen's University Press.

- Whitelaw, A. (2010). Art institutions in the twentieth century. In Whitelaw, A., Foss, B., and Paikowsky, S. (Eds.), *The Visual Arts in Canada—The Twentieth Century* (pp. 3-15). Don Mills, ON: University of Oxford Press.

- Wright, D. (2000). Gender and the professionalization of history in English Canada before 1960. *Canadian Historical Review*, 81(1), 29-66.

Structures and Agency

IV

Adult female learners undergo a potentially transformative experience when they re-engage with post-secondary education.
Adobe Stock image.

21

Adult Female Learner
Is That a Real Thing?

Female students now outnumber male students at Canadian post-secondary institutions, yet our institutions seldom fully reflect this demographic shift in terms of faculty complement or services. In 2009, only 33% of full-time faculty was female (Statistics Canada, 2011). In terms of curriculum, universities largely still teach "androcentric and Eurocentric, [that exemplify] white, male, middle class, hetero-sexual and able-bodied norms which are taken for granted" (Wagner, Acker, and Mayuzumi, 2008, p. 11). University culture is still primarily geared towards the *traditional* student who enrolls in full-time daytime studies. Since, according to Statistics Canada (2013), women now make up 56% of Canada's undergraduate students and 50% of graduate students, it is increasingly difficult to describe them as non-traditional students, yet there they often remain.

Jan Duerden

In this chapter I argue that this group is not a marginal but rather an important demographic. These are women who are re-entering academic study—or perhaps entering it for the first time after raising their children—after a successful career or due to changes they wish to make in their careers or lives. These adult female learners bring to their post-secondary experience very different kinds of strengths, knowledge, and needs, all of which must be reflected in a modern post-secondary institution. The topic of this chapter is an important part of the larger discussion about adult and higher education in Canada, not only because women will play an increasing role in our post-secondary landscape but also because the histories of both adult education and post-secondary education are connected in rich ways and both have a tendency to ignore women.

I became conscious of the issue/difference of adult female learners in my own post-secondary classroom. I teach first-year academic writing; however, I have a unique situation in that I teach writing classes for programs, including those in our Schools of Social Work, Education and Nursing that often include a significant number of adult female students. My sense has always been that these students are undergoing significant changes in their lives and that "re-engaging" with post-secondary education is a part of this process. Consequently, I am curious about the lived experience of these women learners and the potential transformative quality of the experience, as well as how to support it. I also sensed that my own teaching was largely shaped by adult female learners and I needed to explore what it meant to be an adult woman studying at university. I therefore developed a study that would tell me more about women's history within adult and post-secondary education, and how they experienced the post-secondary classroom in their own words.

Women and Adult Education in Canada: A Critical Past

This brings me to the title of this chapter. Whenever I attempted to explain my study to colleagues or friends, I was met with a response that can be best summarized as "An adult female learner ... is that a real thing?" This reaction highlights the need for this type of study even more.

I begin my chapter with a look at the past, drawing attention to Frontier College in Toronto, the YWCA, and the Women's Institutes movements. From there, I provide an historical overview of Canadian women's engagement with post-secondary institutions and then finish with a look at an exciting area of research that brings together the traditions of adult education and higher education through the experiences of adult female learners.

A definitive compilation of women's contributions to adult education in Canada is hardly possible, and I have chosen to reach back into our history to highlight but a few examples that illustrate links between women's experience in adult and post-secondary education. When researching the women whose work and lives created adult education in Canada, it is important to realize that they were taking enormous risks and were up against powerful societal norms, often manifest in the courses and foci of education that must at times have seemed insurmountable. Their strength and determination cannot be ignored, and one realizes it is crucial to bring the same to our post-secondary institutions today.

Women have been a critical presence in adult education, even if the official history has suggested otherwise (Ambrose, 2000; Butterwick, 1998; Wigmore, 1991). We continue to work as adult educators in formal and informal ways, and we work to expand our sphere of influence as scholars researching and writing about learning as experienced by women. The field is notoriously varied (some might say fragmented; some might say fluid) and uncovering the depth of our history is an ongoing process. Examining women's contributions requires reflection on the definitions of learning, education, and influence and the social construction of these concepts. It is critical, however, to make visible the risks women have taken to gain control of their education, both informal and formal, and therefore of their lives. The marginality of women's engagement with adult education in the historical record is troubling, since the "history and foundation of adult education, at least in Canada, is so closely related to the activities of various social movements for social justice" (Butterwick, 1998, p. 105). Equally troubling is the omission of women from the history of post-secondary education, since post-secondary institutions often pride themselves (at least theoretically) on open debate, critical thinking, and the creation of a better society.

Early Connections

The enduring links between events, including early events, in adult education and current trends in Canadian post-secondary education are many and even a brief examination of any single part of the rich history of adult education proves this to be true. Such investigation reveals, among other things, the complex interconnectivity of learning, literacy, economics, and social capital. Consider the following. The influence of women in the well-documented Antigonish Movement was significant. Ida Delaney and Kay Thompson were active insiders—Delaney in fieldwork, teaching, and public relations and Thompson as a creator of teaching materials and editor of the *Maritime Co-operator* (Butterwick,

1998). The impact of these and other pioneers is still seen in St. Francis Xavier University's robust adult education program today, and an indication of the growth of the field is the academic study of it at both the undergraduate and graduate levels. No less than twelve Canadian universities offer graduate programs focused on adult education, and at least two have undergraduate programs. Additionally, the movement's emphasis on social justice and the collective good echoes throughout the history of women's experience at the post-secondary level, including the fight for inclusion as university students and the ongoing struggle to be fully represented in faculty numbers, curriculum, and student services.

Frontier College is another example. Although often still associated with programs for men, it is important to acknowledge that women were also involved as educators and participants. Founder Alfred Fitzpatrick (1999), in his 1920 *The University in Overalls*, was an early advocate for a larger role for women in literacy work. Alex Scott, Mariam Chisholm, and Isabel Mackey worked with female workers in different rural, factory, and retail settings (Wigmore, 1991). University of Toronto graduate Jessie Lucas was the college's secretary-treasurer and registrar during its university phase, holding these posts for a combined forty-three years (Wigmore, 1991). In an early example of historical documentation authored by women, medical graduate and Frontier tutor Margaret Strang maintained a record of her administrative duties and her instruction of labourers in rural camps in western Canada (Wigmore, 1991). After a decrease in efforts to recruit women as tutors or students during and after the Great Depression, there was an eventual increase in their participation in the field, and in the "1970's and 1980's single women and couples were appointed to community projects in eastern, northern and northwestern Canada [and] no longer were their roles thought unusual" (Wigmore, 1991, p. 266). Women are now a critical force in Frontier College, as the organization has moved into new arenas, including programs for female immigrants, domestic workers, and inmates. A 2010 survey of Frontier College graduates suggested that 72% of respondents had gone on to some type of post-secondary education, emphasizing the continuing impact of the organization (Frontier College, 2010). Additionally, Frontier College's practice of self-paced learning has influenced the development of college and university preparation programs, women's bridging programs, and modern online-based learning.

"Alternative" Connections

Women's participation in adult education has been, and in many ways continues to be, poorly supported in conventional historical records (Ambrose, 2000; Butterwick, 1998; Wigmore, 1991). A pervasive societal devaluing (and underfunding) of community and volunteer organizations, parenting networks, and continuing/bridging education programs are not new. Rethinking measures of influence, authority, and outcomes is important, as is making connections between our experiences in these alternative organizations and post-secondary education. Even a selective look at a few of these organizations illustrates such connections. For example, the first YWCA opened in Saint John, New Brunswick, in 1870, followed by centres in Toronto and Montréal (YMCA, 2014, para. 1), before expanding to create a national system of evening classes, lending libraries, reading rooms, and gymnasia for both immigrant and local club-women (Butterwick, 1998). In 1957, the Canadian Association of Adult Education (CAAE) named the YWCA of Canada the most significant contributor "to the adult education field in Canada" (Harshaw, 1966, p. 28). The long-term impact of such educational initiatives on post-secondary education should not be ignored: Montréal YWCA/YMCA classes eventually expanded to become Concordia University in 1926 and, later in 1942, Ottawa's YWCA/YMCA grew to form Carleton University (YMCA, 2014).

By Women for Women

Equally important are other volunteer organizations, established by women, for women. I include here only two early examples that established models for women's activism and leadership that still resonate today. The first Women's Institutes began in Ontario in 1897 (Ambrose, 2000). They brought women from isolated communities together for education in areas such as home economics, childcare, and agriculture (Ambrose, 2000). By 1911 these Institutes were active in every province and, by 1913, the Federal Women's Institutes of Canada (FWIC) was established (Ambrose, 2000). FWIC membership grew substantially until the 1960s and, since then, has moved away from the original more rural focus to a renewed focus on women's health, political activism, literacy, and education, the latter in the form of endowments to universities and student scholarships (British Columbia Women's Institutes, 2008).

Another example of an early grassroots women's organization that worked to create a model of activism and the exercise of contemporary influence on women's post-secondary experience is the Canadian Federation of University Women (CFUW). This group was established in 1919 in response to women's increasing participation in university classes (largely in education, nursing, and social work) and work outside the home (CFUW, 2004). The CFUW's mandate was advocacy for women, particularly around education and health, and the creation of intellectual activity among women, including post-secondary scholarships and bursaries, now awarded in the amount of one million dollars annually (CFUW, 2013).

These are only two organizations that foreshadow the development of a variety of resources that are now a critical component of any post-secondary institution, including women's health and women's resource centres, as well as women's and gender studies programs. These initiatives seek to fill a significant gap in both society at large and specifically post-secondary culture: the devaluing of women's roles, and the knowledge and power those give us.

Women and Canadian Post-Secondary Education

The Canadian post-secondary system has experienced tremendous growth over the past several decades. In 2013, there were almost two million students enrolled in Canadian post-secondary institutions (Statistics Canada, 2013). Despite this significant overall growth in enrollment numbers, many post-secondary institutions are now grappling with declining enrollments within the traditional student demographic (ages 18 to 24). As the "echo-boomers" move through the post-secondary system, this demographic from which universities have historically drawn enrollment is expected to diminish by 10% over the next decade (Association of Universities and Colleges of Canada, 2011). In response, many post-secondary institutions are actively discussing the multi-faceted concepts of student engagement, success, and persistence and, increasingly, this discussion is focused on the retention of non-traditional students.

A review of current post-secondary enrollment statistics does not necessarily suggest that women be considered as non-traditional students. It is important to note however that, historically, women were not considered non-traditional students or even students at all, as our country's oldest universities excluded women for much of their formative years. For example, the oldest formal centre of education in Canada, Université Laval, had existed for 212 years and the oldest public Canadian university, the University of New Brunswick, had existed for 90 years before the first Canadian woman earned a degree (Pernal, 2009).

(Very) Conditional Acceptance

Over two decades ago, Gillett (1998) provided an informative view of the history of women in (Western) post-secondary institutions, dividing that history into four phases. The first period, dating from approximately the late 11th to the early 19th centuries, begins with the emergence of universities out of the European monastic tradition, and centres of learning that "were essentially elite institutions with male students and teachers, patriarchal values, hierarchical structures and curricula, strongly influenced by the writings of the church fathers, Aristotle and, later, Neo-Platonism" (Gillett, 1998, p. 36). Women were excluded from formal education as "higher learning would fit men into appropriate public or leadership positions but was unnecessary for women" (Gillett, 1998, p. 36).

The second period was the result of challenges to intellectual and social traditions led by the Enlightenment, the French and American revolutions, as well as science, industrialization, and urbanization (Gillett, 1998). In the United States, Oberlin College first admitted women in 1837, and all-women colleges were established, including Vassar, in 1861 (Gillett, 1998). Progress was equally slow in Canada. For example, McGill only began to provide the Montréal Ladies' Educational Association with academic lectures in the early 1870s, and it wasn't until 1884 that women were allowed to study on campus, albeit in segregated classrooms (McGill University, 2014). The first Canadian woman to earn a bachelor's degree was Grace Lockhart, who earned her B.Sc. at Mount Allison in 1875 (Gillett, 1998). However, full acceptance within such institutions was hardly evident. For example, in the 1880s, McGill only admitted women to the faculty of arts and gave them few library privileges; the University of Toronto allowed women to sit exams but not attend classes (Gillett, 1998). By 1901, women had attained 12% of the full-time undergraduate and professional enrollments and 30% of full-time graduate students were women (Bellamy and Guppy, 1991). Also worth noting is that once the contentious debate over women's admittance to university waned, other equally contentious debates emerged over residential facilities, appropriate models of co-education, and course content (Bellamy and Guppy, 1991), echoing Caplan's (1993) claim that "when any form of prejudice is labelled as unacceptable, it does not simply vanish; rather it tends to take increasingly subtler forms, thus protecting the prejudiced person from both social and legal accusations of prejudice" (p. 17).

Despite such obstacles, women's participation increased, leading Gillett's (1998) third phase of women's participation in post-secondary education. This increase "reflects intellectual, social and political shifts powered by the civil rights movement, second wave feminism and advances in human rights" (Gillett, 1998, p. 41). The single most significant surge in enrollment in Canada was between 1960 and 1970. By 1985, the number of female students enrolled in post-secondary institutions surpassed that of male students (Bellamy and Guppy, 1991), a trend that continues today.

Women have historically dominated enrollment in post-secondary education in non-university settings, such as teacher colleges, hospitals, and community college. The community college system in Canada grew significantly during this period, and colleges offering academic as well as vocational, technical, academic preparation/bridging, and continuing education programs facilitated women's increased participation. On a curricular level, women's and gender studies programs were developed at many Canadian universities. The first women's studies course was offered at the University of Toronto in 1970: the first degree program was offered at the University of British Columbia in 1971 (Bondy, 2010).

Current Challenges

The fourth phase identified by Gillett (1998), I would argue, is being experienced now and new concerns have arisen. The ongoing expansion of women's participation in post-secondary education co-exists with fiscal restraint, as traditional sources of funding for Canadian universities are cut and a more entrepreneurial style of delivery emerges. Increasing tuition costs, larger classes, fewer permanent or full-time professorships, and cuts to resources can be seen at all campuses. This includes cuts to bridging programs and various literacy and academic upgrading programs that are often adult female learners' first experience with a post-secondary environment. This current global neo-liberal and local deeply conservative political and economic climate has also resulted in direct attacks on smaller academic departments and programs, including women's and gender studies and graduate programs, which by definition house adult learners. Claims that such departments and programs are diminished or shut down to increase economic efficiency must be questioned, because these programs are often sustained through both substantial volunteer hours on the part of faculty, who Reimer (2004) argues are effectively working a double day, and on very lean budgets. The 2009 closure of Guelph University's women's studies program resulted in cutting a mere $78,000 from the university's annual budget, "the cost of two university advertisements in *The Globe and Mail*" (Wendling, as cited in Belyk, 2009, p. 6).

The challenges currently facing women's and gender studies across our post-secondary institutions are of particular interest to scholars of adult education and, specifically, researchers focused on adult female learners, because the fight to maintain these programs echoes similar fights in the past. The current struggle to maintain educational programs designed by women about issues and scholarship important to women and for women would not seem unfamiliar to the many female pioneers who worked hard for representation within adult education and post-secondary landscapes. Additionally, both students and faculty within women's and gender studies programs are often actively engaged with their community and with a variety of social justice issues, carrying on a tradition found across the entire history of adult education in Canada. Students earn academic credit through women-centred co-op placements, practica, and volunteer opportunities (Bondy, 2010). For example, at the University of Victoria (UVic), students:

work in sexual health agencies, in AIDS support groups, they're in queer community groups, in environmental agencies, in homeless youth volunteer work, in anti-violence groups, they're running newspapers, they're on the student government and in proportion to their numbers in the university, they stand out (St. Peter as cited in Bondy, 2010, p. 1).

Post-Secondary and Adult Female Learners: Making the Connection

An exciting area of research that brings together the traditions of adult education and higher education is enquiry into the experience of adult female learners returning to post-secondary education. As noted in the introduction to this chapter, this is a demographic that is understudied in adult education and post-secondary literature. As Pernal (2009) reminds us, "The demographic change in gender and numbers of students in universities is a recognized phenomenon, but little is known about older women students and how their lifelong learning affects society" (p. 3). To deepen understanding of this rich subject and to encourage others to further investigate its complexities, I highlight some of the findings of three recent qualitative studies authored by women (Duerden, 2013; MacFadgen, 2007; Pernal, 2009).

The fact that post-secondary institutions are reflections of society and therefore largely replicate patriarchy and intersectional inequities is proof that scholarship into adult female learners is of

Female students now outnumber male students at Canadian post-secondary institutions.

© Ermolaev Alexander / Shutterstock.

critical importance. As Pernal (2009) illustrates, academia "has little consideration for my permanent full-time position as a mother managing a homeplace or to my positions as a professional employee and volunteer in the larger community" (p. 16). A variety of multidimensional and dynamic themes emerge from these studies, many of which can be subsumed under the main theme of *belonging*. Just because women are a majority in student numbers does not mean they automatically feel they belong, and these studies suggest the same can be said for adult female learners. The studies also demonstrate the tremendous diversity within the experience of attending university as an adult female learner. Sweeping generalizations simply cannot be made; however, the documenting and therefore validating of individual experiences can allow us better understanding.

A Sense of Belonging

For adult women, the sense of whether or not one belongs at university begins long before one even walks on campus. The fact that our patriarchal society has not traditionally supported the education of women is one of the first obstacles faced, reflected in the fact that many women defer personal goals, including educational goals, because society does not at present provide the financial and material support all women need to balance the complexity of work inside and outside the home as well as post-secondary education. Canadian women are still more likely than men to live in poverty, be single parents, be (unpaid) primary caregivers in a dual parent family, and be paid less than men in the workplace, all of which can be obstacles to enrolling in post-secondary education. Because traditional thinking about women's roles persists, returning to school as an adult is still considered by many as unusual.

As mentioned in my introduction, when explaining my research on adult women returning to post-secondary education, more than once I was met with a response that can be best summarized as "An adult female learner—is that a real thing?" Pernal (2009) noted that upon being told that she was returning to post-secondary, others were quizzical about her choice; some asked her to affirm that she really was doing so. Pernal (2009) also suggested that universities needed to value part-time enrolment, a path often chosen by adult female learners, as much as full-time enrolment. All of these attitudes can have a significant impact of one's sense of self, evidenced by one women adult learner's feelings as expressed to me on the night before her first university class: "Should I give this education dream a rest and just accept my place in this world where I am?" (Duerden, 2013, p. 101).

A desire to connect to others, perhaps a very basic human need, is an important component of belonging. This becomes clear whenever we move into a new environment or culture. Post-secondary education is a new culture for all first-year students but, because universities have long been focused on traditional university demographics, it is not surprising that adult learners have concerns about inclusion. Each of these studies suggests that connecting with others, faculty, classmates, and even one's self is an important part of learning and that, for the adult female learner, connecting with faculty and other adult female learners is of great importance.

Connecting with Faculty Members

Making a positive connection with faculty featured prominently in the findings of each of these three studies. Such relationships proved the most influential contributor to what MacFadgen (2007) termed "students' successful integration" (p. 119) into post-secondary culture and what Duerden (2013) called a "genuine sense of belonging" (p. 114). It is interesting to note that in my recent study, which included seven adult female learners newly beginning post-secondary classes, past negative experiences with education almost always involved a memory of a relationship or connection with a teacher. It is also interesting to note that these students were exceptionally curious about faculty before the start of classes. Some were curious if the faculty member would be about the same age as them, and if they might have the same learning/teaching style. Others were worried about how faculty would react to the students' disclosure of a learning or physical exceptionality that required classroom accommodation.

In each of these studies, positive open communication with faculty was pivotal to students' persistence in classes and successful orientation to university culture. Students across all three studies reported that faculty played a large role in introducing them to the social and scholarly practices of post-secondary culture, and that the relationship often felt collaborative in nature. Feeling respected by faculty was crucial to building confidence for these women entering post-secondary because, within that respect, "women as lifelong learners are acknowledged" (Pernal, 2009, p. 183).

Connecting with Classmates

Connections to fellow classmates also play a key role in adult women's experience of post-secondary education. My research revealed evidence of the importance of connecting with other students in a variety of circumstances. One adult female student found herself without adequate funding to continue in school and, while in the financial aid office, wondered "are there others like me?" (Duerden, 2013, p. 112). In a contrasting situation, another research participant, when experiencing pride and accomplishment after having completed her first post-secondary course, claimed "others should do this!" (Duerden, 2013, p. 112). MacFadgen (2007) found that several adult learners expressed a preference for socializing with peers, and Pernal (2009) suggested that students in her study sought out those with similar interests and, in particular, similar motivations. Students in my study also actively sought out other adult female learners in the classroom (Duerden, 2013). However, positive relationships with other classmates should not be discounted. Three of MacFadgen's (2007) research participants "indicated they actually benefitted from the mix of ages and the diverse interaction opportunities in the classroom" (p. 108), and Pernal (2009) found her research participants "enjoyed the diversity of students and the feeling of a sense of community and collegiality" (p. 127).

Such findings make clear that forming connections with faculty and classmates is an integral part of the experience of adult female learners. These are just a few examples of the complexity that makes adult women returning to post-secondary education such an important area of scholarly inquiry.

Conclusions

To answer those who might respond to the idea of adult female learners with "An adult female learner—is that a real thing?" I say loudly and clearly, "Yes, we are real." This chapter has tried, in a brief way, to prove that adult women have always been a critical force in adult education in Canada and, despite enormous (and continuing) obstacles, women of all ages are now creating change in the Canadian post-secondary system, a system that has long replicated societal norms, especially patriarchy. It is important to stay vigilant, since not all women benefit from change equally and multiple forms of oppression cannot be ignored. Additionally, the fact that the expansion of women's participation in post-secondary education co-exists with a trend of extreme financial constraint must be examined, since it is often programs for women, and particularly adult women, that become vulnerable.

There is much more to learn about the impact of adult female learners on both post-secondary education and, longer term, society at large. In fact, I would argue we are just beginning this journey.

References

- Ambrose, L. (2000). *Women's Institutes in Canada: The First One Hundred Years, 1897-1997*. Gloucester, Ontario, Canada: Tri-Co Printing Inc.
- Association of Universities and Colleges of Canada. (2011). *Trends in Higher Education: Volume 1—Enrolment*. Ottawa, Ontario, Canada: Author.
- Bellamy, L. and Guppy, N. (1991). Opportunities and obstacles for women in higher education. In. J. Gaskell and A. McLaren (Eds.), *Women and Education* (2nd ed.). Calgary, AB: Detselig Enterprises Limited.
- Belyk, V. (2009). Women's studies on the chopping block. *Horizons, 23*(1), 6.
- Bondy, R. (2010). Women's studies: Is it time to change course? *Horizons, 24*(2) 16-19.
- British Columbia Women's Institutes. (2008). *100 Years of B.C. Women's Institutes, 1909-2009*. Kamloops, British Columbia, Canada: British Columbia Women's Institutes.
- Butterwick, S. (1998). Lest we forget: Uncovering women's leadership in adult education. In G. Selman, M. Selman, M. Cooke, and P. Dampier (Eds.), *The Foundations of Adult Education in Canada* (pp. 103-116). Toronto, Ontario, Canada: Thompson Educational Publishing.
- Canadian Federation of University Women (CFUW). (2004). CFUW history. Retrieved from: http://www.fcfdu.org/en-ca/aboutus/cfuwhistory.aspx.
- Canadian Federation of University Women (CFUW). (2013). Our Awards. Retrieved from: http://www.fcfdu.org/en-ca/fellowships/fellowshipsandawards.aspx.
- Caplan, P. (1993). *Lifting a Ton of Feathers: A Woman's Guide to Surviving in the Academic World*. Toronto, Ontario, Canada: University of Toronto Press.
- Duerden, J. (2013). *Female Adult Learners' Return to Post-Secondary: Motion, Emotion, and Connection*. Doctoral dissertation, Simon Fraser University, Burnaby, British Columbia, Canada.
- Fitzpatrick, A. (1999). *The University in Overalls: A Plea for Part-Time Study*. Toronto, Ontario, Canada: Thompson Educational Publishing. (Original work published 1920).
- Frontier College. (2010). Frontier College Alumni Survey Highlights. Retrieved from: http://www.frontiercollege.ca/english/success/alumni/alumni_survey_results.pdf.
- Gillett, M. (1998). The four phases of academe: Women in the university. In J. Stalker and S. Prentice (Eds.), *The Illusion of Inclusion: Women in Post-Secondary Education* (pp. 36-47). Halifax, Nova Scotia, Canada: Fernwood Publishing.
- Harshaw, J. (1966). *When Women Work Together: A History of the Young Women's Christian Association in Canada*. Toronto, Ontario, Canada: Ryerson Press.
- MacFadgen, L. (2007). *Mature Students in the Persistence Puzzle: An Exploration of the Factors that Contribute to Adult Learners' Quality of Life and Retention in Post-Secondary Education*. Doctoral dissertation, Simon Fraser University, Burnaby, British Columbia, Canada. Retrieved from: http://summit.sfu.ca/item/8453.
- McGill University. (2014). Blazing Trails: McGill's Women. Retrieved from: http://www.mcgill.ca/about/history/features/mcgill-women.

- Pernal, N. (2009). *Reentry Women Students Who Are Seniors: An Important University Subpopulation*. Unpublished doctoral dissertation. University of Calgary, Calgary, Alberta, Canada.

- Reimer, M. (2004). Will women's studies programs survive the corporate university? In M. Reimer (Ed.), *Inside Corporate U: Women in the Academy Speak Out* (pp. 118-137). Toronto, Ontario, Canada: Sumach Press.

- Statistics Canada. (2011, February). Education Indicators in Canada: Fact sheets: Doctoral Students and University Teaching Staff. Retrieved from: http://www.statcan.gc.ca/pub/81-599-x/81-599-x2011006-eng.htm.

- Statistics Canada. (2013). Post-secondary Enrolments by institution Type, Sex and Field of Study (Females). Retrieved from: http://www.statcan.gc.ca/tables-tableaux/sum-som/l01/cst01/educ72c-eng.htm.

- Wagner, A., Acker, S., and Mayuzumi, K. (2008). *Whose University Is It, Anyway?: Power and Privilege on Gendered Terrain*. Toronto, Ontario, Canada: Sumach Press.

- Wigmore, S. (1991). *The Hidden History of Women in Frontier College*. Proceedings of the 10th Annual Conference of the Canadian Association for the Study of Adult Education (pp. 262-267). Retrieved from: http://files.eric.ed.gov/fulltext/ED349466.pdf.

- YMCA Canada. (2014). History. Retrieved from: http://www.ymca.ca/en/who-we-are/history/ymca-milestones.aspx.

Photo courtesy of UBC ditigal collections.

This vignette was prepared by Shauna Butterwick and Mary Kostandy.

Anne Kincaide Ironside, born May 23, 1936 in Kamloops, British Columbia, grew up in Vancouver. Her father was a physician; of her mother, Anne said, "Had she been born later, she would have been CEO of a large, successful company." Anne had three siblings. She graduated from the University of British Columbia in 1957, with a Bachelor or Science degree in Bacteriology. She worked in mycology research in London before traveling independently to Europe, North Africa, and Russia. Returning to Vancouver, she married Jim Ironside. They had two daughters. Though she had a home and family, she needed intellectual challenges. Anne therefore embarked on a Master of Social Work degree, graduating in 1972. Having studied social work, she noted with a chuckle that "humans are not as predictable as the biological sciences."

Chosen from among 79 candidates, Anne coordinated the Women's Resource Centre—the first in Canada—that opened in 1972. This part-time job was an opportunity to balance family responsibilities and her work life. She discovered this work to be transformative. Anne wrote a proposal for the Deputy Minister of Education describing the benefits of Women's Resource Centres, outlining how centres could be established and run by volunteers. Subsequently, women's centres were set up at community colleges throughout the province. Complications arose, however; the men administering the finances sometimes channeled the funding into existing programs, which led to her identifying a gap between policy and implementation.

Anne joined the Canadian Association for Adult Education (CAAE), recognizing the effect that politics could have on a person's life, and that "Life is politics—women face many external and internal barriers." This step "also broadened my ideas about how to implement change for women." Anne was elected president of the CAAE, the first woman to hold the position. She believed that adult education was the route to positive change for women. In addition, Anne founded the Canadian New Work Institute to support young people in a changing economy and the Bowen Island Lifelong Learning Society, which assisted the community in future planning. She was awarded the Outstanding Adult Educator Award in 1989.

It was a transitional time in the development of the Women's Movement. Anne supported women who were making the transition from a male-dominated society to a society in which women were recognized as having equal insights and capabilities, and she also stated, "I think it's time for us to bring our spiritual and emotional intelligence forward to bear on our concerns." She embraced the ideas of Frithjof Bergmann, who spoke about how being in a relationship with work that we care about is what develops us. Approaching her 60s, she became aware of the demands of achieving equilibrium. She encouraged women to balance equally their "worlds" of work, relationships, and personal development. The structure of work needed to change if women were to combine careers with family life. She felt indebted to the support of her husband; their ability to communicate helped them manage the complexity of their lives.

Anne dedicated her work to improve the lives of women from all walks of life—she was truly a woman ahead of her time. Anne Ironside died on November 22, 2008, leaving an inspiring legacy that can be summarized in her quote: "We need to think about ourselves as Me, Incorporated—we can be the CEOs of our own lives."

Acknowledgements

- We are grateful to Andrea Ironside, Anne's daughter, and Mary Ellen deGrace, Anne's long-time friend, for their contributions to this vignette.

References

- Frithjof Bergmann (n.d.) Centre for New Work Society. http://www.context.org/iclib/ic37/bergmann/

- Deaths. (2008, November 22). The Globe and Mail (1936-Current).

- Finlayson, J. (1999). *Trailblazers: Women Talk about Changing Canada.* Toronto: Doubleday Canada.

- Greene, V. (2008, February 22). What's behind the gender gap in politics. *The Vancouver Sun.*

- http://search.proquest.com.ezproxy.library.ubc.ca/docview/243902664?pq-origsite=summon

- Ironside, A., & Science and Technology British Columbia/Ministry of Education. (1979). Women's access centres: A proposal. Retrieved from http://resolve.library.ubc.ca/cgi-bin/catsearch?bid=242209

- Ironside, A. (1979). Women's access centres: A proposal. Discussion Paper 03/79. Retrieved from http://resolve.library.ubc.ca/cgi-bin/catsearch?bid=3137635

- Rockett, E. (2013). *Ahead of Her Time: Memories of Anne Ironside,* An Echo Memoirs Book.

Woman in a small rural community in Newfoundland, 1939.
Courtesy of The Rooms Provincial Archives Division, VA 14-204, Gustav Anderson,
Newfoundland Tourist Development Board photograph collection.

22

"Don't Relegate Women to the Nursery and Kitchen"
Women and the Memorial University Extension Service

When Memorial College, in St. John's, Newfoundland, became a degree-granting university in 1949, one of its priorities was the creation of an Extension department. In 1953, international consultant Raymond Miller recommended that Memorial create a "people's university," and noted that "Extension plans the world over succeed in direct proportion to the interests of women" (Miller, 1953, 9). He warned that women should not be relegated to the nursery and kitchen. Here, we offer a glimpse into the adult education and community development work by and with women undertaken at Memorial University's Extension Service from its creation in 1959 to its closure in 1991. We ask whether this Extension Service functioned as a means of personal and social transformation for women in rural Newfoundland in the second half of the twentieth century.

Helen Woodrow and Linda Cullum

Our analysis derives from several locations: our own personal experiences as we both worked for Extension Service for sixteen and thirteen years respectively in media, program development, and fieldwork; our conversations with other women workers during and after our time in Extension; and, subsequent reflection, reading, and talking about our work years in Extension. We argue that our unique perspective, as women actually involved in the institution being studied, allows us to reflect critically on how women were viewed at Extension Service and in community work. As a result, in many ways, our experiences can now be set in a wider framework, one that gives a richer sense of the links between personal biography and broader historical events (Mills 1959). Feminists often use the phrase "the personal is political" to express this relationship between women's individual lives and their experiences within the social and political structures that surround us. Our focus here is on the gendering of work and community life, and the effect of gender constructions on the possibility for action and transformation in women's lives. Did Memorial University Extension Service widen the transformative space for women?

To address this question, we examine the experiences of five women who worked for Memorial University Extension Service in rural Newfoundland during the 1970s and 1980s. Regrettably, Extension Service archival records held at Memorial University remain uncatalogued and are inaccessible to researchers. In the available public records, we found that ten women (and twenty-nine men) were hired to work in the field in rural Newfoundland, though not all the women had full-time positions. Many women stayed for only short periods of time; we were unable to trace them all. We set out to interview those women we could locate who worked in the field. We also read closely available primary Extension records and secondary literature on adult education and community development, and examined significant products of Extension Service—the popular *Decks Awash* magazine, organizational reports, films from the Fogo Project (1967-68), and projects in Port aux Choix (1968-69) and Labrador (1969-70)—for representations of women and women's place in communities.

Preparing People for the New Newfoundland

In 1959, with the support of the first Premier of Newfoundland, Joseph R. Smallwood, Memorial University launched a bold project—an Extension Service that would produce social, economic, and cultural development in rural Newfoundland. S.J. Coleman, the first Director, was recruited from England and charged with its creation. He drew on British and American influences: the English tradition brought cultural and intellectual resources of the university to communities by offering courses, often in non-traditional formats or locations; the American land grant college model focused less on a course approach and aimed to work with people in their life situations and problems (Welton, 2013). Coleman argued for an "undoctrinaire and pragmatic approach." He wrote: "People ... have much to learn and adjust to before they can take their full place in the new Newfoundland" (Coleman, 1960, pp. 4-5).

From the beginning, a few Newfoundland women were educators and organizers in this effort: home economist Edna Baird transferred from the university faculty to Extension Service in 1959; Dr. Julia Morgan was hired in 1960 to focus on community development with co-worker Vera Moore at Bonavista; and Neala Griffin was employed as the field representative for Central Newfoundland in 1963. Illness forced Morgan to resign after a few months in Bonavista; she died in 1962 and Vera Moore left Newfoundland. Griffin addressed culture in her region, organizing and directing Extension glee clubs and producing several plays; she died in 1968. Available records indicate their work was probably focused on woman's traditional domains. Some efforts were made to reach women outside the home; for example, Edna Baird spoke to farmers "about the feasibility of starting a farm women's organization" (*Extension News*, 1966, 5).

Gushue's Presidential Report (Memorial University, 1961-62) highlights activities designed to extend knowledge and expertise from the university, and engage in practical work on the problems of communities. These activities included extra-mural university evening classes in St. John's, courses for trade unionists, and discussions on co-operation between fishermen. Nish Rumboldt, Christopher Pratt, and other men were hired to bring cultural and artistic pursuits to rural Newfoundland; community music and drama groups were created and art classes and workshops were offered. Fishers were organized to view and discuss industry developments explored in a television series called *Decks Awash*. Non-credit courses in French, home economics, public affairs, and other subjects were produced for both radio and television. Community development approaches were employed in a number of projects and eight areas were studied for the possibility of ongoing work. Coleman laid the foundation for the Extension Service in Newfoundland, but Don Snowden, appointed Director in 1964, brought an expansive community vision to the organization.

In Snowden's view, the everyday citizens of the province should own the new Newfoundland. Though economic indicators suggested a huge income gap as measured against the Canadian average, Snowden argued that the real poverty in places like rural Newfoundland was the poverty of information, of isolation from decision making, and of lack of organization (see Extension Service, 1970). He built the capacity of Extension to address these needs: increasing full-time staff from 12 in 1964 to 94 in 1974; transforming *Decks Awash* into a regularly published magazine "to serve the interests of people in rural areas of Newfoundland" (1968, p. 1); creating a new film and video facility and working with the National Film Board (Challenge for Change) to use interactive film to engage with social and political questions challenging Newfoundland communities. About thirty-two films were made on Fogo Island alone in 1967-68.

In 1972 Snowden left to chair the Royal Commission on Labrador. Men continued as members of the Extension triumvirate till the early eighties and they were respected by both staff and community members. Tony Williamson was the Head of the Community Development Section and he would become an Associate Director for Extension in Labrador. George Lee, Assistant Director and Head of the Visual and Performing Arts at Extension, was appointed Acting Director during Snowden's leave. Under Lee's leadership the arts flourished and the Community Learning Centre Project (CLC), an experiment in adult education development and communications access involving twenty-six rural and northern communities, was implemented in 1974. Webb (2014) notes that such projects generated "cultural capital" for Extension Service work in rural Newfoundland, and that the prestige gained "enabled it to play a role in the modernization of the province" (p. 84). Whether modernization allowed for the expansion of economic, social, and political opportunities for women in Newfoundland is debatable. How were women's lives and experiences represented in and through Extension work in Newfoundland communities?

Representations of Women

As Stall and Stoecker (1998, p. 731) note, "gender structures and process" shape community organizing, and Shaw (2007) asserts that material circumstances, gender, age, and other social markers structure community relationships. This was borne out by our research of Extension materials. We observed in a randomized selection of films that women were almost entirely absent from discussions on the future of their communities on Fogo Island in the late 1960s; they were not seen as essential subjects in communities. According to Nemtin (1968), "the traditional role of women" created a "reluctance [among men] to discuss serious issues in their presence" (p. 11). Only one film, *A Woman's Place* (Low, 1968), captured the views of women: two unidentified women assert that the knowledge and responsibilities of women made their engagement in discussions of development issues critical, although they identified class and religion as two factors that might be limiting women's participation. Interestingly, those divisions were not seen to affect men on Fogo. The near invisibility of women in local development groups and in the films may have reflected the belief that women were not seen as economic subjects, nor were they expected to engage in important decisions regarding the community's future. Chaulk Murray (1979), Matthews (1976), Porter (1993b, 1995), Cullum and Porter, (2014), Ennis and Woodrow (1996), and Woodrow (2014), among others, have challenged this fallacy in their work on women, communities, and resettlement in Newfoundland.

Intrigued by the absence of women in early Extension work, we explored materials created by the institution in the post-Fogo Project era. Our underlying questions remained: How were women represented in these creations from Extension Service? How might the gender expectations of men and women have silenced the voices of women?

The products we chose for gender analysis included 16 mm films and articles from the *Decks Awash* magazine. We looked for women's interests and work, their perspectives on issues facing their communities, and their roles in local development. The Extension Service Film Unit used the model of film making that evolved on Fogo Island with regional fieldworkers in Port aux Choix in 1968 and on the south coast of Labrador in 1969. As in the Fogo films, local personalities were featured in both Port aux Choix and Labrador, but no women appeared in the Labrador films we sampled (see Memorial University Digital Archive). In the Port aux Choix series, a few women did appear but also, as in Fogo, their views on community needs were minimized in the final products.

Our gender analysis of the popular *Decks Awash* magazine, published from 1968 to 1991, was revealing as well. Issues alternated between regional profiles and resource industries, and on occasion special theme editions appeared. We reviewed all articles that included female interview subjects and sampled every third year between 1968 and 1991 (including 1975, International Women's Year); 438 articles were read in the 50 issues. Forty-two percent of the samples concerned women's paid work, women in small business, and women's history. From the late 1970s through the 1980s, women became more visible in the magazine; they epitomized economic subjects, holding paid work and actively engaging in the development of their families and communities.

An awareness of women as subjects began to emerge in discussions among Extension staff in 1970. At a September meeting, the Head of the Film Unit concluded there was a "great deal of work to be done on the development of women's organizations" on Fogo (Extension Service Film Unit Meeting, 1970, 40). A few months later field staff discussed the hiring of a female field worker. They recognized that women played an important role in the development of communities and must be involved in development efforts. On Fogo Island, women had been involved in workshops, and one man suggested they might be persuaded to become further involved: "it was believed that it would be a great asset if a women were hired to talk with women's groups and to advise them of the role they could play in the development of the community" (Extension Service Field Representatives' Meeting, 1970, 14). Regrettably, no female field worker was dedicated to Fogo Island work. Finally in 1974, two recently hired female staff collaborated on a funding proposal with women's organizations to focus on the changing roles of women in such coastal regions (Extension Service, 1974).

Despite these efforts within the organization, women were not always seen as important subjects in local development. For the most part they were viewed as housewives, even though their direct labour as shore skippers in places like Fogo Island was critical to the economic value of the fishery in the 1960s (Porter, 1995; Antler, 1977; Andrews, 1970). A husband-and-wife team spending a few weeks picking 1200 pounds of bakeapples for 50 cents a pound, or a woman washing and drying salt bulk fish and giving it three days sun for $3 a quintal, earned significant cash income, which was of importance to the household economy in coastal Newfoundland at that time. The seventies did bring more economic opportunity to coastal areas; there were jobs for women in the fish-processing sector, inshore fishing boats were often replaced with mid-shore vessels, and the cashless economy had disappeared.

In our search, we found gendered and contradictory ideas about what it meant to be a woman in rural Newfoundland. Was she a central figure in family and household livelihood, an insignificant contributor to the economy of the household and community, an uninvolved member in community decision making, or an active and engaged participant in community life? How were gender processes and exclusions within Extension Service operating in this complex scenario? To unravel these complexities, we interviewed five women who undertook fieldwork in Extension Service. They offered us more nuanced understandings of rural women and the organization.

Telling Stories: Women in the Field

Extension Service hired Mary Alton Mackey, Laura Jackson, Lynn Best, Agnes Pike, and Elaine Condon between 1973 and 1985. They worked in different regions, at different periods, on different projects; this gives them distinct vantage points on the organization and its work. Laura, Lynn and Elaine were field representatives in Labrador, Central, and the Avalon, and Mary was a Consultant to Rural Women. Agnes was an animator for the Community Learning Centre (CLC) Project, and was later placed on a full-time salary with the project for about twelve months. The women described a vast range of projects, issues, and concerns they tackled in their work, and they reported, with feeling, their experience of working with women and the response of Extension Service to their efforts.

Mary Alton Mackey was recruited for the position of Consultant to Rural Women and came to Extension in September 1973 after she completed her PhD in Nutrition. Mary worked throughout the province responding to requests for workshops from field workers, women's organizations, and various community groups. She also worked for women-centred reforms to existing provincial policies in health, social services, and education and consulted with members of the Faculty of Medicine at Memorial.

Laura Jackson, who went to Labrador with her husband, Lawrie, when he was working with the Snowden Royal Commission on Labrador, created her own job by listening to the needs women expressed in the Commission hearings and in later field trips to the Labrador Straits area. She advised Extension officials she would be going to her husband's job interview because she believed women had particular needs and it would make sense to have someone "working specifically with women." They hired her, but only as a part-time worker.

Lynn Best was hired in 1986, fresh from a development association job. She was informed about basic administrative details such as payroll and employee credit cards, introduced to various people on the university campus, and then told to go find a house and a project to work on in her assigned region.

Elaine Condon, a graduate from the Centre for Community Initiatives at Memorial University, was hired in 1985, after returning to Newfoundland from Saskatchewan. When she was asked about the staff training she received, she laughed and said, "They gave me a key and said, 'There's an office out in Gander ... go do some good work.'"

Agnes Pike was living in the Labrador district in which she worked, and her initial training had taken place at a two-week workshop in St. John's. She recalls that the work she did with Extension had a major impact on her life.

The five women came to Extension Service with different education levels, skills, and experiences behind them, so their work in the field varied considerably. All the attendant social, economic, and political changes in the province also shaped their efforts. Each woman liked aspects of the work, often felt good and productive while doing it, and connected with communities and people in positive ways. For the most part, the five report little explicit support for their work with women, and a lack of larger organizational interest in women in communities.

Working with Women

As Weil (1986) noted, "community organization ... has been a male-dominated preserve" (cited in Stall and Stoecker 1998, p. 729). Memorial University Extension Service was no exception; it lacked an articulated and critical focus on women in communities. When Mary examined the history of community work at Extension in her initial months with the organization, she too was struck by the silencing of women: "With the occasional exception, women were not part of this discussion. Their opinions certainly weren't there." Assigned to a senior position, she worked with the field staff and media unit at Extension as a "bit of a thorn in both of their sides to include women, not as tokens but as real contributors." To accomplish some of this work, Mary allied herself with women in the organization who were interested in similar issues. Other women we interviewed who worked in the field also aimed to empower women and to strategize with them on effective techniques to advocate for themselves. In their narratives, they spoke explicitly of developing women's capacity to engage in shaping their communities and forging a space for their ideas.

Mary recalls the struggle for a fair Matrimonial Property Act and her work on food, child health, and nutrition. Through these "safe," woman-centred projects, rural women could be engaged, skills could be learned, and communication tools—public speaking, meeting management, leadership, and advocacy—developed. In this way, the empowerment of women was structured as a process of skill development, reflection, and action (Stall and Stoecker, 1998). Mary worked with organized groups such as the Women's Institutes, status of women councils, churchwomen, and the Home Economics Association as well.

Mary was acutely aware of gender relations in her activities. She ensured that women were represented in meetings involving men, and she saw a role for men in her work with women. "Even the advocacy I did on matrimonial property involved men because they owned everything... Most of the child development activities were women-focused. For the family-oriented undertakings, we tried to have both. I didn't go out looking for men ... [but I] included them as necessary and useful. Lots of time deliberately, because I was really working on ... giving voice to the women, and challenging them to become active participants."

Mary collaborated with Laura Jackson, who was stationed on the Labrador Straits from 1974 to 1978 as a half-time fieldworker. Agriculture was a significant piece of women's everyday work in the Straits area; "they raised and milked cows, made butter and gardened." Securing the expertise of agricultural representatives, and starting a community garden and greenhouse, which included traditional crops and then-exotic vegetables such as broccoli, garlic, and tomatoes, were just some of the projects Laura took on early in her placement. Work on childcare issues, preschools, and craft marketing captured her attention as well. She remembers these matters were "of special interest to women, and in some cases they seemed to be the exclusive interest of women." Her husband's work— on community councils, development associations, fishers' committees, the road, the ferry—was considered more important than hers to Extension: "They were the 'real' issues. All the women's stuff wasn't well understood or studied."

Lynn Best remembers that working with women specifically was "not on my radar" in the mid-1980s. Rather, economic development was foremost: fishing issues, fishery resources, and formation of co-ops were important. She notes that there was an assumption in some communities that men would lead and women would support.

One particular effort, the Rural Women's Learning Project (RWLP), was very satisfying for Lynn. The RWLP focused on improving women's access to learning opportunities in their regions or communities, through leadership skill development workshops and meetings, as well as a series of video profiles of women leaders from rural areas. Under this project, Lynn worked with farmwomen in more than one community. Farming could be big business, and women's leadership and contribution in the running of that business was important. Women did not easily step into public leadership roles, but Lynn supported and encouraged them by helping them to organize, conducting workshops, facilitating conferences and meetings, and "honouring and acknowledging their contribution to family farms and to the farming industry in the province."

Another large undertaking for Lynn was the Petty Harbour Transmitter Project. Community narrowcasting, as it is sometimes called, "is a media-assisted community development approach" that involves the community in "planning and control of the medium ... the issues or problems to which it is applied, and the length of the actual transmission" via a five-to-fifteen kilometre television signal (Harris, 1992, p. 13). Lynn was responsible for organizing community involvement—everything from the hall space to interviews to individual participation—and preparing educational materials prior to the event. When asked why few women were involved, Lynn replied, "Women were interviewed, absolutely, but ... it was very much a male thing. I'm not kidding when I say that women provided the food after for the [party] ... a very traditional sort of role right?" In part, this was due to a focus on the Petty Harbour Fishermen's Co-operative, a male-dominated fishery organization whose women fish plant workers were not members of the co-op itself. Lynn did not think the contributions of women, the questions they had about their community, key development, or economic issues were valued in the same way as those of men: "I never heard or saw anything that indicated, who's missing from this table, what voices are missing? The question was never asked. There was no deliberate or strategic attempt to engage women in those conversations ... there was no awareness that we need diversity and inclusion." Lynn saw distinct differences in working with women and with men: "For women ... relationships and building relationships was equally as important as the purpose of the work ... how do we support each other ... how do we come together and even socialize .... Coming together was just as important as what you were together for." This parallels argument made by Stall and Stoecker (1998, p. 741) that "in woman-centred organizing, power begins in the private sphere of relationships" and is understood as "limitless and collective."

Elaine worked out of Central Newfoundland and, like other field co-ordinators, served a large field area. She did not wait long for her first request for help: "I was probably sitting in my seat 10 minutes when I got a call ... and she said 'we got a little women's centre over here now, come over and have a chat with us.' And it went on from there." Elaine saw a "double whammy" affecting women and their perception of their importance in communities; "you [are a] rural Newfoundlander who has never had respect from anybody, so therefore you feel you haven't got any skills and knowledge, but you are also a female." Building on this observation, Elaine did many presentations and workshops aimed at the empowerment of women. A feminist approach to paid work, violence, or power in communities was a challenge to some more traditional or government-sponsored women's groups, but, "we developed relationships with some people in some of those communities and kept going back."

Elaine sometimes moved temporarily to live in other communities while she was trying to establish connections and do work in those areas. Being "out in the trenches" was highly valued by some in Extension Service. On the Bonavista Peninsula, she worked with fishermen, one-on-one and in small groups, organizing meetings with government officials and regional fishery conferences, helping the fishermen clarify their ideas and write letters to government on the state of the inshore fishery, and ultimately to document by video men's ideas about the fishery: "They ended up having half a dozen real leaders come out of that region for the fishery." Elaine remembers other Extension staff supported her work in specific community development projects, including training in video recording and editing during her work with inshore fishermen. Elaine also connected with fisherwomen, women development association co-ordinators, women sitting on town councils, and those working in fish plants. She found that, in moving projects forward, women brought experience and skills in community work and in navigating political systems that the men did not possess.

Eventually, much of Elaine's work addressed gender inequality and violence in rural communities, and, by the time she left Extension in 1991, she was working almost exclusively with the women's community: "I was enjoying that work and finding lots of purpose in it and lots of ... really good work to do. And lots of women that were eager to engage, scared to engage, but eager to engage as well."

Agnes Pike's relationship with Extension Service was somewhat different than the others we interviewed. For about eighteen months, she worked as an animator with the CLC Project on the Labrador Straits for an honorarium of $600 a year. In the 1970s, Agnes was very involved as a volunteer on community projects in her region and she was highly recommended for the position by the field staff, Lawrie and Laura Jackson. After the project evaluation, she was placed on a full-time contract for a year. When Agnes agreed to take on the low-paid work of a community animator, she was brought to St. John's for two weeks of training. "You were anxious to get out and do that job the best way you saw fit. It wasn't about money. It was about getting your work done." She found women enthusiastic and willing to work hard to get things accomplished in their communities; "[they] were always anxious to see results," whether in craft development or forming a branch of the Women's Institute. Agnes remembers that, "One of the things I did was get craft instructors to come to the coast ... [they] did some workshops in the summer ... People were so excited by it ... That was one of the things that got the craft movement on the coast."

Agnes used portable video equipment to record important events or document problems in communities, such as poor road development or fishery issues, as well as encourage public speaking skills with students. When her contract with Extension Service ended, she was offered a job with the provincial department responsible for rural development. It would have meant moving to Goose Bay, so she accepted a supervisory position with the first fresh fish plant on the coast.

Agnes generally found little difference in working with women or men, but noted that, "there were people out there who were threatened by women. If you are more knowledgeable or a much harder worker, you'll be shunned." She links this attitude to traditional gender ideologies, which saw women tending to family, children, and the home and men doing paid work. She remembers some women feeling that they couldn't "speak their mind," and being told, "That's not your business, stay out of this," an attitude that shocked Agnes. She thought the CLC Project was a good program, as it reached a lot of people on the Straits; it "had a major impact on my way of thinking right to the present time .... It was a great education for me. I learned a lot by getting involved in that project." Agnes became frustrated with the pace of work and some of the attitudes she saw in particular Extension staff outside her region: "Maybe some staff felt they were doing a lot of great work. Perhaps it was only me who didn't see that. More could have been done."

Mary Alton Mackey believes some administrators in the university did not value education as a tool to be used "as a catalyst for development," regardless of whether men or women were involved in the community activities. Specific organizational goals "to empower women ... to give them some priority," were missing from the university vision of education as well as from the Extension mission, specific planning, and actions. That, coupled with individual "negative attitudes about women" and a "lot of lip service, but not a lot of commitment at the leadership [level]" to work with women, led to "doing what was culturally acceptable," rather than "pushing the envelope" and challenging women's constrained role in communities.

Concluding Thoughts

In this initial exploration of Memorial University Extension Service activities, we found women were usually excluded as active subjects in modernization efforts in the province. Despite Miller's (1953) advice, Extension Service, as a division within a larger university system, seldom considered women in communities beyond their role in the family. It was as though men, within Extension and Memorial University, were blind to rural women's labour, activities, and broader social roles. Working with women on "women's issues" was not highly valued, nor seen as a legitimate focus of attention; there were no organizational goals aimed at achieving the integration of women into decision making in communities. In the 1970s and 1980s, more women were hired as field co-ordinators but, despite the intensity and diversity of activities undertaken by them, a focus on women in communities remained an individual pursuit by particular field workers and a few staff. Sometimes those efforts tested women's traditional role in communities and opened a space for limited personal and social transformation for some women.

As Extension Service headed towards oblivion, its approach meant that the institution was not functioning as it could have, for the betterment of all citizens of rural Newfoundland. Memorial had lost its status as a "people's university" well before the closure in 1991.

References

Primary Sources—Interviews

- Lynn Best, September 2014, St. John's, NL.
- Elaine Condon, September 2014, by telephone, Hopedale, NL.
- Laura Jackson, September 2014, St. John's, NL.
- Mary Alton Mackey, September 2014, by telephone, Toronto, Ontario.
- Agnes Pike, October 2014, by telephone, West Ste. Modeste, NL.

Secondary Sources

- Andrews, R.A. (1970). *Female Participation in the Port de Grave Fishery.* St. John's, NL.

- Antler, E. (1977). Women's work in Newfoundland fishing families. *Atlantis* 2, (Spring 1977, Part 2), 106-113.

- Coleman, S.J. (1960). Memorial University of Newfoundland Extension Service, 3 May, 1960. Smallwood Papers, Coll 075, 3.09.045, Archives and Special Collections, QEII Library, MUN.

- Chaulk Murray, H. (1979). *More than Fifty Percent: Woman's Life in a Newfoundland Outport, 1900-1950.* St. John's, NL: Breakwater Books.

- Cullum, L. and Porter, M. (Eds.). (2014). *Creating This Place: Women, Family and Class in St. John's, 1900-1950.* Montréal: McGill-Queen's University Press.

- Decks Awash, A Rural Magazine. (1968). *Decks Awash,* 1(1). Retrieved from: http://collections.mun.ca/cdm/compoundobject/collection/cns_decks/id/147/rec/10.

- *Decks Awash.* (1968-1991). 1(1) -20(2). St. John's, NL: Memorial University Extension Service.

- Division of Extension Service. Annual Report. 1984/85-1988/89. [St. John's, Nfld]: Memorial University of Newfoundland.

- Ennis, F., Woodrow, H. (Eds.) (1996). *Strong as the Ocean. Women's Work in the Newfoundland and Labrador Fisheries.* St. John's, NL: Harrish Press.

- Extension Service (1970). Brief Submitted to the Special Senate Committee on Poverty. MUN Extension Service. St. John's, NL: Memorial University.

- Extension Service (1974). A Proposal by Extension Service, Memorial University of Newfoundland, on Behalf of the Newfoundland and Labrador Women's Institutes ... [et al.]. Newfoundland and Labrador women in perspective, 1974. St. John's, Nfld.: Extension Service, 1974.

- Extension Service Annual Report. 1960/61-1983/84. [St. John's, Nfld]: Memorial University of Newfoundland.

- Extension Service Field Representatives' Meeting, St. John's, NL, Nov 16-20. (1970). [St. John's, Nfld]: Memorial University of Newfoundland.

- Extension Service Film Unit Meeting, Gander, NL, Oct 18-19. (1970). [St. John's, Nfld]: Memorial University of Newfoundland.

- *Extension News,* 1(2), April 1966. [St. John's, Nfld: Extension Service]: Memorial University of Newfoundland.

- Harris, E. (1992). *Dreaming Reality: Small Media in Community Development as Critical Educational Practice: A Case Study of Community Narrowcasting in the Town of Buchans, Newfoundland, Canada.* Unpublished thesis, University of Toronto.

- Low, Colin (1967). *A Woman's Place.* (1967). Retrieved from: https://www.nfb.ca/film/womans_place.

- Matthews, R. (1976). *There's No Better Place than Here.* Toronto, ON: Peter Martin Associates.

- Memorial University Digital Archive. Extension Collection. Retrieved from: http:// collections.mun.ca/cdm/landingpage/collection/extension

- Memorial University, Report of the President, 1961-62. (1962). Retrieved from: http://collections.mun.ca/PDFs/cns/ReportofthePresidentofMemorialUniversity19611961.pdf.

- Miller, R.W. (1953). Preliminary Report on Extension to the Board of Regents, January 30, 1953. Memorial University of Newfoundland. Washington, DC.: [s.n.].

- Mills, C. W. (1959). *The Sociological Imagination.* Oxford, UK: Oxford University Press.

- Nemtin, W. (1968). Fogo Island film and community development project. Retrieved from: http://onf-nfb.gc.ca/medias/download/documents/pdf/1968-fogo-island-film-and-community-development-project.pdf.

- Porter, M. (1993). "A tangly bunch": The political culture of outport women in Newfoundland. In M. Hanrahan (Ed.) *Through a Mirror Dimly: Essays on Newfoundland Society and Culture* (pp. 95-118). St. John's, NL: Breakwater.

- Porter, M. (1995). "She was skipper of the shore-crew:" Notes on the sexual division of labour in Newfoundland. In C. McGrath, B. Neis, and M. Porter (Eds.), *Their Lives and Times: Women in Newfoundland and Labrador: A Collage* (pp. 33-47). St. John's, NL: Killick Press.

- Shaw, M. (2008). Community development and the politics of community. *Community Development Journal,* 43(1), 24-36.

- Stall, S. and Stoecker, R. (1998). Community organizing or organized community? Gender and the crafts of empowerment. *Gender and society,* 12(6), 729-756.

- Webb, J. (2014). The rise and fall of Memorial University's Extension Service, 1959-1991. *Newfoundland and Labrador Studies* 29(1), 84-116.

- Welton, M. (2013). *Unearthing Canada's Hidden Past: A Short History of Adult Education.* Toronto: Thompson Educational Publishing.

- Woodrow, H. (2014). Julia Salter Earle: Seeking social justice. In L. Cullum and M. Porter (Eds.), *Creating this Place: Women, Family and Class in St. John's, 1900-1950,* (pp. 71-88). Montréal, QC: McGill-Queen's University Press.

Researchers at UNESCO's Institute of Lifelong Learning, a non-profit, policy-driven research, training, and information centre.
Photo: Courtesy of Leona English.

23

Critical and Creative Transformative Learning
"Longing for the Sea" in Feminist Non-Profit Organizations

> If you want to build a ship, don't herd people together to collect wood and don't assign them tasks and work, but rather teach them to long for the endless immensity of the sea. Your task is not to foresee the future, but to enable it.
> —Antoine de Saint-Exupéry (1952)

Women who work for women in the community non-profit sector are engaged in the rewarding work of "longing for the sea." Their task is not only to engage in resistance, but also to help other women envisage a world that is sustainable, equitable, and safe. Even though non-profit women's centres, transition houses, safe housing, and movements for women's literacy are often depicted as places of scarcity and extremity (English, 2005a; 2006, 2007, 2011), these non-profits are in actuality spaces that facilitate creative transformative learning for social change.

Leona M. English

The creativity of non-profit organizations is shown in a variety of ways, including collective efforts of leaders to work together in the community, as articulated by Marg, an executive director of a feminist non-profit organization:[1]

> So all the women's centres, all the transition houses and all the men's programs, we all got together and formed a loose coalition to address these funding cuts which at this point they have, they've stopped. They put a hold on it. So we did this whole kind of reaction to that and our communities basically told the government to leave us alone, that we are very much appreciated and the dollars we get are well used. So the government had to back down, temporarily.

Marg strategically joined with a number of other leaders to keep their non-profit organizations running, even if they were all a bit shattered in the process. She was typical of the women leaders I have interviewed over a decade or more.

It seems to me from my research that feminist non-profit organizations (and leaders) in Canada are often in fragile situations when it comes to funding and leadership. Given the lack of support for housing, income, safety, and childcare, there is much scurrying, rallying, and strategizing. And, somehow, these leaders rise to the challenge, committed as they are to women, social transformation, and a different type of future. Yet, we know relatively few details about how they function, what their challenges are, and how they creatively manage perpetual scarcity. Their stories of creative response and change are needed to counterbalance the stories of regression, want, and scarcity.

This chapter focuses directly on women's transformative and creative learning experience in these feminist non-profits in Canada in order to help shed light on the intricacies and challenges of their experience. As a feminist researcher, I am committed to telling their stories and revealing their challenges as a way of resisting patriarchy and neglect of our most vital sector: the non-profit world.

The Context

As an increasingly neo-liberal country, Canada has by and large dropped the ball on support for the poor and marginalized, those on the lowest end of the socio-economic ladder. Sadly, women are overrepresented in this group, and it falls to the community sector, the non-profit organizations, to work with women who face the effects of poverty on a daily basis.

Non-profit leaders who run housing projects, anti-poverty coalitions, literacy centres, and anti-violence programming know this situation all too well: their organizations are mostly unsupported and underfunded. Their public face, their website and Internet profiles, when they exist, are often unusable and unhelpful as their financial and human resources are strained (Irving and English, 2011). Even a casual observer knows that there is virtually no women's infrastructure left in this country to rally for policy change or funding for women. The Status of Women organizations, once provincial and territorial mainstays, are basically defunct, as is the National Action Committee (NAC) on the Status of Women. To add insult to injury, the federal government recently took away the Thérèse Casgrain Volunteer Award, established in honour of Casgrain's role in securing the vote for women in Québec and for being the first woman to lead a federal party in this country (Stoddart, 2014). These trends in Canada have made the Canadian non-profit sector a challenging place. There are reports of similar challenges around the globe, including in countries such as Norway (Wollebæk and Selle, 2004). Yet, the ways in which non-profit directors and association members in Canada function and lead are inspiring—rather than seeing themselves as bereft and hopeless, they resist the label of marginality and take on life-affirming causes and initiatives (English, 2011).

Feminist non-profit organizations share political goals of social and creative transformation, and work for structural changes to improve the conditions and rights of women globally. Some organizations focus on advocacy and human rights, whereas others provide services such as education, literacy, and protection for women experiencing partner abuse (Hasenfeld and Gidron, 2005). In the face of an increasingly neo-liberal agenda at all levels, women's non-profit organizations struggle with problematic government policies, such as limiting literacy funding to employment-related goals and restricting the right of these organizations to lobby for change if they receive government funds. Despite these challenges around governance (Muthien, 2006) and funding (English, 2006), women's non-profit organizations are sites of critical transformative learning for both female participants and leaders.

Critical and Creative Transformative Learning

Against this regressive political and social background—funding cuts, low priority for women, and increased neo-liberal policies—it is nothing short of remarkable that feminist non-profits continue to function at the grassroots level to empower and support women's transformation, both individually and collectively. While Mezirow's initial study on transformation (1978; also Mezirow and Taylor, 2009) focused on individual women returning to school, much of the later research focused almost exclusively on women in crisis (Nash, 2007). There has been scant attention paid to the experience of women leaders and participants in these NGOs and how they learn to create change. Although there have been some attempts to investigate this phenomenon (English and Peters, 2012; English and Irving, 2013), more investigation is needed. Insight into this transformation is crucial in a time when feminist NGOs need all the resources they can get in order to attract younger women (Alpízar and Wilson, 2005), women of colour (Scott, 2005), and women from diverse socio-economic and faith backgrounds.

Insights from the transformative learning literature can help us understand social transformation in women's non-profit organizations. Tisdell (2012), for instance, identifies three ways of understanding transformative learning theory: (a) the individually and rationally focused tradition of Mezirow; (b) the planetary and ecological focus of O'Sullivan; and (c) the social transformation tradition in the spirit of Freire. To these three strands, Tisdell adds an important dimension, possibly creating a fourth strand: transformative learning for creativity and insight. In this strand, she holds out for a deeper engagement with the whole person, with spirituality, and the richness of aesthetic experience as a way forward to social change and creativity. Though this fourth element of creativity draws on the other three strands, it is unique in its connections to women's experience and its stress on innate creative potential, as it pushes beyond the cognitive limits of the other three; in Tisdell's words, it is "Spiralling in, spiralling out, reflecting the themes and variation of transformative learning" (p. 21).

The ability to think beyond the gamut of rational thought, respond to crises, and imagine a new future are at the heart of the mission of feminist non-profit organizations, and at the heart of what Tisdell (2012) calls spiralling. Such a critical and transformative learning theory draws indirectly on early twentieth-century theorists such as Mary Parker Follett (1924), who viewed organizational power as creatively working *with* each other, not over each other. Follett saw the strength that is possible when people work together to build organizations and to exercise collective power in the process. The discussion also draws on the work of Clover (2012), who has added the insights of the arts and aesthetic experience to her feminist theorizing on social change, women's leadership, and resistance. Writers such as these see that new and thoughtful ways of working are the essence of transformation.

Facilitating Creative Transformation in Feminist NGOs

The literature on facilitating transformative learning identifies three supporting elements that make transformation possible: individual experience, critical reflection, and dialogue. To these elements, Taylor (2009) adds three more: awareness of context, holistic experience, and authentic relationships. These elements would appear to be common to good teaching, and perhaps for understanding transformative learning experiences generally, but it is not clear that they accurately describe the experience of women in non-profit organizations. Here, I draw on data from a decade of qualitative studies in gender, feminism, community-based feminist non-profit organizations in Canada, to name some key components in support of women's personal and collective transformation in feminist non-profit organizations (see English and Peters, 2012; Irving and English, 2011). The studies are available in a variety of adult education journals and books (see also English, 2010).

One concern identified as a limit to transformative learning is rationality, defined as a western bias that privileges cognition. Studies of transformative learning among women in non-profit organizations show that this focus on the mind (to the exclusion of the body) is constraining and is simply not borne out by the data on how women experience transformation (English and Peter,

2012). Tisdell's (2012) notion of creativity comes to mind here when we think of how the body is such an important part of how women relate and how they function in organizations. Indeed, feminist non-profit organizations are among the few places in society where the rights of a woman's body are protected. Learning from and through the body in an organization whether in service delivery or in advocacy work eclipses any notion that transformation is limited to a rational, cognitive process that Mezirow (1978) envisaged. In the feminist non-profit organization, the body becomes the subject of discussion and the site of the learning for many.

The body is central to the functioning of a women's organization as there is priority placed on meetings, encounters, and often consensus-based decision making. It is the body that is at the heart of many struggles, such as Take Back the Night marches and rallying for social causes (such as the Raging Grannies; e.g., Roy, 2012). A case that comes to mind from my qualitative research is Selma, a senior and a leader in a non-profit organization focused on women with disabilities, who talked about how she decided to forego basic captivity in her home to become the leader of an organization for people with disabilities. Selma moved from watching TV to saying "The hell with this!" as she began a lifelong pursuit of rights and policies for the disabled, especially women. Under her leadership, the organization that she is part of has been a space for learning and advocating for change. Through listening to her body, she has increasingly acknowledged the real need to become more involved in her community, and to become part of the disability social movement. For many women, it is the body— through its experience of intuition, pain, stress, or joy—that speaks to them and facilitates change. Yet, the body is mostly seen as the enemy—as the site of sickness, weight, and other issues. A close look at the experience in women's non-profit organizations helps to resist this narrow reading and to reclaim the body as a site of hope and change.

The body is also the place where the arts and music encounter the person and the issues requiring change. It is no accident that feminist popular education efforts are based in the body and movement, as recent collections such as one by Manicom and Walters (2012) illustrate. The body is the site for feminist popular theatre, for creative dance, and for resistance (Madres de Plaza Mayo). So, when a leader in a feminist organization in the community feels the stress of leading, of doing overwork for underpay, she may readily relate this as "in her body" or as causing "jealousy, feeling unequal, and that you are being treated differently." The other side, of course, is that joy and elation at effecting change are also felt in the body. The body is the place of incredible possibility, which is not acknowledged by traditional versions of transformative learning theory (see Mezirow, 1978).

Relationships and Transformation

Relationships—intricate and personal connections—are also an impetus for transformative learning, as acknowledged by theorists such as Taylor (2009). However, he stops short of naming their importance for women. It is likely that relationships are a very important aspect of women's transformation, as their ways of knowing are often connected and collaborative (Hayes and Flannery, 2000). Certainly, it is women who too often take on the burden of emotional labour or caring for participants, co-workers, and the community (Guenther, 2009). In the context of feminist non-profit organizations, relationships take on a particular significance as these organizations are oriented to the caring and support for women, often those at the grassroots.

Relationships were at the core of the successes in Second Wave feminism and even now in Third Wave feminism, despite the latter's attention to individuality and self-expression (Code, 2000). Caring relationships take quite a toll as a result of lack of resources, money, people, and support. Yet, time and again, women's centre directors and board members say that these collective struggles are all part of the process; they are integral to the lifelong learning journey in the organization.

Scholar Susan Bracken (2011) reminds us that women's organizations need to give themselves the freedom to be ordinary in these relationships—not to be flawless and to set the bar so as to avoid any difference and discord. Sheila, a director of a non-profit organization, talked about it this way:

> We talk it out and we discuss issues when they come up. Personally, I feel that healthy organizations do have conflict. I feel that conflict occurs when there is a difference of opinion or when others feel that they do not have a voice. When I experience conflict, I like to address it in a respectful way. If it is a conflict between a colleague and myself, I will sit down and talk to them about how I am feeling. I feel that conflict must be addressed in order for someone to feel respected and safe in an organization. I don't know how conflict is dealt with in other organizations in the community.

Sheila sees the conflict as part of the experience and at times necessary for change to come about. Community change and transformation take hard work and diligence and they call for creative solutions, not rules and rigid boundaries.

Another non-profit leader talked about her own interpretations of rules and boundaries, and how she had learned to negotiate these in ways that made sense to her and her ethics:

> Now I understand a whole lot more about boundaries and that kind of stuff than I did then. Yeah, technically speaking, I probably did overstep some of the boundaries by having this young woman as a guest in our home and by taking a very personal interest in helping her…. You know what, I'd do it again. There are times when you have to heed this stuff and times when you have to deliberately decide that the circumstances warrant you taking a different approach.

Of course, not every leader will (or should) transgress a boundary in this way, but the point is that she did what was authentic to her and she made a decision she could live with when faced with an incredibly difficult situation. Creative change takes bold moves like this.

Power and Context

Power is not an explicitly named dimension (or facilitator) of transformative learning theory, as the theory tends to be oriented to constructivism and humanism, which prioritize meaning making. Yet, my own studies of women in non-profit organizations do show that in naming and tracing power and its effects, we can deepen our understanding of how power works in women's non-profit organizations to facilitate personal and societal transformation.

Within a non-profit organization, located in and working for the community, power is a given, and it is helpful to see power as a source of creativity and change, not oppression. This is the kind of power that Mary Parker Follett (1924) envisaged, as shaping and being shaped by the people in an organization. It is the kind of power that can often be productive, for example, when it moves participants into collective action to demand change or when non-profit organizational leaders protest government cutbacks or unfair laws, and thus make change happen. On good days, this power is regenerative and can result in transformation. On bad days, it is less creative and more repressive. Here is how one leader of a women's centre described the use of power in the board and amongs its members, and the effect that it has had on her ability to be effective in creating change. Mary says:

> One of the things that has kept me going during some not terribly wonderful times internally has been the external battles... When things aren't going well inside the organization, when we've got a really strong rallying point, or, you know, the external enemy ... the government.

Power in this case is directed at the perceived enemy. From this perspective, it is women who are reworking power and, as Mary Follett Parker (1924) once argued, using more often "power with" and not "power over." Of course, there can be a repressive power, such as the clamping down on younger members by the original founders, but there can also be the resistance to that power which is, and can be, productive (English and Peters, 2011). This oppressive power also meets resistance from younger members who ask for space to lead and take part in the organization, to claim their voice as the new leaders. Kate, a young woman, related her own experience of trying to get the original board members (founders) to acknowledge new laws around contracts, hiring, and negotiations:

> We've just had a great big to-do over a contract ... the contract is outdated. We heard howls of protest saying we've never been sued yet and we haven't had any problems and it's worked for us. We had all kinds of trouble getting them to see this was not 30 years ago, that we are living in an electronic time now.

In her willingness to push forward and to challenge the old guard, Kate has been able to create space for younger members, to help the women's movement welcome youth and new voices, to resist stagnation, and to join with other movements to create societal change. She is enacting a creative form of change that is intergenerational and spirited. While the designated leader in any non-profit organization must work to keep the coffers full, which can be very hard to do when the expected support is not forthcoming, the undesignated leaders such as Kate also have a key role to play in facilitating change. And the older leaders do, too. Annie said that for most of her five years, she "was a junior person ... now with them [the founders] gone, it is like this little vacuum; all of a sudden it's like who is going to do that now?" There is valuable recognition at times of the varying age cohorts and levels of expertise needed to move forward.

Within any organization or collective of persons, the issues of who sets direction and who takes responsibility are at the forefront. In a women's non-profit organization, this is no different. With stress on these organizations to build and grow, to include young women and women of difference, and to manage the tension between inclusion and constancy, the challenge is all the harder. An understanding of how power functions and how it can facilitate transformational change is important, especially for organizations that may think that peace and harmony are the ideal. Indeed, creativity requires movement, challenge, and a variety of views to happen. In recognizing the location of power and how it functions, we can strengthen our understanding of transformative learning theory and community-based organizations.

Time and Age

Although transformative learning theorists have come to recognize that change can be incremental (occurring over time) or epochal (sudden and enormous; see Cranton, 2006), there has been no specific attempt to name time as a facilitator of transformative learning for women. Yet, time and age have a special place in the transformation related to women's non-profit organizations engaged in work for the long haul and for societal, environmental, and economic change. Shelters for women who are victims of abuse are part of a lifelong effort to create alternatives for women and to change the relationships between men and women to make them equal. The nature of this feminist work—support, struggle, resistance—is such that it requires a long-term commitment from those involved. As with all organizations, some members and leaders age with the organization and others join at different points, and all are longing for a better future. These women have to be committed to incremental change and to the hope for transformation over time.

Commitment over time and contributions from people of different ages are both important elements. Women in non-profit organizations often work towards change over a lifetime, with guidelines and structures in place to support such change (e.g., boards of directors, meetings, consensus). Both time and age—knowing over time that not all problems have to be solved today and that some things take time—can be facilitators for the transformation that women's organizations and the social movement of feminism(s) envisage. Despite possible frustration with government agencies and regressive policies, there is a need to wait and listen and to keep inching forward. Sudden results in governance are rare and one needs to think long and hard about them.

When one non-profit leader talked about how to bring in new and younger people, she remembered fondly back to her early experiences in the association:

> An older woman said, "You young ones are doing such a good job!" And I thought, she never stood up and said, "This is all baloney!" ... I found that so supportive. I'm sure she didn't always think that [what we were doing was good], but she encouraged [us].

The excitement over new voices creates a sense of possibility and the vitality for an organization to flourish. Acceptance and willingness to encourage, to wait, as hard as it is, leaves doors open and helps us to work our way forward to creative change. And of course, societal transformation can be problematic for even the most open-minded. As society's views on women, gender relations, and identity change over time, members of a non-profit centre—even one comprised mainly of feminists—can be as slow to change as members of the general public. In one organization, there was resistance around group composition. A leader reported on this resistance:

> When one of the members said, "I don't want to come because this is gays and straights together," Naomi responded, "Well, you know, that's our law. You have a right to believe what you do, but you don't have a right to say how they live."

Clearly, then, there is a need to avoid making assumptions about what everyone in an organization believes about any one topic or issue. Non-profit organizations, if they are healthy, feature a diversity of voices. These organizations typically value grassroots decision making, and thus can face the same difficulty in making decisions as do other groups.

Creative Transformation: Discussion

This discussion of creatively oriented change contributes to the theory of transformative learning, which has largely privileged western women and their personal growth and development. The theory, by and large, has bypassed the notions of critical and social transformation necessary to transform civil society, especially as it pertains to women. This chapter helps address the lacuna not only in the literature on women and learning, especially women's transformative learning, but also the literature on feminists who are engaged in societal transformation.

A danger of the traditional writing and thinking about transformative learning for women is that it tends to essentialize or focus on the breaking points, the turning points, and the negative experiences that women have. Also, it tends to see age and slow change as problematic. I would argue our focus has to shift to Tisdell's (2012) ideas around creatively transforming our understanding of relationships in the name of social transformation and creatively transforming the place and the role of women within that movement. There is no real learning if it does not focus on possibility and challenge, or critique and creativity, as all are essential to the slow growth of life in organizations. If there is no life and no creativity—no purposeful going forward—then organizations die and the movement dies, too. Creative change can be facilitated by paying closer attention to the role of the body, relationships, power, time, and age.

Historically, women's organizations in Canada, such as the Women's Institutes and the Women's Christian Temperance Union (WCTU), have found ways to be innovative—for example, by creating visible protest around temperance and suffrage, as well as including younger women and even male allies. Our present time is not much different in that the challenges are huge but our commitments are still strong. Attending to marginalization, inequality, and abuse is important, and we must also look to the transformative potential that exists in de Saint-Exupéry's "longing for the sea" and to the creative impulse that undergirds all meaningful transformation (Tisdell, 2012). Heeding creativity allows us to think of how we might negotiate conflict and challenges; the ability to move beyond critique is essential to understanding transformation. What I have found in my own studies is that women's lives are forever altered by their involvement with each/one another, and especially involvement with issues that have a material dimension—food, clothing, health, shelter, education, and safety—for women. The potential for personal and social transformative learning in non-profit organizations that deal with these issues is immense, as they seed the possibility of collective and political action to transform society.

Women experience transformation in their own lives through relationships, the body, and exercises of power, and the non-profit organization is transformed in the process. Critical and creative transformative learning theory is enhanced by examination of the experience in women's non-profit organizations. We need to be people of hope, of trust in the long haul and in one another. Even this short glance at women's organizations points to how we can shift our thinking to "longing for the sea."

Endnote

[1] Non-profit is the word used here as it is the one most often used in Canada and the United States to describe organizations that are in the civil society sector and that are not oriented to profit. In contrast, the term non-governmental organization (NGO) is used by international agencies and development workers.

References

- Alpízar, L. and Wilson, S. (2005, March). Making waves: How young women can (and do) transform organizations and movements. *Spotlight*, 5, 1-15.
- Bracken, S. (2011). Understanding program planning theory and practice in a feminist community-based organization. *Adult Education Quarterly*, 61(2), 121-138.
- Clover, D. E. (2012). Feminist artists and popular education: The creative turn. In L. Manicom and S. Walters (Eds.), *Feminist Popular Education in Transnational Debates: Building Pedagogies of Possibility* (pp. 193-208). New York, NY: Palgrave MacMillan.
- Code, L. (Ed.).(2000). *Encyclopaedia of Feminist Theories*. New York, NY: Routledge.
- Cranton, P. (2006). *Understanding and Promoting Transformative Learning* (2nd ed.). San Francisco: Jossey-Bass.
- de Saint-Exupéry, A. (1950). *Wisdom of the Sands*. New York, NY: Harcourt and Brace.
- English, L. M. (2005). Foucault, feminists and funders: A study of power and policy in feminist organizations. *Studies in the Education of Adults*, 37(2), 137-150.
- English, L. M. (2006). A Foucauldian reading of learning in feminist non-profit organizations. *Adult Education Quarterly*, 56(2), 85-101.
- English, L. M. (2007). Feminists, factions, and fictions in rural Canada. In L.A. Duran, N.D. Payne, and A. Russo (Eds.), *Building Feminist Movements and Organizations* (pp. 87-95). London and New York: Zed Publications.
- English, L. M. (2011). Power, resistance and informal pathways: Lifelong learning in feminist nonprofit organizations. In S. Jackson, K. Thomas, and I. Malcolm (Eds.), *Gendered Choices and Transitions in Lifelong Learning: Part-Time Pathways, Full-Time Lives* (pp. 209-226). London, UK: Springer.
- English, L. M. and Irving, C. J. (2012). Women and transformative learning. In E.W. Taylor and P. Cranton (Eds.), *Handbook of Transformative Learning* (pp. 245-259). San Francisco: Jossey-Bass.
- English, L. M. and Peters, N. (2012). Transformative learning in feminist organizations: A feminist interpretive inquiry. *Adult Education Quarterly*, 62(2), 103-119. doi:10.1177/0741713610392771.
- English, L. M. and Peters, N. (2011). Founders' Syndrome in women's nonprofit organizations: Implications for practice and organizational life. *Nonprofit Management and Leadership*, 22(2), 159-171. doi:10.1002/nml.20047.
- Follett, M. P. (1924). *Creative Experience*. New York, NY: Longman Green and Co.
- Guenther, K. J. (2009). The impact of emotional opportunities on the emotion cultures of feminist organizations. *Gender & Society*, 23(3), 337-362.
- Hasenfeld, Y. and Gidron, B. (2005). Understanding multi-purpose hybrid voluntary organizations: The contributions of theories on civil society, social movements and non-profit organizations. *Journal of Civil Society*, 1(2), 97-112.
- Irving, C. and English, L.M. (2011). Community in cyberspace: Gender, social movement learning and the Internet. *Adult Education Quarterly*, 61(3), 262-278.
- Manicom, L. and Walters, S. (Eds.). (2012). *Feminist Popular Education in Transnational Debates: Building Pedagogies of Possibility*. New York, NY: Palgrave Macmillan.
- Mezirow, J. (1978). *Education for Perspective Transformation; Women's Re-Entry Programs in Community Colleges*. New York, NY: Teacher's College, Columbia University.
- Mezirow, J., Taylor, E. W., and Associates (Eds.) (2009). *Transformative Learning in Practice: Insights from Community, Workplace, and Higher Education*. San Francisco, CA: Jossey-Bass.
- Muthien, B. (2006). Leadership and renewal: Cite, site and sight in women's movements. *Development*, 49(1), 99-101.
- Roy, C. (2002). The transformative power of creative dissent. The Raging Grannies' legacy. In E. O'Sullivan, A. Morrell, and M.A. O'Connor (Eds.), *Expanding the Boundaries of Transformative Learning. Essays on Theory and Praxis* (pp. 257-271). New York and Basingstoke, UK: Palgrave.
- Scott, E. K. (2005). Beyond tokenism: The making of racially diverse feminist organizations. *Social Problems*, 52(2), 232-254.
- Stoddart, J. (2014). Thérèse Casgrain. *The Canadian Encyclopedia*. (Revised by M.-E .Lambert and A. McIntosh, 2014; originally prepared in 2008) http://www.thecanadianencyclopedia.ca/en/article/therese-casgrain.
- Taylor, E. W. T. (2009). Fostering transformative learning. In J. Mezirow, E. W. Taylor, and Associates (Eds.), *Transformative Learning in Practice: Insights from Community, Workplace, and Higher Education* (pp. 3-17). San Francisco: Jossey-Bass.
- Tisdell, E. J. (2012). Themes and variations of transformational learning: Interdisciplinary perspectives on forms that transform. In E.W. Taylor and P. Cranton (Eds.), *Handbook of Transformative Learning* (pp. 21-36). San Francisco: Jossey-Bass.
- Wollebæk, D. and Selle, P. (2004). The role of women in the transformation of the organizational society in Norway. *Nonprofit and Voluntary Sector Quarterly*, 33, 120.

Acknowledgements

- Thanks to Cynthia Flood, Isabel's niece and to Jonathan Fisher, MEd student, for their assistance with our research into Isabel's life.

References

- Butterwick, S., & Fisher, J. (2014). The vision and pedagogical sensibility of Isabel Wilson: Giving credit where credit is due. In S. Imel & G. Bersch (Eds.), The Handbook of North American Early Women Adult Educators: 1925-1950 (pp. 253-259). Charlotte, NC: Information Age Publishers.

- Canadian Association for Adult Education. (December 7, 1950). Equal pay for equal work: Are women getting a fair deal? Citizens' Forum.

- Corbett, E.A. (1957). *We Have with Us Tonight*. Toronto: The Ryerson Press.

- Faris, R. (1975). *The Passionate Educators: Voluntary Associations and the Struggle for Control of Adult Educational Broadcasting in Canada 1919-52*. Toronto: Peter Martin Associates Limited.

- Flood, C. (n.d.). *A Life in Quotations*. Unpublished memoir. Vancouver, BC.

- Funeral Service Program. (1983, October 27). Biographical Note. Private Collection of Cynthia Flood. Vancouver, BC.

- McKenzie, R. (1970, October 23). [Letter to Isabel Wilson]. Private Collection of Cynthia Flood. Vancouver, BC.

- Sandwell, R.W. (2012). Read, listen, discuss, act: Adult education, rural citizenship and the National Farm Radio Forum, 1941-1965. *Historical Studies in Education*, v. 24, n.1, pp. 170-194.

- Wilson, I. (1980). *Citizens' Forum: "Canada's National Platform."* Ontario Institute for Studies in Education, Department of Adult Education, Toronto.

Photo courtesy of Cynthia Flood (Isabel's niece).

This vignette was prepared by Shauna Butterwick.

Isabel Wilson was born Mary Isabel Creighton in Toronto in 1904, the youngest of three children and the only daughter of Laura Harvie Creighton and William Black Creighton, who was a Methodist minister and an editor of two Christian newspapers in Toronto. She attended Howard Park Public (primary) School, Humberside Collegiate (secondary), and the University of Toronto's Library School. Graduating in 1926, she began working in the Toronto library system. In 1938, she married Harold Godfrey Wilson. Isabel moved to Saskatoon for a brief time, where she took on a "radio job" (Flood, n.d., p.11), returning to Toronto in 1944, mainly to care for her ailing parents. After they died, Isabel and her husband remained in Toronto, where Harold died in 1971. She and her husband did not have any children but Isabel had close relationships with some of her nieces and nephews.

In 1944 Isabel was hired by the Canadian Association for Adult Education (CAAE) to be the National Secretary of the popular CAAE and CBC (Canadian Broadcasting Corporation) joint project called Citizens' Forum (CF). Her previous experience in radio broadcasting gave her an advantage when she began working on CF in 1944. As National Secretary of CF, Isabel oversaw the research and editing of more than 300 listening group pamphlets.

CF ran for 20 years and was one of the CAAE's most high-profile and ambitious projects, regarded as a key contributor to the creation of the post-war ideal of a unified Canada. Isabel was not only responsible for the research but also for crafting a balanced view of oftentimes controversial topics covered in the study pamphlets. In her report on this 20-year project, Isabel wrote, "The world must be rebuilt, old errors and injustices swept away, economic and political wrongs righted" (Wilson, 1980, p. 4). Isabel's commitment to impartiality meant that no pamphlet author, other than the CAAE, was ever identified. While there were many volunteers contributing to the study pamphlets' content, it was Isabel who held the process together.

One of the CF topics that Isabel was particularly passionate about was the 1950 CAAE pamphlet and campaign called "Equal Pay for Work of Equal Value: Are Women Getting a Fair Deal?" This pamplet had the highest distribution numbers compared with any other single CF program. Along with other feminist colleagues within the CAAE, such as Clare Clark (who became the head of CAAE's Joint Planning Commission), Isabel was instrumental in ensuring the great success of this consciousness-raising campaign that pushed the boundaries of Canadian societal norms.

CF was a highly successful, widely popular, and technologically groundbreaking instance of Canadian Adult Education through mass media. While CF was a joint endeavour of the CAAE and the CBC, the actual curriculum and Adult Education pedagogy were shaped by Isabel Wilson, who remained the uncredited editor of these pamphlets for much of CF's 20-year broadcast run. The more than 300 CF study pamphlets that Wilson edited are clear evidence of the power of her words and her deep commitment to her work.

Vignette: Isabel Wilson, 1904–1983

Teaching adult literacy in a landscape of inequalities requires a complexity of practice and skills that go beyond a "kind and patient" disposition.
Photo: Courtesy of Suzanne Smythe.

24

"Neither Kind nor Patient"
Canadian Women Literacy Educators Working in the Spaces of Neo-Liberalism

> [Kindness and patience] are virtues associated most closely with women, and the stereotype raises its ugly head again: lower level students, adult basic literacy students, can (should) be taught by women because of their warm and nurturing natures; students at a higher level need to be taught by people with real skills and knowledge of subject matter.
> —Kate Nonesuch, 2013, para. 3

As an undergraduate student in Montréal in the late 1980s, I attended a two-hour literacy training session by Laubach Literacy's "Each One, Teach One" literacy project. According to Laubach, "the 'Each One, Teach One' philosophy means that if you can read, you can teach another person to read. No teaching experience is required."

Suzanne Smythe

After a brief orientation, and armed with word and spelling games to play with adults who wanted to improve their reading, I was placed in a parent education class in the community of Saint-Henri in the southwest of Montréal. The class met one morning a week and my job was to help the parents with their English and French literacy skills.

All these parents were women and, after taking their older children to school, they arrived at the community centre with younger children and babies, who during the class sat or slept in someone's lap or played on the floor. The space was small, the tables rickety, and the toys and books supplied for the women and children had seen better days.

In my first few weeks at the Saint-Henri program I sat awkwardly, looking for an opportunity to impart my literacy knowledge. Some of the other tutors, more experienced, would make a show of reading and discussing vocabulary worksheets, at least for the first ten minutes or so, and then other texts would appear on the table: bills, letters from the school, rental notices, government forms, health information from the clinic, or a flyer about an employment training program.

Still other texts circulated in the air: "Where is there affordable childcare?" "Anyone know of an apartment for rent?" "There is chicken on sale at Provigo." These were the literacies of women in Canada raising young children, often alone and on low incomes, of which I had no experience or knowledge. I could decode the words on the page but I knew nothing of their meanings or how to interpret them, nor did I have any experience teaching adults, or anyone else for that matter. I was a novice in this setting and everyone knew it. Yet, this was considered less important than a caring and patient disposition and a desire to help: "If you care, you can teach someone to read."

Literacy, Inequality, and Gender Relations

Along with Nonesuch (2013), Belzer (2006) critiques the Each One, Teach One and other volunteer literacy tutoring models:

> It is poor instructional planning to match those who experienced the most difficulty learning to read (for whatever reason) with tutors who may be the least experienced, least trained, and potentially least committed practitioners in the field (Sandlin and St. Clair, 2005); those who read at a higher level are frequently placed in classes with paid (and presumably better trained) teachers. (Belzer, 2006, p. 651)

In a field in which 86% of workers are women (CLLN, 2013, p. 4) and volunteers make up over half of the positions, the organization of adult literacy classes suggests how gender, race, and class shape how literacy work is carried out, valued, and administered.

I joined Each One, Teach One at the time of growing panic around the literacy crisis in Canada, captured by Kathleen Rockhill (1987) as the emergence of literacy as a form of governance:

> This shift from "literacies" to "literacy" as ideology is integral to its use as a means of governance. Whereas once the state feared the development of literacy among the working class, by the mid-nineteenth century, literacy was being mandated as a means of social and moral regulation in industrialised countries. (Rockhill, 1987, p. 156)

As Rockhill (1987) observed, literacy became a prerequisite to equality; an "it" that individuals, particularly low-income, racialized women, had a responsibility to acquire in the interests of good mothering and good economic citizenship. Yet as dire as the need for women's literacy is made out to be, the solution is the mobilization of an army of well-meaning, well-educated volunteers, many of whom are also women. Luttrell (1996) pointed out that this contradiction between the "crisis" in literacy education and the marginalization of literacy education itself as a form of educational practice stems from "twisted" gender relations that make it difficult to distinguish "what is labour and what is love" (p. 249). Luttrell (1996) noted that the well-worn belief that "if you can read and you are caring, you can teach" makes invisible the considerable skills required to support literacy learning among new readers and writers. Griffith and Smith (1991) link these "twisted" gender relations to the reliance of modern educational systems on a gender division of labour in which women are depended upon to carry out basic education, whether for children or adults, as an extension of their caregiving roles.

These gender relations have become more deeply entrenched in the unfolding neo-liberal education policy regimes the past thirty years. Neo-liberalism is both an economic ideology and a practice of governance, recognizable as a vision of a free market and economic growth generated by "competition, tax reductions, deregulation, trade liberalization, incentives to the private sector and reductions in the role of government and in public expenditures" (Carpenter, Weber, and Schugurensky, 2012, p. 147). The sum total of this global educational vision is a much-reduced role of government services in the lives of citizens and a faith in the market to distribute equality of economic and educational outcomes. In democracies, neo-liberalism requires the creation of a particular kind of economic and educational subject, one who will "invest" in herself, take responsibility for her choices and skills, and ensure these skills align to ever-shifting labour market needs. Atkinson (2013), borrowing from

Rose (1999), describes this as *responsibilization*, a technology of neo-liberalism in which "subjects are responsible for meeting their own basic needs and governing themselves. Those who are not economically self-sufficient and actively investing in their own development are constructed as a problem" (Atkinson, 2013, p. 93).

Women's Literacy in the In-Between Spaces

As I revisit the work of Rockhill (1987), Griffith and Smith (1990), and Luttrell (1996) in writing this chapter, I am struck by their astute sketching of what we now recognize as neo-liberalism, manifest as a set of unruly contradictions: Volunteerism in literacy programs is promoted as expectations rise for children's and adult's literacy; meanings of literacy are simplified and narrowed amidst the complexities of people's lives; and the governance of literacy programs is devolved to poorly paid or voluntary community groups as regimes of auditing and regulation intensify.

I explore these contradictions through my experiences as a literacy educator and researcher in Montréal, Québec (for a short time), Johannesburg, South Africa, and Vancouver, Canada. Because neo-liberal policies circulate in the local and the global, this narrative spans kitchen tables in Vancouver, church basements in Johannesburg, and literacy research projects across Canada. Through anecdotes and everyday texts, encounters with literacy policy flavours of the month and my interview research with adult educators about their professional practice, I trace in the pages that follow one trajectory of the unfolding of neo-liberal governance in Canada. I argue that in the past thirty years women's literacy education has become more deeply marginalized, but women have also taken up the contradictory spaces of neo-liberalism for important forms of critique and social action.

Volunteerism and Standardization

When I graduated from university, I left the Saint-Henri program in Montréal, joining a sea of volunteers to drift through this and so many other literacy programs on my way to other things. I moved back to Vancouver and worked as an assistant in a childcare centre, saving money to travel. But I missed the Saint-Henri literacy group, working with people side by side, reading and thinking about texts together, building relationships and meanings that went far beyond menial worksheet exercises. I started to do some volunteer literacy work at Carnegie Learning Centre in downtown Vancouver in the evenings. It was near where I lived at the time, and where I met a woman I will call "D." D had approached the Learning Centre looking for help to improve her reading and writing. Her children were in their teens and about to graduate from secondary school and she and her husband had plans to start a small business together. Her life was changing, and she wanted to fulfill a long-held intention to read a novel, and to write confidently without relying on her children or husband.

D and I met at the Carnegie once a week. We read together, she wrote to me, I wrote back to her, we read one another's writing together and she developed her own voice, reflecting on her life as a mother, wife, and worker. When Vancouver's dark winter descended, we started to meet at her house because she did not feel safe walking to the Learning Centre at night. We sat side by side in her kitchen while her kids tip-toed in and out, pouring themselves a glass of milk, making a peanut-butter sandwich, and glancing over at us. Her husband greeted me when I arrived but left us on our own. "This is something for me," D would say. Over the next few months we continued to meet regularly and D made plans to return to college. She began to take an active role in the house finances, reading the bills and planning the budget, tasks that had previously belonged to her husband. This put a strain on their relationship and, by the time I told D that I was going to South Africa for the summer, she informed me that she and her husband were separating.

Our lives went separate ways, too, and the letters we first exchanged when I was in South Africa eventually stopped. But I still think of D when I pass by where she used to live. I wonder how she is, more now as I realize with hindsight that our time together traced well-worn pathways laid by women who pursue education for purposes "beyond the everyday" (Horsman, 1990) and who carve out, with much struggle, a space for "literacies for themselves" (Mace, 1998).

I ended up moving to South Africa, to the lively inner-city Johannesburg neighbourhood of Yeoville. Two evenings a week I tutored at the Yeoville Adult Learning Group, in the basement of St. Mark's Church. This was in 1993 and 1994, the dying days of Apartheid; Mandela had been released, but Apartheid geographies were very much in place and most South Africans had to migrate to mines or to cities to find work as domestic workers and garden boys, living in the peripheral spaces of the rooftop rooms and khayas (out-buildings) of their employers. If their employers had no more need for them that day, these women arrived for classes after dinner, with their youngest children tied to their backs, to learn to read and write in English. The coordinator of the program was organized and determined, grouping learners according to their performance on literacy placement tests he had designed in-house. The women crowded into small, cubby-like rooms separated by cardboard or thin plywood, designed for the children of the Sunday school. Babies slept or observed closely as their mothers and grandmothers bowed over *Learn and Teach* and *Active Voice*, Freireian-inspired adult learning materials that reflected the voices of South African adults. They were oriented to learning about and preparing for a new, non-racial, democratic South Africa. No churned-out worksheets on domestic vocabulary here. People were learning for a new life.

It was ironic indeed, when the new South Africa was born, that these learning materials and their literacies of aspiration were swept away in the new "Adult Basic Education and Training" (ABET) curriculum, designed to streamline, centralize, standardize, and measure adult learning activities along a grid of learning outcomes aligned to various levels of certification. The new regulatory frameworks reached into the Yeoville Adult Learning Group as some of the more proficient learners began to prepare for and write exams to climb the ABET ladder. All this was to ensure that South African adults had access to high-quality educational opportunities to prepare them for new economic participation in the new South Africa. H.S. Bhola (1997) captured the moment thus:

> The long struggle for freedom in South Africa had been carried out in the name of all the suffering people [...] all sworn to negating the legacy of Apartheid and to give all citizens, black and white, a place in the sun in a non-racial democracy (p. 5).

But Bhola (1997) warned that by emphasizing the "T" in ABET, and orienting adult learning to the needs of the formal economy, the new ABET apparatus "has squeezed out of adult basic education the multitudes not in the formal economy. In addition, education for democratization of communities and institutions is completely sidelined" (p. 6). Betsy Alkenbrack, a Canadian literacy educator who also worked in the Yeoville Adult Learning Group, put it this way: "The government is now the driving force for adult literacy rather than a fragmented NGO movement. But I worry about the loss of creativity and learner-centredness" (2001, p. 2).

Herein lies the contradiction of adult literacy education work for and by women: the imperative of access to literacy education as a social and economic right can lead to the installation of testing regimes and standardizations in teaching practice that takes the heart and meaning out of literacy education as a responsive practice attuned to people's actual lives and uses for literacy.

Women's Right to Literacy for Others: Rising Expectations and Literacy Cuts

In the small, dark room in Saint-Henri, Montréal, in D's kitchen in Vancouver, and in the church basement in Johannesburg, with its small cubbies designed for Sunday School children, women's literacy programs that I experienced in the 1990s took place in spaces designed for other purposes; and more often than not, women's learning was harnessed for the benefit of others: children, employers, healthy populations, democratic and productive nations. Eldred, Pant, Nabi, Chopra, Nussey, and Brown (2014) capture this enduring tension in women's literacy:

> Much of the discussion and debate around women's literacy and learning reflects a functional perspective that involves advocating learning for specific outcomes relating to, for example, health or economic development, rather than for personal purposes, growth and fulfillment. A different perspective, a rights-based approach, advocates lifelong learning programs that enable women to participate in all levels of society as equal human beings and to realise the intrinsic value of education. For many millions of women, this includes developing their literacy knowledge and skills. (p. 659)

A "rights-based" approach to literacy for women was challenged by the rise of the family literacy movement. When I returned to Canada in the early 2000s, the clear message was that women's literacy was important to the extent that women raised healthy and school-ready children: The dictum "teach the mother and teach the child," Sticht and McDonald (1990, p. 1) argued, captured the problem of the "intergenerational cycle of literacy" (p. 3-4), in which illiterate mothers were believed to pose health and economic risks to the broader population because they raised illiterate children. Mace (1998) challenged the formulation of this "intergenerational cycle," observing that the focus on mothers' literacy skills coincided with cuts in public education:

> The evidence of the literacy problem in industrialized countries with mass schooling systems has revealed that schools cannot alone meet this need. Families must therefore be recruited to do their bit, too. This is where the spotlight falls on the mother. She it is who must ensure that the young child arrives at school ready for school literacy, and preferably already literate. (p. 5)

Over time, the family movement has contributed to new subjectivities in which families have come to been seen as responsible for the educational outcomes of their children. The smooth transition to formal schooling and education "success" has become an individual family accomplishment in which governments play a supporting role through the publication of advice texts and the creation of parenting centres to help parents and guardians fulfill their roles as "their child's first and most important teachers" (Achieve BC, 2005, p. 2).

The family literacy movement also challenged the work of adult literacy education. It became more difficult to receive funding for adult literacy programs that did not involve an intergenerational literacy or parenting component. Women care about their children and certainly many women come to literacy programs hoping to find pathways into work and lives that help them to support their children financially and educationally. In this way, family literacy programs were able to exploit this human pull to caring. Yet, even when caring for children and loved ones are at the centre of people's motivations for learning, this is not the sum total of people's learning identities. The problem of how to tell a story of women's right to education without abstracting women from their webs of family and social relations, is also a problem of how to capture the power of literacies education beyond the limits of individual skill for entry-level employment. The Research-in-Practice movement represented one of the spaces created by educators to tell these complex stories.

Research-in-Practice: Narrow Literacies and Complex Lives

In 2001, adult literacy educator Evelyn Battell responded to the policy and research emphasis in Canada on large-scale surveys and standardized literacy measurement apparatus in a ground-breaking, collaborative practitioner inquiry project entitled "Naming the Magic." This work called attention to intricate, life-changing learning outcomes that defied measurement by the rather blunt instruments that tracked rapidity of literacy gains up a ladder. Naming the Magic was one of the first projects to emerge from the Research-in-Practice in Adult Literacy (RIPAL) movement in Canada. Exercising decision-making power that government employees could only dream of today, Yvette Souque of the National Literacy Secretariat and Audrey Thomas of the BC Ministry of Advanced Education created a funding climate that encouraged literacy educators to engage in research into their own teaching practices. This fulfilled the goals of the Ministries at the time to enhance theory-building, professional learning, and instructional approaches in literacy education. But the RIPAL movement was also a space to counter simplistic castings of literacy as equated with employment and "success," with more complex accounts of the actualities of people's lives and learning.

Another collaborative inquiry project, "Hardwired for Hope" (Battell, Gesser, Rose, Sawyer, & Twiss, 2004), documented how practitioners conceptualized their adult literacy work in the context of deep and ongoing cuts to their programs and to the social safety nets upon which many of their learners depended. They framed adult literacy work at the critical intersection of caring and politics:

> The majority of students find real power, not to mention pleasure, in finding they are not alone; they have situations, problems and learning challenges just like others. They can also learn from each other and become politicized by each other. (Politicized means beginning to see things as located in the culture/society/community, not just in themselves, but beginning to see in more specifics how this might work and how they might work to change things) (p. 74). (parentheses in text).

In their interviews with adult literacy educators in British Columbia, Battell, Gesser, et al. (2004) created a portrait of "effective literacy educators" as those who oriented their instructional strategies and program design to recognize that literacy education cannot solve (and nor does it cause) entrenched gender, class, and racial inequalities, but literacy classes can be a place to make these inequalities more visible for discussion and social action, as this interview respondent explains:

I became deeply involved in women's initiatives as it was called at that time, trying to get some support for women in abusive relationships. I felt like that was really connected to the college and to the programs that we were trying to run, but it was triggered by working within the college realizing I cannot begin to talk about adding fractions to somebody who's in an abusive relationship and there's no services in Grand Forks. They have to leave. So that was the impetus to basically spearhead with other interested parties the services for women and children in violent situations (Battell, Gesser, Rose, Sawyer & Tavis, pp. 96-97).

The collegial working relationship the literacy field enjoyed with the National Literacy Secretariat came to an end in 2006. Riding on "a trend of distrust of institutions, particularly public institutions, politicians, and public officials" (Hayes, 2013, para. 7), the Conservative government (an alliance of the Progressive Conservative and Reform Parties) was elected on a mandate to increase accountability and end perceived government corruption. The NLS, along with other government departments, were subject to increased oversight and regulation, and a complete re-working of their relationships to their constituents: "We were no longer able to work side-by-side with partners to develop proposals and strategies. What once was an effort in community development now became transactional—you applied, we supplied" (Hayes, 2013, para. 7). This transition marked the emergence of new relations of accountability for the literacy field (currently renamed the Literacy and Essential Skills or LES field), in the form of more stringent reporting requirements and onerous funding application processes for a smaller funding pot. The International Adult Literacy Skills Survey (IALSS) and LES (Literacy and Essential Skills) frameworks were given new prominence, as federally funded literacy and skills training programs were required to demonstrate: "a) whether "clients" became employed or b) how many levels up the IALS Levels ladder literacy skills increase based on pre- and post-tests (from Levels 1 or 2 to Level 3)" (Hayes, 2013, para. 4).

Before 2006, many of the regulatory regimes that narrowed and constrained literacy education work were implemented by a strong, hands-on government presence. This began to change in the late 2000s, when the new regimes of accountability were accompanied by a devolution of literacy work to communities. Devolving power to communities to decide what kinds of literacy education they most need was an attractive alternative to standardized programming that excluded so many people. But it also further de-valued literacy education work. This brings us to the final contradiction, one that defines the current neo-liberal moment.

Communities as Caring Spaces and Intensified Audit and Regulation

Literacy Now is a BC government initiative introduced in 2007 after Vancouver-Whistler won the bid to host the 2010 Winter Olympics. The initiative promised to bring sustainability to the literacy field by way of a legacy of the Vancouver/Whistler Winter Olympics. The mission of Literacy Now was to encourage communities to "identify local literacy needs and increase participation, sustainability and performance through partnerships, mentoring and communities" (Walker, 2008, p. 464). Communities were asked to form committees of literacy stakeholders, including school districts, libraries, adult learning centres, local businesses, early learning organizations, and even police, to identify literacy assets and gaps in their community and to develop an action plan to address the community's greatest priorities. Each group was awarded $10,000 to hire a coordinator to guide the community planning process, and an additional $30,000 to implement their literacy plan over three years. Eventually 102 communities in BC had a literacy plan.

Literacy Now involves a shift in responsibility for literacy planning, delivery, and funding from government ministries of education to local communities, non-governmental organizations, and new social enterprise and corporate entities; all in an effort to create a learning community in which "all participate and contribute to sustain and enhance the benefits of citizenship in a free and democratic society" (Legacies Now, 2006, p. 72). But it was never clear who the "community" should include. And as well-meaning as the planning and coordinating committees are, in the absence of a coordinated vision of adult literacy education in BC, committees can be swayed by dominant voices that prefer to focus on literacy programs for young children and family literacy rather than adults. In interviews I carried out in 2012 about community literacy programs, one respondent replied, "I believe when we began funding these [community literacy] programs, we all thought the target to be adults who are not able to read … but this is not always so" (Personal communication, May 20, 2012). Of the 102 participating communities, most coordinators are paid about $20 per hour and 98 percent are women. These coordinators keep the roundtables going, relying on community partnerships and the sharing of resources, on donations from local employers (sometimes), and on volunteers to do actual literacy education work. Literacy educators voice their concerns that a few hundred dollars for a literacy program will not improve literacy levels:

> Due to the seriousness of the latest economic downturn to the resource industries, many families suffering from poverty—affecting housing, transportation, utilities, mental health (depression); ability to access services is impacted; motivation to attend literacy services is not seen as a priority when people have personal barriers that are a higher priority. (Personal communication, March 26, 2013)

Indeed, expectations for literacy outcomes and accountability requirements often outstrip the resources at hand. Literacy coordinators file annual reports of their activities with detailed statistical records, evidence of social and economic change, social cohesion, and other achievements that flow from community work and from the very small amount of money they have to make stretch. But these efforts never seem to result in increased support, and some literacy workers have expressed doubt whether government employees even read these reports.

Given the high expectations and anemic financial support, why don't these communities simply stop doing the work? The answer was brought home to me recently in a conversation in a community centre about how to sustain a digital literacy program with no funding for computers, tutors, or Internet modems. The outreach worker remarked as she prepared to leave: "The thing is, they know that we will continue this work even when they cut our funding because they know that we can't turn our backs on our community."

Conclusions: Powerful Caring and Literacy

I have traced in this chapter an assemblage of personal experiences, research insights, and critical moments in literacy education that tell one story of adult literacy as invisible women's work. The complexity of practices and skills required to support adult literacy learning in a landscape of inequalities is subsumed in representations of literacy education as a project of charity, an extension of women's traditional work as caregivers requiring little skill beyond a "kind and patient" disposition.

So, rather than settling for policy tinkering to make things a little better (Atkinson, 2013), my hope is that literacy workers will *lose* patience as they tell difficult and complex stories about the realities of the work. Indeed, it is in the everyday teaching and learning in church basements, at kitchen tables, in community centres, on collaborative inquiry projects, and in community literacy planning, where we find forms of solidarity and resistance that may be, in Foucault's terms, "a starting point for an opposing strategy" (pp. 100-101), one in which literacy work and caring are powerfully and politically intertwined.

References

- Achieve BC (2005). *Reading for Families*. Retrieved November 21, 2014 from: http://www2.gov.bc.ca/gov/DownloadAsset?assetId=D73550A71FCA4EDF8B4090231FB9E76E&filename=reading_for_families.pdf.

- Alkenbrack, B. (2001). *Letters Home*. Literacy BC: Vancouver.

- Atkinson, T. (2013). *Negotiating Responsibilization: Power at the Threshold of Capable Literate Conduct in Ontario*. Unpublished PhD thesis. Ontario Institute for Studies in Education: University of Toronto.

- Ball, S. (2010). New states, new governance and new education policy. In Apple, M., Ball, S., and Gandin, L. (2010). *The Routledge International Handbook of the Sociology of Education*, pp. 155-163.

- Battell, E. (2001). *Naming the Magic: Non-Academic Outcomes in Basic Literacy*. Victoria, BC: Province of British Columbia, Ministry of Advanced Education.

- Battell, E., Gesser, L., Rose, J., Sawyer, J., and Twiss, D. (2004). *Hardwired for Hope: Effective/ABE/Literacy Educators*. Ottawa, ON: National Literacy Secretariat/HRSDC.

- Belzer, A. (2006). What are they doing in there? Case studies of volunteer tutors and adult literacy learners. *Journal of Adolescent and Adult Literacy*, 49(7), 560-572.

- Bhola, H. (1997). Transnational forces and national realities of Adult Basic Education and Training (ABET). *Convergence*, 30, 2/3, 41, June.

- Canadian Literacy and Learning Network (December, 2013). Who We Are: The Realities of Working in the Literacy and Essential Skills Field. Retrieved April 28, 2014 from: http://lesworkforce.ca/wp-content/uploads/2013/01/LMS-survey-results-English.pdf.

- Carpenter, S., Weber, N., and Schugurensky, D. (2012). Views from the blackboard: Neoliberal education reforms and the practice of teaching in Ontario, Canada. *Globalisation, Societies and Education*, 10(2), 145-161.

- Eldred, J., Robinson-Pant, A., Nabi, R., Chopra, P., Nussey, C., and Bown, L. (2014). Women's right to learning and literacy. *Compare: A Journal of Comparative and International Education*, 44(4), 655-675.

- Foucault, Michel (1998). *The History of Sexuality: The Will to Knowledge*. London: Penguin.

- Griffith, A. and Smith, D. E. (1990). What did you do in school today? Mothering schooling and social class. In G. Miller and J. Holstein (Eds.), *Perspectives on Social Problems*. Greenwich, CT: JAI.

- Hayes, B. (May 27, 2013). Adult literacy in Canada: Where Have We Been? Where Should We Be Going? Retrieved from: http://sarn.ca/?p=1159.

- Laubach Literacy Ontario (2014). Each One, Teach One. Retrieved from: http://www.laubach-on.ca/getinvolved/aboutus/eachone.

- Legacies Now (2006). Community Literacy Planning Guide. Legacies 2010. Retrieved from http://www.bced.gov.bc.ca/pls/clp_guide.pdf.

- Luttrell, W. (1996). Taking care of literacy: One feminist's critique. *Educational Policy*, 10(3), 342.

- Mace, J. (1998). *Playing with Time: Mothers and the Meanings of Literacy*. London: UCL Press Limited.

- Nonesuch, K. (May 6, 2013). "Neither Kind Nor Patient." Retrieved from: http://katenonesuch.com.

- Rockhill, K. (1987). Gender, language and the politics of literacy. *British Journal of Sociology of Education*, 8(2), 153-167.

- Rose, N. (1999). *Powers of Freedom: Reframing Political Thought*. Cambridge, UK: Cambridge University Press.

- Sandlin, J. and St. Clair, R. (2005). Volunteers in adult literacy education. In J. Coming, B. Garner, and C. Smith (Eds.), *Review of Adult Learning and Literacy*, Vol. 5, pp. 125–154. Mahwah, NJ: Erlbaum.

- Sticht, T. and McDonald, B. (1990). Teach the mother and reach the child: Literacy across generations. *Literacy Lessons*. Retrieved from: http://files.eric.ed.gov/fulltext/ED321063.pdf.

- Walker, J. (2008). Going for gold in 2010: An analysis of British Columbia's literacy goal. *International Journal of Lifelong Education*, 27(4), 463-482.

This vignette was prepared by Leona English.

Ruth Isabel McKenzie was born on a farm in Wellington County, close to the town of Clifford, Ontario, the youngest of seven in a Scottish Presbyterian family headed by Alexander McKenzie and Isabella Jane Douglas. Ruth was a graduate of Normal School in Toronto, Queens University (B.A.), and the University of Toronto (B.L.S.). She was the intellectual force behind the Canadian Association for Adult Education's (CAAE) flagship program, the National Farm Radio Forum, which aired weekly on the CBC during the fall and winter months from 1941-1965. Ruth served as the National Editor and Research Director from 1943-1953, during which time she organized study clubs, wrote study bulletins for regional distribution, and conducted annual evaluations of the Forum's radio programs and publications. In addition, she contributed articles and columns to the CAAE journal *Food for Thought* and served on its editorial board. Given her staff position at the Forum, she likely is also the author of many of the uncredited Farm Forum updates that appeared in *Food for Thought*. Ruth was first a member of the Farm Forum staff, but was later named the National Research Secretary (her colleague Isabel Wilson experienced a similar work trajectory with the Citizens' Forum).

Under Ruth's guidance, Farm Forum exercised a leadership role in stimulating discussion and action among farmers all across Canada. She was responsible for preparing, testing, and producing the weekly guide for the study clubs in Farm Forum. The significance of this Forum and Ruth's involvement in it cannot be underestimated. Following a UNESCO report in 1954, the Forum was replicated globally; it exists today in a similar format in countries such as Ghana, making it a major Canadian contribution to international education.

Much of what we know about Ruth comes from her own deposit of personal effects in Library and Archives Canada (LAC) in 1982. A researcher with a sense of her place in history, she knew the value of cataloguing and depositing her manuscripts, research notes, and Farm Forum papers in LAC where they could be readily accessed. As well, she funded an eponymous scholarship at Queen's University, her alma mater, as another way of keeping her legacy alive.

Ruth's body of work was considerable. Following her editing, researching, and writing for Farm Forum, she edited the *Citizen* publication of the federal government's Department of Citizenship and Immigration, which continued her interests in cultivating a vibrant and active civil society. When Ruth took an early retirement from her career in government, she began researching and writing works of history. Her publications include: *Leeds and Grenville, Their First Two Hundred Years* (McKenzie, 1967); *Laura Secord, The Legend and the Lady* (McKenzie, 1971); and *James FitzGibbon, Defender of Upper Canada* (McKenzie, 1983). As well, she edited *The St. Lawrence Survey Journals* of Henry Wolsey Bayfield (two volumes, Bayfield, 1984, 1986), and contributed an article on Laura Secord to the *Dictionary of Canadian Biography* (McKenzie, 1976).

Ruth stands proud in our history as an intellectual contributor to the early years of the CAAE and to the development of adult education in Canada.

References:

• National Farm Radio Fonds. (1937-1965). National Archives of Canada. Archival reference no. R2807-0-4-E (formerly MG28-I68).

Photo courtesy of National Archives of Canada.

A new genre of writing, mommy blogs have emerged as a feminist community of practice with strengths as well as limitations.
© Monkey Business Images / Shutterstock.

25

Mommy Blogs
A Feminist Community of Practice

This chapter explores the phenomena of mommy blogging through a feminist "community of practice" framework. Feminist approaches make visible the experiences of women from their standpoint, and by doing so challenge dominant, persistent gendered ideologies. I was drawn to the practice of mommy blogging as a woman, a stepmother, an academic, and a feminist. Previously, I have explored the experiences of women who were both mothers of young children and academics (Careless, 2012). My current research explores how Canadian stepmothers learn to navigate the complexities of this role, with an underlying focus on learning through social media as public pedagogy.

Erin J. Careless

My research interests brought me to blogs written by women who are, among other things, mothers. These women use this space to articulate their lives as mothers publicly and it strikes me that this could be seen as a type of consciousness-raising—of making visible work that historically has been (and in many ways continues to be) devalued. Using Wenger's (1998) framework of "a community of practice," in this chapter I discuss the emergence of weblogs (web + blogs) generally and mommy blogs as a feminist community of practice. I explore the potential as well as the limitations of mommy blogging.

Web2.0 and the Weblog

The term "Internet" was first used in 1974 and, in the decades since then, it has become integral to work, learning, and communications. Even daily practices from grocery shopping to reading the news have changed dramatically as a result of online media. In 2010, when the world's population was approaching seven billion, two billion people identified as Internet users (Robinson, 2011).

One of the most significant technological advancements related to the Internet has been the move from the initial one-way access of information, referred to as Web1.0, to Web2.0 technology that allows users to generate knowledge in a two-way exchange (Greenhow, Robelia, and Hughes, 2009). According to McLoughlin and Lee (2007), Web2.0 is a "more personalized, communicative form of the World Wide Web that emphasizes active participation, connectivity, collaboration and sharing of knowledge and ideas among users" (p. 665). Janks (2012) argues that this technology has the ability now to disseminate counter-discourses, and to question and destabilize power, particularly through the use of social media and weblog platforms. These are significant because of the various "socio-technical dynamics" that have "unfolded as millions of people embraced the technology and used it to collaborate, share information, and socialize" (Ellison and Boyd, 2013, p. 9). Information is no longer primarily delivered from one "expert" source to a wide audience, as in the broadcast model; rather, information is generated, shaped, delivered, and accessed in a many-to-many network model.

Weblogs for Everyone!

Part of the Web2.0 approach to knowledge sharing has been the explosion of the personal blog. The use of blogs has expanded and evolved since their inception as online journals in 1994. Their use is widely accessible to a range of skill levels through digital blog-creation services—the first of which was called Blogger (*New York Times*, 2006). Originally called weblogs, these sites were used simply to maintain ongoing commentaries in a diary-like fashion. They served as "cultural guideposts as the interests and biases of the user … would be known" (Hagenah, 2013, p. 3).

Like other Web2.0 tools, blogs are distinguished by their interactive nature. Readers can respond to the contents of the blog in a designated comments section. Blog writers often link their various social media outlets and communicate with readers in these forums. More than mere diaries, blogs:

> Illustrate the fusion of key elements of human desire—to express one's identity, to create community, to structure one's past and present experiences temporally—with the main technological features of 21st century digital communication (speed, reach, anonymity, interactivity, broadband, wide user base). In this sense, blogs can serve as a lens to observe the way in which people currently use digital technologies and, in return, transform some of the traditional cultural norms—such as those between the public and the private (Gurak and Antonijevic, 2008, p. 67).

The practice of blogging is private and public, individual and collective. Blogging signifies the interconnection between society and the media, and has reframed our notion of identity construction within social practice (Hagenah, 2013). In 2003, *The Oxford English Dictionary* added the term "blog" as both a noun and a verb—individuals blog as a practice and, in so doing, they create and maintain a blog. Boyd (2006), therefore, positions the practice of blogging as active, "where the blogger produces semi-regular expressions that build on top of each other under the same digital roof. Each new expression is connected with earlier expressions" (n/p). As media of communication, blogs can be used to respond to, shift, and even disrupt assumptions of social interaction and private and public discourses.

Mommy Blogs

As a growing genre, there are approximately four million "mommy bloggers" in North America (*Globe and Mail*, 2012). While some mommy bloggers have become quite famous for their writing, women who write these blogs generally write to an "intimate public" or tight-knit community, sharing their experiences and receiving feedback from their readers through the site's comment features (Morrison, 2011). Lopez (2009) argues "nothing is off limits to these writers, and yet the recurrent theme of writing about children positions these women in the category of 'mommy blogger'—a title not wholly unwarranted, as many blogs contain the word 'mommy,' 'mama,' 'mum' or 'mother' in their title" (p. 734). Women who engage in this blogging practice illustrate that there is no one or "right" way to parent, challenge the good mother/bad mother pressures women face today, and tell stories of experiences that relate them to their readers (Lopez, 2009; Powell, 2010).

Feminism and the Mommy Blog

For Luke (1992), repositioning women's lives and experiences from the periphery to the centre "of social analysis is a central task for feminist theorists, regardless of diverse disciplinary perspectives and theoretical standpoints" (p. 25). The aim has been to illuminate and end sexual discrimination and violence. For decades, feminist discourse has stressed that the personal is political, and that research must begin within individual bodily experience and then look outwards to structures that have an impact upon individuals (Smith, 2006). This standpoint perspective relates to a process whereby women's experiences are explored in relation to the dominant culture in order to understand their lived reality (English, 2005).

Popular culture, in the form of television, magazines, and now the Internet, is awash in parenting discourses and ideology. Representations of mothers have "helped mold the notion and performance of motherhood into a problem that causes many women frustration and anxiety" (Lopez, 2009, p. 731). Dominant discourses in Western society have frequently idealized the notion of the "good mother" as someone who devotes their lives to the care of their children, creating problematic and unrealistic expectations for women (e.g., Hartmann, 2004; Gorman and Fritzsche, 2002). According to Correll et al. (2007), "Contemporary cultural beliefs about the mother role include a normative expectation that mothers will and should engage in 'intensive' mothering that prioritizes meeting the needs of dependent children above all other activities" (p. 1306). Douglas and Michaels (2004) refer to this phenomenon as the "new mom-ism" in which the role of mother is highly romanticized and yet all-encompassing—an impossible standard for anyone to meet. Privileging the experience of mothers from their actual standpoint is, therefore, essential in challenging these ideologies, and digital technology is one powerful way of creating space for these stories and experiences to be heard.

In a series of published talks around the social and moral impacts of technology, feminist physicist Ursula Franklin (1990) discusses the "real" world of technology; that is, the reality of everyday life which is both political and personal. Almost twenty-five years ago, she predicted changes that would come with the growth of technology, particularly in what she called "direct experience" (p. 40). Blogs, as free, virtually non-hierarchical tools, are in fact tools that bring "direct experience" to a public forum and, in the case of women, make visible their everyday lives.

The Importance of Voice

Central to feminist theory is the notion of voice. Belenky, Clinchy, Goldberger, and Tarule (1986) used the concept of voice as a metaphor for women's experiences, a marker of a woman's sense of self and agency. English (2005) asks "under what conditions can and do women speak their truths?" (p. 259). Speaking one's truth must necessarily include listening, as women's voices must be heard to be valued and understood. Naming one's experience as a woman, as a mother, and sharing that with others, is a critical practice in today's Canadian society,and in the media that is shaped by patriarchal, neo-conservative, capitalist values. Web2.0 technology, although by no means perfect at this point, has given a new space for the voice of women, and thereby provided a place of counter-gender normative discourse.

Blogging Motherhood as Communities of Practice

I use a "community of practice" framework for this chapter, which is defined as groups of people connected by a common area of interest (Wenger, McDermott, and Snyder, 2002). Based on the belief that learning is a social phenomenon, Wenger et al. (2002) argue that "*communities of practice can be thought of as shared histories of learning*" (p. 86, emphasis in original). Members share information, support one another, and claim their identity in relation to these communities.

We all belong to many communities of practice, but access to technology has increased and shifted the ways in which we participate as social beings (Wenger, 1998). Lave and Wenger (1991) argue that learning and, particularly, situated learning is a key feature inherent in communities of practice. Situated learning involves individuals being participants in the world and actively making meaning for themselves, and for those entering into a community of practice "the purpose is not to learn from talk ... it is to learn to talk" (Lave and Wenger, 1991, pp. 108-109). There are three defining characteristics of communities of practice: the domain, the community, and the practice. Below I explore each characterisitc in connection to the practice of mommy blogs, supported by excerpts from several mommy blogs.

The Domain

A domain of knowledge is about creating "common ground and a sense of common identity" (Wenger, McDermott, and Snyder, 2002, p. 27). This feature of a community of practice shapes what is discussed between members and how knowledge is organized. As communities of practice form around a multitude of interests, the domain is what brings members together (Byington, 2011). Historically, this was frequently limited by geography—at least for many women who were confined to the domestic sphere. However, as far back as 1998, Wenger identified the emerging connection between communities of practice and cyberspace: "Across a worldwide web of computers, people congregate in virtual spaces and develop shared ways of pursuing their common interests" (p. 7).

Just as there are communities of practice around a multitude of interests, there are millions of blogs discussing every topic imaginable. The growing genre of the mommy blog covers a diverse range of topics from popular culture, to schooling, to financial issues, and much more. There are many domains within the larger group of mommy bloggers; groups that support one another's work and have common interests. As a way of bringing women bloggers together to network and share knowledge, BlogHer runs an annual conference that has grown in size from 300 participants in 2005, to approximately 5,200 in 2012 (*Globe and Mail*, 2012). These events aim to enhance connections formed online.

The common domain of mommy blogs is, as the name suggests, the identity of motherhood, but of course that encompasses a great deal. Morrison (2011), who self-identifies as a mommy blogger, defines mommy blogging as:

> Purposive and deliberate social engagement, a creative as well as interpersonal practice that mitigates the assorted ills (physical isolation, role confusion, lack of realistic role models, etc.)

and celebrates the particular joys of contemporary mothering, especially in the earliest years of parenting (p. 38).

As noted earlier, Mommy bloggers typically start blogging with a goal of sharing their stories and experiences and supporting other mothers. In her humorous blog, Mother Blogger, Vicky writes:

> So this is my first official blog entry. It's for working mothers, which includes all mothers, really. (Stay-at-home mothers have one of the hardest jobs on earth, next to lion tamers and North Atlantic crab fishermen). But I won't bore you with things you already know. I'm here to say something different. Of course, I'm not sure what that is yet. I'll just wing it and see what comes out, kinda like giving birth.... We know we shouldn't wish our time away—life is short! We're fully aware that in 10 to 20 years, our hearts will ache for these days of choo-choo trains and apple sauce. And yet we urge time onward. Because in spite of our superhuman, multi-tasking maternal skills, we are human. I don't have time for anything. Especially not this blog (Time waits for no mom, October 12, 2010).

Other mothers write about life's major challenges. For example, Lisa, who writes a blog called Forever in Mom Genes, was a teacher who chose to stay home full-time when her second child was diagnosed with a rare genetic condition. In her first entry, Lisa discussed this life shift: "If you had told me years ago that I was going to leave my job and stay home full-time, I would have rolled my eyes and mocked you" (Why I'm a Proud SAHM, April 17, 2009). Her blog posts over the years deal with the trials and triumphs of daily life.

An example of a mother who blogged about a specific life experience is Heather of Globetrotting Mama. She is a travel writer who blogged about an around-the-world trip with her husband and two sons: "We dreamed of seeing the world with our kids. We imagined having more time to do nothing (and everything) together. We hoped that one day we'd make it happen. And then one day we decided to do it" (About Us page). Entwined with stories of travel, adventure, and food are Heather's reflections on parenting and articulations of motherhood:

> What I expect will get me through those parenting moments is the knowledge that even as my children pull away, just like my own parents have done for my siblings and myself, my fingers will linger outstretched in the distance waiting to be grasped in any moment that they decide they need it. I'm betting that, if you think about it, you feel the same way (Parenting: Lifetime Love and the Myth of "18 Summers," November 26, 2014).

The Community

While the domain defines the issues or topics to be explored in a community of practice, the community is the group of individuals who care about these issues or topics. And it is the community that "creates the social fabric of learning. A strong community fosters interactions and relationships based on mutual respect and trust" (Wenger, McDermott, and Snyder, 2002, p. 28). Members of a community of practice have a shared repertoire, which "includes routines, words, tools, ways of doing things, stories, gestures, symbols, genres, actions, or concepts that the community has produced or adopted in the course of its existence, and which have become part of its practice" (Wenger, 1998, p. 83). With changes in membership, engagement, and learning, communities of practice are historically, socially, and culturally contextualized.

Many of us engage in social practices with others. In digital communication spaces, individuals connect with multiple and more fluid networks (Rainie and Wellman, 2012). The Internet allows individuals who have access to computers and Wi-Fi to connect with others, regardless of geographic location; the capacity to blog from the comfort of one's own home is an added benefit for mothers at home with their children. As the boundaries of communities of practice are fluid, so is the knowledge generated and shared through this engagement.

The key is that knowledge is shaped by members: "Truly reciprocal, with the boundaries of the community determined by adherence to group social norms and guided by deep emotional attachment between participants, personal mommy blogging creates intimate communities wholly guided by their members" (Morrison, 2011, p. 44). These discourses challenge some of the perceptions of motherhood as presented by the media and popular culture, which in turn empowers women and expands our hegemonic beliefs of parenting (Lopez, 2009). From East Coast Mommy, Gina writes:

> I am like most moms out there ... I am a hard working mom trying my best to create a good childhood for my boys ... My goal is to *inspire* and *support* other moms. I know being a mom is a tough job, and I want to take this opportunity to thank all the moms out there who support and inspire me ("I am NOT a Supermom," January 6, 2012).

Perhaps the clearest indicator of the community this blogger is a part of is the long list of supportive comments that follow this post—other women agreeing and thanking Gina for sharing: "Love it Gina. It sounds just like me ... Makes me feel like I am not alone!!!"; "Staying at home to be a full time Mom is new to me, and let me just say I have NEVER worked as hard as I do now ... it just doesn't stop! I really enjoy following you!!"; "The memories we make with our children are worth all the unfolded laundry and sticky floors. I have added your blog to my faves list. Thank you for sharing your life with the rest of us." These are just a few examples of the many responses that illustrate the reciprocal relationships that can develop through these online communities.

The Practice

Practice consists of "a set of frameworks, ideas, tools, information, styles, language, stories, and documents that community members share" (Wenger, McDermott, and Snyder, 2002, p. 29). It denotes a socially defined way of doing things in a specific domain and, if the group primarily engages with one another online, this practice involves a certain level of technological know-how and access to tools. While this may sound a fairly simple facet of communities of practice, Wenger (1998) argues that participation "refers not just to local events of engagement in certain activities with certain people, but to a more encompassing process of being active participants in the practices of social communities and constructing *identities* in relation to these communities" (p. 4, emphasis in original). This participation shapes what we do, who "we are and how we interpret what we do" (p. 4). What this means to me is that, while we often focus on the tools or technical features being used to facilitate practice, such as Web2.0 applications, we must also focus on how these tools are used in practice.

Many mommy bloggers engage with their readership not only through their blog, but also through other social networking sites (or tools of practice), such as Facebook and Twitter. In fact, most of the blogs I explored had links to not only Facebook and Twitter, but also to Instagram and Pinterest. Expanding their arenas of practice in this way not only generates a stronger voice and online presence, but also strengthens the visibility of counter-discourses: "The things people could produce for one another using their free time and working without markets or managers were [previously] limited" (Shirky, 2010, p. 119). Now, online communication platforms are almost ubiquitous in their presence and accessibility, and are clearly being used by women who support one another in their experiences and lives as mothers. Deelle, author of the Mother & Fitness blog, says:

> It is very important as moms for us to take a step back for a moment and recognize the amount of things we do. We deserve a pat on the back every now and then from others but also from ourselves. Be proud of yourself and of everything you do because it is A LOT! Celebrate the fact that you are a mom and are able to accomplish so much (The Many Lives of a Mom, February 28, 2013).

This social practice of supporting one another, sharing experiences, and making lives visible is the practice element of communities of practice.

Limitations and Challenges

While blogs and other Web2.0 tools have had a significant impact on the ability of users to connect, collaborate, and engage in discourse, there are limitations and challenges related to the use of these media. One is accessibility. Many blog hosting sites are available for interested users and, while the cost may be low or free and the necessary skill set minimal, there is still a need for basic technological know-how and access. A computer with access to the Internet is not found in each and every home, just as every mother does not have the time or skills or interest to engage in blogging and learning how to blog.

A second challenge or limitation is language. "Historical, social, and economic factors ... favor (sic) English use in cross-cultural online contexts" (Herring, Paolillo, Ramos-Vielba, Kouper, Wright, Stoerger, Scheidt, and Clark, 2007, p. 10). Similar to critiques of first wave of feminism, there is a lack of diversity among mommy bloggers as a group:

> Personal mommy blogging describes this different kind of public sphere, one whose production practices work to create a new "semi-public" or "semi-private" discourse of femininity— particularly, of contemporary middle-class Western maternity as an identity category and set of embodied practices in the world (Morrison, 2011, p. 51).

Blogs are used by some mothers whose children have disabilities and/or special needs, again to share their experiences and at times advocate for change and support. Bloom, for example, is a blog for parents of children with disabilities. On this site, mother Sue Robins shared an emotional account of her feelings of invisibility as a parent in her child's school:

> In the foyer of every elementary school there's a gaggle of moms standing in a tight circle, waiting to pick up their kids. You'll find these same circles at mom and baby yoga, the new moms' group, the kids' hip hop class and community soccer. In the 10 years I've parented my son Aaron, I've never cracked that circle. I've walked past the circle hundreds of times and nobody has ever shifted—ever so slightly—to give me room to join in. I'm the invisible mom. You've seen me—the mom with the son with the visible disability (The Invisible Mom, June 26, 2013).

Less common are blogs written by mothers with disabilities, although some do exist. For example, Raising a Child as a Disabled Mother: The Joys, Challenges and Victories is written by a woman named Heather, a woman born with Athetoid Cerebral Palsy. Heather is a busy mother working outside of the home, and her blog contributes valuable discourse around the diversity of motherhood. In her own words, "I'm tough and I'm stubborn. Where there's a will, there's a way" (About Me, September 2010). However, many more blogs are written by mothers whose children have been diagnosed with an illness or disability, rather than the mothers themselves. What does this say about the accessibility of these tools, and the voices that are privileged through them?

Another challenge of using Web2.0 tools is the advertising. When a group gains visibility quickly, such as mommy bloggers, marketplace ears perk up. Lopez (2009) reminded us that "with the combination of thousands of eyeballs and an undeniable consumer market for all manners of baby products, it was only a matter of time before advertisers began snatching up real estate on the best blogs" (p. 739). This is a complicated debate among bloggers and theorists. On the one hand, selling advertising is a way to generate financial support for women; but, on the other, it ties bloggers and readers to a consumer culture that may influence their discourses.

In a study exploring word-of-mouth (WOM) marketing in online communities, Kozinets, de Valck, Wojnicki, and Wilner (2012) discussed several blogger communication strategies used in response to the tension between commercial and communal norms: "Word-of-mouth marketing operates through a complex process that transforms commercial information into cultural stories relevant to the members of particular communities" (p. 86). The mommy blogger participant in this study received negative comments when she began reviewing products on her site, and the authors interpreted this as friction between the personal framework of the blog and the commercial aspect of the reviews.

The majority of blogs I reviewed for this chapter include advertisements, and many bloggers engage in product reviews. On one side of this argument, any opportunity for women to support their families doing work of their choosing is a shift of power towards mothers as political subjects with influence on the consumer system (Fejes, 2002). On the other side, and although there are few women making significant money through blogging, it is a reminder of the power of a neo-liberal consumer society and its hold on the "personal."

Conclusions

Women are bombarded by social and cultural expectations of how to be a woman, a mother, a wife, a success. In Western society, girls and women are told that they can "do it all"—balancing a career outside of the home, being a supportive partner, and, above all, striving to be the idealized "good mother." Counter-discourses that are written by and for mothers through mommy blogs provide support, enhance knowledge sharing, and challenge dominant and oppressive ideologies. Web2.0 technologies enable interactive discussions among users with common interests. They constitute an important domain, and a new practice of communication. This is important because "When we change the way we communicate, we change society" (Shirky, 2008, p. 17).

In anticipating the future impact of mommy blogs, historian, feminist, academic, and mommy blogger May Friedman (2010) states:

> I imagine that far away woman holding out some gratitude for the multitudes of women who took the time to document the details of their lives, the mundane and terrifying moments of new motherhood held up before the backdrop of Good Motherhood. (p. 206)

Here's to mothers, and here's to their stories.

References

- Belenky, M., Clinchy, B., Goldberger, N., and Tarule, J. (1986). *Women's Ways of Knowing: The Development of Self, Voice, and Mind*. New York, NY: Basic Books.
- BLOOM (June 26, 2013). The Invisible Mom [blog post]. Retrieved from: http://bloom-parentingkidswithdisabilities.blogspot.ca/2013/06/the-invisible-mom.html.
- boyd, d. (2006). A blogger's blog: Exploring the definition of a medium. *Reconstruction*, 6(4), http://www.danah.org/papers/ABloggersBlog.pdf.
- boyd, d. (2007). The significance of social software. In T.N. Burg and J. Schmidt (Eds.), *Blogtalks Reloaded: Social Software Research and Cases* (pp. 15-30). Norderstedt, Germany: Books on Demand.
- Byington, T. (2011). Communities of practice: Using blogs to increase collaboration. *Intervention in School and Clinic*, 46(5), 280-291.
- Correll, S., Benard, S., and Paik, I. (2007). Getting a job: Is there a motherhood penalty? *American Journal of Sociology*, 112(5), 1297-1339.
- Douglas, S. and Michaels, M. (2004). *The Mommy Myth: The Idealization of Motherhood and How It Has Undermined All Women*. New York, NY: Free Press.
- East Coast Mommy (January 6, 2012). I Am NOT a Supermom [blog post]. Retrieved from: http://eastcoastmommyblog.blogspot.ca/2012/01/i-am-not-supermom.html.
- Ellison, N. & boyd, d. (2013). Sociality through social network sites. In W.H. Dutton (Ed.), *The Oxford Handbook of Internet Studies* (pp. 151-172). Oxford: Oxford University Press.
- English, L. (Ed.). (2005). *International Encyclopedia of Adult Education*. Hampshire, UK: Palgrave MacMillan.
- Fejes, F. (2002). Advertising and political economy of lesbian/gay identity. In E.R. Meehan and E. Riordan (Eds.), *Sex and Money* (pp. 196-208). Minneapolis, MN: University of Minnesota Press.
- Forever in Mom Genes. About/Contact page [webpage]. Retrieved from: http://www.foreverinmomgenes.com/p/mom_05.html.
- Forever in Mom Genes (April 17, 2009). Why I'm a Proud SAHM [blog post]. Retrieved from: http://www.foreverinmomgenes.com/2009/04/two-reasons-why-im-proud-sahm.html.
- Franklin, U. (1990). *The Real World of Technology*. Toronto, ON: CBC Enterprises.
- Friedman, M. (2010). On mommyblogging: Notes to a future feminist historian. *Journal of Women's History*, 22(4), 196-208.
- Friesen, N. and Lowe, S. (2012). The questionable promise of social media for education: Connective learning and the commercial imperative. *Journal of Computer Assisted Learning*, 28, 183-194.
- *Globe and Mail* (August 9, 2012). Mommy bloggers are gaining clout—and retailers are taking notice. Retrieved from: http://www.theglobeandmail.com/life/parenting/mommy-bloggers-are-gaining-clout-and-retailers-are-taking-notice/article4472076/.
- Gorman, K. and Fritzsche, B. (2002). The good-mother stereotype: Stay at home (or wish that you did!). *Journal of Applied Social Psychology*, 32(10), 2190-2201.
- Greenhow, C., Robelia, B., and Hughes, J. (2009). Learning, teaching, and scholarship in the digital age. Web2.0 and classroom research: What path should we take now? *Educational Researcher*, 38(4), 246-259.
- Gurak, L. and Antonijevic, S. (2008). The psychology of blogging: You, me, and everyone in between. *American Behavioral Scientist*, 52(1), 60-68.
- Hagenah, N. (2013). *The Collaborative Self: From Collectivity to Individuality and What Blogs Can Teach Us about Identity*. University of Waterloo M.A. thesis. Retrieved from: https://uwspace.uwaterloo.ca/bitstream/handle/10012/8187/Hagenah_Nathan.pdf?sequence=3.
- Hartmann, H. (2004). Policy alternatives for solving work-family conflict. *The ANNALS of the American Academy of Political and Social Science*, 596, 226-231.

- Herring, S., Paolillo, J., Ramos-Vielba, I., Kouper, I., Wright, E., Stoerger, S., Scheidt, L., and Clark, B. (2007). *Language networks on LiveJournal.* Proceedings of the Fortieth Hawai'i International Conference on System Sciences. Los Alamitos. Retrieved from: http://citeseerx.ist.psu.edu/viewdoc/download?doi=10.1.1.92.7654&rep1&type=pdf.

- Janks, H. (2012). The importance of critical literacy. *English Teaching: Practice and Critique*, 11(1), 150-163.

- Kozinets, R., de Valck, K., Wojnicki, A., and Wilner, S. (2010). Networked narratives: Understanding word-of-mouth marketing in online communities. *Journal of Marketing*, 74, 71-89.

- Lave, J. and Wenger, E. (1991). *Situated Learning: Legitimate Peripheral Participation.* Cambridge, UK: Cambridge University Press.

- Lopez, L. (2009). The radical act of "mommy blogging": Redefining motherhood through the blogosphere. *New Media Society*, 11(5), 729-747.

- Luke, C. (1992). Feminist politics in radical pedagogy. In C. Luke and J. Gore (Eds.), *Feminisms and Critical Pedagogy* (pp. 25-53). New York, NY: Routledge.

- McLoughlin, C. and Lee, M. (2007). Social software and participatory learning: Pedagogical choices with technology affordances in the Web2.0 era. In *ICT: Providing Choices for Learners and Learning.* Proceedings ascilite Singapore 2007. Retrieved from: http://www.ascilite.org.au/conferences/singapore07/procs/mcloughlin.pdf.

- Mom-ology (2015). About Me [blog post]. Retrieved from: http://mom-ology.ca/wordpress/about-me/.

- Morrison, A. (2011). Suffused by feeling and affect: The intimate public of personal mommy blogging. *Biography*, 34(1), 37-55.

- Mother & Fitness (February 28, 2013). The Many Lives of a Mom. Retrieved from: http://motherandfitness.com/the-many-lives-of-a-mom/.

- Mother Blogger (October 12, 2010). Time Waits for No Mom. Retrieved from: http://www.motherblogger.ca/time-waits-for-no-mom/2010/10/#sthash.rISleR5s.dpbs.

- *New York Times* (February 20, 2006). The History of Blogging. Retrieved from: http://nymag.com/news/media/15971/.

- Powell, R. (2010). Good mothers, bad mothers and mommy bloggers: Rhetorical resistance and fluid subjectivities. *MP: An Online Feminist Journal*, 2(5), 37-50.

- Rainie, L. and Wellman, B. (2012). The individual in a networked world. *The Futurist* (July-August), 24-27.

- Raising a Child as a Disabled Mother (September 2010). About Me [blog post]. Retrieved from: http://thelindseyohana.blogspot.ca/p/home.html.

- Robinson, K. (2011). *Out of Our Minds: Learning to be Creative.* West Sussex, UK: Capstone.

- Shirky, C. (2008). *Here Comes Everybody: The Power of Organizing without Organizations.* New York, NY: Penguin.

- Shirky, C. (2010). *Cognitive Surplus: How Technology Makes Consumers into Collaborators.* New York, NY: Penguin.

- Smith, D. (2006). *Institutional Ethnography as Practice.* Lanham, MD: Rowman & Littlefield.

- Wenger, E. (1998). *Communities of Practice: Learning, Meaning, and Identity.* Cambridge, UK: Cambridge University Press.

- Wenger, E., McDermott, R., and Snyder, W. (2002). *Cultivating Communities of Practice: A Guide to Managing Knowledge.* Boston, MA: Harvard Business School Publishing.

When she became a carpenter by default, Kate Braid discovered the joys of using her body and building a structure that would last beyond her lifetime.
Photo: Dan Scott, courtesy of the *Vancouver Sun*.

26

Swinging a Hammer in a Man's World
Learning, Adapting, and Celebrating

I never planned to be a carpenter. If you were raised in the 1950s and 1960s, as I was, and if you weren't planning to grow up, get married, and have babies, which was what Nice Girls were supposed to do, then you could be a nurse, a teacher, or a secretary. Period. Being a Nice Girl, I chose secretary but I was awful at it, and it was by accident that years later I stumbled into the field of construction. In 1977, I was living on Pender Island, British Columbia. At a party one evening I told a small circle of men friends I would have to leave the island to find work. One said he'd just quit his job as a carpenter building the new school, a huge project for our small island, so why didn't I apply? But, in 1977, no one had heard of a woman doing this work; it was unimaginable. When I said the obvious, "I've never built anything," he replied calmly, "Lie." [1]

Kate Braid

The men around us nodded as if this was normal. It was my first lesson in construction; if the foreman asks if you can do something, you say "Sure. No problem," whether you've done it or not. Nice Girls call it lying. Nice Girls say, "I've only had three courses in it and I came top of the class but I've only done it twice. So I'm not sure...." But construction workers call it bullshitting and brag when they get away with it, which is most of the time. "Fake it 'til you make it!," as a carpenter once told me with a cheerful slap on the back.

So one man lent me a hammer, another a tool belt, and I had steel-toed boots from a job piling lumber in Fort St. James the previous summer. The next morning, shaking like a leaf but driven by a desperate need for work, I lied—I mean, I faked it—and told the foreman I'd built houses "up north," where I hoped he couldn't check. I would find out later that he went home that night and said to his wife, "You'll never guess what happened today; a woman wants a job as a carpenter!"

"Hire her," his wife said.

So he did, as a labourer rather than as a carpenter, only because the guys had been slowing down and he figured the presence of a woman on the job, even a useless woman, might make them show off. He didn't reckon that within days I would fall in love, smitten with construction work.

First, of course, came the exhaustion, as it does for everyone—staggering home to have a nap before finding the energy for a quick stir-fry and falling back into bed. Then came the pleasure. Why had no one told me about the joys of working outdoors, using my body, feeling strong and fit, being a part of building a structure that would last beyond my lifetime? Why hadn't anyone ever suggested I could make double the money I'd make as a teaching assistant, receptionist, or secretary by doing "men's work"?

Women in Blue-Collar Work

If you read the results of the latest Canadian census, we still don't seem to be suggesting trades or blue-collar work to our daughters. That was 1977; today, almost forty years later, most women still work in low-paying clerical, sales, and service jobs. I suspect that a smart, physically active young woman today might be directed towards a job—perhaps not as secretary—as a Fitness Trainer or gym teacher, but not as a boilermaker or electrician or carpenter.

I loved the work, but after a couple of months the doubts crept in. Walking onto that construction site was like a slow-motion drive into a brick wall, even if the "bricks" were friendly ones. Part of the problem was the way the guys talked. At break time on the first morning, I collapsed onto a stack of plywood with the other labourers, feeling like a hero. I'd made it through two hours of construction! One of them, a close friend, said, "Last night, eh?" Someone replied, "You bet!" and "Twenty-four, eh?" There was much laughter, and the wisp of satisfaction I'd felt at blending in, vanished. I hadn't the faintest clue what they were talking about. Why couldn't they talk in sentences?

Some of it was the vocabulary. One day a carpenter working on the roof asked me to fetch his crescent wrench. Crescent wrench? He drew it on a scrap of lumber—lollipop with a long handle. "Silver," he said and I slunk away to look for it, ready to be fired at any minute. How could I be so stupid?

Years later, when I began to teach construction to apprentices at the British Columbia Institute of Technology, I'd marvel at how familiar the men were with the tools. But they'd hung out with their dads in the family garage and worked summers in construction. I'd never done any of that, though I knew the vocabulary of the kitchen: stew, simmer, braise....

Another aspect of the vocabulary that struck me was how, on a worksite that's been male for a thousand years, the language tends to be sexual and to reflect the female body that's otherwise conspicuously missing. Every small thing that sticks out is a tit. There are male-female connectors, even lesbian (female-female) ones. Plumbers talk about ballcocks. Carpenters erect vertical framing members called studs. There's a foreman, a powderman, a journeyman. The odd time I dared point this out, the men would insist it didn't mean anything though goddess help me if I proposed "crew manager" or "journeyperson" instead or commented on the pin-ups. After four years of apprenticeship when I got my journeyman papers, addressed to Brother Kate, I suggested that the sign above the union dispatch board that read Journeymen be changed to Carpenters. Which it was, until we got a new dispatcher who changed it back. When I asked why we were again called journeymen, when some (two) of us were journeywomen, the men said I was being too sensitive; it made no difference. However, when I suggested that therefore it wouldn't matter if we all called ourselves journeywomen, it was clear the word indeed mattered—a lot!

But it wasn't just the vocabulary; it was the way they used it, in one-liners, making flat, closed statements. This was what so confused me on my first day. Women have whole conversations about what happened around the table last night and how we felt about it, often ending with a question mark, you know? Men talk impersonally, mostly about sports and cars—neutral subjects—aiming to be not just funny but, even better, to put the other guy down just a little. Everything is competitive, even if gently so. Men pick on the weakest and every exchange is a subtle test. If you're the only woman, or First Nation, or man of colour, you're fair game.

My confusion was that, as a woman, I'd been taught that if someone picks on me it's harassment, and for years I responded defensively, taking it personally, suffering considerable anguish. I learned this lesson—like most of them—the hard way when I was a second or third-year apprentice and one of the men on a high rise job in Vancouver wouldn't stop giving me a hard time. I tried being nice to him (I could never stop being that Nice Girl), tried teasing him, then ignoring him, but nothing worked. Finally one day without thinking I snapped, "Fuck off!" And he transformed; suddenly we were best buddies. He'd just wanted to know where my limits were and I'd told him, not in a Nice Girl way but as another construction worker. Is this why many men have trouble understanding what we women are "whining" about when we talk about some of the issues of sexual harassment? On the job we learned to call it "being assertive" and a woman or other minority in a white-male-dominated workplace can't have enough of it.

When I taught creative writing many years later, I caught myself coming back at student comments with one-liners that were a little bit funny, a little bit of a "put-down." I had learned the men's language too well and had to backtrack to academic language, which is much closer to the feminine, and by this I mean to encourage and support, not just to challenge or to mock.

After two years of working on the island as a labourer and carpenter's helper, my boss, seeing my interest in learning more, asked if I'd ever thought of apprenticeship. I'd never heard of apprenticeship. He explained it was the traditional way of learning the trade, like a Bachelor of Arts for carpenters. It would take four years of work, six weeks each year in school learning theory and the rest of the year— most important in the trades—learning how to apply theory to practice. I would also have to find a boss willing to hire and apprentice me. In return, my salary would start at half journeyman's rate, going up every six months to reflect that I was becoming increasingly skilled.

But I was nervous about not knowing enough (there was that Nice Girl again), so I started my formal training by taking a four-month pre-apprentice course. In hindsight, it was a wise move. Though I knew a lot about how to carry, how to move, and how to talk on a work site, I lacked a lot of the basics— like confidence, which I at first took to be the basis of another problem that showed up in school where the only two students who ever had their hands up to ask questions were the two women. (A friend had signed up with me because some day she wanted to build her own house.)

"Yes, girls?" the instructor would ask with only the slightest hint of condescension. The question we asked repeatedly was, "Why?" Why is a right-angled triangle the best way to square a foundation? Why do we drop the hip rafter? It had been the same at work; I was always bugging the carpenters with questions. "Why are we doing it this way? Why?" On the job, I'd figured it was because everything was new. In school, since none of the men were asking, we "girls" assumed the men already knew this stuff and we were the stupid ones. Maybe we couldn't do this?

That was the nub of it; no one ever overtly said "Women can't do this work," but we all knew that was what they—and often, we—were thinking. So were my questions the proof? Maybe this was why you never saw women as blue-collar workers in advertisements or on movies or TV? Maybe we should give it up and go back to being clerks and secretaries?

But one of the good things about the 1970s and 1980s was that if a feminist woman had a question, she asked another feminist. So two of us called a meeting in Vancouver on International Women's

Day and were amazed when twenty women turned up to talk about being women in the trades. It was 1980 and there were no cell phones, few computers, and no one had yet heard the words "social media." We formed a group, Women in Trades, in Vancouver, then nationally as Women in Trades, Technologies and Blue Collar Work, and met once a month face to face. I would never have stayed in the trade if I hadn't had those women to talk to and laugh with; other women doing this crazy thing, who understood that the challenges and difficulties weren't because we were stupid or "just women." They weren't personal. These were just the difficulties of being the "first."

~ ~ ~

Being able to talk to other women was what kept me in the trade. Back when I was still new at it, after two years of working on Pender Island, I'd been torn by my new identity. I loved talking to the men about construction but I also loved talking to the women about relationships and feelings. I wore blue jeans and dirt at work and came home to a lacy nightgown at night. There was no gender word for women like me. Men often defaulted to "lesbian" but I was heterosexual. So what was I: male or female? The only way I could carry on was to talk to other tradeswomen, to see how they felt and how they were handling this.

Between the time of working on the island and starting the pre-apprentice course in Vancouver, I travelled through British Columbia to interview twenty-two women doing blue collar work. The resulting master's thesis from Simon Fraser University was called *Invisible Women: Women in Non-Traditional Occupations in BC* and one of my conclusions was that as long as we women tried to act like Ladies on the job (another name for Nice Girls) and the men like Gentlemen, we would never feel at ease with each other. With new roles, old definitions had to go.

Later I travelled across Canada, interviewing women in every province and Yukon Territory to produce tradeswomen's profiles for what was then the Women's Bureau of Labour Canada. The women's voices were so compelling that I interviewed even more and created a radio program called "A Journey of Women" for CBC Ideas. In 1986, I attended a conference in Holland where, for the first time, a group of international women discussed the issues of women in blue collar work. What was striking in all these conversations was that all of us shared a remarkably similar experience. The problems we faced integrating into the male culture were identical, even if spoken in different accents.

It was a relief, for example, to find out at a conference, put on by the Women in Trades National Network, that all those "whys?" I'd felt driven to ask came from a learning style very common to the women I met. They, learners like me, always needed to see the big picture before they/we could take in the parts. Don't lift the hood of a car and say, "Here's a carburetor." First tell us how an engine works so we know *why* we need the carburetor, then we can hear the lesson on *how* carburetors work. Furthermore, women and other learners like me don't know what we know until we say it, which is why so many of us do so well in small group learning situations, talking to each other.

But, when I started in the trade, I had no one to talk to, so I talked to my own personal journals, every night pouring out page after page about what strange things had gone on at work that day. I always felt better when it was down on paper, but I was tired and over time the lines got shorter, more condensed. One of the gifts of construction was that it taught me to be a writer and a poet.

~ ~ ~

Still, it was difficult to adjust to how the men treated each other. I always worked hard in construction, not just because I loved the work and had a good work ethic (though that was important) but also because I was afraid I'd never be fast enough, good enough. I knew they were watching The Girl. Whenever a foreman corrected me, I felt awful; he hated me, I was about to be fired, I couldn't do this. One day the carpenter working beside me made a mistake and the foreman gave him a reaming out that included some pretty personal references. Construction language is, if nothing else, colourful. So I was confused when at 4 o'clock the two went off together for a beer. Weren't they mad at each other?

My mistake was taking it all personally. My partner at home, a welder, had said a thousand times, "Stop taking it personally!" but I had no idea what he meant. How could I not take it personally when someone was yelling at me? As a woman, I'd been taught to take things personally, to be sensitive.

I was a fully accredited, ticketed carpenter working on a Vancouver high rise when they gave me an apprentice who—I later discovered—no one else could work with. The man wouldn't take direction and when you're an apprentice, taking direction is the only thing you're supposed to be doing; it's how you learn your trade. We were under a tight deadline and when I asked him for the second time to help me carry several heavy sheets of treated plywood to where we were working—finally going for them myself—he cheerfully announced he was going to change our saw blade instead. And I sort of lost it: "sort of," because I was calm. I knew my job, I knew his job, and I knew I was perfectly in the right when I told him—using every swear word in my by-then extensive vocabulary—to get his ass over there to help me with this ply, so-help-me-God. There was severe shock on the face of a kindly older carpenter working nearby, but my apprentice leaped to my aid. Suddenly I understood that anger could be a tool. I'd used it—impersonally—and it had worked.

It was the sociolinguist Deborah Tannen in her 1990 book *You Just Don't Understand: Women and Men in Conversation* who most clearly helped me understand the gender-based difference in language. She argues that from childhood, North American children have different approaches to communication. Women are raised to focus on connection; men are raised to give factual reporting, no emotion. Women's talk seeks rapport; men's talk seeks status and independence.

In construction, women become bilingual. We learn the talk and we learn the attitude. We learn to focus on the project at hand, on our one assigned job, and to stop worrying about how we're going to get materials up here while the crane's broken down; that's the foreman's job. Though when I became a contractor in my own small renovations company, multi-tasking again became valuable. As one carpenter-contractor told me, having three kids was the best experience she could have had for running a construction company. Order the next day's materials while arranging to get another labourer, meanwhile preparing supper and keeping an ear out for the kids? No problem!

~ ~ ~

The numbers tell the story. In 1977, before Statistics Canada was keeping figures on women in blue collar work, I found out by a series of phone calls to industry around BC that the number of women in trades, excluding chefs and hairdressers, was between two and three percent. When I did the same research 30 years later, the number was still around three percent. Despite federal, provincial, and corporate support programs, despite Human Rights legislation and a Charter of Rights and Freedoms, despite equity legislation (that oddly excluded construction—the sector where most tradeswomen work), despite the existence of small numbers of trained journeywomen as role models and of special courses to introduce women to trades and prepare them for its unique culture, despite summer courses for girls to familiarize them with physical work, despite courses in assertiveness training and health and safety and sexual harassment (a word we hadn't heard until the late '80s)—despite all this, the number of women in trades hasn't budged in over 30 years. Over that period, report after report had asked: "Why—in the face of a shortage of skilled trades—why are there not more women?"

I believe the issue of the male construction culture is part of the answer. But in the face of employers having to look overseas to Ireland, Mexico, and other countries for trained tradespeople (who also happen to be predominately white males), why are we not first looking and training locally, starting with the other 51 percent of the population—the women—not to mention hiring and training people of colour and First Nations?

Looking at the glum statistics, we can only conclude that our tactics to date have failed.

~ ~ ~

In 1989, I was working on building an addition to the Vancouver General Hospital where I'd been assigned a labourer who hated me. "Nothing personal," as another guy once told me, "just that you're a woman." Labourers may not have a lot of status on a construction job but they have a lot of power. If they aren't bringing you materials promptly, the foreman doesn't say "What's the matter with your labourer?" he says, "What's the matter with you? You're not producing." And soon you're off the job. So one day when we were coming out of the lunch shack and my labourer made another of his stupid, put-down comments, the carpenter behind me, a foreman, said, "Lay off." But when he said it, casually, it was as if the skies had opened and God had spoken. From that day, my labourer couldn't do enough for me. It was the only time in 15 years that a man spoke up for me when another was giving me a hard time, and the effect was electric.

Years later I was giving a talk at a local high school where the shop teacher was concerned that he had so few young women in his classes. He seemed a decent man, so I got up the nerve to ask him something that had been on my mind for a long time. "Every time someone—anyone—is being hassled on a crew, everyone knows it but no one says a word." (Except my one foreman, that one time.) The teacher nodded, "Yes, that's right." So I asked him why the men don't speak up, don't defend the one being picked on. He looked at me a moment to see if I was serious. "But that would be implying you couldn't look after yourself!" he said, as if amazed this wasn't obvious.

My turn to be amazed, but it made perfect sense—man sense. When women walk onto a construction site, we're walking into a man's world, a man's unique culture. And though we can—and must—learn to get along, becoming bilingual by learning the men's language, the men don't learn ours. Why should they? There's only one of us. In that all-male world, "looking after yourself" is equivalent to looking after your male pride, your manhood, so of course, someone else "interfering" would be seen as demeaning even if, in most women's way of thinking, someone speaking up for us is seen as a kindness, as caring.

Of course, there are exceptions. Once, when a Vancouver friend was looking for a welder for his shipbuilding company, I recommended a woman, Hilary, who was highly skilled. One day (Hilary told me later), an older man in the shop who didn't know a lot about the high-tech equipment she was using, made a disparaging comment related to her being a woman. A younger man nearby told him to be quiet, and that—Hilary said—was shock enough. But then not only did the owner call her in to apologize, telling her that in his shop everyone gets treated with respect, but the older guy himself apologized to her. Hilary had never seen anything like it.

"Unbelievable!" she said, "I'm in heaven here."

A few years later, when I did research with Dr. Marjorie Griffin Cohen (2003) on the impact on women and First Nations of the building of Vancouver Island Highway under employment equity requirements, I asked a front-line foreman—another decent man—what the effect had been of the compulsory hiring of women and Aboriginal people on his job. He said "The first reaction of 80 percent of the guys when a woman or First Nation person walked on my job was pure hatred."

I'm hoping that number was a little unusual, a little high. However, clearly he and presumably most foremen have a problem on their hands when a woman or other "minority" walks on the job. The woman may be superior in her skills, both technical and social—all of us who survive in the trades have to learn how to get along—and always there are some men who are respectful, or who are won over no matter how reluctantly, when they see that the woman "knows her stuff" and does her work well and safely. But many men are not, and some will go to considerable lengths to get rid of her.

Women can do this work. In the last forty years we've proved that, over and over. In fact, often the ones who stick it out are particularly good at what they do and have an excellent attitude. That foreman in the bush told me that one of the best grader operators he'd ever had was a woman. But, in the past forty years of asking "Why Aren't There More Women in Trades?," we've concentrated on the women and study after study comes up with the same data, the same suggestions. They all agree: the problem isn't recruitment. If you make it clear that women are welcome on your job, they will come. Forty dollars an hour? Are you kidding? The problem isn't recruitment; it's retention.

Based on the stories above, I'd say that, in addition to continuing to train the women, it's time to train the managers, especially front-line managers—the foremen. We forget that the foremen are as much pioneers as the few women who go to work for them. How do you handle the fact that 80 percent of your crew hate the new guy—or in this case, the new gal? You're out in the bush and you're behind schedule. Of course, it's easiest to get rid of her. I understand this. It's why tradeswomen—no matter how skilled or how experienced—are chronically under-employed.

The lack of women in trades is a management problem.

Employers need to train and prepare the women, yes, but first they need to train their front-line managers. That foreman out in the bush had a telephone, a computer, an iPad. What if he'd taken a course on handling staff? What if there was someone he could phone the minute something didn't look good or he was having a problem or foresaw trouble? And here's a novel idea, what if he knew senior management would get rid of him—not her—if he didn't integrate her successfully onto his crew?

This isn't my idea; it's my dad's. My father, Harry Braid, was one of those men who started as stock boy for the Hudson's Bay Company and ended up president of a national textile company. We didn't always see eye-to-eye but it was my father who always said: "If there's trouble in a company, it's a management problem." This from a man who was no great friend of unions. The lack of trained tradespeople isn't just a women's problem; it's a leadership problem.

Of course, it can't all be done from the top. After almost forty years, what women in the trades are doing is hard. They are still pioneers, more closely watched and more strictly judged than any man on the job. Though it can be enormously rewarding—both financially and personally—the work isn't easy and training helps. And when you're on the job, there's no one who understands exactly what you're experiencing like another woman in trades, especially when you're meeting in person. So far, online support groups and social media don't seem to work very well. There's something about the knowing glance, a laugh or eyes rolled at exactly the right minute that tells you more than any Tweet that you're understood, you're not alone.

Trades work is important and profoundly satisfying. Some of the smartest people I know are men with an extraordinary ability, learned over years of hands-on experience, to make wood and steel and concrete do what they want them to do to become shelter. With more awareness we may pass this gift on to our sisters and our daughters. I conclude with this poem from my first—as well as my third— book of poetry about construction, entitled: *Covering Rough Ground*:[2]

These Hips

Some hips are made for bearing
children, built like stools
square and easy, right
for the passage of birth.

Others are built like mine.
A child's head might never pass
but load me up with two-by-fours
and watch me
bear.

When the men carry sacks of concrete
they hold them high, like boys.
I bear mine low, like a girl
on small, strong hips
built for the birth
of buildings.

Endnotes

[1] Much of this introductory material is taken from my memoir, *Journeywoman: Swinging a Hammer in a Man's World* (Caitlin Press, 2012).

[2] Braid, Kate (2015). *Rough Ground Revisited*. Halfmoon Bay, BC: Caitlin Press.

References

• Cohen, M.G. (2003). *Training the Excluded for Work: Access and Equity for Women, Immigrants, First Nations, Youth, and People with Low Income*. Vancouver, Toronto: UBC Press.

• Tannen, D. (1990). *You Just Don't Understand: Women and Men in Conversation*. New York, NY: Harper Collins.

Michèle Stanton-Jean represented the government of Québec within the Permanent Delegation of Canada to UNESCO from 2011-2014.

Photo: Permanent Delegation of Canada to UNESCO, Paris.

27

My Long Journey in Adult Education
From the "Me" to the "We"

I have been involved in adult education since 1966, wearing different hats.
In this chapter I reflect back on my career and my growing awareness of
women's inequality, and of adult education as a significant area for expanding
opportunities, most particularly for women. Following this, I outline what I
believe are the past, present, and future challenges for adult education. This
chapter is based on my keynote speech given at the opening plenary of the 2015
CASAE conference held at the University of Montréal on June 9, 2015. Special
thanks to Arpi Hamalian for suggesting my name and to Shauna Butterwick and
Darlene Clover for their editing assistance.

Michèle Stanton-Jean

After obtaining a college degree, I wanted to continue on to university but, being the eldest of five girls, my father told me that it would be better to attend Mother House Secretarial College run by the Congrégation de Notre-Dame in Montréal to provide young women with employment opportunities. During that period, I began to realize that things were different for girls.

I had also noticed this lack of opportunity in relation to sports; I was a good skier and tennis player and involved in tournaments, but I found that girls were not receiving the same support as boys. Something was not working for girls, I thought, and this did not please me. I started looking for work and found an advertisement in *Le Soleil*, a daily newspaper in Québec that was looking for a journalist for the *page feminine* (women's pages). I applied and got the job with the condition that I had to know how to type my own articles. So I rented a typewriter and practised for two weeks before starting my position.

There was a great deal of on-the-job, experiential learning over the three years I held that position. I learned how to interview people, take notes, and write my articles quickly (no laptops at that time), and also produce a weekly page on youth, cinema, music, and artwork critiques, which at that time were all under the responsibility of the "women's pages."

A Journey of Formal and Non-Formal Learning

Before leaving my position as a journalist with *Le Soleil*, I was asked to write five articles on women and work. My knowledge of gender disparities deepened as I learned and wrote about the inequities in salaries and other difficulties women faced in the labour force, including ghettos, glass ceilings, few job promotions, no maternity leaves, etc. I also discovered there was little data on women in the labour force in Canadian publications.

I then married, moved to Montréal, had my first three children, and stayed home with them for a couple of years. But I continued to write articles for daily newspapers and magazines, especially on the status of women. In 1966, I decided to go back to university with the view of eventually returning to work as a journalist. Finding a program that would fit my situation was a nightmare. Here again, I became aware of the lack of opportunities for adults, especially women with children, to pursue their education and how the system was unable and unwilling to recognize prior learning.

My first choice was psychology, but at that time the program required a residency, which was not possible due to reproductive demands. I then decided to take history, thinking that that discipline would be useful if I returned to journalism or entered teaching. There was no part-time program available, and they would not recognize any credit for my former college degree nor any of the credits in literature, art history, and human geography that I had taken from the University of Montréal via distance education offered through television. They also did not recognize all the learning, writing, and research experience I had from the work at *Le Soleil*. But when I finally met Rose Bernier, a woman working in the registration department, I was able to explain my problem. Her response was simple yet profound: "I will help you." She organized my agenda so that I could take courses two days a week and provided me with credits for my former "formal" courses.

There was no daycare provided at that time, so I had to find a babysitter and that was a huge challenge. Through an agency, I hired several women who were not good caregivers for various reasons. Finally, I found a woman who looked after the children and she did so for almost ten years. Once I had my children's care organized, I attended my first course. The professor announced on the first day that he had decided to change the day of the lecture. I had to redo all my planning, but I finally managed to complete a Master's in History in 1975, having had a fourth child in 1970.

While working on my Master's of History degree, I learned that if I wanted to teach I would need a degree in pedagogy, but I decided upon a Master's in Andragogy at the University of Montréal. The Director for my Master's in History readily agreed to my pursuing two masters together, as he felt andragogy was, in fact, useless.

Discovering the Field of Adult Education

After receiving my Master's in Andragogy in 1974, I became a counsellor in adult education in the Cegep Bois de Boulogne in Montréal. I believe that I was the first full-time counsellor in adult education in Québec. As a counsellor, I had the opportunity and the funding to put in place many modules and workshop for educators who, while being experts in different fields, had never taught adults. The Vocational Training Agreement, financed by the federal government for students who had dropped out of school and for those with disabilities or were unemployed, funded many of the courses I organized.

In 1977, Monica Matte started the program Nouveau Départ in collaboration with the Fédération des femmes du Québec, the YWCA, and the College Bois-de-Boulogne where I was working. This program was open to women who, after having spent some years at home to bring up their children, wanted to do something else either by going back to school, getting involved in their community, or going back to work. I worked with Monica on the planning of the program and took charge of the part dealing with going back to school, in part because I was working in adult education and also because I myself had gone through that process. During my presentation, I explained ways they could get organized, the types of study skills required, and techniques to convince their family that this was a good decision.

Working on "Herstory"

During all those years, I continued to I to build my collection of facts related to women's history. One day I showed this data to the Editor of the University of Montréal newspaper who invited me to give some lectures on the history of women in Québec in the Faculty of Lifelong Learning. These lectures were part of an afternoon course for women called "When women write." I requested that the women students prepare a paper on a topic related to their own history beforehand. This was unusual but was accepted.

At first, the women students were terrified because they had never written a university paper. I told them I would help and showed them how to use a methodology we called "study skills." I also invited Thérèse Casgrain, a prominent feminist activist, to speak to them about her life and fight to get women the right to vote. In the final class, the students presented their work. Some were so thrilled to present their writing that they cried. This experience led me to write my first book entitled *Québécoises du XXe siècle* and an article for the magazine *Forces*: "Does the 'Québécoise' have a history?" (Jean, 1974). Finally, due to the lack of books on women's history, I co-wrote and published, with three other historians, a book entitled *Québec Women: A History*, which was published by The Clio Collective in 1987.

From Teaching to Policy Development

In December 1979, the then Québec Minister of Education, Camille Laurin, delivered a speech that stated:

> What we need is a holistic policy [in adult education], one that can meet educational, cultural development, social development and economic development requirements. We need a coherent and integrated policy adapted to our population....We need as much a global adult education on lifelong learning policy, that meets all the challenges of our society, adapted to all the sectors: socio-cultural, vocational training and general education.

During the same month, this Minister called me and explained that the Québec Government wanted to organize a Commission of Inquiry into adult vocational and socio-cultural education and to develop a policy on that topic. He asked me if I would Chair the Inquiry; I was quite surprised by the invitation and told him that I would think about it. The next day, his Deputy called and I agreed.

The Commission, usually referred to as The Jean Commission, was given a very broad mandate covering all aspects of adult education. Moreover, all members had a lengthy experience in adult education. Instead of travelling to different countries to learn about others' expertise, we decided to tap into the knowledge available within our own province. To that end, we devoted a large part of our two and a half million budget to regional consultations. We undertook fifteen regional workshops with secondary, college, and university teachers and students, as well as administrators. In the end, we met with about eleven thousand people. We also received a large number of briefs from schools, colleges, universities, businesses, non-governmental organizations, and cultural and socio-cultural organizations.

We discovered a lot of problems and obstacles within the system, including difficulties with access, lack of prior learning assessment processes, and overlaps between courses at the secondary, college, and university levels. In many places, people had to redo the same courses at those levels, given by the same teacher, because there was no system in place to assess and recognize their prior learning. We also learned, through our research, that business was doing almost nothing in training or retraining their employees. We recommended that one percent of their payroll be allocated to training.

Through another study, we learned that a large percentage of the labour force was functionally illiterate, even though many had secondary-school diplomas. In response, we recommended that a campaign of adult literacy be built into a strong basic education system. This did not please the Department of Education because it demonstrated serious problems in the system.

We tabled our report in 1982 (Québec, Ministère des Communications, 1982). It contained recommendations on the national and regional organization of adult education, material on content and methods, and a financial scheme allowing lifelong learning with educational leave. Above all, it was grounded in a vision of democratization, transformation of practices, empowerment of adults, and the development of adults' potential as full human beings, not just their economic capital. We also recommended recognition for prior learning and access to participation in decision making about the development of peoples' community policies and practices.

From Local to Transnational Policy to Federal Policy Development

After the Commission, I was invited by the UNESCO International Institute of Planning in Education (based in Paris) to provide seminars as part of the elaboration of policies in adult education on citizen participation. Having read about our consultation process during the Commission of Inquiry, the Director of that Institute was intrigued. Many students at the Institute, he had observed, were from countries where adult education policies were frequently designed behind closed doors. Thus, the policies were not understood by the population and were difficult to implement. Citizenship participation was not a common practice. I accepted that new challenge and moved to Paris for five months, and then back to my former job at the CEGEP.

In April 1984, two years after our Report was released, the Québec Government put forward its own policy (Québec, 1984). That policy was using the Report of the Commission only partially. It was more focused on vocational training than on community education, a sector on which we had made many recommendations, but it had many interesting parts on prior learning assessment, on literacy, and on labour force training, which was transferred from the Department of Education to the Department of Manpower and Social Security. I was asked to comment on the Policy and I expressed my positive and negative views very frankly.

Shortly after the release of its policy, the Québec government offered me a position as Assistant Deputy Minister and Director General of Vocational Training in the Department of Manpower (sic) and Social Security. Even though I had vowed never to work in government, having grown up in Québec City and having been the daughter of a Deputy Minister who talked a great deal about his work, I accepted the job. During my tenure in the Québec government, we organized three programs for unemployed youth: Returning to School, Stage en milieu de travail (On-the-job Training), and Community Development.

I also was in charge of negotiating with the former federal Employment and Immigration Department the Québec Vocational Training Agreement. This was a time when vocational training was federally funded and negotiations with each province were undertaken as to how the funding was to be used. Instead of using a confrontational approach, I worked (successfully) with the federal government to find ways to smoothly harmonize our programs. My negotiation skills led to being invited in 1988 to take up a position in Ottawa in the then Department of Employment and Immigration. I accepted the offer and became Executive Director of Employment Services. In that position I negotiated the training agreements with all the provinces and I also was in charge of the application of the Federal Employment Equity Act. Following this I became Under Secretary of State (1992) in the former Secretary of State Department, which had programs on Literacy and also on Aboriginal Languages. In 1993, I became Deputy Minister at Health Canada where we had the responsibility of the Canada Health Act (1985), the approval of drugs, and some programs for children, Aboriginal peoples, and seniors. There, I discovered how literacy skills are an important aspect of good health in terms of the capacity to read a prescription, to understand what your physician is telling you, and so forth. In November 1993, the Department received the Report on New Reproductive Technologies, entitled Proceed with Care. We had to work on the implementation of that Report. This is how I discovered all the new ethical issues that were coming at us with the ongoing developments of science and technology, especially in genetics and genomics.

In 1998, I was appointed to Brussels to work with the Canadian Permanent Delegation with the European Commission as an Advisor to the Minister of Foreign Affairs in Health and Social Affairs, Brussels. There, I had the opportunity to work on European education strategies. During that time, I became a member of the International Bioethics Committee (IBC), a UNESCO committee composed of thirty-six independent experts coming from different countries and professional backgrounds. I chaired this committee from 2002 to 2005 during the preparation of the International Declaration on Bioethics and Human Rights adopted by UNESCO in 2005.

In 2000, I left the federal government and joined the University of Montréal, in the Faculty of Higher Education, and was in charge of developing new multidisciplinary programs. Being in the university milieu and having my experience in bioethics, I decided to complete a PhD in Bioethics, obtained in 2011. While I was interested in that area of study, in the back of my mind, I also wanted to show that your brain is still functioning even if you are more than 70 years old!

The Gap Between What We Know and What We Do

What I had learned as an adult student—going through all the challenges that you have to meet in dealing with a job, a family, and your study program—strongly influenced the decisions I have made in my work as an advisor, a teacher, a deputy minister, or a researcher. I am still very much preoccupied by the fact that we know a lot but we do not manage to implement what we know.

During my three years at UNESCO (2011-2014) as the Québec Representative within the Canadian Delegation, I had the opportunity to watch 195 countries discuss adult education. Although there has been some progress made, data continue to show that, as of 2012, there were still 58 million children out of school, of which 48% are girls. Furthermore, progress in reducing this number has stalled (EFA, 2015). There are also 781 million illiterate adults. Although there is plenty of research and evidence of these gaps (e.g., see reports from OECD, UNESCO, and other international agencies), these facts did not seem to bother the ambassadors too much. We have known for years that some countries, such as those in the Nordic region, are doing very well in adult education; we know that if you have the proper methods and programs, resources, and well-trained educators, adults can learn at any age. We know that sciences, technology, and the digital age are changing our lives, making lifelong education even more important. So, why are we not doing a better job?

Basically, and unfortunately, we have to admit that knowledge is power and those who have the knowledge and the power do not always care about sharing that power with the poor and with vulnerable people, either at the national or the international level. CASAE's *25th Anniversary Memory Book* states:

> Canada's stature in the field of adult education was demonstrated in 1960, when UNESCO's Second World Conference on Adult Education was held in Montréal and J.R. Kidd was elected as its President. The conference articulated the conviction that adult education had passed the stage of being seen largely as a remedial activity—something one engaged in to make up for what was missed earlier. It was seen instead as part of a normal pattern of lifelong learning in which all persons would expect to take part as a customary dimension of adult life (p. 12).

Fifty-five years later, we are still looking for the implementation of such an approach across the world. From 2011 to 2014, while working at UNESCO, I had the opportunity to attend many meetings preparing the follow-up of the 2000 Millennium Goals, a process that will be completed during the autumn in New York. As Irina Bokova, the UNESCO Director General, argued:

> Education is a right that transforms lives when accessible to all, relevant and underpinned by core shared values. Because quality education is the most influential force for alleviating poverty, improving health and livelihoods, increasing prosperity and shaping more inclusive, sustainable

and peaceful societies, it is in everyone's interest to ensure that it is at the centre of the post-2015 development agenda (UNESCO, 2015, p. 1).

Furthermorw, education can contribute to the promotion of peace and social cohesion as long as it includes consideration of "cultural practices, and traditions, ethnic identities and language" (p. 2). UNESCO advocates for a single, clearly defined global education agenda, with a global overarching goal to "Ensure equitable quality education and lifelong learning for all by 2030" (p. 2).

This goal can be seen in the United Nations Open Working Group's document. Their Goal 4 states: "Ensure inclusive and equitable quality education and promote lifelong learning opportunities for all" (Open Working Group, 2014, n.p.). They have added the term "inclusive," which broadens the idea and they also added the idea of "quality." This suggests that access is not all that matters, but that excellence too is important in new, lifelong learning discourse.

Paragraph 4.5 of the same document states that, "By 2030, eliminate gender disparities in education and ensure equal access to all levels of education and vocational training for the vulnerable, including persons with disabilities, Indigenous peoples and children in vulnerable situations." There are also references to women and teachers, promoting international cooperation, teacher training, and increasing the quality of teachers. Will it be possible this time to reach these new goals? Will it be possible for countries to do a better job? Will it be possible to put aside unethical agendas prone to buying and selling ammunition instead of providing the resources to their education systems? Countries have been asked to come up with a percentage increase of their budget in education and with precise indicators and targets. Will this happen? This agenda will be discussed and adopted in New York during the UN General Assembly in the fall of 2015. Will this agenda be adopted as is and will it be implemented?

The 2012 CMEC report entitled *Adult Learning and Education, Canada Progress Report for the UNESCO Global Report on Adult learning* states that: "Canada faces various challenges in its efforts to increase adult literacy and essential skills" (CMEC, 2011, p. 54). These challenges, as identified by the provinces, included the following. The first challenge is assessment data and evaluation; there is lack of consistent data collection to inform policy decisions. This is important for research because policy must be founded on evidence. The second challenge is recognition of non-formal learning and certification/credentials. Some jurisdictions lack frameworks to recognize and articulate non-formal learning, while many employers still insist on academic credentials. The third challenge is coordination of program delivery. Other challenges listed by the CMEC include funding; lack of capacity and learning methods/delivery models/tools, and resources; partnership and citizen engagement; culturally appropriate programming; and increasing access. In relation to access, the report notes the need to overcome a variety of non-financial barriers faced by adults with low skills, which include stigma and unwillingness to admit literacy issues, inability to navigate the learning, literacy, and essential-skills system, and a lack of access to opportunities. Learners' recruitment and government commitment are also listed as challenges (CMEC, 2012).

Malcolm Knowles (1980), Paulo Freire (2000), the *Delors Report*, (1996), the *Faure Report* (1972), and others have been basically saying the same thing: lifelong learning needs to be positioned as an investment, not an expense. Employers and governments have yet to understand that. Some progress has been made. Now business firms are required to put forward 1% of their payroll to training, a policy we recommended over thirty years ago. I am told that the business sector is now more conscious about the importance of training and retraining their workforce. There are, even if they are not perfect, some services for adults who want to go back to school. But we need to do much more.

Back to the Future

We live in a national and international context where, more than ever, adult education should be seen in a lifelong learning perspective. As the gap between those who have access and those who do not is increasing, as the digital age is already present in our daily lives, we need to continue to struggle to meet the challenge of not leaving anyone behind. Angel Gurria, head of the OECD, has called for "inclusive growth." That concept relates well with adult education principles. He recently argued that inequality was "a critical social and economic challenge. Widening disparities weaken the structures that hold our societies together and threaten our ability to move" (OECD, 2015, n.p.). A recent OECD Report adds that the competencies needed in the twenty-first century are not only technical competencies but also cognitive and emotional competencies, like self-esteem (OECD, 2015). Of course, women have known that for ages, but the statement is important because it is now coming directly from the OECD.

On average, across OECD (2012) countries, 16% of those between the ages of 15 and 29 are neither employed, nor in education or training. This is higher among women than men. According to the *Program for the International Assessment of Adult Competencies* (PIAAC), the first-ever OECD (2013) study of adult skills needed in the twenty-first century, 10% of all recent graduates have poor literacy skills and 14% have poor numeracy skills. Literacy and numeracy skills are no longer based on a simple binary division between literacy and illiteracy but on a continuum of skills where the level of literacy and numeracy can be assessed.

Even though Canadians are among those most equipped with the new skills demanded in the twenty-first century, there is still a lot of work to do to reach all those who are left behind. In technology-rich environments, the challenges facing those with lower proficiency in literacy and numeracy contribute to the digital divide. Seventeen percent of the Canadian population is at the lowest proficiency levels in literacy and 23% are at the lowest levels in numeracy. "There is a clear relationship between participation in organized adult learning and proficiency. But those who could benefit most from adult learning are not always those who access it" (OECD, 2012, p. 2). That data show us that adult educators will have a lot of work to do in the coming decades.

What also concerns me is that we do not value enough the importance of the quality of teachers in adult education. Students who are in a regular program and with no interruptions in their schooling are very different from those who have dropped out, or an adult returning to school to complete a program or to ameliorate their competences. But going further, teachers are central to adult education and they should be recognized as such. In Finland, teaching is seen as a very prestigious and important profession and there is great competition to enter programs; of the students who apply to teacher education programs, almost 50% do not succeed.

The adult education context is complex, with students coming from different socio-economic backgrounds, different cultural and family backgrounds, and different schooling backgrounds. These are factors that will influence their attitudes in the learning environment. Some of them have bad memories of school and this too has an impact. I recall a course I taught on study skills to a group of unionized members—all men—who were doing a certificate in human resources. During the first lesson, they told me that in their course on statistics they had not received the professor's notes because no more copies were available. I told them: "You are all big guys, working in different unions, negotiating contracts and you are not able to ask, or even request those notes? You have paid for this course, so go demand your notes!" The following week they returned with the notes. But it made very clear the real-life negative impact of earlier experiences of school, which leaves grown men in fear of what Freire (2000) called professional authority. Past experiences at school do influence the way adult learners act and their levels of confidence.

Conclusions

My questions about how we can implement what we know works in education and where we need to take action takes me back to the *CASAE Memory Book* in general and, in particular, a quotation by Alan Thomas:

> In our increasingly complex and demanding globalized world, it is critical that those involved in the practice of adult education pay attention to policy and the role of government, as well as the needs of adult learners. It is critical to remember that participation in adult education must be viewed both from the perspective of the student and that of the agencies providing courses and other educational opportunities (cited in Grace and Kellard, 2006, p. 24).

But it also brings me back to women, those like me who have important stories to tell. Over the centuries, women have been some of the best educators as mothers, sisters, spouses, nuns, and/or nurses. But their access to education in all forms and at all levels has been hampered by power, stigma, and discrimination and overall by a profound and unrelenting message that they should restrict themselves to the home. Despite that, they have fought for their rights to vote, to join the labour force, and to have equal access to higher education training.

What I have illustrated in this chapter is my own journey in adult education as an educator, counsellor, and policy maker. What is clear to me, looking back, is that to ensure the goal of "Education for All," we must create systems that are accessible to all, and this requires an emphasis on women and inequity.

References

- CMEC (Council of Ministers of Education) (2012). Adult learning and education. In UNESCO, *Global Report on Adult Learning and Education* (GRALE). Retrieved from: www.CMEC.ca.
- Delors, J. (1996). *Learning: The Treasure Within*. Report to UNESCO of the International Commission on Education for the Twenty-first Century. Paris: UNESCO.
- Faure, E., et al. (1972). *Learning To Be*. Paris: UNESCO. Retrieved from: www.unesdoc.unesco.org.
- Freire, P. (2000). *Pedagogy of the Oppressed*. New York, NY: Continuum.
- Grace, A. and Kelland, J. (2006). *The 25th Anniversary Memory Book: 1981-2006*. Ottawa: CASAE.
- Jean, M. (1974). *Québécoises du XXe siècle*. Montréal, QC: Éditions de l'Homme.

- Jean, M. (1974). Does the "Québécoise" have a history, or A brief history of the evolution of the feminine condition in Québec (1900-1974). *Forces*, 27, 49-52.

- Education for All (2015). Global Monitoring Report. Retrieved from: http://www.unesdoc.unesco.org.

- Gurria, A. (n.d.). Tackling inequality. *OECD Observer*. Retrieved from: http://www.oecdobserver.org.

- Knowles, M. (1980). *The Modern Practice of Adult Education: From Pedagogy to Andragogy*. Englewood Cliffs, NJ: Prentice Hall.

- Laurin. C. (1980). L'éducation des adultes et son proche avenir. Speech in Québec.

- OECD (2012). Education at a Glance: Highlights. Retrieved from: www.oecd.org.

- OECD (2012; 2). OECD Programme for the International Assessment of Adult Competencies, PIAAC in Canada. Retrieved from: www.piaac.ca .

- OECD (2013). Skills in Canada: Programme for the International Assessment of Adult Competencies (PIAAC). Retrieved from: www.statcan.gc.ca.

- OECD (2015). Skills for Social Progress: The Power of Social and Emotional Skills. Retrieved from: www.oecd-library.org .

- Ottawa, Royal Commission on New Reproductive Technologies (1993). *Proceed with Care*. Retrieved from: https://en.wikipedia.org/wiki/Royal_Commission_on_New_Reproductive_Technologies.

- The Clio Collective (1987). *Québec: Women History*. Toronto, ON: The Women's Press.

- Turan, B. (n.d). Why quotas work for gender equality. *OECD Observer*. Retrieved from: http://www.oecd.org/social/quotas-gender-equality.htm.

- Québec Ministère des Communications (1982). Rapport de la Commission d'étude sur la formation professionnelle et socio-culturelle des adultes : Apprendre une action volontaire et responsable. Retrieved from: www.cedeaf.ca .

- Québec Ministère des Communications (1984). Un projet d'éducation permanente. Énoncé d'orientation et plan d'action en éducation des adultes. Retrieved from: www.catalogue.cdeaf.ca .

- UNESCO (2015). Position Paper on Education Post-2015. Retrieved from: ED-14/EFA/POST-2015/1.

- United Nations (2014). Open Working Group Proposal for Sustainable Development Goals. Retrieved from: http:/undocs.org/A/68/970.

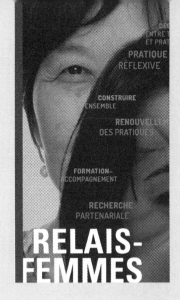

RELAIS-FEMMES

Vignette: Relais-femmes

This vignette was prepared in both English and French by Darlene E. Clover.

Relais-femmes (Montréal) was created in 1980 alongside a rapidly growing women's movement. Its aim was to document the situation of women in Québec society as a way to meet the needs of practitioners, organizations, academics, and women working in government. Its mission was, and remains, primarily action research training.

Two years following the creation of Relais-femmes, members took the decisive step to work more closely with universities, by signing an agreement with the Université de Québec à Montréal (UQAM). Through the Community Services Department, they established a formal, multidisciplinary community-university partnership (UQAM/ Relais-femmes Protocol) and they have added other collaborations with universities to this model over the years.

Between 1980 and 2000, Relais-femmes focused primarily on fulfilling the role of liaison between women's groups and academic researchers. These community-university partnerships were exercised through projects that originated with women's groups who required research assistance. Relais-femmes played the role of coordinating and facilitating research training and undertook its own research when funds permitted. The sharing of research results was done mainly through reports and the organization of knowledge mobilization workshops, seminars, and symposia.

Beginning at the turn of this century, knowledge mobilization began to be done on a much larger scale. Relais-femmes consolidated its team and expanded its "Training of Trainers" model to include more women's groups in Québec, as well as other groups such as community organizations, workers/labour groups, and other public sector agencies.

To move beyond some of the limitations of normative "Training of Trainers" models, Relias-femmes engages actively in experimentation, as well as post-training workshop evaluations. These mechanisms are designed to be able to better support organizations wishing to engage in the dynamic and demanding process of renewal. By supporting endeavours such as the development of professional, research, and organizational skills building, Relais-femmes contributes to organizational sustainability.

Relais-femmes has now reached maturity and is a unique player on the chessboard of knowledge mobilization and training. It differs from other community organisations in terms of both the scope of its training as well as its specific capabilities in the analysis of gender relations. The intellectual and educational independence of Relais-femmes allows the organisation to be bold, and to advance knowledge in the interests of innovation and equality.

354

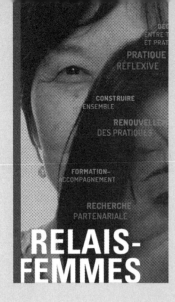

PRATIQUE
RÉFLEXIVE

CONSTRUIRE
ENSEMBLE

RENOUVELLER
DES PRATIQUES

FORMATION-
ACCOMPAGNEMENT

RECHERCHE
PARTENARIALE

RELAIS-FEMMES

Relais-femmes voit le jour en 1980, alors que le mouvement des femmes connaît une forte expansion. Créé dans le but de documenter la situation des femmes et de répondre ainsi aux besoins exprimés par des praticiennes, des universitaires et des femmes provenant de l'appareil d'État. Sa mission s'oriente principalement vers la recherche-action.

À peine deux ans après sa création, Relais-femmes franchit une étape décisive pour sa consolidation et son développement en signant une entente avec l'UQAM. Par l'entremise du Service aux collectivités, l'organisme établit un partenariat multidisciplinaire formel (Protocole UQAM/Relais-femmes). Depuis, des collaborations avec d'autres universités sont venues enrichir le parcours de Relais-femmes.

Entre 1980 et 2000, Relais-femmes concentre son travail sur son rôle d'agent de liaison entre les groupes de femmes et les chercheures universitaires. Cette fonction s'exerce dans le cadre de la réalisation de projets en partenariat qui répondent à des demandes provenant de groupes de femmes. Relais-femmes joue déjà, à l'époque, un rôle de coordination et de médiation dans les partenariats de recherche et de formation. Lorsqu'il dispose des ressources nécessaires, l'organisme conduit aussi ses propres recherches. Le transfert des résultats des recherches s'effectue alors essentiellement par la production de rapports vulgarisés et l'organisation d'ateliers, de séminaires et de colloques.

Avec les années 2000, le transfert des connaissances prend une plus grande envergure. Relais-femmes consolide son équipe et ses pratiques de formation. Cette voie connaît une évolution rapide et favorise l'appropriation des connaissances par un plus grand nombre de personnes. À cette étape de développement de ses pratiques, l'organisme utilise la formule « formation de formatrices ». C'est aussi à cette période que Relais-femmes élargit sensiblement son rayonnement. Il étend ses activités non seulement aux groupes de femmes, mais aussi aux groupes mixtes, tant communautaires, syndicales, publics que parapublics.

Prenant conscience des limites de la formule « formation de formatrices », Relais-femmes n'hésite pas à se lancer dans l'expérimentation et l'évaluation de plusieurs mécanismes d'accompagnement post-formation entre 2005 et 2007. Ces mécanismes visent à soutenir plus étroitement les organismes qui souhaitent renouveler leurs pratiques. Les résultats s'avèrent concluants et la formule d'accompagnement post-formation fait dorénavant partie de l'éventail d'outils intégrés au modèle de transfert des connaissances de Relais-femmes. Relais-femmes propose, entre autres, d'accompagner les organisations tout au long du processus de renouvellement de leur intervention ou de leurs pratiques. Son savoir-faire en accompagnement renforce la capacité des organismes à s'engager avec confiance dans une démarche exigeante. En soutenant ainsi le développement des compétences professionnelles et organisationnelles des organismes, Relais-femmes contribue à leur pérennisation.

Relais-femmes a aujourd'hui atteint sa maturité et revêt un caractère unique sur l'échiquier de la mobilisation des connaissances et il se distingue toutefois des autres organismes communautaires de formation par son champ d'action et ses compétences spécifiques sur l'analyse des rapports sociaux de sexe. L'indépendance intellectuelle de Relais-femmes lui permet d'expérimenter, de faire preuve d'audace et de continuellement faire progresser son modèle de transfert des connaissances. L'organisme entretient ainsi une véritable dynamique d'innovation sociale en matière d'égalité.

355

Index